Brentano's Philosophical System

Brentano's Philosophical System

Mind, Being, Value

Uriah Kriegel

OXFORD
UNIVERSITY PRESS

OXFORD

UNIVERSITY PRESS

Great Clarendon Street, Oxford, OX2 6DP,
United Kingdom

Oxford University Press is a department of the University of Oxford.
It furthers the University's objective of excellence in research, scholarship,
and education by publishing worldwide. Oxford is a registered trade mark of
Oxford University Press in the UK and in certain other countries

Published in the United States of America by Oxford University Press
198 Madison Avenue, New York, NY 10016, United States of America

British Library Cataloguing in Publication Data
Data available

Library of Congress Control Number: 2017955295

ISBN 978-0-19-879148-5

Printed and bound by
CPI Group (UK) Ltd, Croydon, CR0 4YY

for Solo

It is thyself, mine own self's better part;
Mine eye's clear eye, my dear heart's dearer heart,
My food, my fortune, and my sweet hope's aim,
My sole earth's heaven, and my heaven's claim.

(Shakespeare, *A Comedy of Errors*)

Contents

Introduction

Why Brentano?

This is a book about the late-nineteenth-century/early-twentieth-century Austro-German philosopher Franz Brentano. It attempts to present Brentano's philosophical system, especially as it pertains to the connection between mind and reality, in terms that would be natural to contemporary analytic philosophers; to develop Brentano's central ideas where they are overly programmatic or do not take into account philosophical developments that have taken place since Brentano's death a century ago; and to offer a partial defense of Brentano's system as quite plausible and in any case extraordinarily creative and thought-provoking.

Why write a book about Brentano? For me personally, the primary motivation to study Brentano in detail has been the combination of creativity and plausibility I have found in his work. It seems to me filled with gems that are not so much under-appreciated as virtually unknown by contemporary analytic philosophers. To convince the reader of this is the mandate of the bulk of this book. But there are also metaphilosophical as well as historical reasons to take interest in Brentano. Historically, Brentano's influence runs much deeper, at a subterranean level, than a cursory acquaintance with the prehistory of twentieth-century philosophy might suggest. Metaphilosophically, Brentano's conception of philosophy itself – how and why it is to be done – merits attentive consideration. For Brentano combines the clarity and precision of the analytic philosopher with the sweeping vision of the continental philosopher. He pays careful attention to important distinctions, conscientiously defines key notions, presents precise arguments for his claims, judiciously considers potential objections to them, and in general proceeds in a very methodical manner – yet he does so not as an end in itself, but as a *means* to something else. The *end* in the service of which he employs these analytical means is the crafting of a grand philosophical system in the classical sense, attempting to produce nothing less than a unified theory of the true, the good, and the beautiful.

The book's primary goal is to make clear to the reader both the grand system Brentano pursued and the analytical means he employed in this pursuit. A further task is to consider the plausibility of various components of the system and propose fixes and improvements where possible. This introduction, meanwhile, has two tasks. In §1,

I develop a little more the historical and metaphilosophical themes just aired. In §2, I offer a roadmap to the book and address some scholarly matters pertaining to sources, translations, and so on.

1. Brentano's Significance

This section presents succinctly the historical and metaphilosophical significance I find in Brentano. I start (§1.1) with a bit of historical background about Brentano, for those interested; this part can be safely skipped, from a purely philosophical standpoint. I then (§1.2) try to explain why I take Brentano to be such an important philosopher, in terms of his conception of how philosophy should be done and what the point of doing it is.

1.1. Historical significance: the Brentano School and beyond

Brentano was born in a small Bavarian village in 1838 and in his youth was mostly home-schooled. By age 24 he had submitted his doctoral dissertation (on Aristotle on existence) in Tübingen, and at 26 he was ordained as a Catholic priest in Würzburg. Two years later Brentano defended his 'habilitation' (on Aristotle's psychology) and became a philosophy professor at Würzburg. Brentano's alienation from Catholicism started early on, but was exacerbated when the Vatican adopted the dogma of Papal infallibility in 1870. Thinking this dogma absurd, Brentano started delving into past dogmas and found that many of them were actually inconsistent. By 1873, he withdrew from the priesthood, and in connection with that had to resign his professorship in Würzburg. The following year he was appointed full professor in Vienna. When he married in 1880, in contravention of rules for ex-priests, he had to resign his Viennese professorship as well. He continued to teach in Vienna as a sort of unpaid adjunct ('*Privatdozent*') until 1895. He then moved to Florence, and ultimately died in Zurich in 1917.

Brentano's oeuvre divides into two very different parts. There is the limited number of works he published during his lifetime, which are all extremely methodical and analytic in style. And there is the wealth of posthumous material published by devoted students and students' students, material which is often messy, sketchy, and coalesced from a motley collection of sources. Someone who reads one of Brentano's posthumous books might get the impression of a creative but undisciplined thinker stumbling from one exciting idea to the next. But one only needs to read a few pages from Brentano's magnum opus, *Psychology from an Empirical Standpoint* (Brentano 1874), to realize he was a bona fide analytic philosopher thirty years before Russell and Moore. Not only did his style resemble Moore's and Russell's in its clarity and precision, at a substantive level his sense of bringing forth a renewal of philosophy was tied up with vehement opposition to German idealism – just as theirs was suffused with rejection of British idealism.

One could argue that Brentano not only presaged early British analytic philosophy, but actually played a causal role in its inception. The Cambridge philosopher George Stout was thoroughly acquainted with, and influenced by, Brentano's work. In 1896, Stout published a book titled *Analytic Psychology* (Stout 1896), which closely follows Brentano's *Psychology from an Empirical Standpoint* thematically, organizationally, and sometimes doctrinally. Intriguingly, in 1894 Stout was the tutor at Cambridge of both Moore and Russell, and both read *Analytic Psychology* carefully. They must therefore have been well aware of Brentano from the outset. Russell repeatedly discusses Brentano's 'doctrine of intentionality' in *The Analysis of Mind* (Russell 1921). Moore sings the praises of Brentano's metaethical work in the preface to *Principia Ethica* and engages with it in a review to be discussed in Chap. 8 (Moore 1903a, 1903b).[1]

In the US, Brentano's thought was a late arrival. In 1937, his quasi-student Hugo Bergman delivered a lecture on Brentano at the Harvard Philosophical Society (Bergman forthcoming).[2] In it he emphasized Brentano's view that the method of philosophy is continuous with the method of science (Brentano 1866) – what after Quine (1951) came to be known in analytic circles as 'naturalism.' Since Quine lectured at Harvard already from 1934, one could only speculate about his presence at Bergman's lecture. A year after that lecture, Roderick Chisholm arrived at Harvard as a first-year graduate student. It is during his doctoral work there that Chisholm was first exposed to Brentano, in a seminar by Edwin Boring. Some years later, reading Russell's *Analysis of Mind*, he was drawn to Brentano's work on intentionality and started reading Brentano himself (Chisholm 1997: 7–8). He would later become Brentano's chief American advocate (see especially Chisholm 1952, 1982, 1986). In the seventies and eighties, Chisholm spawned a number of students whose work focused on Brentano (notably Susan Krantz Gabriel, Linda McAlister, and Lynn Pasquerella) or at least centrally addressed him (Dale Jacquette, Matthias Steup). Chishom's last student, Dean Zimmerman, discussed in his 1992 dissertation (on extended simples) Brentano's mereology and topology in some detail (see Zimmerman 1992, 1996a, 1996b).[3]

Brentano's most direct influence, however, was on the European continent. It is there that arose the 'Brentano School,' which was a live philosophical framework, especially in Austro-Hungary and later in Austria and Czechoslovakia, more or less until the German invasion and occupation of Czechoslovakia in 1939 forced Oskar Kraus and Georg Katkov into exile (more on those two momentarily).

Brentano's most celebrated student is Husserl, who of course came to exercise momentous influence on European philosophy. Husserl spent 1884–6 in Vienna working with Brentano, who then sent him to finish his studies in Halle with Carl Stumpf, Brentano's very first student. (Brentano had lost his professorship by then and could not supervise doctoral students himself.) Husserl and Brentano exchanged letters until about a year before Brentano's death (Husserl 1994), whereafter Husserl wrote a touching piece of 'reminiscences' about his old teacher (Husserl 1919). Reportedly Husserl once said, 'without Brentano I could not have written a word of philosophy' (Brück 1933: 3).[4] In addition to Husserl, Stumpf had a number of relatively high-profile students, some of whom went on to be central figures of Gestalt psychology (notably Koffka, Köhler, and Wertheimer).[5] And indeed, both phenomenology and Gestalt psychology clearly bear Brentano's imprint. (At this point I avoid getting into actual ideas, so just trust me on this!)

Brentano's other major student was Alexius Meinong, known to analytic philosophers mostly for his ontology of nonexistent objects (Meinong 1904). In fact, Meinong made important contributions to a range of research areas cast as central by Brentano, such as value theory, the classification of mental phenomena, and the theory of consciousness (see Meinong 1894, 1902, 1906 respectively). Meinong studied with Brentano from 1875 to 1878 and wrote under him his *Habilitationsschrift* (on Hume and nominalism). Although their personal relationship was rather tense (Marek 2017), as a professor in Graz Meinong supervised a number of students who took on Brentanian themes, including two of Brentano's own students, Christian Ehrenfels and Alois Höfler, whom Brentano referred to him in the early eighties. In addition, Meinong taught a number of prominent psychologists (e.g., Stephan Witasek) and had a number of Italian students (e.g., Vittorio Benussi) who went on to establish something of a Brentanian strand in Italian philosophy (see Albertazzi and Poli 1993).

Brentano's most loyal student was probably Anton Marty, who studied with him already in Würzburg and who developed a philosophy of language modeled to a large extent on Brentano's philosophy of mind (Marty 1908). Marty established in Prague a veritable Brentanian orthodoxy, raising generations of students on a steady diet of Brentanian doctrine and method. Marty's students include the three philosophers who went on to edit and publish most of Brentano's posthumous books: Oskar Kraus, Alfred Kastil, and Franziska Mayer-Hillebrand. All three taught at some point at Innsbruck, which for many decades constituted a sort of Brentanian 'franchise' (Baumgartner 2017). Kraus had his own series of Brentanian students – notably the creative Russian philosopher Georg Katkov (see, e.g., Katkov 1930) – who represent a third generation of Brentanian philospohers (if we take Brentano himself as Generation Zero). Other students of Marty's included the philosopher of art Emil Utitz, the godfather of Israeli philosophy Hugo Bergman, and even Franz Kafka and his friend and editor Max Brod. (All four were schoolmates, born into German-speaking Jewish families in Prague in 1883–4.) For many years, a weekly meeting of these and other Marty students at the Café Louvre in Prague (where one can still get a very good schnitzel!) was dedicated to discussing various minutiae of Brentano exegesis. Arguably, the main obstacle to the philosophical growth of the Brentano School in Prague and Innsbruck, accounting for its eventual atrophy, was its excessively reverential approach to the master's teachings.[6]

One could go on and on about the further-flung influences of Brentano. He exercised considerable influence on Polish philosophy, stubbornly analytic in its character, via his student Kasimierz Twardowski.[7] One of his students, Tomáš Masaryk, was the first president of Czechoslovakia and one of a handful of twentieth-century intellectuals who served as heads of state. Freud followed Brentano's lectures in Vienna and in one letter describes himself as a Brentano student (Merlan 1945: 375). Rudolf Steiner, the esoteric thinker and inspirer of the Waldorf-Steiner educational approach, followed Brentano's seminar on 'practical philosophy' and was strongly influenced by him (Steiner 1917: chap. 3). Thus the tentacles of Brentanian thought run deep through philosophy on the European continent, reach Anglo-American analytic philosophy, and go beyond philosophy to Gestalt psychology, psychoanalysis, and pedagogy.

This book takes a decidedly analytic approach to Brentano's thought, if for no other reason than that this is how Brentano himself meant it. Although he did not use the expression 'analytic philosophy,' he both practiced and preached a style of philosophy characterized by no-fluff prose that puts a premium on clarity and precision and proceeding methodically from a clear statement of a central thesis, through consideration of arguments in its favor and objections against it, to an approximatively impartial assessment of the thesis' overall plausibility. It is a style of philosophy that makes assertions about the phenomena themselves rather than about previous thinkers' texts about the phenomena. In all these ways it bears the unmistakable mark of analytic philosophy.

1.2. Metaphilosophical optimism

Analytic philosophy faces today two major internal challenges: hyper-specialization and excessive technophilia. The phenomenon of specialization is not peculiar to (analytic) philosophy, of course. Specialization is on the rise throughout the sciences and the humanities. On the whole, this is a positive phenomenon, indeed an inevitable byproduct of intellectual progress: the more knowledge we acquire, the more we need to zero in on as yet unknown details. To that extent, the kind of specialization we have witnessed in academic philosophy over the past century, too, can be seen as a welcome symptom of underlying progress. On the other hand, philosophy is dissimilar to other disciplines insofar as understanding the 'Big Picture' is inherent to the aims of philosophical inquiry. Wilfred Sellars put it crisply: 'The aim of philosophy, abstractly formulated, is to understand how things in the broadest possible sense of the term hang together in the broadest possible sense of the term' (Sellars 1963: 1). Thus while specialization in every other discipline is an unmitigated good, in philosophy it invites a measure of ambivalence: it is a symptom of intellectual progress, but its effect may undermine the distinctive aim of philosophy. Moreover, one worries that such specialization reflects an unfortunate combination of increased *knowledge* with decreased *understanding* – especially if a central part of what (philosophical) understanding consists in is precisely seeing how different bits of knowledge 'hang together.'

Not unrelatedly, analytic philosophy of the last quarter-century also exhibits increased emphasis on technical work. The most flourishing areas of twenty-first-century philosophical research have by and large been technically accented.[8] And large tracts of philosophical research are dedicated to the developing and perfecting of apparatus rather than to seeking insights that target the deep nexus of the perennial problems of philosophy. Such research is seductive insofar as it offers precise and unambiguous answers to the questions it addresses. It provides objective standards of quality assessment readily applicable to philosophers' output. If one is insecure about whether open-ended ruminations on knowledge of the external world, the mind-body problem, determinism and free will, the existence of abstract objects, and so forth are of genuine and lasting value, one would be comforted by engaging in the kind of work which produces concrete results (say, a proof in confirmation theory) instead of roaming in a constant state of intellectual disorientation through the blasted landscape of those intractable-seeming perennial problems of philosophy.

At bottom, I suspect the wave of technophilia washing through current analytic philosophy is a symptom of an underlying malaise: a deep skepticism about what philosophy can really achieve and what value its achievements really have. In the background is a subtle hopelessness about the prospects for genuine illumination on the philosophical core of the aforementioned perennial problems, and more deeply about whether philosophy (as compared to physics and biology, say) can generate quantum leaps in our understanding of the universe. Given twenty-five-hundred years of trying to settle the mind-body problem, or to establish the existence or nonexistence of abstract objects, and given war and famine and misery and desperation in various corners of the globe, should philosophers not try to contribute something more tangible to the society bankrolling these ruminations of theirs, which by the way never issue in any resolution of anything? After all, it is not an altogether unrespectable metaphilosophical position that the perennial problems of philosophy simply do not *have* the kinds of answer philosophers seek for them.

Whatever its merits, this line of thought was not shared by Brentano, who apparently radiated an almost messianic optimism about the value of philosophical activity. His view – highly plausible, as it seems to me – was that this kind of skepticism and hopelessness about philosophy is but a cyclical phenomenon.[9] More importantly, when we wonder what philosophy might be good *for*, the answer depends on what we want to obtain *ultimately*. Western societies are currently laboring under the adopted goal of increasing *economic growth*. But if economic growth has any value, surely it is only *instrumental* value (increase in the amount of stuff produced does not inherently capture the meaning of life!). Utilitarians have a more perspicuous conception of that which we ultimately want, namely, maximum pleasure and minimum pain. But as we will see in Chap. 9, while Brentano's ethics adopts the general form of a consequentialist theory, it rejects the notion that pleasure is our *only* final end. Another end – of greater value, actually – is *knowledge of reality*. Insofar as it is the mandate of philosophy to synthesize the knowledge obtained in all other disciplines and produce a regimented total theory of the world, philosophy delivers a product with the highest intrinsic value. This is what economic growth is *for* – it gives us means to make people happier, and even more importantly for Brentano, it gives us means to develop our unified, total theory of the world. Crucially, having such a theory is not valuable (only) for making anyone happier. It is valuable *in and of itself.*

Furthermore, genuine progress in philosophy is possible, though for Brentano philosophical quantum leaps are a cyclical phenomenon too.[10] The progress Brentano has in mind is of the robustly realist kind, consisting of actually closing in on the truth. It is true perhaps that in comparison to scientific progress, philosophical progress produces less of a consensus within the community of inquiry. But from a Brentanian standpoint, consensus is merely a sociological *symptom* of scientific progress, not what scientific progress consists in. And if philosophical progress does not exhibit a similar symptom, that by itself does not impugn the existence of underlying progress. Suppose that Avicenna's philosophy, say, provides the right framework for producing a preponderance of true philosophical beliefs. Then for Brentano any philosophers working within the Avicennist framework are carrying the torch of philosophical progress, however anonymously they may be laboring.

I do not personally share Brentano's robustly realist conception of philosophical progress. My view, very roughly, is that philosophical progress consists in explicitation and articulation of the structure of logical space, not in closing in on a 'true' neighborhood within that space. I also do not share Brentano's view that knowledge of reality is intrinsically valuable. At the same time, I hold that philosophical insight affords a kind of delight which is both intrinsically valuable and irreproducible by any non-philosophical means. To that extent, I share Brentano's sunny optimism about philosophy.

Although as we will see Brentano did belabor the technical details of some of his theories, this remained a secondary goal for him. The primary goal was to fashion as stable and as unified a framework for a total theory of the world as he could. In other words, working out the technical apparatus was for him of crucial importance, but only as a *means.* The *end* was to produce a unified theory of everything. Indeed, as I hope to convince the reader by the end of Chap. 10, Brentano actually had a *grand system* in the classical sense of a unified account of the true, the good, and the beautiful. As a committed empiricist, Brentano had no truck with Hegel-style systems that proceed from the top down, imposing theory on the phenomena. Rather, he believed in evidence-driven theorization progressing through a series of local studies – but all the while having in sight their ultimate integration into a cohesive, total system.

In sum, in Brentano's conception of philosophy, specialization and technical sophistication are both of crucial importance, but only as means. As long as we keep in mind a clear and constant awareness of what is an end and what is a means in philosophical work, *hyper*-specialization and technophilia should be kept at bay. For me, this is another reason to take a close look at Brentano's philosophical work – to see what it looks like when a philosopher adopts the standards of clarity and precision dear to analytic philosophy, but does so in the service of the more romantic goal of constructing a stable total theory of the world.

2. Plan of the Book

This section offers a brief overview of the coming chapters (§2.1) and addresses some scholarly and methodological matters that may not, I confess, fascinate readers ill versed in Brentano scholarship (§2.2).

2.1. Roadmap

As we will see, Brentano's philosophical system is grounded in his philosophy of mind. Accordingly, this book is divided into three parts. The first part discusses the core of Brentano's highly sophisticated philosophy of mind, the second the way his philosophy of mind grounds his 'theoretical philosophy,' and the third the way it grounds his 'practical philosophy.' Each of the three parts is itself divided into three chapters (an organization that would doubtless please Brentano's aesthetic sensibilities!).

The first part includes a chapter on consciousness, a chapter on intentionality, and a chapter on the different 'modes' of conscious intentionality. The rationale for starting with consciousness is as follows. As noted, Brentano's philosophy of mind is the keystone of his system. Crucially, however, Brentano holds that all mental states are conscious. As we will see, this rather implausible claim can be excised from his system without much repercussion. But what it means is that his philosophy of mind is at bottom really just a philosophy of consciousness. Accordingly, the book's opening chapter is an interpretation and defense of Brentano's theory of consciousness. The chapter attempts to do two things: first, to engage the secondary literature on Brentano's theory of consciousness and offer a new interpretation based on a particular understanding of Brentano's mereology; second, to show that Brentano's theory of consciousness, as interpreted in the chapter, is actually superior in some key respects to leading accounts of consciousness in the contemporary literature.

Chap. 2 is about intentionality, the notion Brentano is best known for. Because this area of Brentano scholarship is well trodden, there is a special premium on saying something really *new* on the topic. In this chapter, I push two ideas. The first is that the idea of 'intentionality as the mark of the mental,' popularized by Chisholm, should really be understood, given what was shown in the previous chapter, as 'intentionality as the mark of the *conscious*.' More specifically, I provide textual evidence that Brentano took intentionality to be a *phenomenal* feature of conscious states, and to that extent anticipated the currently widely discussed notion of 'phenomenal intentionality.' The second line I push is a nonrelational, broadly 'adverbialist' interpretation of Brentano's *mature* theory of intentionality, as presented in various writings from the final decade of his life (and three decades after the publication of his *Psychology from an Empirical Standpoint*, often the main source consulted in relevant discussions).

The upshot of the first two chapters is that there is a kind of conscious intentionality, or felt aboutness, which for Brentano is the essential characteristic of the mental. Chap. 3 offers a systematic reconstruction of Brentano's taxonomy of kinds of mental state, which is grounded in a more basic taxonomy of *modes* of conscious intentionality.

Brentano's notion of intentional mode is fundamental to his entire philosophy, but is relatively under-discussed in the secondary literature. Accordingly this is a rather lengthy chapter that tries to get into the finer details of Brentano psychological taxonomy. What makes the notion of intentional mode so important, as we get to see later in the book, is that there are two modes of intentionality – what Brentano calls 'judgment' and 'interest' – that serve as a basis for his theoretical philosophy and practical philosophy respectively.

So much for the book's first part, titled 'Mind.' The second part, titled 'Being,' starts with a chapter on Brentano's heterodox theory of judgment, moves on to Brentano's metaontology (his theory of what we do when we say that something exists), and closes with a chapter on Brentano's ontology (his theory of what actually exists).

The theory of judgment is so heterodox, in fact, that it is hard to even make sense of it within the framework of current philosophy of mind. Accordingly, the main contribution of Chap. 4 is to offer a way of thinking of Brentano's theory of judgment in the terminology of today's philosophy of mind. Specifically, I propose to understand the fundamental idea as the thesis that as far as the psychological reality of belief is concerned, all our beliefs are beliefs-in rather than beliefs-that. Modern philosophy of mind presupposes exactly the opposite: belief-that is taken to be basic, and reports such as 'Jimmy believes in ghosts' are construed as elliptical for 'Jimmy believes that there are ghosts.' Brentano's surprising claim is that *the opposite* is true: reports such as 'Jimmy believes that some ghosts are scary' are just misleading formulations for 'Jimmy believes in scary ghosts,' while reports such as 'Jimmy believes that all ghosts are scary' should be paraphrased as 'Jimmy disbelieves in non-scary ghosts.' Having formulated the view, I spend much of the chapter trying to push as far as possible a defense of it. In particular, I consider what kinds of paraphrase into (dis)belief-in talk can be offered for *difficult cases* of apparent belief-that (negative beliefs, modal beliefs, disjunctive beliefs, and so on). I close by conceding that there are two major liabilities to this extraordinary theory of Brentano's. The main *advantage* of the theory is to become apparent in the subsequent two chapters: it provides the foundations for a responsible brand of nominalist ontology.

Chap. 5 is about Brentano's highly original metaontology. Brentano embraces the Kantian thought that 'existence is not a real predicate,' but draws from it a surprising lesson. According to Brentano, to say that something exists is to say that the right attitude to take toward it is that of *believing in it*. For example, to say that ducks exist is not to characterize ducks in any way, but is rather to say that it is appropriate or fitting to believe in ducks. (Likewise, to say that the ether does not exist is to say that the right attitude to take toward the ether is that of disbelieving in it.) Here we start to see the sense in which Brentano's metaphysics is grounded in his philosophy of mind, specifically his theory of judgment.

Chap. 6 is about Brentano's ontology – what he actually think there is. The short answer is that he thinks there are only concrete particulars and mereological sums thereof. Properties and states of affairs are eliminated. However, in order to do justice to the phenomena, Brentano ends up embracing certain quite unusual concrete particulars. We will see the details in due course, but Brentano's basic innovation is this: in addition to ducks, there are also (collocated with ducks) such things as brown-ducks and winged-ducks. Take a brown duck named Duckie. Where Duckie is, it is natural for us to say that there is only one concrete particular, Duckie, but several states of affairs, including Duckie's-being-brown and Duckie-having-wings (states of affairs that have the properties of being brown and being winged as constituents). But according to Brentano, as I interpret him, in Duckie's location there are *many* collocated concrete particulars: Duckie, brown-Duckie, winged-Duckie, and so on. At the same time, there are no states of affairs and no properties (nor property instances). The chapter attempts to make this view clearer and more systematic and to defend its plausibility. Here too, I identify two major costs, but also point out that accepting those costs enables a highly elegant and parsimonious ontology. I close the chapter with a discussion of a virtually forgotten manuscript by Brentano, dictated two years before his death, in which he appears to anticipate the kind of monism about material objects that has attracted so much attention in recent metaphysics.

The book's third part, titled 'Value,' is dedicated to Brentano's practical philosophy and is structured analogously to the second part: first there is a chapter on the crucial types of mental state we must understand in order to understand Brentano's theory of value, then a chapter on Brentano's metaethics (his theory of what we do when we say that something is good), and finally a chapter on Brentano's first-order normative ethics (his theory of what is actually good).

The chapter on the relevant type of mental state, Chap. 7, covers three phenomena that in modern philosophy of mind are often treated in separation: states of the will, emotional states, and pleasure and pain. The chapter tries to show that Brentano has a unified account of all three as characterized by a distinctive, inherently evaluative mode or attitude. Interestingly, in today's philosophy of mind the account is widely accepted for certain mental states but not others. In particular, it is quite popular for such states as desire and intention, but gets less play for emotions. In the chapter, I try to leverage the view's popularity for desire to argue that it should extend rather well to emotion and pleasure/pain. The unified account of all three phenomena does raise a problem of how to *distinguish* them; I appeal to relatively unknown manuscripts of Brentano's to address this problem.

Chap. 8 focuses on Brentano's metaethics. In it, I try to show that Brentano's account of what it means to say that something is good closely parallels his account of what it means to say that something exists. There, the view was that 'ducks exist' means that the right attitude to take toward ducks is that of believing in them. Here, the view is that 'generosity is good' means that the right attitude to take toward generosity is a positive state of *interest* – what we call today a 'pro attitude.' Here we see that Brentano anticipated the currently 'hot' fitting-attitude account of value. The chapter's main focus is on distinguishing Brentano's version of the fitting-attitude theory from later versions. It considers potential advantages of Brentano's version, as well as potential costs. It also discusses Brentano's main *argument* for his fitting-attitude account, which, strikingly, is essentially Moore's open question argument – but developed at least a decade earlier. Toward the end of the chapter, the question is taken up of how one might be able to distinguish *moral* from *aesthetic* goodness. To answer this question, I go into Brentano's aesthetics and his theory of beauty. The theory parallels Brentano's account of the true and the good and may be called a 'fitting delight theory of beauty': very roughly, to say that a thing is beautiful is to say that it is fitting to be delighted with it.

Chap. 9 presents Brentano's normative ethics. Brentano's is an old-fashioned ethical theory, the kind of bold theory that tries to guide us in life – to tell us *what to do*. Brentano's consequentialist answer is that we should maximize the good in the world, that is, maximize that which it is fitting to have a pro attitude toward. The question is: what *is* it fitting to have a pro attitude toward, ultimately? Brentano's response is to list *four* different things that are intrinsically good, that is, merit a pro attitude in and of themselves. Granting that pleasure is one such thing, he adds three others: (i) conscious activity, (ii) knowledge, and (iii) fitting attitudes. The chapter presents this ethical system and Brentano's case for it, defending it in some places and sounding a more skeptical note in others.

The book's final and concluding chapter pulls together the main ideas from the previous chapters to present the general structure of Brentano's overall philosophical system: his structurally symmetric theories of the true, the good, and the beautiful. As we will have seen by then, for Brentano, we grasp the natures of the true, the good, and the beautiful by grasping (i) three types of mental state – belief, pro attitude, and delight – and (ii) the standard of fittingness for each. The true is that which it is fitting to believe, and more poignantly, the real is that *in* which it is fitting to believe; the good is that toward which it is fitting to have a pro attitude; the beautiful is that with which it is fitting to be delighted. Some of the notions used in these three formulations can be understood in terms of others. For example, the notion of delight can be analyzed in terms of a certain combination of first-order awareness and second-order pleasure taken in that awareness. Ultimately, however, I show that Brentano's system involves five primitive notions. These cannot be understood via analysis. The only way to grasp the nature of the phenomena they denote, for Brentano, is by direct experiential acquaintance. Thus the relevant experiential acquaintance ultimately underpins our grasp of the true, the good, and the beautiful.

2.2. Methodological

I have spoken time and again of 'Brentano's system.' But those familiar with Brentano's career may find this strange, given that the man continuously changed his mind on just about everything. Husserl tells us that Brentano's thinking 'never stood still' (Husserl 1919: 50). And indeed, in Brentano's writings one can often find different views in different texts. How can one speak of *a* system given this?

Here is how I understand what Brentano was about. He had a set of core convictions on which he never seriously changed his mind. These include prominently the notions that intentionality is the mark of the conscious, that there are three fundamental modes of conscious intentionality, and that the true, the good, and the beautiful can be made intelligible only in terms of the fittingness of reactions characterized by those modes. How to construct a stable system around these convictions, in a way that does justice to the phenomena, was the defining challenge of Brentano's adult life. In pursuit of this project, he developed many different lines of thought, in an attempt to see which will serve the purpose best. There are often tensions, or even inconsistencies, between these lines of thought, but this is partly because they were not intended to be held *together*. And some of these lines of thought he endorsed more fully than others. Finally, there is a collection of views closest to his heart (that is, most fully endorsed) that together do constitute a stable system. These views were likely held all at once, with a reasonable degree of confidence, from around 1904 to 1915 – but I suspect were held at other times as well, perhaps with lesser conviction. It is the system arising from this coalition of views that I present here.

In deciding which views are closest to Brentano's heart, and more generally in developing my interpretation of Brentano's system, I have followed a number of methodological principles. First and foremost, I give priority to the texts Brentano published in his lifetime. Brentano's writings can be divided into three kinds: (i) works he published himself during his lifetime, (ii) works published posthumously by others, and (iii) unpublished manuscripts (mostly archived in Graz, Würzburg, and at Harvard's Houghton Library). There is reason to put interpretive premium on the material Brentano himself decided to publish, as more likely to reflect what he was willing to actually endorse – all the more so given that Brentano apparently instructed his students to publish sparingly, and only material in genuinely good shape.[11] So, whenever writings from group (i) appear to clash with writings from groups (ii) and (iii), I have given greater weight to the former.

Secondly, I have taken special care with materials from group (ii). Many of these works were heavily and intrusively edited by the three aforementioned Innsbruck-based editors of Brentano's literary estate (his 'Nachlass'). Some of the materials were originally lecture notes not necessarily written in full sentences. Others were short fragments dictated by Brentano in the last years of his life, when he was functionally blind. To create intelligible texts out of these materials, the editors essentially needed to do some of the writing themselves. In some cases they took paragraphs from different fragments and put them together into new texts they deemed reflective of Brentano's ideas. Obviously, this process is fraught with risks, and whenever I have used this material, I made sure to consult the original manuscripts to ensure as much as possible that Brentano's ideas are faithfully presented.

Thirdly, when quoting Brentano's work, I have virtually always relied on my own translation, though informed and often helped by the existing English translations. Translating German into English is a delicate affair: English does not work well with long, complex sentences embedding multiple nested phrases – but that is just what German writing *is*. Wisely, the English translators working with Chisholm have by and large chosen not to respect the German grammar of Brentano's sentences, instead breaking long Germanic sentences into several more straightforward English sentences. This renders the English texts more legible, but in a way it involves a measure of rewriting as well. It incorporates a certain understanding of what the sentence is trying to say. For the most part, the translators' understanding matched my own – but not always. In particular, the fact that I have a specific systemic interpretation of what Brentano is trying to do at the level of the big picture perforce affects my understanding of individual sentences – whereas the translators had no need to share my systemic interpretation of Brentano.

In some cases, I also think the common translation of certain key Brentanian phrases are misguided. Perhaps the most striking example is Brentano's locution *als richtig charakterisiert*, which plays a crucial role in Brentano's metaethics as well as metaontology. English translators, I suspect under Chisholm's guidance, have translated this as 'experienced as being correct.' This seems to me to commit to a substantive thesis that Brentano may not have shared, and that on philosophical grounds I think he would do well not to adopt (for details, see Chaps. 5 and 8). Accordingly, I offer a more literal translation of *als richtig charakterisiert* as 'with the character of correctness.'[12] At the same time, my interpretation of Brentano's metaethics and metaontology sees his use of *richtig* as in some ways closer to 'fitting' than to 'correct' (here my preferred translation is in a sense *less* literal). There are other cases in which individual words receive a different translation in my hands. Thus, another central Brentanian notion is that of *Evidenz*, which is universally translated as 'evidence' but which I translate as 'self-evidence.'[13] *Bewusstsein* is universally translated as 'consciousness,' but in some contexts 'awareness' seems to me more apt.[14] There are other examples, but where the choice of adopting a nonstandard translation reflects an element of interpretation, I flag this in my discussion.

Because I use my own translations, I refer first to pages of a German edition, followed by the pages in the English translation in brackets (when it exists).

I should mention that throughout the book, I use a device foreign to the annals of translation: when a key German word is not perfectly captured by any one English word, I offer in my translation several relevant English words, separated by slash signs. The idea is that many German words (like non-German words!) have a nuanced meaning better understood when one contemplates what is common across several English words that may legitimately be taken to render it. The device is intended to give a better sense of the original word's 'living sense.' It is telling, I find, that when asked in everyday life for the meaning of some word in a foreign language, we usually proffer two or three words in the home language. Only rarely and for the simplest words do we offer a single perfect match. I have simply decided to do the same in writing.

I should not hide that my intense work on Brentano over the past half-decade has filled me with something of an adolescent admiration for him. Indeed, I have come to the opinion that Brentano is one of a handful of towering geniuses in the history of philosophy, on a par with the likes of Aristotle and Kant – though rarely if ever mentioned in one breath with such figures. I hope this book manages to convey the grounds for my enthusiasm to the reader. At the same time, I have tried to rescue Brentano scholarship from the reverential approach that characterized so much work within the Brentano School. One aspect of doing so is not to adopt wholesale Brentano's own terminology in presenting and discussing his ideas, instead imposing on them (where possible) the terminology most natural to contemporary analytic philosophy. I suspect this exercise might seem to some Brentano scholars to do violence to Brentano's own thought, and to some extent it surely does. The rationale behind, and ultimate justification for, the decision to do this violence is that it casts Brentano's thought not only as a great historical edifice, but also as a *live philosophical program*.[15]

Notes to Introduction

1. On the link between Brentano, Stout, Russell, and Moore, see Valentine 2003, Nasim 2008, and Schaar 2013, 2017.

2. Bergman was a direct student of Brentano's favorite student, Anton Marty (more on him shortly), and visited Brentano in his summer house at least five times between 1905 and 1911 (Fréchette 2017), and the two exchanged letters for many years (see Bergmann 1946). As a Jew and a Zionist, Bergman's professional prospects in Austro-Hungry were virtually nonexistent, and he eventually emigrated to Palestine, where in 1935 he became the first Rector of the Hebrew University of Jerusalem.

3. Outside analytic philosophy, there is also the context of American phenomenology. Marvin Farber, who studied with Husserl and founded *Philosophy and Phenomenological Research* (and then edited it until Chisholm took over in 1980), was fully aware of Brentano's crucial role in the inception of Husserlian phenomenology (see Farber 1943).

4. Philosophically, Husserl's early phenomenology is largely derivative from Brentano's project of 'descriptive psychology', the project of *describing* psychological phenomena before we start trying to *explain* them. (Compare: zoologists first describe the zoological phenomena, *then* try to develop explanatory theories about them.) Starting circa 1905, Husserl's phenomenology acquires a broadly Kantian, 'transcendental' dimension foreign to Brentano's thought. Nonetheless, the project retains the Brentanian traces of descriptive psychology.

5. As we will see already in Chap. 1, it is central to Brentano's mereology that at least some kinds of parthood involve the whole's priority to its parts – a theme taken up in part by Stumpf (1890) himself.

6. An aspect of this was neglect of developments elsewhere in the philosophical world. Kastil himself wondered about this aloud in a 1948 letter to Wittgenstein's editor Rush Rhees (Baumgartner 2017).

7. The latter was the teacher of the most prominent twentieth-century Polish philosophers, some of whom seem to have taken up Brentanian themes. The best known among them is Tarski, who is known for developing the original deflationary theory of truth – though some argue that Brentano already had a deflationary theory (C. Parsons 2004, Brandl 2017), which Twardowski may have appreciated. Leśniewski developed the first formal mereology, but mereological thinking is already present in Brentano (see Chap. 1) and Twardowski

(1894). Kotarbiński developed a brand of nominalism that he himself took to be inherited from Brentano (see Kotarbiński 1966). And yet, some scholars maintain that Brentano's main influence on Polish philosophy was in style rather than content, method rather than doctrine (see Betti 2017).

8. Consider some of the most flourishing areas of research in contemporary philosophy: in epistemology, formal epistemology and confirmation theory; in philosophy of science, highly specialized parts of the philosophy of physics, the philosophy of chemistry, and the like; in philosophy of mind, experimental philosophy and philosophy of cognitive science; in metaphysics, extremely technical issues in mereology and the ontology of material objects; in moral philosophy, decision theory, game theory, and increasingly technical concerns surrounding the regimentation of expressivist language.

9. Brentano actually had a comprehensive theory about the history of philosophy, according to which it proceeds in cycles of four recurring phases: the phase of genuine growth, the phase of popularization, the phase of skepticism, and the phase of gratuitous mysterianism (Brentano 1895). I do not wish to endorse this somewhat odd and ham-fisted theory, with its seemingly megalomaniac subtext. (The point of the theory is that post-Kantian German idealism is the mysterian phase of the last cycle before Brentano, and Brentano himself represents the renewal and regeneration of philosophy as the opening phase of a new cycle. It is possible to interpret Brentano's curious theory more charitably, though, as partly ironic, taking on a distinctly Hegelian form that makes it feel ham-fisted; this ingenious interpretation was suggested to me in conversation by Guillaume Fréchette.)

10. See note 9, and consider the kind of philosophical progress analytic philosophy witnessed around the 1970s. Sandwiched between the present technophiliac phase and the logical-positivism-inspired one, fully a generation of exciting philosophical activity had addressed the core issues of philosophy, from direct-reference theory in philosophy of language and reliabilism in epistemology, through non-reductive materialism in philosophy of mind and the Armstrong-Lewis revival of systematic ontology, to virtue ethics in moral philosophy and Rawlsian liberalism in political philosophy.

11. Consider this passage from a letter Husserl wrote to Brentano in 1889: 'My behavior to this point has demonstrated that the ambition to see my name in print as quickly and as often as possible has not driven me to premature publications. I am certain of your approval in this matter. I will only publish what I deem really useful (*nützlich*)...' (Ierna 2015: 71).

12. I note that while the widely used English translation of Brentano 1889 is the 1969 translation by Chisholm and Elizabeth Schneewind, which indeed translates *als richtig charakterisiert* as 'experienced as correct,' there exists also a 1902 translation, by one Cecil Hague, which translates the same locution as 'with the character of rightness.'

13. Although the English word 'evidence' has a meaning that suggests demonstrative force, its more dominant meaning suggests exactly the opposite – a non-demonstrative relationship between that which is evidence and that which it is evidence for (as when we say that the big footprints are evidence of a male burglar). The German word that best fits this dominant English sense of 'evidence' is *Beweis*, but it is clear that Brentano's *Evidenz* is nothing like *Beweis* – it concerns precisely the demonstrative phenomenon. Hence my preference for 'self-evidence.' (Interestingly, this problem arises only for nouns. For the corresponding adjective the dominant meanings align much better: 'evident' means more or less the same as 'self-evident' in everyday English and suggests something with demonstrative force.)

14. English is generous in providing both 'consciousness' and 'awareness' – many languages, including German, have only one corresponding word, that is, only one word into which either 'consciousness' or 'awareness' would be translated. There are certain subtle differences, however, in particular the fact that the more dominant use of 'awareness' is as a transitive verb (although there is also an intransitive use) whereas the more dominant use of 'consciousness' is as a transitive verb (though there is also an intransitive use). This subtle difference is useful in capturing certain subtleties of Brentano's theory of consciousness – see Chap. 1.

15. Work on this book was supported by the French National Research Agency's grants ANR-11-0001-02 PSL* and ANR-10-LABX-0087. It was also supported, in an array of alternative ways, by my wife Lizzie, whose wise meta-level prompts have often helped me move forward when I felt stuck. Yet another type of support I have derived from the Brentano community at large, and in particular Arnaud Dewalque, Guillaume Fréchette, Kevin Mulligan, Hamid Taieb, and Mark Textor. I have also benefited from a pair of seminars on Brentano that I led at the *École normale supérieure* in Paris. I am grateful to the 30-odd students who participated in those seminars. Sadly I do not remember all their names, but here are those I remember: Mathilde Berger-Perrin, Iris Bernadac, Géraldine Carranante, Lucie Cheyer, Victor de Castelbajac, Lionel Djadaojee, Anna Giustina, Vincent Grandjean, Zdenek Lenner, Jean-Pierre Lesage, Valentin Lewandowski, Alice Martin, Florent Papin, Lylian Paquet, Manon Piette, Mikaël Quesseveur, Mathilde Tahar, and Justin Winzenrieth. Finally, I would also like to thank profusely the two anonymous referees for OUP, whose input improved the book considerably both at sentence level and with respect to key arguments, as well as my friend and student Anna Giustina, whose input on various class lectures, conference talks, and chapter drafts has more than once saved me from a wrong turn and set me on the right course.

PART I
Mind

1

Consciousness

This book makes two main *historical* claims. The first is that Franz Brentano's contributions to philosophy amounted to a philosophical *system*: they offer a unified, structurally symmetric account of the true, the good, and the beautiful. The second is that Brentano's system is grounded in his philosophy of mind. Philosophy of mind serves in it as *first philosophy*, in a sense that will come through in due course.

Importantly, however, Brentano held the problematic view that all mental life is conscious – there are no unconscious mental states. To that extent, his philosophy of mind is more precisely a philosophy of consciousness. Thus it is ultimately Brentano's theory of consciousness that serves as the basis for his entire philosophical system. This is why I open with a chapter on Brentano's account of the nature of consciousness. I argue that for Brentano, a conscious perception of a tree is a single mental state that can be (accurately) conceived of, or framed, either as a perception of a tree or as a perception *of a perception* of a tree. I further argue that this interpretation casts Brentano's theory as quite a bit more plausible than it is commonly taken to be – indeed more plausible than many modern theories of consciousness!

1. Phenomenal Consciousness and the Awareness Principle

Before starting, we should consider whether by 'consciousness' Brentano has in mind the notion that has attracted so much attention in contemporary philosophy of mind, namely, the notion of *phenomenal* consciousness, the what-it-is-like aspect of experience. Obviously, Brentano does not use the *term* 'phenomenal consciousness.' And crucially, while some of the contemporary discussion of phenomenal consciousness has focused on purely sensory phenomena, for Brentano consciousness comes both in sensory and nonsensory varieties. (More on this in Chap. 3.) Nonetheless, I contend, it is reasonable to suppose that phenomenal consciousness is precisely the phenomenon his discussion targets.

On one view, the phenomenal notion of consciousness is the pre-theoretic notion familiar to each of us from our personal experience. This is the approach suggested by Block's (1978) remark that the correct response to the question 'What is phenomenal consciousness?' is just 'If you have to ask, you ain't never gonna know.' If this is how we conceive of phenomenal consciousness, then unless an author indicates otherwise, his or her discussion of consciousness probably targets phenomenal consciousness. Against this background, it would be natural to take Brentano to target phenomenal consciousness – since he in fact does not indicate otherwise.

Another view is that the phenomenal notion of consciousness is a highly technical notion – the notion of something that at least *appears* to be categorically different from physical reality, inducing an appearance of an *explanatory gap*. Thus, elsewhere Block suggests that we appeal to the explanatory gap 'by way of pointing to [phenomenal] consciousness: *that's* the entity to which the mentioned explanatory gap applies' (Block 1995: 382).[1] Against *this* background, we should suppose that Brentano targets phenomenal consciousness only if the phenomenon he has in mind is that which appears so categorically different from matter as to raise the specter of an explanatory gap. It seems to me that this is indeed the phenomenon Brentano has in mind. In his *Psychology from an Empirical Standpoint* (Brentano 1874), he writes:

In reality, physiological processes seem to differ from chemical and physical processes only in their greater complexity … [By contrast,] if one turns one's attention from the outer to the inner realm (*Welt*), it feels like one has switched to a new realm. The phenomena are absolutely heterogeneous …   (Brentano 1874: 71–2 [50–1])

This passage suggests that Brentano thinks vitalists were demonstrably wrong in holding that biological phenomena were *categorically* distinct from physical and chemical phenomena, involving something extra (the *élan vital*). In reality, the former differ from the latter only in *degree*, not in *kind* – their degree of complexity is simply higher. However, a genuinely categorical difference ('absolute heterogeneity') does characterize the gap between physical, chemical, and biological phenomena, on the one hand, and conscious phenomena, on the other. Here the difference 'feels like' one of kind, not degree.

Thus Brentano's concern is clearly with phenomenal consciousness, whether under-stood technically or pre-theoretically. In saying this, I do not mean to claim that he is interested only in *sensory* consciousness. Rather, I mean that he is interested in that very phenomenon which we know more intimately than all others but which nonetheless creates an imposing sense of explanatory gap with the rest of reality. It is a separate question whether or not this phenomenon occurs only in the sensory domain.

The starting point of Brentano's theory of consciousness is the following claim:

(C1)   There is no unconscious consciousness.

As Brentano explicitly notes, this is not meant as a tautology (Brentano 1874: I, 143 [102]). But the only way C1 can be non-tautological is if the two consciousness-terms in it are used in different senses. Oddly, Brentano specifies the two senses only in a footnote:

We use the term 'unconscious' in two ways. First, in an active sense, speaking of a person who is not conscious of a thing; secondly, in a passive sense, speaking of a thing of which we are not conscious.   (Brentano 1874: I, 143* [102‡])

The passive sense of 'conscious' may be understood as follows: a mental state M of a subject S is conscious$_p$ iff S is conscious *of* M. The active sense is rather something like this: a mental state M of subject S is conscious$_a$ iff M is a state of S's consciousness.[2] As Brentano makes clear toward the end of this footnote, the intended reading of C1 is:

(C2)   There is no unconscious$_p$ consciousness$_a$.

This thesis no longer carries the air of tautology. What it means is that no subject is in a state of consciousness of which she is not conscious. To further dissipate any appearance of triviality, let us replace one occurrence of a consciousness term with 'awareness' (since *Bewusstsein* corresponds to both 'consciousness' and 'awareness' in English). We obtain the following thesis:

(C3)   For any mental state M of a subject S, if M is a state of S's consciousness, then S is aware of M.

I will call this the *awareness principle*, as it foreshadows David Rosenthal's (2005) 'transitivity principle.'[3] Brentano's theorizing on consciousness grows out of the awareness principle. (I will conduct the discussion in terms of 'states' and not 'acts' – the latter is Brentano's preferred term – because of the prevalence of state talk in current philosophy of mind. There are of course important differences between states and acts, but they do not affect the goals of this chapter.)

Many different theories of consciousness are compatible with the awareness principle. They differ among them on two principal issues. The first concerns the nature of S's awareness of M. In particular, there is a choice to be made between perceptualist and intellectualist construals of this awareness. On one view, S is aware of M in a perception-like manner, as though shining a flashlight on M. On another view, S is aware of M in a thought-like manner, as though mentally describing M. The second issue concerns the metaphysical relationship between M and the awareness-of-M. On one view, the two are distinct: S is aware of M in virtue of being in some other mental state. On a second view, they are *not* distinct: S is aware of M in virtue of being in M itself. In other words: S is aware of M in virtue of being in M*, but is M* ≠ M or is M* = M? This second issue will take up the core of this chapter (§§4–7). But first I want to address the first issue.

2. Inner Awareness and Inner Perception

A conscious experience of a tree involves awareness of a tree. According to the awareness principle, it also involves an awareness of the awareness of the tree. But is this second-order awareness (i) a *perception*-of-awareness-of-tree, (ii) a *thought*-about-awareness-of-tree, or (iii) something else? In other words, is M* (i) a perceptual awareness of M, (ii) an intellectual or cognitive awareness of M, or (iii) something else?

There is no doubt that Brentano opts for (i): M* is an *inner perception* of M. From the earliest chapters of the *Psychology*, Brentano stresses that all conscious states are inner-perceived, ultimately claiming that this demarcates them as mental (1874: I, 128–9 [91–2]). Accordingly, C3 could be sharpened into the following:

(C4)   For any mental state M of a subject S, if M is a state of S's consciousness, then S inner-perceives M.

That this is Brentano's view might be obscured by the fact that in various places Brentano describes M* not as an inner perception (*Wahrnehmung*), but as an inner presentation (*Vorstellung*), inner judgment (*Urteil*), inner cognition/acquaintance (*Erkenntnis*), or inner consciousness/awareness (*Bewusstsein*). However, this multiplicity of expressions reflects, for the most part, various substantive views Brentano held about those mental states. We will encounter many of these views in later chapters; but a preliminary glance is necessary to see why Brentano is committed to C4.

A central task of a serious theory of consciousness, according to Brentano, is to offer a 'fundamental classification' of conscious states. Brentano's own classification divides conscious states into three fundamental categories, one of which he calls 'judgment.' As we will see in more detail in Chap. 3, this category covers all conscious states that can be assessed as true, veridical, or accurate. Since perception can be assessed as veridical or accurate, it qualifies, for Brentano, as a form of judgment in this sense. Perception is a *species* of the genus judgment. Accordingly, any state which can be described as a perception can also be described, at a higher level of abstraction, as a judgment. This explains why Brentano sometimes describes M* as a *judgment*. To our modern ears, describing a mental state as a judgment marks first and foremost a contrast with perception. But for Brentano, the real contrast is with mental states that are not assessable as true or veridical (such as desire, anger, and contemplation). The inner-perceiving of a banana-smoothie experience affirms the existence of that experience, as well as its character, hence can be assessed as accurate or inaccurate. It is therefore a judgment in Brentano's technical sense.

For a similar reason, Brentano sometimes describes M* as an awareness. Brentano uses the term 'awareness' or 'consciousness' (*Bewusstsein*) for the most generic kind of mental state. Indeed, awareness is the genus of which judgment itself is a species. So, anything which is an inner perception can at an even higher level of abstraction be described as an awareness.

As for the term 'cognition,' this is a somewhat unhappy translation of *Erkenntnis*. In English, the verb 'knows' describes two very different relations. We say 'I know that Chalmers is smart,' but also 'I know Chalmers.' In the first case, we ostensibly report a relation to a proposition, fact, or state of affairs. In the second, we report a relation to an individual. In most languages, two different verbs are used for these two relations, but in English we use 'know' for both. At the same time, we can also say 'I am acquainted with Chalmers,' meaning essentially the same as 'I know Chalmers.' In Brentano's mouth, *Erkenntnis* is the kind of state denoted in such reports: a state of acquaintance, or of objectual (as opposed to propositional) knowledge. Crucially, now, one way to be acquainted with an individual is to perceive it. So it stands to reason that Brentano should sometimes describe inner perception as inner *Erkenntnis*.[4]

A further substantive Brentanian position, to be discussed in Chap. 3 as well, is that every mental state is grounded in a presentation. For example, judging that *p* involves harboring a presentation of *p* and accepting or affirming the content presented. Other types of mental state involve other modifications of the same fundamental act of presenting (Brentano 1874: I, 112 [80]; II, 34 [198]). This applies to perception as well, indeed to *inner* perception: S's inner perception of M involves a specific modification of an inner *presentation* of M. This explains why Brentano also ascribes to the subject an inner presentation of her conscious state.

This battery of substantive positions thus explains the multiplicity of expressions Brentano uses to describe our awareness of our conscious states. It is in light of all this that passages such as the following make perfect sense:

Every [conscious] act, therefore, is accompanied by a twofold inner awareness, by a presentation which refers to it and a judgment which refers to it, the so-called inner perception, which is an immediate, self-evident acquaintance with the act.   (Brentano 1874: I, 203 [143])

In this passage, it is clear that 'judgment', 'perception', and 'acquaintance' are used to describe the same element of experience. My suggestion is that they do so by describing that element at different levels of abstraction: a perception is a species of acquaintance, which itself is a species of judgment, which in turn is a species of awareness. Meanwhile, 'presentation' is used to describe a second aspect of the awareness, though one that grounds, and is thus presupposed by, the inner perception. So the fundamental claim, a claim independent of all these substantive positions, is that we inner-perceive our conscious states.

(In the first edition of the *Psychology*, Brentano also posits a third kind of inner awareness of M, beyond the inner perception and its presupposed inner presentation. The third kind is an 'inner feeling' of pleasure or displeasure toward M. Brentano later dropped this view – see Brentano 1911: II, 139 [276] – so I will mostly ignore it here.)

It is legitimate, then, to think of Brentano's view as simply invoking a perceptual awareness of conscious states. In this, he belongs to a long philosophical tradition. Locke wrote: 'It [is] impossible for any one to perceive, without perceiving, that he does perceive' (*An Essay Concerning Human Understanding* 2.27.9). A similar view is attributed to Aristotle by Brentano himself, and more expansively by Caston (2002). In contemporary philosophy of mind, the view is represented by Lycan (1990) among others.[5] In contemporary presentations, however, the inner awareness is typically qualified as *quasi*-perceptual, to mark the fact that it is also importantly different from standard sensory perception. Brentano too recognizes that there are important differences here. But his terminological choice is the opposite: he considers inner perception to be perception 'in the strict sense' and sensory perception of external objects to be merely 'so-called perception' (Brentano 1874: I, 128–9 [91]). We might say that for him, this sensory awareness of external objects is *quasi*-perceptual, while inner perception is the only kind of full-blooded perception.[6] The reason for this is partly etymological: the German *Wahrnehmung* means literally something like 'grabbing the true.' The term thus intimates a kind of direct contact with the perceived. As we will see in the next section, Brentano holds that such direct contact characterizes inner perception but not sensory ('outer') perception.

3.   What Is Inner Perception?

To the modern reader, it might seem that what Brentano calls inner perception is just what we call introspection. However, Brentano explicitly distinguishes between inner perception (*Wahrnehmung*) and inner *observation* (*Beobachtung*), and identifies introspection with the latter. The distinction is important, because according to Brentano inner observation of one's current conscious experience is in fact impossible.[7]

To appreciate the difference between the two, consider Brentano's argument against introspection:

…inner perception and not introspection, i.e. inner observation, constitutes [the] primary source of psychology…In observation, we direct our full attention to a phenomenon in order to apprehend it accurately. But with objects of inner perception this is absolutely impossible. This is especially clear with regard to certain mental phenomena such as anger. If someone is in a state in which he wants to observe his own anger raging within him, the anger must already be somewhat diminished, and so his original object of observation would have disappeared.
(1874: I, 40–1 [29–30]; see also 1874: I, 180–1 [128])

It is a central aspect of the phenomenology of raging anger that one is *consumed* by one's anger. If the subject has the presence of mind to attend to her anger, to reflect on it, she is no longer consumed by it. She has managed to 'take some distance' from it. Thus in introspecting one's experience, one would perforce be presented with a milder, unconsuming variety of anger. The anger experience one was originally undergoing – the experience one wished to examine by introspecting – was different, a stronger and more violent anger. In this way, the introspecting *alters* the quality of the anger introspected. To that extent, one's lived experience eludes introspection – as soon as one turns one's attention to it, it goes out of existence and is replaced by another experience with a slightly different phenomenal character. Therefore, it is (nomically) impossible to introspect raging anger. (The modality here is presumably nomic, since if the laws of psychology were different, it might have been possible to introspect our experiences without altering their intensity.)

It might be objected that while the felt intensity of an anger experience is an aspect of its phenomenal character, it is not an *essential* aspect and does not go to its identity conditions. It is still the same anger experience, only experienced more mildly. Accordingly, although introspecting an anger alters it, it does not *destroy* it. And therefore, it is still possible to introspect one's anger, albeit altered. In response, Brentano might insist that every aspect of an experience's phenomenal character is essential to its identity. But more cautiously, we might retreat from the claim that introspection is nomically impossible to the following weaker claim: it is nomically impossible to introspect one's anger experience *as it is independently of being introspected*.

It might still be objected that not all experiences are like anger in this respect. Perhaps it is impossible to introspect anger without altering it, but nothing prevents us from introspecting a visual experience of the blue sky without altering it (Textor 2015). To this objection, Brentano might respond that while the altering of anger by introspection is particularly dramatic, it occurs in a more subdued fashion with other experiences as well. The visual experience of the sky *is* altered by being introspected: it is ever so slightly more vivid, perhaps, just as a headache hurts just a little bit more when we attend to it. Hill (1988) captures this by noting that introspection functions as 'volume control' of our experience, in the sense that introspecting an experience alters its 'phenomenal intensity.' There is an important asymmetry here of course: introspecting *decreases* the anger's phenomenal intensity but *increases* the headache's and visual experience's. Nonetheless, Brentano might insist, it always alters *in some way* the phenomenal character of the introspected experience.

More cautiously yet, we might make an analogous but merely epistemic claim: for any experience E, it is nomically impossible *to know* whether E's character is the same when E is introspected as when E is not introspected. This seems to me quite a plausible claim.

Regardless of whether Brentano's argument against introspection is cogent, we may use it to clarify his notion of inner perception, as opposed to inner observation. What creates the problem for inner observation, according to the argument, is its attentive nature. It is part of the very notion of introspection, for Brentano, that the exercise of introspection involves the control and guidance of attention. (Recall: 'In observation, we direct our full attention to a phenomenon in order to apprehend it accurately.') The problem is that attending to a conscious experience alters its phenomenal intensity (if nothing else). The attentiveness of introspection implies further properties, such as voluntariness. Normally, we can *decide* to introspect, and equally, we can decide *not* to introspect, or to *stop* introspecting. By and large, attending, and hence introspecting, are up to us. Accordingly, introspecting is not ubiquitous: sometimes we introspect, sometimes we do not.

From the fact that Brentano's argument is not supposed to apply to inner *perception*, we may now infer that inner perception differs on these scores: it is non-attentive, involuntary, and ubiquitous. The claim is that we have a broadly perceptual kind of inner awareness that proceeds independently of attention and goes on in us involuntarily and at all times. When one undergoes an experience of consuming anger, one is *aware* of it, but aware of it (i) non-attentively, insofar as one attends rather to the angering stimulus, and (ii) involuntarily, insofar as one cannot stop being aware of one's anger at will. This non-attentive and involuntary awareness is, according to Brentano, pervasive in our conscious experience.

To appreciate this kind of awareness, consider an analogy with *sensory* ('outer') perception and observation. Right now, I am visually aware of a scene involving a desk, a laptop, a cup of coffee, a book, and a lamp. Visually, I am attentively aware of the laptop. I am not visually attending to the lamp or the cup. Yet I am clearly visually *aware* of them, though in a peripheral, non-attentive sort of way. Brentano would put this by saying that I visually *perceive* the desk, laptop, cup, book, and lamp, but visually *observe* only the laptop. Now, I can deliberately *decide* to start attending to the cup to my right (even without moving my eyes), and to that extent can *decide* to no longer attend to the laptop. I can decide, that is, what I want to observe. But as long as my eyes are open and I do not intervene in the scene before me, I cannot decide what I want to *perceive*. I cannot decide to *shut down* my peripheral visual awareness of the book and the lamp. Thus unlike visual observation, visual perception is not voluntary and need not be attentive.

The same characteristics distinguish *inner* perception and observation. Right now, I am undergoing a complex episode involving visual experience of the scene just described, auditory experience of my dog snoring softly, tactile experience of the soles of my shoes, a mild experience of anxiety about an afternoon appointment, and occasionally a number of fleeting thoughts and episodic memories about last night's film. Of these, I am attentively aware only of the visual experience (since I am trying to describe it). I am not attending at all to the auditory, tactile, emotional, and mnemonic components of my overall experience. Yet I am clearly aware of them too, though in a peripheral, non-attentive sort of way. In Brentano's terms, I have inner *observation* only of the visual component of my overall experience, but have inner *perception* of the auditory, tactile, emotional, and mnemonic components as well.[8,9] As before, I can *decide* to shift around my attention, to stop attending to the visual experience of the scene before me and attend instead, say, to the auditory experience of my dog's snoring.[10] But although I can decide what I want to attend to, I cannot similarly decide what I want to be aware of. I can stop attending to my visual experience, but I cannot at will stop being aware of it. I have control over inner observation, but not over inner perception.

Imagine a paralyzed person who can neither move her neck nor close her eyes at will. She has no control over what appears to her visually, though she can decide to attend to one or another element in her visual field. According to Brentano, we are all in this position when it comes to our awareness of our own stream of consciousness: we have no control over what appears to us, though we can decide to attend to one or another element in our stream of consciousness. That by which our own conscious life appears to us nonattentively, involuntarily, and ubiquitously is what Brentano calls inner perception.

᪣

Inner perception, then, is the non-attentive, involuntary, ubiquitous awareness we have of our conscious life. These are the *psychological* characteristics of inner perception. In addition, inner perception is centrally characterized by its *epistemic* properties:

...besides the fact that it has a special object [namely, mental phenomena], inner perception possesses another distinguishing characteristic: its immediate (*unmittelbare*), infallible (*untrügliche*) self-evidence (*Evidenz*). Of all the types of knowledge (*Erkentnissen*) of the objects of experience, inner perception alone possesses this characteristic.   (Brentano 1874: I, 128 [91])

Inner perception has at least three epistemic properties that separate it from other types of awareness: (a) it is *immediate*, in that its justification is not based upon, or mediated by, anything else's; (b) it is *infallible*, in that inner-*mis*perception is impossible; and it is (c) *self-evident*, where self-evidence is a primitive, unanalyzable notion.

I will expand on the primitive notion of self-evidence (*Evidenz*) in Chap. 5.[11] But one may reasonably suspect that with its primitive status comes a certain *foundational* status. After considering a number of arguments for the infallibility of inner perception, Brentano concludes thus:

These attempts to establish the infallibility of inner perception are, therefore, complete failures, and the same is true of any other attempt which might be suggested instead. The correctness (*Richtigkeit*) of inner perception cannot be proved in any way. But it has something more than proof; it is immediately self-evident. If anyone were to mount a skeptical attack against this ultimate foundation of cognition/knowledge (*Erkenntnis*), he would find no other foundation upon which to erect an edifice of knowledge (*Wissens*).   (1874: I, 198 [140])

There is no argument for the infallibility of inner perception. The only reason to accept the proposition <inner perception is infallible>, for Brentano, is that it is itself self-evident. We may presume that the same holds of the *immediacy* of inner perception: there is no argument for it, but it is self-evident. To that extent, self-evidence is the most basic of inner perception's epistemic properties.

As for self-evidence itself, there is no argument for it either, the passage suggests, except perhaps a *transcendental* one: if inner perception were *not* self-evident, all knowledge would be impossible. Brentano seems to assume here a form of classical foundationalism, where the epistemic justification of all beliefs derives ultimately from the self-evidence of inner perception (compare BonJour 2000). We will assess the special role of the notion of self-evidence in Brentano's system in Chap. 5. The only point I want to make now is that for Brentano, none of these epistemic properties characterize introspection. Thus Brentano holds that there is no appearance/reality gap for consciousness, but not with respect to *introspective* appearances – his claim concerns only *inner-perceptual* appearances.

Brentano has no real argument for the self-evidence and infallibility of inner perception, then, but he does have an *explanation* for them. The explanation is that a conscious experience and one's inner perception of it are in fact not numerically distinct mental states; rather, they are intimately connected in such a way as to exclude any daylight between the experience and the inner perceiving of it:

Whenever a mental act is the object of an accompanying inner cognition/acquaintance (*Erkenntnis*), it contains itself in its entirety as presented and cognized/acquainted with (*erkannt*)...This alone makes possible the infallibility and immediate self-evidence of inner perception. If the cognition/acquaintance which accompanies a mental act were an act in its own right, a second act added on to the first one,...how could it be certain in and of itself?

(1874: I, 196 [139])

Recall that the inner perception of an experience can also be described, at a higher level of abstraction, as an inner acquaintance. What gives this inner perception or acquaintance its special epistemic properties, says Brentano, is the fact that it is not really separate from the mental state inner-perceived. Underlying the special epistemic properties of inner perception, then, is an involved view on the internal structure of every conscious experience. It is to this important view that we turn next.

In conclusion, inner perception is a broadly perceptual awareness of our conscious experience that is (i) non-attentive, (ii) involuntary, (iii) ubiquitous, (iv) immediate, (v) infallible, and (vi) self-evident. Brentano spends precisely zero time arguing that there *is* such a thing. The existence of this self-evident inner perception seems to be a foundational insight, something without which the rest of the system cannot work.

4. Inner Perception and the Inner-Perceived: An Elusive Intimacy

Granted that all conscious states are states the subject inner-perceives, as per C4, it remains to ask whether a conscious state and its inner perception are numerically distinct or numerically identical.[12] As we have just seen, it is central to Brentano's view that the two cannot be entirely distinct. They are intimately connected, or inner perception could not be self-evident and infallible. Brentano is categorical on this:

People have misconstrued the true character of inner self-perception, holding that it is not co-encapsulated (*mitbeschlossen*) in the activity perceived and is not co-given (*mitgegeben*), as Aristotle said, *en parergo* ['on the side']; that it is sometimes entirely absent, and that when it is present, it is not exactly simultaneous but rather follows somewhat as an effect follows a cause as closely as possible...Such a theory eliminates the special characteristic (*Eigentümliche*) that makes possible the immediate self-evidence of self-perception: it omits *the identity of the perceiving and the perceived.* (Brentano 1928: 8 [7–8]; my italics)

Based on passages such as this, many have taken Brentano to hold that a conscious experience and its inner perception are one and the same mental state (e.g., Caston 2002, Hossack 2002, Kriegel 2003a). Already in the *Psychology*, Brentano writes:

In *the same* mental act in which the sound is present to our minds we simultaneously apprehend the mental act itself. What is more, we apprehend it in accordance with its dual nature insofar as it has the sound as content within it, and insofar as it has itself as content at the same time. (Brentano 1874: I, 179–80 [127]; my italics)

That is, it is one and the same mental state that constitutes (i) our hearing a trumpet and (ii) our being (inner-perceptually) aware of hearing a trumpet.

Brentano's use of the expressions 'identity of' and 'the same' in these passages, and of similar locutions in others, suggests that he takes a conscious state and one's awareness of it to be strictly *identical*. This is what Keith Hossack (2002) calls the 'identity thesis':

The thesis I now wish to consider…which was endorsed by Brentano, is the claim that any conscious state is identical with knowledge of its own occurrence, and that this is in fact the criterion of whether a state is conscious.   (Hossack 2002: 174)

Hossack relies on the following passage from Brentano:

While we have the presentation of a sound, we are conscious of having it…[T]here is a special connection between the object of inner presentation and the presentation itself, and…both belong to one and the same mental act. The presentation of the sound and the presentation of the presentation of the sound form a single mental phenomenon.

(Brentano 1874: I, 176–9 [126–7], quoted in Hossack 2002: 174 fn14)

We may call this the 'identity interpretation' of Brentano's view on the relationship between a conscious state M and the awareness of it M*.

Observe, however, that the passage Hossack relies on does not quite say that M and M* are *identical*. Instead, Brentano speaks of a 'special connection between,' or rather special *interweaving* (*Verwebung*) of, M and M*. He says that M and M* 'belong' to the same mental act, not that they *are* the same mental act; that they 'form' a single mental phenomenon, not that they *are* a single mental phenomenon. In other places, Brentano speaks of the 'peculiarly intimate bond (*Verbindung*) of the mental act [M] with the accompanying presentation which refers to it [M*]' (1874: I, 187 [133]). He writes:

…the presentation of the sound is connected/bound (*verbunden*) with the presentation of the presentation of the sound in such a peculiarly intimate (*eigentümlich inniger*) way that its being at the same time contributes inwardly to the being of the other.   (Brentano 1874: I, 179 [127])

Now, one intimate relation is certainly the *identity* relation. But arguably, if Brentano thought that the 'special' and 'intimate' relation at play was simply identity, he would have put his claims in terms of identity. The fact that he does not may suggest, on reflection, that he thinks there is something more nuanced going on.

According to Textor (2006), talk about M and M* 'belonging to,' or 'forming,' a single mental state suggests a *mereological* relation: M and M* are two *parts* of a single mental state. We may call this the 'fusion interpretation': a conscious experience of a tree is a mereological fusion of an awareness-of-tree and an awareness-of-awareness-of-tree. Textor writes:

If in painting A and painting A hitting B, I have painted A only once, the two acts of painting *cannot be distinct*. It seems natural to say that the painting of A is contained in my painting A hitting B. Similarly, if the sound is not presented twice over, once in the first-order presentation, a second time in the higher-order presentation, the presentations cannot be distinct. The mental acts are *interwoven or fused*. This should be taken literally.

(Textor 2006: 418; my italics)

There is no question Brentano often frames his view in mereological terms, for instance when speaking of the 'peculiar fusion (*eigentümliche Verschmelzung*) of awareness and the object of awareness' (1874: I, 196 [139]) we find in inner awareness. On this basis, Textor (2006: 422) asserts that Hossack's identity thesis, while perhaps attractive, is simply not Brentano's view.

Over the next four sections, I want to defend the identity interpretation over the fusion interpretation, while doing justice to the basic motivation for a fusion interpretation. I proceed in two steps. First, I present a novel interpretation of Brentano's view that casts M and M* as, strictly speaking, identical. I will then show why Brentano sometimes uses mereological language to express his particular version of the identity view. The two basic ideas may be put initially as follows:

(1) Brentano holds that a conscious experience of *x* is a mental state that can be framed, or conceived of, equally accurately as (i) awareness of *x* or (ii) awareness of awareness of *x*.

(2) Brentano's mereology distinguishes two parthood relations, a real-parthood relation and a conceptual-parthood relation, and the awareness of *x* and the awareness of the awareness of *x* are merely conceptual parts of the same state.

What follows elaborates on these two ideas: §5 develops the first idea, §6 presents Brentano's mereology, and §7 elaborates on the second idea in light of Brentano's mereology; §8 defends the emerging theory of consciousness against substantive objections.

5. A New Interpretation of Brentano's Theory of Consciousness

On the interpretation of Brentano's theory I want to offer, a conscious experience of a tree involves the occurrence of a single mental state, but one that lends itself to *characterization* either as an awareness of a tree or as an awareness of an awareness of a tree. On this interpretation, there is an element of identity cited in Brentano's account as well as an element of difference. The identity pertains to the *state itself*; the difference pertains to *ways of construing* the state, or of *framing* it, or *conceptualizing* what it is. Nonetheless, at bottom what there is in the subject's mind is a single mental state.

It is natural for us today to articulate this kind of position in terms of Fregean identity. Hesperus and Phosphorus are one entity, but there are two completely separate ways of *conceiving* of that entity: via the MORNING STAR concept and via the EVENING STAR concept. (This is a case of a posteriori identity regarding a concrete particular, but there are also cases of a posteriori identity regarding properties, events, states of affairs, and so on.) The way I see things, this is exactly Brentano's position on conscious experience: the awareness of X and the awareness of the awareness of X are one and the same entity; the concepts, or conceptualizations, AWARENESS OF X and AWARENESS OF AWARENESS OF X are distinct ways of picking out that entity. Crucially, both conceptualizations are equally legitimate, indeed equally *accurate*. When you point at Venus and say 'This is the morning star,' you speak truly, and so do you when you point at Venus and say 'This is the evening star.' By the same token, you speak truly, while 'pointing at' a conscious experience of a tree, either if you say 'This is an awareness of a tree' or if you say 'This is an awareness of an awareness of a tree.'

Lacking Frege's machinery, I contend, Brentano continuously sought ways of articulating this kind of view.[13] Sometime during the 1880s, he settled on a way of articulating it that involved mereological language; I will discuss this articulation in §§6–7. But already in the *Psychology* (from 1874) one can find passages in which the idea is all but explicit. Consider:

The presentation of the sound [M] and the presentation of the presentation of the sound [M*] form a single mental phenomenon; it is only by considering/regarding/viewing (*betrachten*) it in its relation to two different objects, one of which is a physical phenomenon and the other a mental phenomenon, that we divide it conceptually [i.e., in thought] into two presentations.

(Brentano 1874: I, 179 [127])

In reality, says Brentano, there is only one thing here – the subject's experience. It is just that we can *consider* or *regard* it in two different ways, depending on whether we consider it as an intentional relation to a sound or as an intentional relation to an awareness of a sound. Accordingly, the subject's experience can be *grasped* either qua presentation-of-sound or qua presentation-of-presentation-of-sound. But the thing itself is one. (Note that already in this passage Brentano alludes, somewhat cryptically, to a 'conceptual division' of the experience into two presentations. Talk of division, or partition, brings in a mereological dimension as yet undeveloped. We will see its fuller development in Brentano's later writings in §6.2.)

Brentano repeats this formulation in terms of *betrachten* elsewhere in the *Psychology*. For example:

…every [conscious] act, even the simplest, has [several] aspects (*Seite*) under which it may be considered/regarded/viewed (*betrachtet*). It may be considered/regarded as a presentation of its primary object…; however, it may also be considered/regarded as a presentation of itself…   (1874: I, 218–19 [154])

A conscious thought of the Eiffel Tower can be *viewed* as an act of contemplating the Eiffel Tower or, just as accurately, as an act of contemplating a contemplation of the Eiffel Tower. These are in some sense two different aspects under which the thought can be conceived. But these 'aspects' should not be thought of as separate *constituents* of the thought. Rather, they are different ways one and the same thing can be *considered* or *regarded*. The point is stated simply and crisply by Brentano's *Enkelschüler* ('grand-student') Hugo Bergman in his remarkable 1908 study of inner perception. Referring to an act of inner perception as an 'inner act,' he writes:

An inner act [M*] and its object [M] are one and the same (*sind eins*), and are only conceptually distinguished (*beggrifflich unterschieden*).   (Bergmann 1908: 12)

It is this exact position that I want to ascribe to Brentano. As we will see in §6, talk of conceptual distinguishability comes directly from Brentano's mereology.

Call this the *Fregean identity interpretation* of Brentano's theory of consciousness. According to this interpretation, the point of Brentano's theory may be summarized as follows: if you want to know what a conscious state is, imagine a mental state that lends itself at once to understanding as a presentation of something and as a presentation of a presentation of that thing. Such a mental state is what a conscious state *is*. This account of the *nature* of consciousness is striking in its originality: none of the current theories of consciousness offers quite this perspective on what makes something a conscious state (with the possible exception of Nida-Rümelin 2017), and to my knowledge, there is no precedent for this view in the history of Western philosophy.

As such, the view also raises certain immediate question marks. In particular, one might wonder whether there is not *something about* a conscious state that makes it lend itself to two equally accurate framings, something that *grounds* this 'dual-framability' of conscious states. If there is not, the view might seem a tad mysterious. But if there is, then the nature of consciousness should be identified rather with that which *grounds* the dual-framability, whatever that is. We will return to this very real difficulty in §8. For now, let me only stress that it would be a misunderstanding to take Brentano to simply be making the point that a conscious experience of a tree has both the property of presenting a tree and the property of presenting a presentation of a tree. Rather, his point is that there is *no difference* between the property of presenting a tree and the property of presenting a presentation of a tree. They are one and the same property, framed in two different ways. It is a crucial part of the view that the multiplicity of potential framings of a conscious experience is not explicable in terms of a multiplicity of properties or components of the experience. On the contrary, it is only by appreciating the fact that one and the same thing – be it a state or a property – admits of two equally good characterizations that we grasp the essence of consciousness. (More on this in §8.)

6. Brentano's Mereology

Starting in his 1867 metaphysics lectures at Würzburg and up until his death, Brentano continuously developed systematic ideas about part-whole relations. The first published discussion is the chapter on the unity of consciousness in the *Psychology*. But more serious developments, partially abstracted from the psychological context, appear in his Vienna lectures from the late 1880s, published posthumously as Chap. 2 of *Descriptive Psychology* (Brentano 1982). The most systematic and topic-neutral presentation of his mereological ideas published to date is in various dictations from 1908 and 1914–15, collated by Alfred Kastil into chaps. 1 and 2 of *The Theory of Categories* (Brentano 1933).

Brentano never presented an axiomatic mereological system with proofs of consistency and completeness. But his mereological ideas directly influenced work in this direction by his students Stumpf (1890), Ehrenfels (1890), Twardowski (1894), and Husserl (1901).[14] It was a student of Twardowski's, Leśniewski, who first developed a formal system of so-called Classical Mereology (Leśniewski 1916). My approach to the exposition of Brentano's mereology is to first introduce the basics of Classical Mereology and then point out the respects in which Brentano's mereology deviates from it (§6.1); one deviation is particularly important for our present purposes and will be examined in special depth (§6.2).

6.1. *Classical Mereology and Brentano's mereology*

Classical Mereology (CM) is most naturally axiomatized in terms of six propositions, couched in logical vocabulary plus four mereological notions: part, proper part, overlap, and sum. The four notions are interdefinable, and it is possible in principle to take a single notion and define the others in terms of it (plus the logical vocabulary). Typically mereologists take 'part' as their basic notion, but sometimes they opt for 'proper part' (e.g., Simons 1987a). As I find 'proper part' to be the more intuitive notion, I will use it as the basic notion here. We may then say that a *part* of A is something which is either a proper part of A or identical to A; A and B *overlap* when they have a part in common; and the *sum* of A and B is anything that has A and B as parts such that any *other* part it has must overlap them. More formally:

(Def$_1$)   A is a part of B iff (i) A is a proper part of B or (ii) A = B.
(Def$_2$)   A overlaps B iff there is a C, such that (i) C is a part of A and (ii) C is a part of B.
(Def$_3$)   S is a sum of A and B iff any C that overlaps S overlaps either A or B.

In this construction, we define 'sum' in terms of 'overlap', 'overlap' in terms of 'part', and 'part' in terms of 'proper part'. The term 'proper part' remains undefined, a primitive of the system.

The axioms of CM divide into two groups. The first are axioms that describe the proper-parthood relation as a strict partial order (irreflexive, asymmetric, and transitive):

(CM$_{Ar}$)   A is never a proper part of A.
(CM$_{As}$)   If A is a proper part of B, then B is not a proper part of A.
(CM$_T$)   If A is a proper part of B and B is a proper part of C, then A is a proper part of C.

Not every strict partial ordering is proper-parthood, however. So CM includes also three more substantive axioms. One is the axiom of unrestricted composition: for any plurality of things, there is a sum composed of them. Another is the 'axiom of supplementation': if one thing is a proper part of a second, the second must have an additional proper part (to make it whole, so to speak). The last is the 'axiom of extensionality': having the same parts implies being identical and vice versa. More formally:

(CM$_U$)   For any plurality of items A, B, ..., there is a X that is the sum of A, B, ...

(CM$_S$)   If A is a proper part of B, then there is a C, such that (i) C is a proper part of B and (ii) C does not overlap A.

(CM$_E$)   A = B iff every part of A is a part of B and every part of B is part of A.

These axioms employ the terms 'sum', 'part', and 'overlap', but can be reformulated entirely in terms of 'proper part' and logical vocabulary (by using Def$_1$–Def$_3$). As noted, however, CM can also be formulated in terms of six axioms that use only logical vocabulary plus 'part'.

So much, then, for CM. How does Brentano's mereology (BM) differ? Brentano explicitly accepts unrestricted composition: 'Every plurality (*Mehrheit*) of things is a thing' (Brentano 1933: 11 [19]; see also 1933: 5 [16]). He also defends the thesis of 'composition as identity' (Brentano 1933: 5 [16], 50 [46]), which is commonly thought to lead rather straightforwardly to the axiom of extensionality. There are two main differences, however, between BM and CM.

One is that in BM the axiom of supplementation does not hold generally (though it does hold for *substances*, that is, for entities capable of independent existence). The reasons for this odd claim are complex and derive from Brentano's nominalist agenda; they will be explained and motivated in Chap. 6. As these issues bear nowise on the interpretation of Brentano's theory of consciousness, I set them aside here.[15]

The most important difference between CM and BM concerns the primitive notion of (proper-)parthood. In CM, there is a single, univocal notion at play. This does not seem to be the case for Brentano:

> ...one may be able to distinguish parts that are actually *separable/detachable* (*ablösbar*) from one another, until one reaches parts where such...separation can no longer take place.... However, even these ultimate actually separate parts, in some sense, can be said to have further parts.... To differentiate these from others, we may refer to them as *distinctional* parts.
>
> (Brentano 1982: 13 [16]; my italics)

Brentano seems to distinguish two types of proper part: *separable* and *distinctional*. Here is one example where they come apart:

> Someone who believes in [mereological] atoms believes in corpuscles which cannot be dissolved into smaller bodies. But even so he can speak of halves, quarters, etc. of atoms: parts which are distinguishable even though they are not actually separable. (Brentano 1982: 13 [16])

By 'atoms' Brentano means not the entities referred to as atoms in physics, but the entities genuinely admitting of no physical division. A 'physics-atom' with one proton and three electrons does have separable parts, since we can separate the electrons from the proton – this is called 'splitting the atom'. The proton too has separable parts – the quarks making it up. But the electrons have no separable parts. It is impossible to 'split the electron'.[16] Still, even though we cannot separate *in reality* different parts of electron E, we can distinguish *in thought* different parts of it. We can call the top half of E

'Jimmy' and the bottom half 'Johnny.' (Or perhaps better: since E has a determinate mass m, we can divide m by two and consider each of E's two halves independently.) Jimmy and Johnny are thus *distinguishable* parts of E, but not *separable* parts. We may say that they are *merely*-distinguishable parts; Brentano often calls such parts *divisiva*.

It would seem, then, that Brentano distinguishes two notions of (proper-)parthood, which we may call *parthood-as-separability* and *parthood-as-distinguishability*.[17] Accordingly, he recognizes two kinds of (proper) part: separables and distinguishables. The former are separable *in reality*, the latter are distinguishable *in thought*. It may well turn out that whatever is separable in reality is distinguishable in thought, but clearly, not everything which is distinguishable in thought is separable in reality – as the electron case shows.

6.2. *Merely-distinguishable parts*

The notion of merely-distinguishable part does not feature in current mainstream mereology. But many cases appear to suggest it, beside the electron case. Consider the difference between Marie Antoinette's head and Marie Antoinette's smile. There is a sense in which Marie Antoinette's head is part of Marie Antoinette, and there is also a sense in which her smile is a part of her. But these do not seem to be the *same* sense. Remarkably, Marie Antoinette's head is manifestly a separable part of her, whereas her smile is merely-distinguishable. So one way of making sense of the difference between these two kinds of parthood is in terms of Brentano's separable/distinguishable distinction.

The relationship between a person and her smile is a special case of the more general relation between a 3D object and (any portion of) its 2D surface: the surface cannot be separated from the object and exist on its own.[18] There is a clear intuition that although it is a genuine part of the object, the surface is such in a different sense from any physically separable component of that object. In general, any n-dimensional part of an $n+m$-dimensional object ($n, m > 0$) is intuitively a part of that object in a special sense worth labeling.

There is more than just intuition here, however. There is a real and deep difference between two kinds of part: some parts are *ontologically independent* of the wholes of which they are parts; others are ontologically *dependent*. We may mark this difference any way we want, but it is deeper than many other distinctions routinely made in current mereology. One perfectly natural way to mark the difference is to call the former separable parts and the latter merely-distinguishable parts. When P is a separable part of some whole W, P is ontologically independent of W. For it can exist *without* W. Accordingly, the destruction of W does not entail the destruction of P. By contrast, when P is a merely-distinguishable part of W, it is very much ontologically dependent upon W. Since it cannot be separated from W, it cannot exist without W. The existence of W is a precondition for its existence. Accordingly, the destruction of W entails the destruction of P.[19]

These characteristics of the merely-distinguishable part have clear implications for its ontological status. Brentano tells us that merely-distinguishable parts 'cannot be called *realia*' (Brentano 1956: 232). In lecture notes from the 1860s, he explicitly contrasts the status of divisiva (i.e., merely distinguishable parts) and 'real beings':

> The metaphysical parts, such as bigness, thought, virtue, lions' nature, and so forth are not real beings (*wahren Seienden*), but rather *divisiva*.   (MS 31534, quoted in Baumgartner 2013: 236, though here I offer my own translation)

What does Brentano mean when he says that merely-distinguishable parts are not 'real beings', not *realia*? The answer is far from obvious, but I would propose the following. When we say that P is a merely-distinguishable part of W, it may seem that 'P' is a referring expression picking out some individual item. But in truth, our statement is just an indirect way of describing an aspect of W's *structure*. It is an infelicitous way of saying that W is structured P-ly. Thus while the truthmaker of 'The ear is part of Marie's face' consists in a parthood relation between two items, Marie's ear and her face, the truthmaker of 'The smile is part of Marie's face' does *not* consist in a parthood relation between two items, Marie's smile and her face. Rather, it consists in one item, Marie's face, being structured in a certain way, that is, in Marie's face being smiley. From this perspective, the point of the notion of a merely-distinguishable part, for Brentano, is to recognize that a thing may have no (separable) parts and yet have *structure*. It is not simple in the sense of being structureless, even though it is simple in the sense of being (in reality) partless. These are two different and non-coextensive kinds of simplicity.

Consider: when we say that Marie is two-legged, what makes our statement true is that Marie has two separable parts each of which is a leg; but when we say that Marie is smiling, something must make this statement true as well, even though Marie does not have any separable part which is a smile. That is, even though there are no such entities as smiles, we speak truly when we say that Marie is smiling. Moreover, this is a truth *cum fundamentum in re* – there is something *about Marie* (something about the structure of her face) that makes it true. Talk of merely-distinguishable parts is a device for *describing* this structure. More generally, it is a device for describing structure-without-separable-parts. But we must keep in mind that since merely-distinguishable parts are by definition distinguishable only in thought, what there is in reality is just the structure: although parts are more fundamental than structure when it comes to separable parts, structure is more fundamental than parts when we are dealing with merely-distinguishable parts.

It might be objected that Brentano's notion of a merely-distinguishable part is still unmotivated, on the grounds that Brentano imposes on us parthood talk where property talk would do just fine. The atom has the *property* of having a mass (or occupying a space) divisible by half, Marie Antoinette has the *property* of smiling, a 3D object has the *property* of having a 2D surface, and so on. Merely-distinguishable parthood is thus entirely dispensable.

For Brentano, however, the important thing is that in conscious experience, there is no *real distinction* between awareness of *x* and awareness of awareness of *x* – whatever ontological category we slot awareness under. So even if we speak of the *property* of being an awareness of *x* and the *property* of being an awareness of an awareness of *x*, Brentano would claim that these are *in reality* one and the same property. And yet *in thought* we can discern in that property two 'dimensions', or 'aspects', or indeed merely-distinguishable parts...Thus it appears that the role played by the notion of merely-distinguishable part is needed whether we think of awareness in terms of states or in terms of properties. (Moreover, even if the distinguishable-part role could be played by properties, for Brentano the more important fact is that the property role can be played by parts! Because of his nominalism, which we will discuss more fully in Chap. 6, Brentano needs to be able to say everything he wants to say without ever mentioning properties. More accurately, he needs to paraphrase truths whose truthmakers ostensibly involve a property as constituent into truths whose ostensible truthmakers do not. Thus, he wants to find a truthmaker for 'There is a smile on Marie Antoinette's face' that does not involve the property of having a smile as constituent. His way of doing this is to recognize Marie Antoinette's smile as a merely-distinguishable part of Marie. In Chap. 6, we will see how Brentano's mereological innovations allow him to handle a wider array of apparent truths without invoking properties.)

7. The Mereology of Consciousness

Brentano's distinction between separable and merely-distinguishable parts means that when he uses mereological language to express his view of consciousness, there are two very different things he might have in mind. In saying that an awareness of *x* and an awareness of an awareness of *x* are parts of a single state, he might have in mind (a) that they are separable parts of some 'greater' whole, or (b) that they are merely-distinguishable parts of a single thing.

In the *Psychology*, the distinction between the two parthood relations is nowhere explicitly drawn. But where it is drawn – in lecture notes from the late 1880s, at least – Brentano is explicit that parthood-as-distinguishability is what connects an experience M and the awareness of it M*. He speaks of

...the *inseparable connection/fusion* (*untrennbar Verbindung*) of a primary [M] and a concomitant [M*] mental reference (*psychischen Beziehung*). Every consciousness, upon whatever object it is primarily directed [e.g., a tree], is concomitantly directed at itself [the experience of the tree].   (Brentano 1982: 22 [25]; my italics)

In describing the connection between M and M* as *inseparable*, Brentano intimates mere-distinguishability. This becomes more explicit further along, where Brentano considers the internal unity of an audiovisual experience. Imagine having the audiovisual experience of a loud airplane flying overhead. We may distinguish three parts in this experience: (i) the visual awareness of the airplane's shape and color, (ii) the auditory awareness of the airplane's sound, and (iii) the *inner* awareness of the overall experience. Brentano holds that while (i) and (ii) are separable from each other, (i) and (iii) are merely-distinguishable, as are (ii) and (iii).[20] The contrast is clear:

> Whereas the separation of parts considered there [the auditory and visual parts] can only be actual, the parts considered here [the visual part and the inner-awareness part] can only be separated *distinctionally*. This is why, having referred to the former as *actually separable* mental parts, it is probably not wholly inappropriate to call the latter *inseparable (distinctional) parts*.
>
> (1982: 25 [27]; my italics)

In an audiovisual experience, the auditory aspect and the visual aspect are ontologically independent. If while looking at the airplane you suddenly went deaf, your visual experience would persist without the auditory component; if you instead suddenly went blind, the auditory experience would persist without the visual component. But for Brentano, there is no conceivable event that could bring apart your visual experience and your awareness of your visual experience, or your auditory experience and your awareness of it. These are merely distinguishable parts of a single underlying reality.

Recall now that while separable parts can be separated *in reality*, merely-distinguishable parts can only be distinguished *in thought*. They do not have any individual existence *in reality*. It is only *conceptually*, or *in thought*, that we can pull them apart. If so, when we say that an awareness-of-tree M and an awareness-of-awareness-of-tree M* are merely-distinguishable, it would seem to follow that M and M* are not two separate items in reality; it is only in thought that we can pull them apart. More specifically, it is only in thought that we can pull an awareness-of-tree apart from the overall conscious experience of the tree, and at the same time, it is only in thought that we can pull an awareness-of-awareness-of tree apart from that experience. Neither the awareness-of-tree nor the awareness-of-awareness-of tree can exist on its own. The destruction of the experience entails the destruction of the awareness-of-tree, as it does the destruction of the awareness-of-awareness-of tree.

My suggestion can be summarized as follows, then: all Brentano has in mind, when using mereological language to describe the relationship between M and M*, is that in a single, simple, and indivisible mental state, one can *distinguish in thought* M and one can likewise *distinguish in thought* M*. There is no claim about *real* separability, that is, of *parthood-in-reality*. There is only a claim about different ways the one simple thing in reality can be thought of. This is perfectly consistent, then, with the Fregean identity interpretation of Brentano's theory of consciousness. For it suggests precisely that awareness-of-tree and awareness-of-awareness-of-tree are simply two different ways of thinking of a single mental state.

⊱⊰

On the Fregean identity interpretation defended here, Brentano holds that M and M* are merely-distinguishable parts of a single mental state. What this means, I have suggested, is that *in reality* there is only one thing, but we can think of it, or regard it, in two different ways. Just as Venus can be thought of, equally legitimately, as the morning star or as the evening star, a tree experience can be thought of, equally legitimately, as an awareness of a tree or as an awareness of an awareness of a tree.

On this interpretation, it is natural to say that the awareness-of-tree and the awareness-of-awareness-of-tree are *not* numerically distinct, because in reality they are one and the same thing. To repeat, this is *not* meant as the idea that a conscious state has both the property of being an awareness of some object and the property of being an awareness of an awareness of that object; rather, it is meant as the idea that in a conscious state, the property of being an awareness of an object and the property of being an awareness of an awareness of that object are one and the same. The difference is only in how that one property is *regarded*. At the same time, we are missing something if we just assert that conscious experience involves the subject being in a single mental state, or the subject instantiating a single relevant property, and leave it at that. What we are missing, moreover, is the definitive aspect of conscious experience – the way it envelops awareness and awareness-of-awareness in a single mental state. We might therefore say, doubtless somewhat impressionistically, that *qua regarded* the awareness and the awareness-of-awareness are different, even though in and of themselves they are identical. Compare a single duck-rabbit drawing. If we do not see *two* potential book covers here – one suitable for *The Ugly Duckling* and the other appropriate for *The Tales of Peter Rabbit* – we are missing something. Likewise, we can frame the conscious state as M or frame it as M*, and these are different framings.

This explains, I suggest, why Brentano stresses in some contexts the non-distinctness of M and M* and in others their non-identity. When designing a cover for *The Ugly Duckling* or *The Tales of Peter Rabbit*, we would stress the difference between the duck drawing and the rabbit drawing. But when the bill for the copyright fees arrives, we might stress sameness, arguing that we only used one drawing. Likewise, in the context of discussing the internal *structure* of a conscious state (e.g., in Chap. 3 and 4 of Book 2 of the *Psychology*), Brentano stresses the *difference* between the state's various distinguishable parts (M is not the same *distinguishable part* as M*); but in discussing the threat of infinite regress (e.g., in Chap. 2 of Book 2 of the *Psychology*), Brentano stresses the *sameness* of the state itself.

It is in this light that we should understand passages that appear to underline the non-identity of M and M*. Consider this example:

> ...it is clear that such a real identity never holds between our concurrent mental activities, and that it will never be found between the diverse aspects of the simplest act which were differentiated earlier...They are divisives of the same reality, but that does not make them really identical with it and thus with one another.   (Brentano 1874: I, 229 [161])

Textor (2006: 423) relies on this passage to argue for the implausibility of the identity interpretation – as well he should, given the explicit denial of identity in the passage. I would suggest, however, that Brentano is trying, in such passages, to highlight the difference between a conscious state qua awareness of a tree and a conscious state qua awareness of awareness of a tree. Anyone who simply stated that there is just one mental state here, and left it at that, would be missing *the* crucial feature of conscious states – the fact that they lend themselves to conceptualization in two very different yet equally accurate ways. It is this kind of opponent, who does not even recognize the sense in which conscious states essentially involve awareness-of-awareness, that Brentano has in his sights in passages such as this.

This Fregean-identity interpretation is more flexible than either Hossack's flatter identity interpretation or Textor's fusion interpretation. In expounding his identity interpretation, Hossack (2002) appears to make no provision for the mereological subtleties of Brentano's account (although see Hossack 2006 for some distancing from the straight-up identity interpretation). In defending the fusion interpretation, Textor (2006) explicitly recognizes that M* is a divisive (i.e., a merely-distinguishable part) of M. What he fails to recognize, however, is that this means there is only *one* mental state involved. Textor says that 'A "divisive" is an object that can be distinguished in another object as a part, although it cannot be separated from it' (Textor 2006: 423). This seems to directly contradict Brentano's own treatment of parts of a conscious whole as merely *apparent parts*: Brentano tells us that these 'constitute apparent-parts/part-appearances (*Teilphänomene*) of a mental phenomenon, the elements of which are neither distinct things nor parts of distinct things' (1874: I, 232 [164]). Saying that a divisive is 'part of *another* object' suggests that what we have on our hands here are two different items, the conscious state and its awareness-of-awareness part; yet as we have seen for Brentano there is in reality only one item. The inner perception of a tree perception is not a part of *another* state, that of perceiving a tree. Thus just as Hossack's identity interpretation has difficulties making sense of fusion-leaning passages (see esp. Brentano 1874: I, 228–9 [161]), Textor's fusion interpretation has difficulties making sense of the identity-leaning passages (see esp. 1874: I, 179–80 [127]). The interpretation presented here makes sense of both. It is, strictly speaking, an identity interpretation, but one that mobilizes a fuller understanding of Brentano's mereology to do justice to mereological-sounding passages.

8. Brentano's Theory of Consciousness Revisited

Higher-order and self-representational theories are motivated by the intuitiveness of the awareness principle: conscious states are states we are aware of having. It has proven difficult, however, to accommodate the principle (and its intuitiveness) without incurring structural problems in one's theory.

Higher-order theories face a dilemma. They must construe the higher-order state they invoke either as conscious or as unconscious. If they construe it as unconscious, they cannot account for the *intuitiveness* of the awareness principle: it is unclear why conscious states should immediately strike us as states we are aware of if the relevant awareness is but a sub-personal event (and why the awareness principle should be intuitive if conscious states do *not* immediately strike us as states we are aware of). But if the higher-order state is construed as conscious, an infinite regress immediately ensues: the higher-order state would have to be conscious in virtue of being targeted by a yet *higher*-order state (since it is itself a state the subject is aware of), which would have to be targeted by a further higher-order state, and so on.

Self-representational theories attempt to circumvent the regress problem by claiming that one is aware of one's conscious state in virtue of being in that very conscious state. Since that state represents itself, and is conscious, the state is *consciously* represented – which explains the intuitiveness of the awareness principle. However, self-representationalists face a different dilemma. Not all properties of a phenomenally conscious state are themselves phenomenally conscious: my experience's property of occurring on a Wednesday, for example, contributes nothing to what it is like for me to have the experience. Presumably, self-representationalists would say that a state's phenomenal properties are those which the state represents itself as having. But then a question arises: does the conscious state represent only its non-representational properties or also its representational ones? If it represents only its non-representational properties, it is unclear why the state's directedness at the outside world is phenomenally manifest. If it represents also its representational properties, we are off on a regress again: the state would have to represent its self-representing, and then represent its so representing, and so on. An infinite regress of states is avoided, but an infinite regress of representational properties replaces it.

Within Brentano's framework, the problem is much less pressing. The worst-case scenario would be an infinite regress of accurate ways of conceiving of a conscious state – plainly a less troubling prospect, all told, than an infinite regress of states or properties. In truth, however, it is unclear that any kind of regress attends the Brentanian picture. The view is that a conscious state is a single state which lends itself to framing both as awareness-of-*x* and as awareness-of-awareness-of-*x*. But there is no discernible pressure to invoke some third-order awareness-of-awareness-of-awareness-of-*x* to illuminate the fact that the conscious state lends itself to a second-order framing as awareness-of-awareness-of-*x*.

In the extant literature, perhaps the most persistent challenge to higher-order theories is that surrounding the 'division of phenomenal labor.' In general, mental states can misrepresent – and that in two ways: (i) by misrepresenting something to have properties it does not in reality have, or (ii) by misrepresenting something to exist that in reality does not. The same applies to the higher-order states that target conscious states: nothing prevents the occurrence of a higher-order state with the content <I am having a reddish experience> when in reality (i) one is having a greenish experience, or even when (ii) one is having no relevant experience at all. It was originally argued that higher-order theories lead to paradoxical results whatever they choose to say about such cases (Byrne 1997, Neander 1998, Levine 2001: chap. 3, Caston 2002, Kriegel 2009: chap. 4). More recently, it has also been argued that the problem applies with equal force to self-representational theories (Weisberg 2008, 2011, Picciuto 2011). Bracketing the plausibility of such arguments, it is clear that they do not apply to Brentano's theory.

For according to him, there is only one thing in reality, without any division of labor between a first-order representation and a higher-order or self-representation. Some experiences can be accurately framed both as a reddish perception and as an inner perception of a reddish perception. Others can be accurately framed both as greenish perception and as inner perception of greenish perception. But there is simply no experience which can be accurately framed both as a *reddish* perception and as an inner perception of a *greenish* perception.[21]

Rosenthal (1990) once argued that Brentano's theory is incoherent when it comes to conscious desires. For a mental state cannot be both a desire and an awareness of a desire. This is because desire involves a world-to-mind direction of fit whereas awareness involves a mind-to-world direction of fit.[22] According to Rosenthal, a single mental state cannot have both directions of fit at once. However, the principle that a single mental state cannot involve both directions of fit is entirely unsupported. When S is glad that *p*, S presumably both desires that *p* and believes that *p*. If gladness can involve both directions of fit, then conscious desire can as well. (For longer discussion, see Kriegel 2003b.)

๙๘

Some objections to Brentano's theory can be handled in light of his notion of merely-distinguishable parts. Zahavi (2004) and Drummond (2006), for example, have pressed the following Husserlian complaint against Brentano's theory of consciousness: if a conscious experience of a tree performs double duty as a perception of the tree and a perception of a perception of the tree, the tree would appear in consciousness *twice*. Now, Brentano himself insists that the tree appears only once in consciousness:

> We have recognized that the seeing and the presentation of the seeing are connected/bound (*verbunden*) in such a way that the color, as the content of the seeing, at the same time contributes to/constitutes (*beträgt*) the content of the presentation of the seeing. The color, therefore, even though it is presented both in the seeing and in the presentation of the seeing, is still presented only once.   (Brentano 1874: I, 188–9 [134])

The Husserlian complaint, presumably, is that nothing *entitles* Brentano to say this. However, there very clearly *is* something that entitles Brentano to say this, namely, his distinction between separable and distinguishable parts, and his claim that the perception of the tree and the perception of the perception of the tree are merely-distinguishable. The tree qua showing up in M's content and the tree qua showing up in M*'s content are one and the same – even though that one tree can be *regarded* in different ways (as perceived and as perceived to be perceived).

The very appeal to the separable/distinguishable distinction may be questioned, though. In particular, it might well be asked: what is the point of insisting on distinguishing different aspects of a single entity *in thought*, if the entity has no parts *in reality*? Indeed, if a thing has no parts in reality, distinguishing in it parts in thought would appear to be in some sense nonveridical or inappropriate. To my knowledge, Brentano nowhere addresses this worry. As noted in §6.2, however, his basic motivation for the notion of a merely-distinguishable part appears to be to recognize that a thing may have no (separable) parts and yet have *structure*. And thoughts (and statements) about that structure *can* be veridical (or true); it is just that they must be properly understood – as indirectly concerned with structure.

This relates to what is perhaps the deepest objection to Brentano's theory of consciousness (as interpreted here). Granted that a conscious state is a state that lends itself to framing either as an awareness of *x* or as an awareness of an awareness of *x*, we may ask *what it is* about the conscious state that makes it so lend itself. This creates a dilemma for Brentano: either he can cite something in the state itself that grounds its dual-framability, or he cannot. If he can, then whatever he cites should be taken to constitute the essence of consciousness, preempting the dual-framability feature. If he cannot cite anything, then the theory ends up being quite mysterian: we are left with an inexplicable oddity in the midst of the natural world.

As before, Brentano does not address this issue anywhere. But if we apply the general point just made about the relationship between merely-distinguishable parts and structure, we obtain the following response to the dilemma. On the one hand, we must recognize that both 'This experience involves awareness of a tree' and 'This experience involves awareness of an awareness of a tree' are true *cum fundamentum in re*. This means that there definitely is something about the experience that makes it 'dually framable' – a certain intrinsic *structure* that grounds its lending itself to two equally accurate framings. We can use talk of merely-distinguishable parts to indirectly *describe* this structure. But this should not tempt us to start thinking of merely-distinguishable parts as what the account bottoms out in. On the contrary, we must keep in mind that in the case of merely-distinguishable parts, structure is more fundamental than them. Brentano's basic idea, then, would seem to be that, at bottom, there is no way to *characterize* what the special structure of a conscious experience is other than by saying that it is the kind of structure which licenses both a framing as awareness-of-*x* and a framing as awareness-of-awareness-of-*x*. This can be put more economically, but less perspicuously, by saying that it is the kind of structure that may be described in terms of the merely-distinguishable parts *awareness-of-x* and *awareness-of-awareness-of-x*.

The bitter pill one must take to accept Brentano's account is the notion that an entity's being structured need not consist in its having real parts with different properties. A simple, partless entity may sill boast an irreducibly structural character. This is certainly a problematic idea, but one defended by several philosophers on independent grounds (J. Parsons 2004, Horgan and Potrč 2008). Brentano essentially proposes to join forces with them, while continuing to use part talk to capture structure. From his perspective, it is only by successfully wrapping our minds around the notion of a mental state which is equally awareness of *x* and awareness of awareness of *x* that we can understand the special structure characteristic of conscious states. This is a cognitive achievement without which we cannot successfully grasp the nature of consciousness.[23]

9. The Unconscious

A discussion of Brentano's theory of consciousness would be incomplete without mention of his least plausible claim about consciousness: that all mental states possess it. Around the time Brentano wrote, it was still possible to deny the existence of the unconscious purely out of dogmatism. (Although the idea of the unconscious had become steadily more central in nineteenth-century literature – from Stendhal in the thirties through Dostoevsky in the sixties to Strindberg in the nineties – it took time for psychological research to catch up.) Nonetheless, Brentano takes pains to develop a sustained *argument* against unconscious mental states; this consumes the long chap. 2 of *Psychology* II.

The argument can be represented as a destructive dilemma: Brentano considers four ways in which the existence of unconscious mental states may be supported, then rebuts each. The four ways are (1874: I, 147–8 [105]): (a) positing them as *causes* of conscious states; (b) positing them as *effects* of conscious states; (c) discovering a function *f* from the intensity of mental states to the intensity of awareness of them, such that for some non-zero value of the former the value of the latter is zero (with the result that some mental states are accompanied by zero awareness and are thus unconscious); (d) positing unconscious mental states as infinite-regress-stoppers. Against (a), Brentano argues that for every existing unconscious-invoking causal explanation of some conscious phenomenon, he can adduce a better explanation that does not invoke unconscious mental states (1874: I, 149–56 [106–11]). Against (b), he argues that all existing attempts to posit unconscious effects of conscious states have violated the principle of 'same effects, same causes' (1874: I, 163–7 [116–19]). Against (c), he offers the following argument: 1) the intensity of an intentional state is always identical to the intensity with which the state's intentional object is presented; so, 2) the intensity of an awareness of a mental state M is always identical to the intensity of M; therefore, 3) there is no M, such that the intensity of M is non-zero but the intensity of the awareness of M is zero (Brentano 1874: I, 169–70 [120–1]). Against (d), we have already seen that Brentano thinks he can avoid the regress without invoking the unconscious.

The argument is extremely carefully prosecuted, but it ignores a *fifth* basis for positing unconscious mental states, which basis has been in fact most operative, in both psychological and literary contexts. This is the idea that we must posit unconscious mental states to causally explain, not conscious states, but certain *behaviors*. The idea recurs in Freudian deep psychology, folk psychology, and experimental psychology.

Its clearest application is in the Freudian case. Suppose a person has no awareness of anger toward her father, but consistently behaves toward him in a variety of inappropriately aggressive, petty, or defensive ways. Because these behaviors would be both explained and rendered intelligible by assuming the person harbors an *unconscious* anger toward her father, we are inclined – quite justifiably, it seems to me – to make this assumption. In doing so, we adopt none of Brentano's (a)–(d). Instead, we make an inference to the best explanation from behavioral explananda to unconscious explanantia.

Similar reasoning appears implicit in folk-psychological explanations of behavior. Much of your friends' and colleagues' everyday behavior is strictly unintelligible if you do not attribute to them a *desire to be happy*. This desire remains tacit, dispositional, and unconscious for most of your friends' and colleagues' lives: for the most part they are not inner-perceiving their desire to be happy. Some of Brentano's remarks on character traits and other apparently mental dispositions may suggest the following response: we do not actually have a dispositional desire to be happy, but only a disposition to desire to be happy.[24] When the disposition is manifested, we have an occurrent, conscious desire which we do inner-perceive. But as long as the disposition is not manifested, we are not in any mental state – we are merely disposed to be in one. More generally, while we have dispositions to enter (conscious) mental states, for Brentano these dispositions are not themselves mental states. This is not an entirely implausible response, but it does face its own dilemma: Brentano must either (a) deny that a person fast asleep wants to be happy or (b) accept that she wants to be happy but deny that this want of hers is properly considered a mental state. It might be thought simpler to just accept unconscious desires as mental states.

Consider finally experimental grounds for unconscious mental events. Already Sidis (1898) and Dunlap (1900) posited such events to explain behavior in experimentally induced circumstances. Imagine a Müller-Lyer arrow in which the arrowheads are extremely thin and light (see Figure 1.1). If you stand very close to such an arrow, you will be able to detect the arrowheads. If you stand very far, you will not see the arrowheads, and the arrows' lines will seem equi-sized to you (that is, you will not fall victim to the Müller-Lyer illusion). But as Dunlap showed, there is also an intermediary distance where human subjects report not seeing the arrowheads but also report one line seeming to be longer than the other (that is, they *are* victim to the Müller-Lyer illusion). The natural explanation of these reports is that subjects at that distance do *see* (or 'visually detect,' if we prefer) the arrowheads, but *unconsciously*. The subject has a visual representation of the arrowheads that affects downstream visual processing, but at no time is *aware* of that visual representation. This visual representation non-consciously primes the conscious Müller-Lyer illusion. Thus a behavioral datum – the subjects' reports – is best explained by the position of unconscious visual states.

Brentano might respond that the real datum here is not the subjects' reports, but the conscious visual illusions being reported. This would make the case fit the first group of reasons for unconscious mentality Brentano rebuts: the unconscious mental states posited to causally explain conscious mental states. Accordingly, Brentano's response would be to claim that there is a better explanation of the experience of different

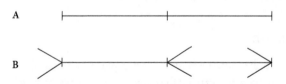

Figure 1.1. Stimuli used by Dunlap (1900: 436)

lengths, one which does not appeal to unconscious visual states. Often, Brentano's better explanation appeals to association laws more (neuro-)physiological than psychological (see Brentano 1874: I, 155 [111]). In this instance, the idea would be that the visual experience of different line lengths is caused by a merely neural representation of the arrowheads, a representation in visual cortex that does not itself qualify as mental. From the vantage point of modern cognitive science and philosophy of mind, the fact that the visual representation is neural does not exclude its being a *mental* representation. In fact, given the representation's role in inducing the conscious illusion and shaping the attendant behavior, it rather *merits* qualifying as mental. But this is where Brentano's substance dualism comes in. Since he takes physiological and mental phenomena to pertain to different kinds of substance, in classifying the visual representation as neural (hence physical) he considers that he has thereby excluded it from the mental realm.[25] The problem with this response, obviously, is its reliance on a strong strand of dualism, in which even a neurophysiological *token* cannot be identical to any mental token.

✌︎☙

In general, Brentano's case against unconscious mentality may fare reasonably well against the background of substance dualism: behaviors we explain by citing Freudian suppressed emotions and tacit folk desires can all be reinterpreted as caused by non-mental physiological states. However, anyone who accepts the kind of minimal physicalism whereby mental states can be token-identical to neurophysiological ones would be unimpressed by Brentano's case.[26] For against this minimally physicalist background (consistent with *property* dualism), all the neurophysiological states invoked to causally explain intelligible behavior are naturally seen as unconscious *mental* states.

To some extent, the thesis that all mental states are conscious (and the substance dualism that underwrites it) can be excised from Brentano's theory of consciousness with limited repercussions. It is perfectly coherent to hold that some mental states can be accurately framed either as perceptions-of-x or as perceptions-of-perception-of-x, while others can be accurately framed only as perceptions-of-x. The former are conscious mental states, the latter unconscious mental states. Both may be token-identical with some neurophysiological states. The upshot would be a picture that incorporates Brentano's theory of consciousness, as interpreted here, into a wider outlook which is consistent with minimal physicalism in the above sense and is hospitable to unconscious mentality. This is not Brentano's view, but it is a coherent view, and what its coherence shows is the logical independence of Brentano's theory of consciousness from both his substance dualism and his rejection of unconscious mentality.

Conclusion

Although the rejection of unconscious mentality may be an excisable part of Brentano's theory of consciousness, it is crucial to remember when examining his philosophy of mind. For it entails a coextension of mentality and consciousness, with the result that many claims which at bottom target consciousness end up being presented, in Brentano's pen, as concerning mentality writ large. For example, when Brentano claims that all mental states involve inner perception of their own occurrence, what he really means is that all *conscious* states are such; he puts the claim in terms of *mental* states only because he thinks that all mental states are conscious. Another important example concerns the doctrine of intentionality, to which we turn in the next chapter.

The goal of the present chapter has been to present a new interpretation of Brentano's theory of consciousness, what I have called the 'Fregean identity interpretation.' I have argued that for Brentano, every conscious state is inner-perceived by its subject, and moreover, that the conscious state and its inner perception are mutually merely-distinguishable. Accordingly, a tree perception and the inner perception of it are just different ways one and the same underlying reality may be (accurately) framed or conceived of. They relate to each other as the morning star and evening stars do, and as the road from Athens to Thebes and the road from Thebes to Athens do. This interpretation, I have claimed, recovers the grain of truth in both the identity and fusion interpretations of Brentano's theory of consciousness. In a sense, it subsumes them under a more fundamental interpretation. More importantly, this new interpretation has the virtue of rendering the theory particularly attractive, imputing on it certain advantages compared to modern alternatives and blunting the force of traditional objections to it.[27]

Notes to Chapter 1

1. I develop this line of thought myself in Kriegel 2009: 5, 271–2; 2015: 47–53.
2. Speaking of a state of consciousness should not be taken to imply that consciousness is a *thing* whose state is being mentioned. Just as we speak of states of *mind* without implying that the mind is a thing in the sense that a chair is, so we can speak of consciousness without that implication.
3. Rosenthal distinguishes between transitive and intransitive notions of consciousness: transitive consciousness is the property ostensibly designated in such statements as 'S is conscious of a tree'; intransitive consciousness is the property ostensibly designated in such statements as 'S's thought of the tree is conscious.' With these notions in place, Rosenthal formulates the following principle: (Intransitively) conscious states are states we are (transitively) conscious of. Given relatively straightforward links between the intransitive/transitive and active/passive distinctions, the transitivity and awareness principles amount to the same.
4. Sometimes Brentano sounds as though he reserves the term *Erkenntnis* to judgments with special epistemic properties: *immediately self-evident* judgments. As we will see in §4, Brentano holds that inner perception *has* those epistemic properties. Since he also takes it to be a judgment, it is clear that inner perception qualifies as *Erkenntnis* from this perspective as well.
5. Lycan's view is very different from Brentano's along the second dimension in which theories inspired by the awareness principle differ: he construes the perceptual awareness as clearly numerically different from the conscious state of which it is an awareness, whereas Brentano does not. Locke is often considered to have been on Lycan's side in this disagreement

(see Guzeldere 1995 among many others), but this is highly questionable (see Coventry and Kriegel 2008).

6. Another formulation: while in contemporary philosophy of mind sensory perception strikes us as paradigmatically perceptual, and inner perception (when it is recognized at all) is considered perceptual only insofar as it sufficiently resembles sensory perception, for Brentano the opposite holds, that is, inner perception is seen as paradigmatically perceptual, and sensory perception qualifies as perceptual only by courtesy of its resemblance to inner perception.

7. Importantly, inner observation of *past* experiences, presumably using episodic memory, is perfectly possible according to Brentano (1874: I, 48 [34]). But without inner perception of current experiences we would be unable to remember them later (1874: I, 60–1 [43]). It is unclear whether inner observation of past experiences deserves the name 'introspection' – Brentano does not seem to grant the name, but others do. Titchener (1912: 491), for example, calls the examination of past conscious experiences in episodic memory 'indirect introspection.' Here I use 'introspection,' in line with Brentano's usage, to denote a 'live' awareness of a simultaneous phenomenon.

8. Thus the distinction between inner observation and inner perception can be accounted for in terms of the focal/peripheral distinction. There is no need to account for it in terms of the disposition/manifestation distinction, as some Brentano commentators repeatedly suggest (e.g., Kim 1978, Rutte 1987).

9. Importantly, though, for Brentano there is no guarantee that the visual experience is the same once I attend to it as it was when I attended to its object (e.g., the laptop). It may well be that the experience's phenomenal character has changed in light of the fact that I started attending to it.

10. This is not yet to say that I can decide to attend to anything that goes on in my mind. If in addition to the conscious anxiety about the afternoon appointment I harbor an unconscious anxiety about my mother's health, I will not be in a position to attend to the latter, since it is unconscious.

11. Throughout this book, I translate *Evidenz* as *self*-evidence. Translators have largely chosen to translate it as 'evidence,' but this seems misleading – the English 'self-evidence' is much closer to Brentano's notion of *Evidenz* (Simons 2013).

12. This question has garnered a considerable amount of attention in recent philosophy of mind (Thomasson 2000, Caston 2002, Hossack 2002, 2006, Kriegel 2003a, 2009, Thomas 2003, D.W. Smith 2004, Zahavi 2004, Drummond 2006, Textor 2006, 2013).

13. In Brentano's immediate world of philosophical reference, the closest case resembling Frege's is Aristotle's case of the *road from Athens to Thebes* and the *road from Thebes to Athens* (*Physics* III.3). Aristotle claimed that these are one and the same 'in number' but different 'in *logos*.' It is not immediately clear what to make of this notion, but the case appears to parallel Frege's: Phosphorus and Hesperus, too, are one in number but different in *logos*! There is only one road, but we can *think of* it in two different ways, indeed *regard* or *consider* it in two different ways; and likewise there is only one planet, which lends itself to conceptualization or appreciation in two different ways. To my knowledge, Brentano nowhere discusses Aristotle's case of the Athens–Thebes road. But Aristotle also mentions in the *Physics* another example of the same phenomenon: A's agency and B's 'patiency' when A acts upon B. Brentano does discuss *this* Aristotelian case, writing in a dictation from 1908: 'Aristotle said that an action and a passion are the same: "A brings about B" and

"B is brought about by A" appear to say the same thing. In such cases, the same accident would be ascribed (*zugeschreiben*) to two things [A and B], though in a different way to each' (Brentano 1933: 55 [49]). Superficially, suggests Brentano, one might think that A's causing B involves the instantiation of two relational properties (accidents): A's property of causing B and B's property of being caused by A. But in reality only one relation is instantiated in such an event, though a relation which may be *ascribed in two different ways*.

14. For more modern studies and developments, see Baumgartner and Simons 1994, and Baumgartner 2013.

15. The rejection of the supplementation axiom has certainly met its share of ridicule (Simons 2006: 92), but with some charity may be made sense of (Chisholm 1978: 202). Note, in any case, that for *substances* (such as Socrates and the Eiffel Tower), the supplementation principle holds: if they have a proper part, then they also have some other proper part that supplements it.

16. I am assuming here what I am perhaps not entitled to, namely, that the spinons, holons, and orbitons 'making up' an electron are not really separable parts of it. As we will see momentarily, the crucial feature of a separable part is that the whole's destruction would not entail *its* destruction. But as far as I understand the physics, it makes no sense to suppose that, if we could destroy an electron, the spinon might be 'left behind.' Spinons are more like electron-tropes than physical electron-parts, though tropes that behave curiously independently in extreme circumstances. I might be wrong about all this, but if so we would just need to change the example, taking a genuinely unsplittable physical constituent as our example.

17. More accurately: there are *at least* two notions of parthood. For reasons that will not concern us here, it is natural to read Brentano as distinguishing in fact *four* notions of parthood (see esp. Brentano 1956 §20.42). For our purposes here, only the central distinction between separable and distinctional parthood will matter.

18. In general, Brentano uses many topological phenomena as examples of distinctional parthood (Brentano 1976). Thus, a boundary between two adjacent regions of space is merely-distinguishable from either region.

19. Here we can see how Husserl's (1901) distinction between pieces and moments is just a rebranding of Brentano's distinction between separable and distinctional parts. Husserl writes: 'Each part that is independent relatively to a whole W we call a Piece (Portion), each part that is non-independent relatively to W we call a Moment (or abstract part) of this same whole W' (Husserl 1901: 29).

20. This may not have been Brentano's view in the *Psychology*, where he describes the auditory and visual parts of an audiovisual experience as 'divisives of one and the same unitary thing' (1874: I, 224 [157]). By 1890, it is clear that he uses 'divisive' and 'distinctional part' to mean the same thing. It may be that Brentano later sharpened his notion of a divisive, and in the *Psychology* it was still intended rather vaguely to pick out a special kind of part, or it may be that he changed his substantive commitments on the relationships between the auditory and visual parts.

21. Accordingly, no gap can open up between the reality of an experience's phenomenal character and its appearance in inner perception, that is, the phenomenal character it in fact has and the one it inner-perceptually appears to have.

22. The notion of direction of fit will be discussed more fully in Chap. 3.

23. There is a kind of *effort* involved in this exercise – an effort not unlike the one we make, say, when we try to wrap our minds around quantum indeterminacy. We may first resist accepting it at face value, attempting to explain the apparent indeterminacy in terms of hidden variables, say. But when eventually the gambit fails, we have to stretch our minds in one way or another, exercising a special kind of theoretical imagination, to grasp a fundamentally and ultimately indeterminate world.

24. For Brentano's discussion of apparently mental dispositions, see Brentano 1874: I, 86 [60]. It must be admitted that to posit a dispositional desire *on top* of the disposition to desire would seem to be explanatorily pointless. Thus dispositional desires, insofar as they are meant to be more than just dispositions to desire, would appear to be explanatorily preempted by the latter. An analogous point on dispositional *beliefs* is made by Audi (1994).

25. Contrary to what some have claimed (e.g., Moran 1996), there is no question that Brentano was a substance dualist. For he believed in the immortality of the soul, which he thought was demonstrated by discontinuities between our mental lives and animals' (see esp. manuscript XPs62: 54011–54012, quoted in Rollinger 2012: 273–4).

26. The definition of physicalism is a contentious matter, but most anyone requires *more* than just token-identity of mental with physical phenomena. Thus, Papineau (1993) defines physicalism as the conjunction of token-identity and the (metaphysical) supervenience of mental types upon physical types. Thus what I refer to in the text as 'minimal physicalism' may in fact be too weak to qualify as physicalism. Weak though it is, however, Brentano seems to reject it.

27. For comments on a previous draft, I am grateful to Anna Giustina, Vincent Grandjean, Marie Guillot, Frank Knappik, Mario Schärli, Nicola Spinelli, Ken Williford, and two anonymous referees for OUP. I have also benefited from presenting drafts of this chapter at the Australian National University, École Normale Supérieure, Kings' College London, LOGOS, the University of Fribourg, the University of Houston, the University of Liege, the University of Texas – Austin, and the University of Warwick. I am grateful to the audiences there, in particular Alexandre Billon, Oliver Black, Bill Brewer, Géraldine Carranante, Steven Gubka, Bob Hale, Robert Koons, Andrew Lee, Katherine Piatti, Denis Seron, Mark Textor, Josh Weisberg, and Ken Williford. In addition, I have benefited from exchanges with Arnaud Dewalque, Leon Leontyev, Cathal O'Madagain, Simon Prosser, François Recanati, Peter Simons, Gianfranco Soldati, and Sebastian Watzl. Some of the material in this chapter overlaps with my article 'Brentano's Dual-Framing Theory of Consciousness,' published in *Philosophy and Phenomenological Research*; I am grateful to the publisher, Wiley, for allowing me to reuse this material.

2

Intentionality

The notion of intentionality is what Brentano is best known for. But disagreements and misunderstandings still surround both the phenomenon he had in mind and the account of it he proposed, that is, both his explanandum and his explanation. In this chapter, I argue for two main claims. Regarding the explanandum, I argue that, unlike the notion of intentionality central to modern philosophy of mind, Brentano's notion of intentionality has nothing to do with mental states' capacity to track elements in the environment; rather, it has to do with a phenomenal feature in virtue of which conscious experiences present something to the subject. Regarding the explanation, I argue that, contrary to common wisdom in Brentano scholarship, there is no real evidence that Brentano took intentionality to be a relation to immanent objects; rather, his mature theory clearly casts intentionality as an *intrinsic, non-relational* property, and a property in the first instance *of subjects* (rather than of subjects' internal states).

1. Intentionality as the Mark of the Conscious

If you know nothing else about Brentano, you know this: he said that intentionality was the mark of the mental. This may be thought of as the following claim:

(I1)   All and only mental states are intentional.

Recall from Chap. 1, however, that Brentano took the mental and the conscious to coextend, and so tended to present theses targeting consciousness as applying to mentality writ large. Ultimately, it seems to me, Brentano derives I1 from two more fundamental claims:

(I2)   All and only conscious states are intentional.
(COEXTENSION)   All and only mental states are conscious.

Clearly, I1 is entailed by I2 plus COEXTENSION. Brentano is committed to all three claims, but the entailment relations work in one specific direction, suggesting that Brentano's more fundamental mark thesis is that intentionality is the mark of the *conscious*. The claim that intentionality is the mark of the mental just falls out of it against the background of COEXTENSION.

This is important, because it shows that Brentano's notion of intentionality is the notion of a feature characteristic *of conscious experience*. To that extent, it is very different from the notion of intentionality discussed in most twentieth-century philosophy of mind, the notion of an objective relation that conscious and nonconscious states alike bear to some environmental feature. While there may well be such object-ive relations between mental states and environmental features, they are simply not the phenomenon Brentano has in mind in speaking of intentionality. What he has in mind is a *subjective* feature special to conscious experiences – a kind of *felt aboutness*, an experience of the mind's endogenous directedness at the outside world.

Accordingly, the only way to grasp what intentionality *is*, for Brentano, is to experi-ence intentionality for oneself. The various descriptions of intentionality he offers – including the celebrated 'intentionality passage' – are intended to help the reader focus her mind on the right phenomenon; but the nature of the phenomenon cannot be appreciated simply by reading those descriptions. It must be experienced directly. In a 1906 piece, for example, he writes:[1]

> The general nature of all mental things, as we experience it, is the having of [intentional] objects. What is said thereby cannot be made distinct without recourse to experience: just as it would be impossible to make clear to a blind man the concept of red, it is impossible to make clear to someone…who has never apprehended himself as a thinker the concept of thinking…and to show him what one means when one says there is no thinking thing without thought object, no mental subject without object.   (Brentano 1966: 339)

Imagine trying to explain to someone what babaganush tastes like, or what nocciola gelato tastes like, or what vegemite tastes like. Indeed, imagine trying to explain to someone congenitally incapable of gustatory experience what experiencing *taste* is like. If you are lucky, your various descriptions may be suggestive and intriguing. Ultimately, however, to fully grasp what it is like to taste nocciola gelato, or to taste at all, a person must be able to experience taste for herself. Similarly, according to Brentano, true appreciation of intentionality requires experiencing for oneself the subjective quality of endogenous directedness, of felt aboutness. This subjective experience is much more general than that of experiencing the taste of nocciola gelato (indeed, for Brentano the latter is a *species* of the former) but both are equally experiential, subjective properties.

In this respect, the notion in current philosophy of mind that dovetails most closely with the phenomenon Brentano has in mind is that of *phenomenal intentionality* (see Loar 1987, 2003, as well as Horgan and Tienson 2002 and Kriegel 2013a,b). Phenomenal intentionality is supposed to be precisely an experiential feature of endogenous directedness at the world. The idea is that our conscious experiences *feel* as though they are directed at something other than themselves. It is something like this felt directedness that Brentano had in mind with his notion of intentionality (Potrč 2002, 2013, Dewalque 2013). Accordingly, it is something like phenomenal intentionality, I contend, that constitutes the explanandum in Brentano's theory of intentionality.[2]

Taking all this into account, it is clear that Brentano's I2, the thesis that intentionality is the mark of the conscious, concerns specifically phenomenal intentionality. We may therefore formulate it more accurately as follows:

(I3)   All and only conscious states exhibit phenomenal intentionality.

We might call this 'phenomenal intentionality as the mark of the conscious.'

Unlike I1, which has met with justifiable resistance, I3 is extremely plausible. It is not tautological, because phenomenal intentionality is not *defined* as the intentionality that conscious states exhibit. In a sense, it is not defined at all, but rather grasped through direct encounter in inner perception. Although not tautological, however, I3 is highly plausible. To see this more clearly, let us start by factorizing I3 into two claims:

(I3a)   *All* conscious states exhibit phenomenal intentionality.
(I3b)   *Only* conscious states exhibit phenomenal intentionality.

It is hard to imagine a counterexample to I3b. Can we think of a nonconscious state exhibiting the kind of felt directedness we encounter in inner perception? Surely not. The only real challenge to I3 must therefore concern I3a: whether *all* conscious states exhibit phenomenal intentionality. In particular, it has sometimes been claimed that (i) algedonic experiences of pain and pleasure and (ii) long-term moods, such as depression and anxiety, are undirected.

Brentano addresses the algedonic worry. He argues that pain and pleasure experiences present sui generis secondary qualities, that is, secondary qualities distinct from color, sound, and the like perceptible properties. He writes:

[When we] say that our foot or our hand hurts, that this or that part of the body is in pain... there is in us not only the idea of a definite spatial location but also a particular sensory quality analogous to color, sound, and other so-called sensory qualities, which is a physical phenomenon and which must be clearly distinguished from the accompanying feeling.

(Brentano 1874: I, 116 [83])

For some perceptual modalities, ordinary language generously provides two terms, one naturally applicable to the experience and one to its object. Taste is a property of gustatory experiences, flavor a property of gustatory objects; smell is a property of olfactory experiences, odor a property of olfactory objects; and so on. Unfortunately, 'pleasure' and 'pain' are ambiguously applicable to both experience and object, and this is what misleads us into non-intentional thinking in this case. Yet:

If we hear a pleasing and mild sound or a shrill one, harmonious chord or a dissonance, it would not occur to anyone to identify the sound with the accompanying feeling of pleasure and pain. But then in cases where a feeling of pain or pleasure is aroused in us by a cut, a burn or a tickle, we must distinguish in the same way between a physical phenomenon, which appears as the object of external perception, and the mental phenomenon of feeling, which accompanies its appearance, even though in this case the superficial observer is rather inclined to confuse them.   (1874: I, 116–17 [83])

In other words, the non-intentional conception of pleasure and pain rests on a linguistic illusion. In reality, an experience of taking pleasure in a piece of music presents two types of secondary quality of the music: its sound properties and its hedonic properties.

I am not familiar with a discussion of moods in Brentano. Perhaps one reason is that Brentano focuses on *occurrent acts*, whereas moods appear to be *states* of some longevity (though not quite *standing* states). Nonetheless, moods are clearly part of our conscious life, and must be brought into the intentional fold if I3 is to be accepted. It is thus a real lacuna in Brentano's discussion that he nowhere (again: to my knowledge) addresses the case of moods. It falls on us, then, to 'supplement' Brentano's case for I3 with an intentionalist account of moods. In contemporary philosophy of mind, the most prominent intentionalist approach to mood construes it as presenting properties of *everything*, or else properties of *the world as a whole* (Crane 1998, 2009, Seager 1999). On the first view, anxiety presents everything as threatening and euphoria presents everything as delightful or exciting; on the second, anxiety presents the world as a whole as a threatening place and euphoria as a delightful, exciting place. A different intentionalist account attempts to capture the undirected character of moods by claiming that they present features but without presenting them as being any*thing's* features (Mendelovici 2013). On this view, anxiety may present threateningness, but not anything's threateningless; instead, it represents a kind of uninstantiated, 'uninhabited' threateningness. It is impossible to know how Brentano would look upon either of these views, but they are at least options.

The next question is: what is Brentano's *account* of phenomenal intentionality? In the remainder of this chapter, I want to argue that Brentano's mature account of intentionality construes it as a non-relational, intrinsic property of subjects. This is twice removed from the notion that intentionality is a relation that conscious states bear to immanent objects: first, insofar as it casts intentionality as intrinsic rather than relational; second, insofar as it casts intentionality as a property of subjects rather than of subjects' internal states. (Note well: I frame the claims being debated in terms of properties just for convenience. As we will see more fully in Chap. 6, Brentano does not have a place for properties in his ontology. Nonetheless, claims that appear to make reference to properties get paraphrased in a way that preserves their truth. This will be the case with claims about intentional properties as well.)

2. Brentano's Non-relational Account of Intentionality

It is striking how little there is in the *Psychology* about the *nature* of intentionality. Long discussions are dedicated to arguing that intentionality is the mark of the mental, but to say this is not yet to say anything about what intentionality *is*. On the issue of the nature of intentionality, all we find in the *Psychology* are the 97 words (in the German original) constituting the 'intentionality passage.' Here is the passage in full:

> Every mental phenomenon is characterized by what the Scholastics of the Middle Ages called the intentional or mental inexistence of an object (*Gegenstandes*), and what we might call, though not wholly unambiguously, reference (*Beziehung*) to a content (*Inhalt*), direction (*Richtung*) toward an object (*Object*) (which is not to be understood here as meaning an entity (*Realität*)), or immanent objecthood (*Gegenständlichkeit*). Every mental phenomenon contains (*enthält*) something as object (*Object*) within itself, although they do not all do so in the same way. In presentation, something is presented, in judgment something is affirmed or denied, in love loved, in hate hated, in desire desired and so on.   (Brentano 1874: I, 124–5 [88])

On the basis of this passage alone, interpretive debates have flourished in more than one philosophical tradition. The dominant interpretation, thought to require the least interpretive 'creativity,' ascribes to Brentano an 'immanentist' account of intentionality. According to this, intentionality is a relation between subjects' intentional acts and immanent objects, objects that exist only 'in the subject's head.' That is, when S perceives a tree, there is (i) a perceptual act taking place in S, (ii) a 'mental tree' or 'tree-idea' in S's mind, and (iii) a primitive intentional relation that (i) bears to (ii). Perhaps partly because this immanentist theory is taken to suffer from fatal flaws,[3] some have attempted to reinterpret the passage so as to ascribe to Brentano a more plausible account (e.g., Moran 1996, Chrudzimski 2001).[4] Proponents of the immanentist interpretation tend to dismiss these endeavors as 'twisting Brentano's words' (Smith 1994: 40; see also Crane 2006).

  My own view is that the passage is too short and underdeveloped to discriminate among a number of importantly different accounts: many accounts of the nature of intentionality will be compatible with Brentano's 97 words. The choice of interpretation is thus strongly underdetermined by *this* textual evidence. Moreover, it is not implausible that at that early stage of his career, Brentano had simply not yet worked out anything very specific, perhaps had not even appreciated the multitude of theoretical options. What is clear, in any case, is that by 1911 Brentano had developed a much more textured account of the nature of intentionality. In 1911, the last four chapters of the *Psychology* were reprinted, in slightly reedited form, along with eleven appendices, under the title *The Classification of Mental Phenomena* (Brentano 1911). In the first of these appendices (1911: 133–8 [271–5]), Brentano presents a more determinate and worked out account of intentionality, to which I will refer as the 'mature account.' In the remainder of this section, I present an interpretation of Brentano's mature account according to which:

  (INTRINSICNESS)   Intentionality is an intrinsic property of subjects.[5]

This thesis has two important elements: (i) it assays intentionality as an intrinsic, non-relational property and (ii) it construes that property as a property not of intentional *acts*, but of *subjects*. I start by developing more fully this interpretation of Brentano's mature theory (§2.1), then discuss Brentano's argument for it (§2.2).

2.1. The view

A first step toward understanding Brentano's view is a correct appreciation of his conception of the intentional object. The notion of an intentional object involves a tangle of substantive and terminological issues. With deliberate artifice, let us pretend that it is a matter of simple terminological decision whether when subject S veridically perceives a tree, the expression 'intentional object' will be used to denote (a) the external tree targeted by S's perception or (b) a different entity which might be called the-presented-tree or the-tree-qua-presented (never mind what exactly that means). On this terminological issue, it is clear that the mature Brentano chose the first route. In a 1905 letter to Anton Marty, he writes:

> It has never been my view that the [intentional] object is identical to the *presented object* (*vorgestelltes Objekt*). A presentation, for example a horse-presentation, has as its [intentional] object not the *presented thing* but rather the *thing*, in this case not a *presented horse* but rather a *horse*.   (Brentano 1930: 87–8 [77])

This 'decision' raises, however, three important questions: (i) how to understand the status of the intentional object in *non*-veridical experiences, (ii) how to understand the nature of the relation between the intentional act and the intentional object, and (iii) whether the intentional relation involves also a third relatum, sometimes called 'content.'

Debates among Brentano's students (Twardowski 1894, Meinong 1904), and Brentano's own reflections on the various theoretical options in the area (see Chrudzimski 2001: chaps. 2–7), have concerned mostly these issues. Perhaps through witnessing the various options' travails, in particular as concerns the accommodation of radical error and hallucination, Brentano, as I read him, had by 1911 come to the position that intentionality is not a relation at all, but a non-relational property of the intentional act, or rather of the subject performing that act. As we will see, this non-relational conception of intentionality goes hand in hand with the claim that in cases of non-veridical experience, *there is no* intentional object.

The title of the relevant 1911 piece already suggests this notion: 'Mental reference (*Beziehung*) as distinguished from relation (*Relation*) in the strict sense.' This already suggests that, *strictly* speaking, intentionality is not a relation.[6] The point is articulated most clearly here:

> The terminus of the *so-called relation* does not in reality need to exist at all. For this reason, one could doubt whether we really are dealing with something relational here, and not rather with something in certain respects *relation-like* (*Relativen Ähnliches*), something which might therefore be called *quasi-relational/relational-ish* (*Relativliches*).
>
> (Brentano 1911: 134 [272]; my italics)

The English translators chose to translate *Relativliches* as 'quasi-relational,' but the expressions 'relational-ish' and 'relation-like' may in truth be more felicitous. The expression 'quasi-relational' suggests a status curiously intermediate between those of being relational and being non-relational. As the rest of the passage shows unequivocally, however, Brentano's idea is rather that intentionality bears some important *similarities* to a relation but strictly speaking is not a relation. This is why Brentano refers to a 'so-called relation' and voices 'doubt whether we are really dealing with something relational' (where this seems to be a stylistically guarded negative assertion rather than genuine doubt). As Moran (1996: 11) puts it, by *Relativliches* Brentano 'seemed to mean that it [intentionality] only looked like a relation.' *Strictly speaking*, intentional properties are non-relational, monadic properties. Brentano works out the similarities between intentional properties and relations in the sentences immediately following this passage, but consistently refers to them as mere similarities.[7] The expression 'relation-like' is thus apt, as it suggests something non-relational that resembles relations in some respects (rather than some intermediate status between relational and non-relational).

Clearly, the surface grammar of intentional reports, such as 'S is thinking of dragons', is relational. Brentano must hold, then, that such statements also have a (very different) 'deep grammar,' one that reflects more accurately the ontological structure of their truthmaker. The challenge is to find the kind of paraphrase whose 'surface grammar' would manifest this non-relational character. The 'deep grammar' claim boils down to this, then: (i) 'S is thinking of dragons' is paraphraseable into some statement P whose grammatical structure is non-relational, and (ii) the ontological structure of the truthmaker of 'S is thinking of dragons' is more accurately reflected in P's grammatical structure. The question is: what exactly is P?

Several options are available. One is *adverbialism*, where 'S is thinking of dragons' is paraphrased into 'S thinking dragon-ly' or 'S is thinking dragon-wise.' Here the grammar suggests that the subject, S, is engaged in a certain *activity*, thinking, and is engaged in it in a certain *manner*, namely dragon-wise. There is no relation between S and a separate entity or group of entities, only a first-order monadic property (thinking) of S and a second-order property (occurring dragon-wise) of the first-order property (or of S's instantiating of the first-order property).[8]

Some scholars ascribe such adverbialism to Brentano (Moran 1996, Chrudzimski and Smith 2004). Presumably, however, what they have in mind is primarily the non-relational construal of intentionality. The adverbialist technique for rendering that construal intelligible is only one option. Another option is what we might call *hyphenism*, where 'S is thinking of dragons' is paraphrased into 'S is thinking-of-dragons.' The purpose of the hyphens is to intimate that 'thinking-of-dragons' is a grammatically simple, unstructured predicate, of which 'dragons' is a merely *morphological*, but not *syntactic*, part. Compare: 'apple' is a morphological but not syntactic part of 'pineapple'; accordingly, something's being a pineapple does not involve its being an apple as part or component. Likewise, someone's thinking-of-dragons does not involve as part dragons: dragons are not constituents of the truthmaker of 'S is thinking-of-dragons.' The only constituents of the truthmaker are S and its monadic property (which, misleadingly, is denoted by a composite-sounding predicate).⁹ As in adverbialism, there is no relation involved. Unlike in adverbialism, no second-order property is invoked either.

Brentano himself appeals neither to adeverbialization nor to hyphenation. The closest he comes to adopting a specific paraphrase technique is in describing the subject, especially in his metaphysical writings (esp. Brentano 1933), as *this kind of thinker* or *that kind of thinker*, in the sense of that-which-thinks (*Denkendes*). This can be developed into what we may call *subjectism*, where 'S is thinking of dragons' is paraphrased into 'S is a dragons-thinker.' Here the grammar suggests a monadic property of the subject, that of being a particular species of the genus Thinker. Brentano writes:

'There is' has its strict or proper meaning when used in connection with genuine logical names [i.e., expressions used to refer to entities], as in 'There is a God' or 'There is a man.' In its other uses, 'there is' must not be taken in its strict sense...[Thus,] 'There is something which is the object of thought (*ein Gedachtes*)' may be equated with [i.e., paraphrased into] 'There is something which thinks (*ein Denkendes*).'   (Brentano 1930: 79 [68])

More generally:

...not the contemplated round thing, but the person contemplating it is what is in the strict sense. This fiction, that there is something which exists as a contemplated thing, may also prove harmless, but unless one realizes that it is a fiction, one may be led into the most glaring absurdities...Once we have translated [paraphrased] statements about such fictive objects into other terms, it becomes clear that the only thing the statement is concerned with is the person who is thinking about the object.   (Brentano 1933: 8 [18])

Here Brentano states that intentional truths require as truthmakers only subjects (thinkers) and their taxonomizing into kinds; only careless constructions in public language mislead us into thinking there are further constituents in these truthmakers.¹⁰

A word on the issue of taxonomizing. A dragon-thinker is a species of a thinker, and a green-dragon-thinker is a subspecies of it. For Brentano, in asserting 'S is thinking of a green dragon,' we talk of an object (a green dragon) to indirectly classify the subject. This phenomenon is more familiar from other parts of our mentalistic discourse. It is often remarked that we have no better way to describe our visual experiences than indirectly, in terms of the color and shape properties of the objects of which they are experiences. Asked to describe your visual experience of a Mondrian, you are likely to fall back on terms which strictly speaking denote properties of the Mondrian you see, not properties of the seeing. If you are hallucinating the Mondrian, it is still true that your experience has the kind of qualitative character that it would have if it veridically presented an horizontal red rectangle at the bottom right corner, a vertical white rectangle next to it, and so on. That is, it is still true that your experience is *as of* a horizontal red rectangle at the bottom right corner, a vertical white rectangle next to it, and so on. For Brentano, we essentially use the same strategy to classify our thoughts, judgments, desires, and other intentional states across the board: we describe them indirectly by using terms for properties of what they are about (or would be about if they were veridical). Thus, we have no better way to describe a thought than by noting that it is *of dragons*, or *about the financial crisis*.

And so when we wish to state how one thinking individual differs from another, it is natural to characterize the thinker by reference to that which he is thinking about and to the way in which he relates to it as a thinker. We thus speak as though we were concerned with a relation between two things... Our language in these cases treats the object of thought as though it were a *thing* along with the person who is thinking.   (Brentano 1933: 15 [22])

For Brentano, then, every intentional state is but an intrinsic modification of a subject, and we parasitically use expressions originally designed to pick out worldly items to indirectly describe these intrinsic modifications. A correct thought is accurately described by describing its object; an incorrect thought is accurately described by describing the object it would have if it were correct. Thus, in a 1911 letter to his *Enkelschüler* Franz Hillebrand, Brentano writes:

[W]e can say that a centaur, if it were to exist, would be a creature whose upper parts are like those of a man and whose lower parts are like those of a horse... [I]n such a case, it would be better to say that one is describing, not a centaur, but someone who is thinking about a centaur...   (Brentano 1930: 114 [101])

Ultimately, it is this reliance on terms for external objects' properties to indirectly describe the intrinsic properties of subjects that has misled philosophers to construe thought as an honest-to-goodness relation between a subject and an object.

It is part of Brentano's view that, in cases of non-veridical presentation, strictly speaking there *are* no intentional objects. Conscious states involve intentional acts, which are intrinsic modifications of the subject, and intentional-object talk is just a device for characterizing different modifications. Importantly, intentional-object talk is still useful in classifying and describing a non-veridical intentional state. For we can still classify an intentional state according to the intentional object there would be if it were correct. Call this kind of 'would-be intentional object' a *merely-intentional object*. The present point could be summarized as follows: it is hard to classify or describe an intentional state without mentioning its intentional or merely-intentional object; all the same, strictly speaking there are no merely-intentional objects. Thus, in a 1904 fragment Brentano writes that 'there is nothing other than things, and "empty space" and "object of thought" (*Gedachtes*) do not name things' (Brentano 1930: 79 [68]). There are certainly objects which are intentional, namely, regular objects when targeted by some intentional act, or more accurately, by a subject suitably modified. But there are no objects which are *merely* intentional, that is, ones that have no other existence but as targeted by some intentional act. To that extent, merely-intentional objects are *useful fictions*: there are no such things, but it is useful to speak as though there are to indirectly describe and classify intentional states. In a 1916 dictation, Brentano explicitly describes intentional objects as useful fictions:

Obvious examples of such fictions are so-called *intentional beings*. We speak of 'a contemplated man,' or of 'a man who is thought about by this or that thinker,' and our statements are like those in which we actually do speak of a man. But in such a case what we are thinking of *in recto* is [just] the person thinking of the man.   (Brentano 1933: 19 [24])

Regardless of whether the man that S contemplates exists, what is really going on when S contemplates the man is that S exists and is intrinsically modified in a specific way, so that he can be described – classified – as a man-contemplator.

2.2. *The argument*

What is Brentano's *argument* for the non-relational account of intentionality? Much of the 1911 piece is dedicated to an analysis of statements about relations among nonexistent putative entities, outside intentional contexts. Brentano's mature position is that such statements are elliptical:

I am not unmindful that some people nowadays, in opposition to Aristotle, deny that both things must exist in order for something to be larger or smaller than another thing. [But...] Someone who says that three is less than a trillion is not positively asserting the existence (*Existenz*) of a relation. He is saying, rather, that if there is a plurality/multitude (*Menge*) of three and a plurality/multitude of a trillion, that relation must obtain (*bestehen*) between them...   (1911: 134–5 [273])

The passage presupposes a mathematical nominalism according to which talk of numbers is just talk of pluralities or multitudes (compare Maddy 1981). But the main point does not depend on such nominalism. It is that a categorical statement such as 'Hobbits are cuter than dragons' only *appears* to assert (read: has a surface grammar suggesting) the obtaining or holding (*bestehen*) of the cuter-than relation. In reality, it is merely elliptical for the hypothetical statement 'If there were hobbits and dragons, the former would be cuter than the latter.' The hypothetical statement does not assert the obtaining, the actual instantiation, of any relation – it only says that *if* certain conditions were met, *then* that relation would obtain/be instantiated. We may suppose that this hypothetical is true, and therefore requires a truthmaker; but the truthmaker will not involve any actual instance of a relation. It is only the original categorical, unparaphrased into the hypothetical, that would require a relation-instance as part of its truthmaker; but the unparaphrased categorical is strictly speaking true, precisely because there is no actual instantiation of the cuter-than relation due to hobbits and dragons.

A similar treatment applies to cases in which one, but only one, relatum does exist. Thus, 'Dogs are cuter than dragons' is elliptical for 'If there were dragons, dogs would be cuter than them.' The paraphrasing hypothetical is true but does not require a relation-instance in its truthmakers, while the unparaphrased categorical is strictly speaking false, so does not require *any* truthmakers. Either way we are spared the need for a relational truthmaker.

Against the background of this analysis, consider now an intentional expression, such as 'thinking of.' The view that thinking of *x* is a matter of bearing a certain relation to x, the thinking-of relation, would lead to odd results. First, given that there are no dragons, it would require us to reinterpret 'S is thinking of dragons' as elliptical for 'If there were dragons, S would be thinking of them.' Secondly, it would require us to consider the unparaphrased categorical 'S is thinking of dragons' as strictly speaking false. But both consequences are implausible. Therefore, we should reject the view that 'thinking-of' denotes a relation. Instead, we should construe it as denoting a non-relational property of the subject, misleadingly denoted by a transitive verb.

Brentano's argument for the non-relational account of intentionality is basically this, then. *Categorical* intentional statements (statements about intentional states) can be true, without being paraphrased into hypotheticals, even where the 'intended object' does not exist. But statements involving relational predicates cannot be true, unparaphrased, in such circumstances. So, the intentional predicates used intentional statements are not really relational predicates.

We may regiment Brentano's argument as follows. Let S be a statement composed of terms or expressions $T_1, \ldots, T_n$ plus logical vocabulary. Let N be a proper subset of $T_1, \ldots, T_n$, whose members ostensibly refer to concrete particulars, and let M be the complement of N in $T_1, \ldots, T_n$. How can we tell whether S is a *relational statement*? A superficial criterion might require M to include a 'relational term' as member, where T is a relational term just if a grammatical statement involving T must involve at least two other terms. The problem with this criterion is that it gets the extension wrong: it correctly classifies as relational the statement 'Jimmy argued with Johnny,' but incorrectly classifies as relational 'Jimmy argued with conviction.' A deeper, more semantic criterion might require M to include a member that successfully refers to a relation, or requires S to have a relation among its truthmaker's constituents. That sort of criterion is surely right, but is dialectically unhelpful in the present context: we want to know whether 'Jimmy is thinking of dragons' is a relational statement, but only because we want to settle precisely the question of whether thinking-of is a relation. What would be useful for us would be a partly semantic criterion that does not presuppose knowledge of whether a relation is denoted. In a way, this is what Brentano offers us. More precisely, from what he offers us we can generate the following criterion, which combines the syntactic condition presented above with a semantic condition that does not presuppose prior knowledge of whether a relation is involved in S's putative truthmaker:

S is relational iff: (i) M includes a relational term and (ii) for S to be both categorical and true, every member of N must successfully refer.

If some member of N fails to refer, S is either false or hypothetical (or else non-relational). For example, if 'Johnny' fails to refer, then the categorical 'Jimmy argued with Johnny' is false, though the hypothetical 'If Johnny existed, Jimmy would have argued with him' may well be true. The key to Brentano's argument is the claim that some intentional statements are categorical and true even though some of the terms ostensibly referring to concrete particulars ('ostensibly singular') fail to refer. For example, 'Jimmy is thinking of Bigfoot' is true and categorical even though 'Bigfoot' fails to refer. Therefore,

'Jimmy is thinking of Bigfoot' is *not* a relational statement. And *there*fore, we have no reason to think that its truthmaker involves a relation as constituent.

In summary, Brentano's argument for the non-relational assay of intentionality may be represented as follows:

1) For any relational statement S, if S is true and categorical, then necessarily, all of S's ostensibly singular expressions successfully refer;
2) For any intentional statement S*, if S* is true and categorical, then possibly, some of S*'s ostensibly singular expressions fail to refer; therefore,
3) For any intentional statement S* and any relational statement S, S* ≠ S.

The modality at play in the premise is *conceptual*: it is part of the concept of a relational statement that it meets the condition cited in Premise 1, and part of the concept of an intentional statement that it allows for the possibility cited in Premise 2. These premises strike me as highly plausible, and they do seem to entail the conclusion. So, I find myself quite convinced by Brentano's argument.

3. Objections and Replies

Let us consider some objections, to the view I ascribe to Brentano (§3.2) but also to the ascribing of it (§3.1).

3.1. Objections to the interpretation

To the ascribing, it might be objected that another interpretation of '*Relativliches*' is possible: intentionality *is* a relation, but a special kind of relation, where only one of the relata need exist. Perhaps this is what a 'quasi-relation' is: a relation whose occurrence or instantiation does not require the existence of all relata.

There is no doubt that Brentano seriously entertained this alternative account. In some of his unpublished fragments, he clearly expounds the idea – see esp. Brentano 1933: 167–9 [126–7], a dictation from 1915. One view might be that Brentano simply changed his mind sometime between 1911 and 1915 (Moran 1996). Another, however, is that Brentano wanted to let the idea play out in private writings but what he *published* should still be taken as his considered view. Regardless, I would argue, charity exhorts us to focus on the 1911 view, because the envisaged notion of quasi-relation is forsooth not altogether intelligible. As far as I can see, saying that a dyadic relation can be instantiated even if only one relatum exists is no more plausible than saying that a monadic property can be instantiated even where there is no instantiator of it. On the face of it, it is absurd to think that the property of having mass m can be instantiated even if there is no object whose mass is m. (I am assuming here that mass is monadic.) It should strike us as equally absurd that some relation R might be instantiated in the absence of an appropriate number of relata.

An objector might insist that the 1915 dictation, being posterior to the 1911 appendix, must be taken to represent Brentano's final, considered position. My main response to this is that if we accept this reasoning, I would simply contend that Brentano took one final wrong turn, and would have done better to stick with his 1911 account. In addition, however, it is not clear that we have to accept this reasoning. For it is significant, in this context, that Brentano *published* the 1911 piece but not the 1915 piece. For all we know, the 1915 piece is just an attempt to let a view play out and see where it goes and how it might be defended.[11]

Another objection to the ascription of a non-relational view to Brentano is that Brentano clearly thinks that in thinking of a tree, one is *aware of* a tree-idea. The tree-idea is the *content* of one's thought. So even if the intentionality of one's thought does not involve a relation to a tree, it does involve a relation to this tree-idea. One way to put this is to say that intentionality is a relation to a content even if it is not a relation to an object. However we put this, though, a relation is involved after all.

This objection relies on a confusion. The expression 'tree-idea' can be read in two ways. One is as denoting a kind of mental tree that resembles worldly trees in some respects but exists only in the subject's mind. So construed, the notion of a tree-idea is both ontologically and phenomenologically suspect, and as we have seen, it is clearly rejected by Brentano. A more plausible construal of a tree-idea is simply as an idea *of* a tree. But in this construal, the idea seems to be the intentional act, not the object (*or* content). Now, it is true that in Brentano's picture one would still be *aware of* the tree-idea, but this is simply because every intentional act is intentionally directed at itself. Insofar as it is its own intentional object, then, the intentional act is something the subject is aware of. Nonetheless, it is still just the intentional act of the tree thought – not the thought's content or (primary) object!

A third objection to the ascription might appeal to Tim Crane's (2006) unusual basis for an immanentist interpretation of Brentano. Crane does not rely primarily on the intentionality passage. Rather, his main reason for ascribing to Brentano an immanentist theory of intentionality is that for Brentano the intentional objects of perceptual experiences are Kantian appearances 'which are signs of an underlying reality but which are not real themselves' (Crane 2006: 23) and instead 'only exist in the mind' (2006: 25).

Crane relies on passages from the opening chapter of the *Psychology*, where Brentano says, for example, that 'light, sound, heat, spatial location . . . are not things which truly and really (*wahrhaft und wirklich*) exist' (Brentano 1874: 28 [19]). Consider a visual experience as of a yellow lemon. Brentano takes the yellow lemon presented by the experience to be a Kantian phenomenon (as opposed to a noumenon). However, Brentano nowhere says that such Kantian phenomena 'only exist in the mind.' On the contrary, he says very explicitly (including in the sentence just quoted) that they *do not exist at all* – not in the mind and not elsewhere. In ascribing the immanentist view to Brentano, Crane is *presupposing* that Kantian phenomena are immanent objects that exist only in the mind. This is quite a common view, of course, but it is not Brentano's. The only view we can ascribe to Brentano is that Kantian phenomena are mere intentional objects of our conscious states. Since Brentano takes talk of intentional objects to be a roundabout way of describing the species of intentional act the subject is performing, this is how he would take talk of Kantian phenomena as well. This explains why he says that Kantian phenomena do not 'really and truly exist.' After all, his view – as interpreted here – is that *merely-intentional objects* do not really and truly exist. They are useful fictions and not *entia realia*.

In addition, Crane's interpretation does not extend to non-perceptual experiences, since those are not directed at Kantian phenomena. But Brentano's theory of intentionality is supposed to apply to non-perceptual acts such as judgments and decisions. So Crane's interpretation has no real chance of applying generally.

3.2. Objections to the view

An immediate objection is that the view ascribed to Brentano fails to do justice to the pull of the relational conception of intentionality. It is not just English or German that have a relational surface grammar for intentional ascriptions; all known languages do. Surely there is some underlying reason why they are all forced to do so.

I have already indicated the reason Brentano is likely to proffer for this phenomenon. The elusiveness of conscious experience forces us to describe its phenomenal character indirectly. There is a kind of 'direct-ineffability' of conscious states, in the sense that such 'effability' as they admit is always indirect. One might wonder why *that* should be the case, but perhaps the contrast between the private character of conscious states and the public nature of language could be part of the explanation here.

One way to appreciate the pull of the relational conception is this. A symptom of the fact that carrying is a relation is that the active-voice 'Jimmy is carrying Johnny' seems to mean the same as the passive-voice 'Johnny is carried by Jimmy.' Remarkably, the same holds for intentional statements: 'Jimmy is thinking of Johnny' means the same as 'Johnny is thought of by Jimmy' (or indeed 'Johnny is the object of Jimmy's thought'). This suggests that thinking-of is just as relational as carrying.

In response, however, Brentano could deny that 'Jimmy is thinking of Johnny' means the same as 'Johnny is thought of by Jimmy' – when left unparaphrased, that is. Statements S_1 and S_2 cannot mean the same if they differ in truth value: given that the world is the same, they must be saying something different about it if one ends up true and the other ends up false. It is significant, then, that 'I am thinking of Bigfoot' and 'Bigfoot is thought of by me' have different truth-values: the first is true but the second untrue. On Russell's (1905a) view, 'Bigfoot is thought of by me' is false, as is 'The present king of France is bald'; on Strawson's (1950) view, 'The present king of France is bald' has a third, 'neutral' truth-value intermediate between truth and falsity – and so does 'Bigfoot is thought of by me.' Using the term 'untrue' to cover both falsity and the neutral truth-value (if there is one), we can say that on all standard semantic views 'Bigfoot is thought of by me' is untrue (again, unless paraphrased). Accordingly, it cannot mean the same as the true 'I am thinking of Bigfoot.'

Another objection in the same spirit is that there is still something hard to swallow in the non-relational account. For the phenomenology of being in an intentional state often involves a feeling of bearing a relation to something in the outside world. This is most obvious with perceptual experience: the phenomenology of having a visual experience of a yellow lemon is a phenomenology of bearing a distinctive perceptual relation to an object standing before one (a *Gegenstand* indeed!).

It is hard to know how Brentano would respond to this objection, but here is one possible line. We may concede this: when I have a visual experience of a yellow lemon, I experience a *feeling of perceptually connecting* to the lemon. In a way, the experience's overall phenomenology says more than 'here is a yellow lemon'; it says something like 'here is a yellow lemon I am perceptually connecting to.' Thus if I am hallucinating a yellow lemon before me, but there happens to be a lemon of the same color, shape, and size just there, it is natural to assess the experience as *non*-veridical, and non-veridical purely in virtue of its phenomenology (Searle 1983, Kroon 2013). If so, the feeling of perceptually connecting to the lemon is a component of the experience's overall phenomenology, in addition to the yellow-lemon component. So it is true that perceptual experience includes a phenomenology of perceptual connection to an object. However, as just noted, this feeling of perceptual connection, like any feeling, may or may not be veridical. And when it is non-veridical, the subject need not *in fact* perceptually connect to anything. Thus although this is a phenomenology *as of* bearing a relation to something, *having* the phenomenology does not require actually bearing a relation to something. The having of a phenomenology never guarantees that the phenomenology is *veridical*. To that extent, the fact that the experience of being in an intentional state involves a phenomenology as of bearing a relation to something does not tell against a non-relational metaphysic of intentionality. The non-relational account can readily admit that intentional states involve such a phenomenology but insist that a relation is actually instantiated only when this phenomenology is veridical. Since what makes an intentional state the intentional state it is, and an intentional state at all, is independent of whether the state is veridical or not, the fact that a veridical intentional state involves a relation does not imply that what makes that state the intentional state it is (and an intentional state at all) is that relation.

Perhaps the most formidable objection to Brentano's mature theory is due to Moran (1996). Adapting Jackson's (1977a) argument against the adverbial theory of perception, Moran (1996: 9–10) claims that Brentano's 'adverbial view' faces a 'daunting problem': it cannot account for the similarity or type-identity among some intentional states. I have suggested that Brentano does not *have* an adverbial view, but a 'subjectist view'; nonetheless, Moran's objection can be reformulated to target that. Compare (a) a dragon-visualizer, (b) a unicorn-visualizer, and (c) a horse-seer. Clearly, (a) resembles (b) more than it resembles (c). The most straightforward explanation of this would be that (a) and (b) share an aspect or component that (c) lacks. But since 'visualizer' is not a syntactic part of 'dragon-visualizer' and 'unicorn-visualizer' (think of 'apple' and 'pineapple' again), Brentano cannot identify a component that (a) and (b) might share. He thus lacks the resources to explain, or even accommodate, this resemblance fact.

One might respond that incomposite, structureless states can also resemble, and the way in which they do could apply to the case of (a)–(c). Someone who believes that colors are simple, monadic, structureless features can still admit that red is more similar to orange than to yellow. Being a dragon-visualizer might resemble being a unicorn-visualizer more than being a horse-seer in the same way. One problem with this response is that the objector may reverse it to claim that a monadic conception of color has no resources to explain resemblance facts. But there is a more serious problem with the response: it seems to misrepresent how one could grasp what a *horse-visualizer* is. On the face of it, once we possess the concepts of dragon-visualizer and horse-seer, we can 'put together' the concept of a horse-visualizer, without having to go through a separate process of concept acquisition.[12] If subjectism is true, however, we would have to acquire the concept of a horse-visualizer in the same laborious way as the concepts of dragon-visualizer and horse-seer. For 'visualizer' is not a component of 'dragon-visualizer' and 'horse' is not a component of 'horse-seer,' so they could not be separated and recombined.[13]

A better response to the objection is called for, then. One distinctly Brentanian response is to claim that although a state such as (a) has in some sense no components, it nonetheless has a *structure*, indeed a structure that behaves in ways that mimic combinatorial components. The obvious problem with this response is that it is unclear how it might work: normally, we think of an entity's *structure* as precisely a matter of its having different parts, or components, bearing certain interrelations. It is unclear, then, how the property of being a dragon-visualizer could have a structure despite having no components.

Here again, however, Brentano's mereological innovations may be helpful. We might suggest that although intentional states are incomposite, in that they do not have *separable parts*, they do have structure, in that they have *distinguishable parts*. On the standard view, intentionality is a relation between an intentional act and an intentional object, each of which is ontologically independent of the other. This casts the act and the object as mutually separable: you can think of a cat even if the cat does not exist, and the cat can exist even if you do not think of him. An alternative picture, however, may construe the intentional act and the (merely-)intentional object as two mutually merely distinguishable parts of a single whole. In that scenario, the intentional state has no *components*, in the sense of separable parts, but it does have *structure*, in the sense that we can *distinguish* different aspects of it. We can *think* of it in different ways, one act-centric and one object-centric, just as we can think of it in terms of aware-ness-of-the-object or in terms of awareness-of-awareness-of-the-object. These dis-tinguishable aspects of an intentional state constitute its structure, and explain, or at least enable, purely combinatorial concept acquisition. A subject who acquired the concepts of dragon-visualizer and horse-seer, could *distinguish* within these concepts (i) an act-aspect to do with visualizing or seeing and (ii) an object-aspect to do with dragons or horses. She could distinguish these even though they can never come apart.

She could then imaginatively 'put together' these aspects in different combinations, thereby acquiring the concepts of a horse-visualizer and dragon-seer.

This suggestion is clearly very speculative, but the model it offers does recover combinatorial concept acquisition while insisting on the non-relational nature of intentionality. Its availability to Brentano is thus good news. Interestingly, there is textual evidence that Brentano indeed took the intentional act and the merely-intentional object to be mutually merely distinguishable:

> As in every relation, two correlates can be found here [in intentionality]. The one correlate is the act of consciousness, the other is that which it is directed upon... The two correlates are *only distinctionally separable from one another.* And so we have here again two purely distinctional parts of the pair of correlates, one of which [the act] is real, the other [the merely-intentional object] is not.   (Brentano 1982: 21–2 [23–4]; my italics)

When S visualizes a yellow lemon, we can distinguish *in thought* a visualization element and a yellow-lemon element. Even if *in reality* there are not two separate entities here, we can tell apart these two distinctional parts of the experience. We should be able, accordingly, to acquire the concept of a visualization experience and the concept of a lemon-ish experience. Once we have, we can recombine these concepts with others like them.

Jackson's (1977a) original objection to adverbialism pressed the compositionality of adverbial paraphrases from another angle as well. Adapted to the subjectist context, we might put Jackson's objection as follows: from 'S is thinking of a dragon,' one can validly infer 'S is thinking'; but from 'S is a dragon-thinker,' one *cannot* infer 'S is a thinker.' For 'dragon-thinker' is a syntactically unstructured predicate, so making this inference would be akin to inferring 'x is an apple' from 'x is a pineapple.'

In response, note first that although 'x is a pineapple, therefore x is an apple' is a bad inference, 'x is a strawberry, therefore x is a berry' is a good one – even though they seem superficially similar. What makes the latter inference good, it seems, is the availability of a certain bridge premise, which we may formulate as 'A strawberry is a species of berry' (contrast 'An apple is a species of pineapple'). The question, then, is whether a similar bridge principle is available to Brentano. And the answer seems positive: 'A dragon-thinker is a species of thinker' is as plausible as 'A strawberry is a species of berry.' Accordingly, it *is* possible to correctly infer 'S is a thinker' from 'S is a dragon-thinker.' The point is that although 'dragon-thinker' is syntactically simple, it is not true that its *only* relation to 'thinker' is morphological. Another relation is the genus/species relation: 'dragon-thinker' picks out a species of what 'thinker' picks out. It is this further relation that licenses the inference (for a fuller discussion of this, see Kriegel 2008).[14]

Conclusion

Perhaps the main reason I am a Brentano fan is simply that I think he got so much *right*, especially when it comes to the most fundamental problems of philosophy. Where I do not share his views, I can usually appreciate the grounds for them (his substance dualism is a case in point!), and can enjoy considering how the system alters if we remove the piece I dislike and replace it with one more to my liking. Importantly, such replacements are usually possible, without excessive reverberations through the system, because they do not go to the system's core. In the whole of Brentano's philosophy, I think there is only one wrong turn that has proven disastrous to his legacy. This is the claim that all mental states are conscious.

As I argued at the end of Chap. 1, Brentano's argument for this is poor. But even if there were strong grounds for the claim, I think Brentano would have done well to cordon off this commitment of his. As it stands, the official agenda of the *Psychology* is to lay methodological and theoretical foundations for the scientific study of the mind. Remarkably, Brentano's proposed foundations have zero relevance to the actual science of the mind that developed around the middle of the twentieth century. The basic reason for this is that Brentano focused on the first-person study of subjective phenomena available to inner perception, whereas much of actual cognitive science concerns the third-person study of processes and mechanisms posited in the context of explaining behavior. In retrospect, it is not clear why it should be so important for Brentano to insist that processes responsible for shaping behavior but inaccessible to inner perception do not deserve the appellation 'mental.' As long as they are clearly distinguished from the inner-perceptible phenomena that interested him more, he could have readily accorded them the courtesy of being called mental. He could then have presented the *Psychology* as a book about the methodological and theoretical foundations of the science of *consciousness*, rather than the science of *mind*, while bracketing the issue of whether anything outside consciousness qualifies as mental.

Crucially for our present purposes, in that scenario intentionality would be cited as the mark of the *conscious* rather than the mental. Its character as a subjective phenomenon accessible to inner perception would be more manifest. It would not be confused by later generations with the objective tracking relations posited in the context of explaining behavior. Informational and teleological accounts of such tracking relations would not be confused for accounts of the phenomenon Brentano was interested in. And the plausibility of Brentano's mature account of the phenomenon *he* was interested in would be more easily appreciated, since it is not all that odd to hold that the phenomenal property of felt directedness is an intrinsic, non-relational property of the conscious subject. But when the claims that all mental states are conscious and that intentionality is the mark of the conscious got fused into one thesis, 'intentionality as the mark of the *mental*,' its various components became invisible, and in consequence, both Brentano's philosophical concerns and his substantive accounts in response to them became invisible to many readers. My goal in this chapter has been to undo that infelicitous fusion and present more cleanly Brentano's basic ideas about intentionality – in particular, that intentionality is an intrinsic property of phenomenal directedness which subjects can fully grasp only if they experience it for themselves.[15]

Notes to Chapter 2

1. I am grateful to Mark Textor for bringing this passage to my attention.

2. The theses that intentionality is in essence a relation between mental states and environmental features and that there exists phenomenal intentionality can be seen as competing theories of the same phenomenon: intentionality as such. But to my mind, it is at least as reasonable to see them (or some versions of them) as targeting two different but related phenomena. One phenomenon is the objective ability of mental states to track environmental features; the other is the subjective feature of felt directedness that some mental states exhibit (see Kriegel 2013c).

3. There are ontological, epistemological, and phenomenological worries: ontologically, it is unclear what to make of the notion of a 'mental tree'; epistemologically, it is thought to raise a 'veil of appearances' between the subject and the external world; phenomenologically, it is in conflict with the so-called transparency of experience, the observation that when attending to our own experience it is hard to pick up on anything other than what the experience represents.

4. The other option would be to defend the immanentist theory, or a slightly modified variant, against the objections to it (see, for example, Brandl 2005).

5. I use the expression 'intrinsic property,' as is common, to denote a property that something has not in virtue of bearing a relation to anything else independent from it. This allows two scenarios: where the thing does not bear a relation to anything, and where it bears a relation to a part of itself (as when a person is intrinsically legged in virtue of having a leg as part). Sometimes the expression 'intrinsic property' is used to denote a property that something cannot exist without having – the property is thus 'intrinsic' to the thing's nature. However, I prefer to use 'essential property' to denote that kind of property.

6. This title does contain some ambiguities, insofar as (i) mental reference might yet be a relation in some loose sense and (ii) it is not immediately transparent that mental reference is the same thing as intentionality. But the passage I discuss in the text next seems to me to remove these ambiguities.

7. The similarity, according to Brentano, is that both when we think of a (two-place) relation and when we think of intentionality, we have in mind two objects, and we think of one of them directly ('*in recto*') and of the other indirectly ('*in obliquo*'). Thus, thinking that Jim is taller than Jane and thinking that Jim is thinking of Jane both involve having two objects in mind, Jim and Jane, and representing Jim directly and Jane indirectly. This is the crucial similarity between intentionality and bona fide relations, according to Brentano. (For what it is worth, it strikes me personally that this claim of similarity is fraught with difficulties, but that other claims in the vicinity would indeed show important similarities between the non-relational property of intentionality and paradigmatic relations and relational properties.)

8. For a more detailed development of the adverbial machinery, and hesitant defense of the underlying philosophical idea, see Kriegel 2011: ch. 4. The original adverbialist theory was developed by Chisholm (1957) and applied just to sensory perception. The gambit here is to apply it to all intentional states.

9. We could obtain the same result with 'sequencing' instead of hyphenation: we could write out 'S is ThinkingOfDragons,' or even 'S is TOD' for short.

10. The *reason* Brentano prefers subjectism over adverbialism and hyphenism seems to do with his particular brand of nominalism, which we will explore in detail in Chap. 6.

11. Recall my methodological principle, presented in the Introduction, of giving priority to materials Brentano decided to publish himself. This is an example of the principle's application – and, I would say, of its plausibility.

12. This capacity is related to, or parallels in some way, what Fodor (1975) called the 'productivity' of thought: the fact that any subject who grasps the proposition that John loves Mary has all the resources needed to grasp the proposition that Mary loves John, needing no further learning or acquisition process.

13. Observe that in the case of colors, it is *not* plausible that we acquire the concept of orange by 'putting together' the concepts of red and yellow. Rather, we seem to require going again through the laborious process of acquiring the concept of orange 'from scratch.' (This claim is compatible with the possibility of acquiring a concept of a missing shade of blue in the more direct way; the point is that this cannot work for such concepts as orange, which are 'too distant,' in some sense, from red and yellow to be acquired in the same way.) In this respect, we can see that the cases of color concepts and intentional-state concepts are disanalogous.

14. It might be objected that 'S is a dragon-thinker' still fails to recover the exact inferential profile of 'S thinks of a dragon,' since the latter supports an inference to 'S thinks' *without* need of a bridge principle, whereas the former does not. This seems right to me, but it also seems like a minor liability on the paraphrase. Arguably, it is permissible for a paraphrase to be *somewhat* revisionary – indeed, this is often the *point* of the paraphrase.

15. For comments on a previous draft, I am grateful to Lionel Djadaojee, Anna Giustina, and two OUP referees. I have also benefited from presenting drafts of this chapter at École Normale Supérieure, Kings' College London, and the University of Liege. I am grateful to the audiences there, in particular Géraldine Carranante, Arnaud Dewalque, Bob Hale, Zdenek Lenner, Alice Martin, Denis Seron, and Mark Textor. For useful exchanges and conversions of relevance, I am grateful to Ben Blumson, Davide Bordini, Johannes Brandl, and Hamid Taieb.

3

The Modes of Conscious Intentionality

In Chap. 1, we saw Brentano's theory of consciousness, and in Chap. 2, his theory of intentionality, the *mark* of the conscious. This chapter lays the foundations for the rest of the book by discussing the three fundamental *modes* of conscious intentionality in Brentano's theory of mind. This three-way distinction is crucial, as we will later see, to Brentano's metaphysics and value theory.

1. Brentano's Attitudinal Classification of Conscious States

Although the topic of psychological taxonomy has not seen much play in contemporary philosophy of mind, in the history of philosophy it has often been regarded as one of the central tasks of a philosophical theory of mind. In *The Republic*, Plato divided the soul into three 'departments': reason, spirit, and appetite. Aristotle had his modifications to make, Aquinas his own, and so on. Brentano takes up the topic in chaps. 5–8 of Book II of the *Psychology*, and considered it one of the most important aspects of that work.[1] So much so, in fact, that in 1911 he published a revised edition of just those four chapters (plus appendices) as a stand-alone book titled *On the Classification of Mental Phenomena* (Brentano 1911). Moreover, he returned to the topic in various manuscripts and lecture notes, some of which were published posthumously – most notably an essay titled 'A Survey of So-Called Sensory and Noetic Objects of Inner Perception' (in Brentano 1928). The bulk of this section is dedicated to exposition and elucidation of the basics of Brentano's classification (§1.1); toward its end I will also present Brentano's *argument* for his classification (§1.2).

1.1. The fundamental classification

The central task in this area, as Brentano sees it, is to identify the 'fundamental classes' of conscious experience. What does 'fundamental class' mean? Brentano's basic assumption is that the domain of consciousness is structured by genus/species relations (observer-independently!), so that some kinds of consciousness are species of others. This assumption he imports from zoology, botany, and chemistry, which had seen an explosion of classificatory research in the eighteenth and nineteenth centuries. Fifteen years before the publication of Brentano's *Psychology*, Darwin already marveled at the 'wonderful fact' that

... all animals and all plants throughout all time and space should be related to each other in group subordinate to group, in the manner which we everywhere behold – namely, varieties of the same species most closely related together, species of the same genus less closely and unequally related together, forming sections and sub-genera, species of distinct genera much less closely related, and genera related in different degrees, forming sub-families, families, orders, subclasses, and classes.   (Darwin 1859: 128)

It is a priority for Brentano's *Psychology*, as a programmatic book designed to lay the foundations of psychology on a footing akin to that of the natural sciences, to show that a similar scheme imposes itself in the realm of consciousness. For example, color consciousness is a species of visual consciousness, which in turn is a species of perceptual consciousness, and so on. The *highest* genus here is consciousness per se. What Brentano calls the 'fundamental classes' are the *second-to-highest* genera – kinds of consciousness which are species of only one higher genus. Any conscious kinds which are species of more than one conscious genus are not fundamental in this sense. Thus, visual consciousness is not a fundamental class of conscious phenomena, since it is a species of both perceptual consciousness and consciousness per se. Only conscious kinds which are species *only* of consciousness per se are fundamental.

So what *is* Brentano's fundamental classification? Here is his crispest presentation of it:

It is clear that all modes of reference (*Beziehungsweisen*) to an object fall into three classes: presentation, judgment, and emotion [or interest]. The second and third modes always presuppose the first, and in both we find a contrast, in that a judgment is either a belief or a denial, and an emotion is either a form of love or hate.   (Brentano 1928: 55 [42])

The three fundamental classes are: presentation (*Vorstellung*), judgment (*Urteil*), and 'interest' (*Interesse*) or 'emotions' (*Gemütsbewegungen*) (see also Brentano 1874: II, 33 [198]). Unlike presentation, judgment and interest are each divided into two opposing kinds: judgment into acceptance (*Anerkennung*) and rejection (*Verwerfung*), interest into love (*Liebe*) and hate (*Hasse*) (see Figure 3.1). Let us expand a little on each of Brentano's three classes, then go slightly deeper into his taxonomic framework.

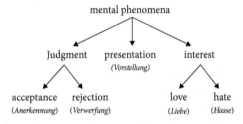

Figure 3.1. Brentano's fundamental classification

Consider first the category Brentano calls judgment. The term 'judgment' is in truth misleading, as it suggests an intellectual exercise of conceptual thought. In reality, Brentano has in mind any conscious act that targets the way things *are* – any state that presents what it does as true, as real, as obtaining, etc. Brentano writes:

By 'judgment' we mean, in accordance with common philosophical usage, acceptance (as true) or rejection (as false).   (Brentano 1874: II, 34 [198])

This includes not only the products of conceptual thought, such as belief, but also perceptual experience. 'Every perception counts as a judgment,' he writes (1874: II, 50 [209]). A visual experience of a yellow lemon has veridicality conditions in the same sense the belief that the lemon is yellow has truth conditions. Both are in the business of *getting things right*. What characterizes Brentano's category of judgment is this kind of concern with *truth*, with how things *are*.

This contrasts with the category of conscious states Brentano calls interest. These are essentially concerned with *goodness*, with how things *ought* to be:

Just as every judgment takes an object to be true or false, analogously every phenomenon which belongs to [the category of interest] takes an object to be good or bad.
(Brentano 1874: II, 36 [199]; see also 1874: II, 88–9 [239])[2]

This category, too, covers a large group of phenomena, including emotion, affect, the will, and pain/pleasure. For this reason, Brentano has no satisfactory name for this class, and calls it alternately interest, emotion, or (often) 'phenomena of love and hate.'[3] What unifies the phenomena in this category is the fact that they present what they do as good or bad – in a suitably generic sense of the word (*not*, mind, in the narrower sense of *moral* goodness). Wanting a beer presents beer as good, but so does taking pleasure in the beer, wishing for beer, liking beer, deciding on beer, and so on. Meanwhile, being disgusted with beer, being displeased with a beer, disliking beer, and being disappointed with a beer all present a beer as bad. In truth, the modern technical notions of 'pro attitude' and 'con attitude' are perfect terms for Brentano's positive ('love') and negative ('hate') kinds of interest.

Brentano's other fundamental class is presentation.[4] This is a kind of intentional state that in itself presents what it does neither as true or false nor as good or bad. Instead, it presents what it does in an entirely 'neutral' manner, without commenting on its object's truth or goodness. Brentano writes:

We speak of a presentation whenever something appears to us.   (Brentano 1874: II, 34 [198])

Brentano holds that every state of judgment or interest involves presentation as a component: to present a beer as good, for example, you have to present it at all. It is a separate question whether a presentation can occur entirely on its own. Brentano's occasional talk of *mere presentation* (*bloße Vorstellung*) suggests this kind of state. And indeed mental states that present an object without taking a stand on the matters of truth and goodness abound in our mental life: entertaining something, contemplating something, apprehending, considering, or supposing something – as well as sensory analogs such as imagining, daydreaming, and visualizing – all seem to be *mere* presentations in this sense.[5] When you merely contemplate *p*, *p* appears to you neither as true/false nor as good/bad; it just appears to you.

❧

It might seem natural to frame Brentano's fundamental classification in terms of the modern notion of *direction of fit*. The idea would be that judgment has a mind-to-world ('thetic') direction of fit, interest a world-to-mind ('telic') direction of fit, and presentation a 'null' direction of fit. This is plausible, but only if we construe direction of fit in terms of modes of presenting an intentional object: presenting as true/false (judgment), presenting as good/bad (interest), and 'mere' presenting (presentation). In current philosophy of mind, direction of fit is often glossed in terms of *functional role*: the mind-to-world direction is cashed out in terms of *inferential* role, the world-to-mind direction in terms of *motivational* role. On this understanding, the difference between judgment and interest would be a difference in functional role. This is certainly not Brentano's view.

One problem with the functionalist gloss is that it is unclear what the distinctive functional role associated with the null direction of fit would be. But Brentano has a more basic argument against the functionalist gloss, namely, that it simply *gets the extension wrong*. For it fails to classify wish with desire, intention, and other states of interest:

Kant indeed defined the faculty of desire (*Begehrung*) simply as 'the capacity to bring into existence the objects of one's presentations through those presentations.' … This is why we find in Kant that curious claim that any wish (*Wünsch*), even if it were recognized to be impossible, such as the wish to have wings for example, is an attempt to obtain what is wished for and contains a presentation of our desire's causal efficacy. This is a desperate attempt to harmonize the boundary between the two classes [interest and causally efficacious states] …

(Brentano 1874: II, 117 [259]; see also Brentano 1907a: 157 [151], quoted in Chap. 7)

It is (nomologically) possible to wish for what is recognizably unachievable (immortality, say), which means that wish is not inherently characterized by a motivational force. Yet wish seems to naturally belong in one class with desire and hope, not with supposition and apprehension (and certainly not with belief). Brentano's own notion of mode of presenting does secure this result, since wishing for immortality presents immortality *as good*.

The moral is: if we want to use the modern notion of direction of fit to elucidate Brentano's trichotomy, we must not construe direction of fit functionally but in terms of presentational modes. That is how I will be understanding direction-of-fit talk hereafter.

The notion of *mode* is crucial here. The idea is that different kinds of conscious state present what they do *in different ways*. The difference between them is not in *what* they present but in *how* they present. Importantly, Brentano's presentational modes are not Frege's – they are not aspects of a state's (fine-grained) *content*. Rather, they are aspects of the state's *attitude*. When you judge that 2+2=4, you are mentally committing to the truth of 2+2=4. But this commitment is built into the attitude you are taking toward 2+2=4, it does not show up in the content of your judgment. You do not judge that 2+2=4 *is true*, but simply that 2+2=4. Nonetheless the judgment is inherently committed to the truth of 2+2=4. This commitment is thus built into the very nature of judgment as a type of mental state.

We may put this by saying that the judgment that 2+2=4 does not present 2+2=4 as true, but rather *presents-as-true* 2+2=4. Presenting-as-true is a mode or modification of the presenting. Compare (a) a pink wall on which a white light is shined with (b) a white wall on which a reddish-pink light is shined, with the result that both walls look the same to a normal perceiver under normal conditions. The wall is cast as pink in both cases, so that it appears the same. But in one case the pinkness comes from the wall being lit, whereas in the other it comes from the light being cast thereon. The truth-element in an act of judging that 2+2=4 is like the pink element in the light cast on a white wall.

The same goes for the other presentational modes. When you *dis*believe that 2+2=5, you are mentally committing to the falsity of 2+2=5, but the commitment is built into the attitude of your disbelief rather than into its content: your disbelief presents-as-false 2+2=5. By the same token, your love of ice cream presents-as-good ice cream and your disapproval of jingoism presents-as-bad jingoism. And the difference between belief and desire is purely *attitudinal*: a belief that *p* and desire that *p* both present *p*, but the former presents-as-true *p* while the latter presents-as-good *p*.

In all these cases, the relevant mental commitment is an 'attitudinal feature' of the conscious state, not a 'content feature.' Accordingly, it does not show up in the state's satisfaction or correctness conditions. Nonetheless, it has an important role with respect to such conditions: namely, it determines *what kind* of satisfaction or correctness conditions are appropriate for the relevant state. Because it is in the nature of belief to present-as-true, belief is evaluated *for truth*, and its appropriate correctness conditions are *truth conditions*. In contrast, since it is in the nature of desire to present-as-good, desire is to be evaluated for goodness, and the appropriate correctness conditions for desire are what we might call goodness conditions.[6]

To summarize the discussion thus far, Brentano divides conscious states into three basic kinds, and locates the fundamental difference between them in the mode of intentionality each uses – the distinctive attitudinal presentational feature characteristic of each. The following exposition of Brentano's basic classification by Chisholm is spot on:

He believes that there are three *ways* in which one's thoughts may be directed upon an object A. First, one may simply contemplate – or think about – the object A. Secondly, one may *take an intellectual stand* with respect to A; this stand consists either in accepting A or in rejecting

A. And, thirdly, one may *take an emotional stand* with respect to A; this emotional stand consists either in taking a pro-attitude toward A or in taking a negative attitude toward A.

(Chisholm 1981a: 4; italics mine)

The term 'intellectual stand' is suboptimal, insofar as it suggests a conceptually sophisticated kind of mental state, but otherwise Chisholm's presentation is perfectly accurate.

If we interpret direction-of-fit talk not in terms of functional role but in terms of Brentanian presentational mode, we can represent Brentano's classification as in Figure 3.2.

1.2. The argument for the fundamental classification

So much, then, for Brentano's *view* on the fundamental classification of conscious states. What is his *argument* for the view?

Brentano's argument focuses on the role of presentational modes in capturing the deep homogeneity and heterogeneity relations among conscious states. Brentano writes:

Nothing distinguishes mental phenomena from physical phenomena more than the fact that something inheres (*inwohnt*) in them object-wise (*gegenständlich*). And that is why it is so understandable that the fundamental differences in the *manner* something inheres in them object-wise constitute the principal class differences among mental phenomena.

(Brentano 1874: II, 32 [197]; my italics)

Insofar as intentionality is the mark of the conscious, different *kinds* of intentionality should distinguish different kinds of consciousness. Compare: insofar as a vehicle is a machine that gets you from A to B, different *kinds* of vehicle are distinguished by the different *ways* they get you from A to B: flying, floating, rolling, and so on. These different *modes* of transportation parallel our different *modes* of intentionality. The underlying idea here is that what makes a vehicle the kind of vehicle it is is intimately connected to what makes it a vehicle at all; and by the same token, what makes a conscious state the kind of conscious state it is is intimately connected to what makes it a conscious state at all. Where intentional directedness is the principle of *demarcation*, it stands to reason that *manner* or *mode* of intentional directedness should serve as principle of *speciation* or *classification*.

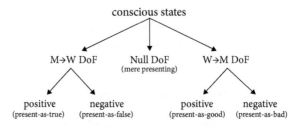

Figure 3.2. Brentano's classification, reframed

Once Brentano adopts this approach to fundamental classification, it straightfor-wardly delivers his classification. We have already quoted this key sentence: 'It is clear that all modes of reference (*Beziehungsweisen*) to an object fall into three classes: presentation, judgment, and emotion [interest]' (Brentano 1928: 55 [42]). Presentation is characterized by the neutral mode of mere-presenting, judgment by the alethic mode of presenting-as-true/false, and emotion or interest by the axiological mode of presenting-as-good/bad.

Brentano's argument for his trichotomy may be reconstructed as follows, then: 1) the correct principle for classifying conscious states is by mode of intentionality; 2) the three fundamental modes of intentionality are presenting-as-true/false (characteristic of judgment), presenting-as-good/bad (characteristic of interest), and mere-present-ing (characteristic of presentation); therefore, 3) the three fundamental classes of conscious state are judgment, interest, and presentation. The argument is clearly valid. What supports Premise 1 is (a) the claim that intentionality demarcates the mental and (b) the idea that the principles of classification and of demarcation should be con-nected in the expected way. What supports Premise 2 is Brentano's careful analysis, in the *Psychology*, of the relation between (i) presentation and judgment (Book II, chap. 7) and (ii) feeling and will (Book II, chap. 8). We will consider both in due course.

For Brentano, the fundamental classification of mental phenomena (which, we should remember, is at bottom a classification of *conscious* phenomena) guides the structure of psychological inquiry. His original, six-book plan for the *Psychology* involved a Book III on presentation, a Book IV on judgment, and a Book V on interest (see Rollinger 2012). Each book was to lay out (among other things) further, *non-fundamental* classifications; some of these are discussed in the next section.[7]

2. More on Brentano's Classification

As noted, in contemporary philosophy of mind the question of psychological tax-onomy has not seen much uptake. Explicit discussions of the matter are few and far between. Implicitly, mainstream research seems to work with a model positing four fundamental types of mental phenomenon: there is input in the form of sensory per-ception, output in the form of intentional action, and a mediating layer consisting of beliefs and desires.[8] These themselves are differentiated by two cross-cutting (inten-tional) distinctions: perception and belief exhibit a mind-to-world direction of fit, desire and action a world-to-mind direction of fit; perception and action are nonprop-ositional, belief and desire are propositional (see Table 3.1).

There are many other mental phenomena, of course, but they can be accounted for in terms of the four fundamental ones: either as species of them (remembering that p is believing that in the past, p), combinations of them (being disappointed that p is a combination of believing that p and desiring that $\sim p$), or combinations of species of them (hoping that p is a combination of desiring that p and believing that possibly, p).

Table 3.1. Mainstream's fundamental classes

	M → W	W → M
Nonpropositional	sensory perception	intentional action
Propositional	belief	desire

Brentano's explicit taxonomy involves many notable differences from today's mainstream implicit taxonomy. The most striking one will be discussed in the next section. In this section, I discuss other important features of Brentano's taxonomic system. I divide the discussion in two: a consideration of Brentano's 'fundamental' taxonomy (§2.1) and a consideration of his non-fundamental taxonomy (§2.2).

2.1. More on the fundamental classification

The most central feature of Brentano's taxonomy is that it is driven almost entirely by attitudinal properties of conscious states, properties such as presenting-as-true and presenting-as-good. This is quite an original take on the essence of conscious states. Consider currently popular theories of the nature of belief. Perhaps the leading theory is functionalist: what distinguishes belief from desire and other mental states is its distinctive functional role. But functional role is a *dispositional* property, and such properties are typically grounded in deeper, more essential *categorical bases*.[9] It would thus be natural to identify the categorical basis of the relevant functional role, rather than the functional role itself, as the essential feature of belief. The property of presenting-as-true is occurrent and might for all we know ground and explain belief's functional role. Likewise, a more recent approach to belief focuses on the distinctive norms governing beliefs: the 'aim' of belief is truth, we are told, and so belief is governed by a truth norm.[10] But here too, one suspects there is something about belief, something nonnormative, that *makes* it governed by the truth norm rather than other norms. After all, belief is an *empirical* phenomenon whose very existence cannot be owed to anything like supra-empirical norms. The thought imposes itself that belief is governed by the truth norm precisely because it is of its essence to present-as-true. Thus Brentano's attitudinal account of the nature of belief seems to go deeper than currently popular approaches. In Chap. 7, I will make a parallel claim about Brentano's attitudinal account of desire and emotion.

A second important feature of Brentano's taxonomy is its division of judgments into two mutually irreducible, *categorically distinct* kinds. On Brentano's view, to disbelieve that p is not just to believe that $\sim p$. (Nor, of course, is it to fail to believe that p.) Rather, it is a sui generis attitude irreducible to belief (Brentano 1874: II, 65–6 [222–3]).[11] On this view, there is a psychologically real difference between believing that $\sim p$ and disbelieving that p. The former involves mental commitment to the truth of $\sim p$, the latter mental commitment to the falsity of p.[12] In this respect, disbelief parallels displeasure: being displeased that p feels nothing like being pleased that $\sim p$.[13] This is a psychologically real categorical difference between two kinds of conscious state. Thus believing and disbelieving can have the same content, and take the judgment attitude toward it, but one takes the positive-judgment attitude while the other takes the negative-judgment attitude.

What motivates this nonreductive account of disbelief? After all, disbelief that p and belief that $\sim p$ seem inferentially equivalent, and it would certainly be more *parsimonious* to treat disbelief that p as nothing but belief that $\sim p$. Moreover, it is not clear that there is any *phenomenological* evidence for a categorical distinction here. So Brentano must adduce some compelling reason why a sui generis disbelief attitude is *needed*. It is quite obvious that Brentano is attracted to this view partly by his evident penchant for aesthetic symmetries, of which a parallelism between positive and negative judgments on the one hand and positive and negative affective states on the other would be an instance.[14] But in addition, there is a genuine dialectical pressure for the nonreductive account of disbelief in the context of trying to account for negation within the framework of Brentano's particular theory of judgment; we will only be in a position to appreciate this pressure in the next chapter.

Thirdly, Brentano takes perceptual states to form a species of judgment. This is *not* intended as the substantive claim that perceptual experiences have a propositional content akin to that of judgments as we ordinarily think of them. Rather, Brentano simply uses the label 'judgment,' unadvisedly, to cover both beliefs and perceptions. What unifies this category is that all mental states belonging to it employ the same attitudinal property in presenting their intentional object. This might seem initially implausible: all beliefs essentially present-as-true, but plausibly, not all perceptions do. When you see that the cat is on the mat, your perception does perhaps present-as-true what it presents. But when you simply *see the cat*, the perception surely does *not* present-as-true the cat. Cats are not truth-bearers, after all. However, this worry does not in fact arise within the Brentanian framework. Again, we will be able to fully appreciate why only in the next chapter. As we will see there, Brentano attempts to reduce all belief-that to belief-in. This matters because believing *in* a cat does not present-as-true the cat, but rather presents-as-existent (or presents-as-real) the cat. Plausibly, now, this is exactly how seeing a cat presents the cat: as-existing.

There is a traditional view that opposes this outlook, holding that a perceptual experience of a cat does not in and of itself commit to the cat's existence. In and of itself, it does not comment on the cat's existence; it merely presents the cat. It is just that perceptual presentations of this sort are typically accompanied by *beliefs* that do commit to the existence of their presented object. Brentano rejects this view, however, holding instead that every act of perceiving x has accepting x as a merely distinguishable part (Brentano 1982: 86–7 [92–3]).[15] His reason for this is that belief in the external world does not feel as though it is acquired *on the basis of* perceptual experience; rather, it feels as though it *comes with* perceptual experience:

Particular evidence in favor of belief in the primary object being contained in [sensory perception] is provided by reflections arising from the question concerning the origin of the belief in an external world. These reflections seem to lead to [the conclusion] that rather than having originally been without such a belief, [and] having only gained it later by realizing that the law-governed connection between the sequence of our mental experiences can be best understood on the basis of such hypotheses, one did trust immediately…The belief [contained] in the fundamental sensory acts thus seems to be involved in the beginning.   (Brentano 1982: 87 [93])

Commitment to the independent reality of a cat seems immediate upon perceiving the external cat; it does not seem based on inference (e.g., to the best explanation) from perception of feline sense-data, as Russell (1912: chap. 2) for example held. Believing and perceiving thus share an attitudinal essence for Brentano, and therefore belong to a single mental category. Obviously, there is also an important *difference* between them; this difference will be discussed in the next subsection.

Fourthly, while the domain of emotion/interest is analogous to that of judgment in dividing into positive and negative attitudes, there is also an important disanalogy between the two: we can present things as *better* or *worse*, but not as truer or falser. Accordingly, Brentano recognizes the need for a third sui generis type of interest state: preference (Brentano 1889: 23 [26], 1907a: 148 [143], 1952: 147 [92]). To prefer x over y is to present x as better than y in the same sense in which to love x is to present x as good. That is, it is to present the superiority of x over y *attitudinally*. To a first approximation, we might say that preferring x to y *presents-as-structured-by-value-superiority* the ordered pair (x, y).[16] Importantly, Brentano adopts a nonreductive account of preference, arguing that preferring x over y is irreducible to loving x more than y. Various intriguing questions arise around this set of ideas; some will be taken up in Chap. 8.

Fifthly, Brentano claims that judgment and interest are 'grounded in' presentation, or have presentation as their grounds/foundations (*Grundlage*). (1874: I, 112 [80]). It is an open question what notion of grounding Brentano has in mind, and whether it is the notion currently widely discussed in metaphysics and beyond (see Fine 2001 for the *locus classicus*). One *similarity* is that Brentanian grounding is a matter of *ontological asymmetric dependence*, what Brentano calls 'unilateral separability.' Since a judgment presents-as-true/false p, a fortiori it presents p. But the converse does not hold: not every presentation presents-as-true/false.[17] Presenting is thus unilaterally separable from presenting-as-true/false: a conscious state can be a presentation without being a judgment, but it cannot be a judgment without being a presentation. (In order to believe that p, one must apprehend p; but one may apprehend p without believing what one apprehends.) To that extent, Brentano's notion of grounding resembles ours. On the other hand, Brentanian grounding is not an *explanatory* relation. The currently much-discussed notion is often thought to provide for a ('vertical' rather than 'horizontal') explanation of the grounded in terms of the ground: the vase is fragile *because* of its microstructure, a car is parked illegally *because* it is parked on the sidewalk, and so on. In contrast, it is clearly not the case that a conscious state is a judgment *because* it is a presentation – its being a presentation leaves many other options open. In summary, we may say that Brentano's notion of *Grundlage* is just the notion of an ineluctable foundation, something without which the grounded cannot come to be, but is not meant to denote an explanatory in-virtue-of relation.

2.2. The non-fundamental classification

While the initial trichotomy exhausts Brentano's *fundamental* classification of conscious states, further classification is possible. In particular, further divisions among conscious states are possible according to their attitudinal properties of presenting-as-F. Notably, both Brentano's 'acceptance' and 'rejection' can come in two varieties: 'assertoric' or 'apodictic.' The former variety presents what it does as *contingent*, the latter as *necessary*. That is to say, assertoric belief that *p* presents-as-contingently-true *p*, while apodictic belief that *p* presents-as-necessarily-true *p*. Meanwhile, assertoric disbelief presents-as-contingently-false, while apodictic disbelief presents-as-necessarily-false, i.e., as impossible (see Brentano 1928: 55 [42]). A parallel distinction applies to interest: apodictic hate of genocide presents-as-necessarily-bad genocide, while assertoric hate of car salesmen presents-as-contingently-bad car salesmen; an assertoric pro attitude toward football presents-as-contingently-good football, while apodictic pro attitude toward *eudaimonia* presents-as-necessarily-good *eudaimonia* (see Brentano 1928: 55 [42–3]). Other attitudinal distinctions apply to both judgment and interest (Brentano 1928: 55 [42–3]).

Just as alethic modality is an attitudinal feature of judgments, so is *temporal* modality. Consider the difference between having a visual experience of rain and having an episodic memory of rain (or of seeing rain). There are in fact many differences between the two, but one of them seems to concern what we might call *temporal orientation*: the episodic memory presents the rain as (having occurred) in the past, whereas the visual experience presents the rain as (in the) present. According to Brentano, this difference is not a content difference (Brentano 1956: 34). It is entirely attitudinal: the episodic memory presents-as-past the rain, while the visual experience presents-as-present the rain. His argument is that only this attitudinal view of temporal orientation can diffuse a certain puzzle about hearing a melody. The puzzle is that at a single moment we seem to enjoy sensuous awareness of both the note currently playing and the note just played. How is it that in such a case we do not experience the audible superposition of both notes? Brentano's answer is that the two awarenesses are kept separate by presenting their objects in different *ways*. Calling the awareness of the current note 'aesthesis' and that of the note just past 'proteraesthesis,' he dictates the following on Boxing Day 1914:

What then could constitute the essential difference in the [experience] of proteraesthesis as compared to aesthesis? The way to the only possible answer is clearly indicated. Sensing is a [kind of] mental reference to an object. Such reference can be distinguished, first, through the difference in objects, and secondly, through the difference in the *manner* of reference to the same object … Admittedly, proteraesthesis has the exact same object as aesthesis, but it refers to that object in a different *manner* … (Brentano 1928: 48 [36]; my emphasis)

The two notes are not experientially superimposed because the aesthesis presents-as-present its note while the proteraesthesis presents-as-past its.

There are also attitudinal distinctions proper to the domain of presentation. Unlike judgment and interest, presentation does not come in a positive variety and a negative one. Nor is there an assertoric/apodictic-like distinction in this case. Nonetheless, other attitudinal distinctions apply. Paramount among these is the distinction between a direct mode (*modus recto*) and an oblique mode (*modus obliquo*). When you contemplate whether your friend wants a vacation, your contemplation presents your friend *directly*, but it also presents a vacation *obliquely* (Brentano 1928: 56 [43]). This distinction does a considerable amount of work for Brentano in the last stage of his philosophical development, but will be largely ignored in this book (see Dewalque 2014 for discussion).[18]

Note the absence in Brentano's classification of what has often been taken to be the most basic division of mental phenomena: between those that are sensory or visceral or 'lower' and those that are cognitive or intellectual or 'higher.' In the above presentation of the current mainstream, the distinction between propositional and nonpropositional states plays this role. Brentano's fundamental classification, however, lumps together sensory perception and abstract thought, on one side, and on the other, sensuous pleasure and considered moral preference. Now, surely Brentano *recognizes* the distinction between the 'lower' senses and the 'higher' intellect. Equally clearly, however, he takes this distinction to be *less fundamental* than the distinction between modes of intentional directedness. The point is that the 'natural homogeneity' between a sensory perception of a eucalyptus and a belief that this is a eucalyptus is greater, for Brentano, than both (i) the natural homogeneity between the belief that this is a eucalyptus and the desire that it be a eucalyptus and (ii) the natural homogeneity between the sensory perception of a eucalyptus and a sensuous pleasure in the eucalyptus' minty odor.

What underlies this assessment of comparative 'natural homogeneity,' or objective similarity, between conscious states? Brentano says almost nothing about this. It might be, however, that he takes the sensory/intellectual distinction to pertain merely to the *contents*, or *objects*, of conscious states. Clearly, for Brentano content distinctions are always 'shallower' than any attitudinal distinction. His taxonomic principle is that the classification of conscious states must start up top with the modes of intentional directedness, which are then divided and subdivided as far as the attitudinal phenomena allow; only when attitudinal distinctions have been exhausted can we start classifying conscious states by their types of content. (This is quite plausible: attitudinal differences go to the very nature of judgment, love, etc. as types of conscious states; the specific types of object they may take are more accidental.) If the sensory/intellectual distinction is a content distinction, then it would stand to reason that it would be subordinate to Brentano's three-way distinction between intentional modes. Perhaps the following passage suggests this content view of the sensory/intellectual distinction:

Let us turn now to the differences that the mental activities we inner-perceive exhibit with regard to their objects. They can be divided into sensory and intelligible (noetic).

(Brentano 1928: 58 [44])

This passage could be seen as suggesting that the most basic distinction between kinds of intentional object is between sensibles and intelligibles. This content construal of the sensory/intellectual distinction explains why Brentano is so confident that the distinction is subordinate to the direction-of-fit distinction in the overall taxonomy of conscious states.

It is a separate question how plausible this content construal of the sensory/intellectual distinction is. On the face of it, one can think about what one perceives, for example a brown dog. Both believing *in* a black swan and *seeing* a black swan present a black swan. This may suggest that the difference between them must ultimately be attitudinal rather than content-based. However, given that both the belief in the black swan and the perceptual experience of the black swan present-as-existent the swan, it is not immediately obvious what the attitudinal difference between the two might be. One promising idea might be that perception goes beyond belief in not merely presenting-as-existent its object, but presenting-as-existent-here-and-now that object. As we have seen, Brentano construes temporal orientation as an attitudinal feature of perception and episodic memory. Something similar might be said about spatial relations. Thus, while a belief in a black swan can be correct even if black swans exist far away from the believer, a perceptual experience of a black swan is veridical only if a black swan is present roughly in the same place as the perceiver. The experience does not count as veridical if there happens to be an indistinguishable swan (identically surrounded) but on another planet. Plausibly, this kind of spatial constraint on veridicality is specified by the very mode of perception – it is in the nature of perception to inform us about the *hic et nunc* (see Recanati 2007: 201, 285).[19]

Brentano's taxonomic efforts push further. One might expect the sensibles to divide according to the five/six senses, for example. Somewhat oddly, Brentano argues instead that there are *three* classes of sensible: colors, sounds, and the rest (1907b: 160–3, 1928: 63 [48]). The reason for this heterodox individuation of the senses is that Brentano's underlying criterion for the individuation, which has to do with the mixability of sensibles (see Massin 2017). I am unaware of a taxonomy of intelligibles in the Brentano corpus.[20]

In summary, Brentano's full taxonomy of conscious states is to be produced in three steps. First, a comprehensive classification of states by attitudinal features is to be produced. Then, a full classification of sensible and intelligible contents is to be produced. Finally, the content classification is to be plugged in at the 'bottom' of the attitudinal classification, such that attitudinally maximally determinate conscious states are to be classified in the first instance by minimally determinate intentional contents they might take. The result is (partially) represented in Figure 3.3.

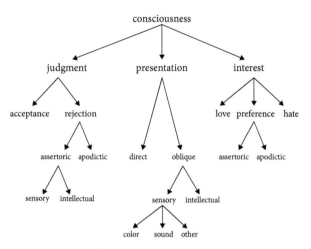

Figure 3.3. Brentano's full taxonomy – fragment

3. Presentation as an Attitudinal Primitive

The fundamental classification of mental states implicit in contemporary philosophy of mind, as presented in Table 3.1, differs from Brentano's in two ways. First, it treats the propositional/nonpropositional (higher/lower) distinction as equally important as the distinction between directions of fit. Second, it divides mental states by direction of fit only into two basic categories: belief-like cognitive states and desire-like conative states. I have already discussed Brentano's reason for diverging from the contemporary approach on the first point: if the propositional/nonpropositional distinction is a content-level distinction, it is perforce subordinate to any attitude-level distinction. In this section, I want to discuss in some length Brentano's reason for diverging on the second point. I want to flesh out a bit more Brentano's view and the way it differs from current-day orthodoxy (§3.1), then assess Brentano's two *arguments* for the view (§§3.2–3.3).

I should note that this section is in some sense 'optional' for the rest of the book and can in principle be skipped. As we will see in Parts II and III of the book, Brentano's theories of judgment and of interest are foundational for his accounts of the true, the good, and the beautiful. In contrast, while Brentano's theory of presentation has some relevance to his account of the beautiful, it does not play the same foundational role as judgment and interest. In particular, the thesis that presentation is a third type of basic attitude, on a par with and irreducible to judgment and interest, is not necessary for the rest of the system to hold together. It is, so to speak, an optional commitment for Brentano's system. This is why this section, which discusses that commitment, is likewise optional for the book. Nonetheless, I think Brentano's view here is both correct and important, so that contemporary philosophy of mind can learn from him on this score.

3.1. The view

Brentano's fundamental classification divides conscious states into states of judgment, interest, and presentation. In contemporary philosophy of mind, the prominent 'belief-desire psychology' suggests analogs of judgment and interest: both Brentano's judgment and our belief are cognitive states with a mind-to-world direction of fit, and both Brentano's interest and our desire are conative states with a world-to-mind direction of fit. However, the state of presentation, which is central to Brentano's classification, lacks a clear counterpart in belief-desire psychology.

In contemporary philosophy of mind, belief and desire are construed as propositional attitudes. Belief reports overtly suggest that belief has propositional content: we say 'Jimmy believes *that* the weather is nice.' Desire reports do not always: we often say things like 'Jimmy desires ice cream.' Nonetheless, it is common to treat 'Jimmy desires ice cream' as just shorthand for 'Jimmy desires *that* he have ice cream,' so that the desire is in fact a propositional attitude. Now, as we will see starting Chap. 4, Brentano's conception of judgment and interest is completely different. In particular, he takes both belief and desire to be *non*-propositional. We may nonetheless indulge here the propositional framework, and ask the following question: is there also a third propositional attitude on a par with belief and desire and irreducible to (any combination of) them?

Belief-desire psychology answers in the negative. It recognizes, of course, the existence of further propositional attitudes; but as already noted, it insists that these can be handled in terms of belief and desire. Some propositional attitudes, such as suspecting and being unwilling, can be construed as simply *species* of belief or desire (S suspects that p just if S believes that p with a sufficiently low degree of conviction; S is unwilling to ϕ just if S desires not to ϕ).[21] Other propositional attitudes, such as gladness and disappointment, can be reduced to logical combinations of belief and desire (being glad that p is just believing that p and desiring that p; being disappointed that p is just believing that p and desiring that $\sim p$). According to belief-desire psychology, *all* propositional attitudes succumb to such a treatment. The only *primitive, irreducible* propositional attitudes are belief and desire.

Brentano's position is different. Still indulging the propositionalist framework, we could say that he holds that in addition to belief and desire, there is a third primitive propositional attitude – what he calls presentation and we may call *entertaining, contemplating*, or *apprehending*. More specifically, in addition to believing that p, which presents-as-true p, and desire that p, which presents-as-good p, there is *entertaining* that p (or contemplating or apprehending p), which merely-presents p (without commenting on p's truth or goodness). According to Brentano, entertaining that p can be considered neither (i) a species of believing, nor (ii) a species of desiring, nor (iii) a 'product' of (some species of) belief and desire. Instead, it is a third attitudinal primitive on a par with belief and desire. At the very least, then, we should replace 'belief-desire psychology' with 'belief-desire-entertaining psychology.'[22]

Brentano does not bother arguing against (i) and (ii). One may conjecture that this is because he thinks it evident that there is no *constitutive* connection between entertaining that *p* and desiring that *q* for any *q*. At bottom, what Brentano argues against is a certain nuanced version of (i) – the notion that belief and entertaining form a single 'natural kind.' This is the idea that the cognitive 'department' of our mind includes such states as believing, suspecting, assuming, supposing, and entertaining, and even though some of these may be reducible to others, they all fall under a single fundamental category of mental activity – they are all in the business of getting the world right. For Brentano, this view fails to do justice to the fundamental difference between belief-like and entertaining-like states: whereas believing, suspecting, and assuming that *p* all present-as-true *p*, entertaining and supposing that *p* do not. This is a fundamental categorical difference that goes to the deep natures of these two types of state, which therefore constitute two different natural kinds.

In the background is Brentano's principle, which we have already seen, that the fundamental classification of mental states appeals to mode of intentionality. If belief and entertaining (judgment and presentation) involve different modes of intentionality, then they are fundamentally distinct classes of mental states. Accordingly, chap. 7 of Book II of the *Psychology* is dedicated to making the case that judgment and presentation indeed differ in their mode of intentionality. Brentano offers there two arguments. The more central argument, pursued in §§1–7 of the chapter, is a deductive argument by elimination – a demonstration of the attitudinal distinction between belief and entertaining *via negativa*. The other argument proceeds *via positiva*, but offers a more abductive route to the same conclusion. I consider the first argument in §3.2, the second in §3.3.

3.2. *The* via negativa *argument*

Brentano's central argument for the attitudinal distinction between belief and entertaining may be summarized as follows:

1) There is some difference between believing and entertaining;
2) The difference between them is not in their extrinsic properties;
3) The intrinsic difference between believing and entertaining is either (i) a difference in intensity/vivacity, (ii) a difference in content, or (iii) an attitudinal difference;
4) The intrinsic difference is not one of intensity;
5) It is not one of content; therefore,
6) The difference between believing and entertaining is attitudinal (they employ different modes of intentionality).

Brentano provides no support for Premises 1 and 3 (both stated explicitly in 1874: II, 39 [202]). He argues for Premise 2 in §2 of Chap. 7, for Premise 4 in §3, and for Premise 5 in §§4–7.

Premise 1 indeed seems beyond reproach. The fact that we have two different *words* here suggests prima facie that we find a *need* to denote two different phenomena. Just as most languages contain one expression for wanting to φ and one for being willing to φ, because we need to be able to speak differently of these two different phenomena, so most languages contain one expression for believing that *p* and one for entertaining that *p*, for a similar reason. Desire and willingness both belong to a single fundamental category of mental state, however: conative states with a world-to-mind direction of fit. The burden of Brentano's argument is to show that the same fate does not attend belief and entertainment.

In defense of Premise 2, Brentano argues against a functionalist account of the belief/entertaining distinction that grounds it in *relations* to different potential effects. One might hold, as Alexander Bain apparently did, that believing that *p* differs from entertaining that *p* in having a more direct impact on the will, and ultimately on behavior. Thus, believing that the weather is nice enough for a picnic has more chances of leading to picnic-pursuing behavior than merely entertaining that the weather is nice enough for a picnic. Nonetheless, Brentano thinks, these differences in functional role must ultimately be grounded in some intrinsic features of belief and entertaining:

> …why is it that the one presentation of the object has such an influence on behavior while the other does not? Just to raise the question is to show very clearly the oversight of which Bain is guilty. There would be no special consequences [for behavior], if there were no special *ground* (*Grund*) for them in the nature/quality (*Beschaffenheit*) of the thought process. Rather than making the assumption of an intrinsic difference between mere presentation and judgment unnecessary, the difference in [behavioral] consequences emphatically points up this intrinsic difference.   (Brentano 1874: II, 40 [202–3]; my italics)

Brentano is exactly right here. Functional role is a dispositional property of conscious states, and dispositional properties are *grounded* in categorical bases. So if there is a functional-role difference between belief and entertaining, ultimately it must be grounded in a categorical, intrinsic difference between them. It is because belief and entertaining have the intrinsic natures they do that they dispose the subject to act in the way they do. If they had different intrinsic natures, they would dispose the subject's behavior differently. The question is what the relevant difference in their intrinsic natures is.

As regards Premise 3, it is hard to think of another candidate intrinsic difference between belief and entertaining than those Brentano cites: intensity, content, and attitude. Certainly Brentano is entitled to consider it his opponent's burden to provide a fourth alternative.

Premise 4 claims that the intrinsic difference is not one of experiential intensity. Importantly, the kind of intensity Brentano has in mind is not a matter of degrees of conviction. The hypothesis under consideration is not that entertaining that *p* is simply a very tentative belief that *p*. (That seems rather to be *suspecting* that *p*.) Rather, the intensity in question is a matter of the degree of vivacity or 'fullness' (*Vollkommenheit*) with which p is *present before the mind* (1874: II, 39 [202]). The hypothesis under consideration, vaguely Humean, is that to believe that p is simply to entertain that p specially vividly. Brentano offers two arguments against this hypothesis. One is that it could not handle disbelief, since it seems to suggest that to disbelieve that p is to entertain that p with *negative* vivacity – a patently absurd proposal (1874: II, 44 [205]). This argument presupposes, of course, Brentano's sui generis account of disbelief. For if, contra Brentano, one were willing to identify disbelief that p with belief that $\sim p$, then one could hold that disbelief that p is just specially vivid entertaining of $\sim p$. Brentano's other argument, however, is more theoretically neutral and thus more compelling. It is that the identification of belief with vivid entertaining is simply extensionally inadequate:

> But even if in certain cases the act of taking something to be true coincides with the greater intensity of a presentation, the presentation is not, on that account, itself a judgment. That is why [a judgment recognized as mistaken] may disappear, while the vividness (*Lebendigkeit*) of the presentation persists. And in other cases we are firmly convinced of the truth of something, even though the content of the judgment is anything but vivid.   (1874: II, 43–4 [205])

Even though the intensity of a presentation can lead us to assent to its content, we sometimes recognize that in fact we should dissent from it without any consequent change in experienced vivacity. A person may suddenly have a strong feeling that her favorite football team will lose this weekend, but upon reflection realize that this feeling is baseless and untrustworthy. She could then stop believing that her team will lose while the proposition that it will remains highly vivid in her mind. (Keep in mind that the relevant kind of vivacity is *not* a degree of conviction-more on this in §3.3.) Conversely, we often find ourselves believing to be true a proposition relatively dully present before the mind. Arduously following through the proof of some complex mathematical theorem, one is liable to feel highly confident in its truth without having a particularly vivid awareness of the theorem itself. Thus entertaining and tentative believing are doubly dissociable.

It might be objected that we may still account for the belief/entertaining distinction in terms of intensity in the sense of degree of conviction. In particular, one might hold that entertaining that p is nothing but having 0.5 credence in p (or better: having 0.5 credence in p and 0.5 credence in $\sim p$). The thought is that when one has 0.5 credence in p and 0.5 credence in $\sim p$, one is committed neither to the truth of p nor to its falsity. One's mental state then merely-presents p. In this model, the belief/entertaining distinction is one of degree rather than kind.

To my knowledge, Brentano does not consider this kind of deflationary hypothesis. But the hypothesis faces several difficulties. First, on the face of it we can entertain propositions in which our credence is much lower than 0.5. Thus, I can entertain the notion that England will win the next World Cup. Indeed, secondly, one may entertain a proposition precisely with a view to establishing some credence in it. I may entertain the proposition that England will win the next World Cup in the context of attempting to know what kinds of bet would be wise for me to make; the episode of entertaining may then span moments in which I am 0.1 credent in the proposition entertained, moments I am 0.15 credent, and indeed moments of thorough indecision. Finally, a rational subject 0.5 credent in p who was also 0.9 credent in q would have 0.45 credence in p & q; whereas an equally rational subject who merely entertained that p, but was also 0.9 credent in q, may not be 0.45 credent in p & q.

I conclude that the belief/entertaining distinction is not one of intensity, as per Premise 4 of Brentano's argument. Premise 5 asserts that the belief/entertaining distinction does not pertain to content. The hypothesis under consideration is that entertaining and believing form a single kind of state, but with two structurally differ-ent kinds of content. Here too, Brentano considers one particular version of the hypothesis: that entertaining that a is F involves a presentation of a and of F, whereas believing that a is F involves that *plus predicating F of* a. That is, belief contents are pre-dicative, whereas entertained contents refer to the same entities but are non-predica-tive. We might say that the content of entertaining is <a, F> whereas the content of believing is <Fa> – with the attitudes themselves being the same. Brentano responds that belief and entertaining often have the same content (1874: II, 44–5 [205]). Indeed, it seems clear that we can sometimes come to believe something precisely by endorsing the content of an entertaining. Thus, I may entertain a philosophical proposition for a few hours, consider its plausibility, and eventually come to accept it. When I do, I seem to simply endorse the content I have been entertaining all along. If so, the entertaining and the believing must have the same content. In addition, Brentano maintains that existential beliefs are *not* predicative (1874: II, 48–9 [208]). As we will see in Chaps. 4–5, in believing that there are ducks, I do not quite predicate existence of ducks. So not all beliefs involve predicative contents.[23]

From Premises 1–5, the conclusion certainly follows: the belief/entertaining dis-tinction must be attitudinal at bottom, and pertain to the manner in which each presents its content. This conclusion, however, falls short of Brentano's full-fledged position in two ways. First, it does not commit to the *nature* of the attitudinal distinc-tion between belief and entertaining, in particular to the notion that belief presents-as-true whereas entertaining merely-presents. Secondly, the conclusion does not specify the *level* at which the attitudinal distinction arises: Brentano means presentation to be an attitudinal primitive at the same ('fundamental') level as judgment and interest, but for all the argument shows, presentation may simply be an attitudinal primitive one level lower, for example at the level of belief and disbelief. In that case, entertaining could turn out to be a species of belief.

One way to fill in the lacunae in Brentano's argument is as follows. First, we might propose the present-as-true/merely-present distinction as the *best explanation* of the belief/entertaining distinction. Secondly, once the belief/entertaining distinction is construed specifically in terms of presenting-as-true and merely-presenting, the notion that entertaining is a species of judgment on a par with belief and disbelief, rather than a species of consciousness on a par with judgment and interest, becomes implausible. For the common feature of all judgments, beliefs and disbeliefs alike, is what we might call their *alethic orientation*, the fact that they are concerned with truth and falsity. *If* merely entertaining that *p* were nothing but having 0.5 credence in *p*, *then* it would be plausible to see entertaining as a third species of judgment. But given that entertaining is by its nature alethically disengaged (if you will), it cannot be a species of judgment – no more than entertaining the idea of ice cream is a third species of interest, in-between loving ice cream and hating ice cream.

I conclude that Brentano's main argument for his account of presentation as an attitudinal primitive is highly plausible, especially when augmented with the just-raised more abductive considerations. Nonetheless, there is a very basic objection to it we must consider: that entertaining cannot be treated as quite on a par with belief and desire, given the much more central role the latter play in the explanation of action and behavior. I will consider this objection in §4. Before that, I want to assess Brentano's subsidiary argument for his view.

3.3. The via positiva *argument*

In §9 of Chap. 7, Brentano presents in rapid succession four asymmetries between judgment and presentation. Each asymmetry *suggests* that belief and entertaining belong to different fundamental categories. Together, they constitute *converging lines of evidence* for Brentano's attitudinal conception of the belief/entertaining distinction; which conception in turn supports the notion that entertaining is an attitudinal primitive on a par with belief and desire.

Brentano's first asymmetry has to do with the existence of contraries in the case of the former but not the latter:

> Among presentations we find no contraries other than those of the objects which are contained in them. Insofar as warm and cold, light and dark, higher and lower pitch, etc., constitute contraries, we can say that the presentation of the one is opposed (*entgegengesetze*) to that of the other... When love and hate enter in, there arises an entirely different kind of opposition. This opposition is not an opposition of objects, for the same object can be loved or hated; it is, rather, an opposition between [intentional] relations (*Beziehungen*) to the object... An entirely analogous opposition manifests itself unmistakably in the domain of mental phenomena when we affirm or deny the presented object instead of directing love or hatred toward it.
>
> (Brentano 1874: II, 65–6 [222–3])

The argument here is straightforward: there is no positive/negative distinction for presentation; there is one for judgment; so, presentation is importantly unlike judgment. Brentano would presumably suggest that the *reason* there is a positive/negative distinction in the case of judgment is that some judgments present-as-true while others present-as-false, so that the former can be thought of as positive and the latter as negative. Since presentations merely-present, no similar distinction is possible for them.

Obviously, this too presupposes Brentano's nonreductive account of disbelief: if disbelief that *p* were just belief that ~*p*, the contrast between belief and disbelief would also be just a content-level contrast. As noted, we will see the main motivation for the nonereductive account in Chap. 4. It is, in any case, clearly controversial.

Brentano's second asymmetry concerns the kinds of intensity we find in judgment and presentation. A presentation is less or more intense depending on the 'sharpness (*Schärfe*) and vivacity' with which its intentional object is present to the mind (1874: II, 66 [223]). I can visualize a purple horse in a somewhat drowsy or inalert manner, and a second later, after drinking a double espresso, imagine it with great liveliness and clarity – even if no further *details* are added to the imagined horse. In judgment, the same kind of intensity occurs as well: I can also *believe* that no horses are purple before and after my espresso! But in the case of judgment, there is also a completely different kind of intensity, to do with the 'degree of certainty in conviction (*Überzeugung*)' (1874: II, 66 [223]). My belief that there are no purple horses is stronger than my belief that there are no purple parrots in a sense unrelated to the vivacity with which I am having these thoughts. I am simply *surer* of the former.

It might be objected that while variation in degrees of conviction is a familiar phenomenon, the notion of variation in an independent degree of vivacity is quite mysterious. However, although this latter phenomenon is quite important to Brentano, it is *not* important in the present dialectical context. For even if there is a single type of intensity in the area, one along which judgments vary but presentations do not, this already creates an asymmetry between the two.

A second objection is that intensity talk is unsuitable even for degrees of conviction. But this too is quite immaterial to Brentano's purposes. What matters for the asymmetry claim is just the idea of purely quantitative variation among judgments. It is plausible that presentations can vary quantitatively in one way at most, whereas judgments may vary quantitatively in an additional way. That is already an asymmetry. Brentano's attitudinal account of the judgment/presentation distinction then provides an elegant *explanation* of this: belief that p presents-as-true p, and can vary quantitatively along the 'presents' dimension or along the 'as-true' dimension; the former is variation in vivacity, the latter variation in conviction. In contrast, entertaining that p merely-presents p, and so can vary quantitatively only along the 'presents' dimension.

A third objection is that judgments do not in fact vary quantitatively in and of themselves. Rather, different beliefs are accompanied by different *second-order* appraisals of their likely plausibility. The idea is that one does not believe that p confidently; rather, one believes that p with confidence. That is, confidence is not an intrinsic modification of a single belief state, but rather involves two mental states: a belief with the content <p> and a confidence state with the content <my belief that p is very likely true>. If this is right, then beliefs in themselves do *not* vary along an intrinsic dimension we may call degree of conviction.[24] This strikes me as a fair objection, one which shows, at the very least, that Brentano's second purported contrast between judgment and presentation carries its own theoretical baggage, just as the first did.

Brentano's third asymmetry concerns normativity: while judgment is governed by a norm, and is evaluable in light of a standard of correctness, neither is the case for presentation. A belief can be evaluated for truth, and is criticizable when false. In contrast, 'there is no virtue, no wickedness, no knowledge, no error in presentation. All this is intrinsically foreign to it' (1874: II, 66–7 [223]). Here too, it is clear that the *reason* belief has a standard of correctness is that it presents-as-true. Indeed, the fact that it presents-as-true determines truth as the kind of correctness by which belief is to be evaluated. As already noted, truth is the norm of belief precisely because belief by its nature presents-as-true its content. In contrast, since there is no F such that entertaining by its nature presents-as-F, there is no F that can serve as a standard of evaluation for entertaining – there is no 'norm of entertaining.' We can entertain whatever we wish without ever exposing ourselves to epistemic blame. Thus the normativity of belief and entertaining serves as indirect evidence for the thesis that the belief/entertaining distinction is an attitudinal distinction to do with the difference between presenting-as-true and merely-presenting.

Here it might be objected that while entertaining cannot be assessed in terms of truth or goodness, there are a host of other dimensions along which it can be: clarity, distinctness, informativeness, detail, and others. A more detailed contemplation of something is in some sense *better than* a less detailed one; conceiving a possible scenario in a more distinct manner (that is, with a stronger grasp of how it differs from other possible scenarios) is superior to conceiving it in a vaguer fashion; and so on. In response, however, Brentano might say that detailed and distinct apprehensions are not in fact better *in and of themselves*. Perhaps they are only better insofar as the judgments that would be formed simply by endorsing them would be better. Perhaps they are better in affording greater joy, especially where the apprehension of an aesthetic object is concerned (see Brentano 1959: 127). But in any case it is not quite *intrinsically* that a clear and distinct idea is better than an unclear and indistinct one. If so, there is no normativity *proper* to the domain of mere presentation.

Finally, Brentano invokes an asymmetry to do with psychological laws governing judgments and presentations:

...besides the general laws governing the succession of presentations...we find special laws, which are particularly valid for judgments, and which bear the same relation to logic as the laws of love and hate do to ethics.   (Brentano 1874: II, 68 [224])

Brentano seems to suggest here that while the only laws governing presentations are the kind of laws posited in 'associationist psychology,' judgments are also governed by the kind of laws posited in 'rational psychology.' The latter dictate that, at least in the well-functioning subject, causal connections among mental states track logical connections (deductive, probabilistic, or whatever) among their contents. This contrasts with 'laws of association,' where causal connections among states track non-logical connections – resemblance, contiguity, etc. – among contents.

Of Brentano's four asymmetry claims, this is probably the most dubious. When one *considers* whether to believe that p, one does not yet believe that p but merely presents p. Thus there is no attitudinal opposite here (there is no such thing as 'dis-considering' whether *p*) and no truth-evaluation is possible (one cannot be said to consider falsely). Yet considering whether *p* will involve considering the evidence for *p*, the implications of *p*, and so on, where logical or 'rational' connections between contents are very much concerned. Similar remarks apply to supposing that *p* (say, in order to see what follows from it). So while there are certainly such states as imagery and contemplation, for which association laws may be in force, rational laws do govern *some* states that merely-present.

In conclusion, of Brentano's four asymmetry claims, only the third is compelling against a neutral theoretical background: plausibly, there is a kind of 'ethics of judgment' but no 'ethics of presentation.' This asymmetry claim *could* be taken all by itself as a springboard for an inference to the best explanation for an attitudinal judgment/presentation distinction. But the idea behind Brentano's *via positiva* argument was more ambitious: that the four asymmetry claims admit of a single, unifying explanation in terms of the idea that the *nature* of judgments is to present-as-true/false whereas the nature of presentations is to merely-present, and as such provide converging lines of evidence in favor of the Brentanian take on the distinction. With only one compelling asymmetry, the force of such an argument is much weakened.

For my part, I am quite convinced by Brentano's claim that entertaining that *p* is an attitudinal primitive on a par with, and irreducible to, belief and desire (see Kriegel 2015: chap. 3). But I find the (suitably strengthened) *via negativa* argument much more effective in making the case for it. In the next section, I consider (what I suspect is) the main reason the Brentanian outlook has not had much traction in contemporary analytic philosophy of mind, where entertaining has been disregarded within belief-desire psychology.[25]

4. Classification and Demarcation: Brentano versus Contemporary Philosophy of Mind

Why is entertaining (and more generally presentation) not treated in contemporary analytic philosophy of mind as on a par with belief and desire? Arguably, the basic reason is that it does not play the kind of *direct role in the explanation of behavior* that belief and desire do. Since Davidson (1963), we are accustomed to working with a straightforward model of action explanation in terms of reasons consisting of belief-desire pairs. Why did Jimmy buy chocolate? Because he *desired* to eat chocolate and *believed* that buying chocolate would enable him to eat some. More generally, if a person φs for reason R, then (a) she has a desire that *p* and a belief that φ-ing would increase the likelihood that *p*, (b) this belief-desire pair constitutes R, and (c) R causes the φ-ing. Clearly, entertaining plays no role in this kind of model. On the one hand, the combination of Jimmy desiring chocolate and him merely entertaining the notion that buying chocolate would enable eating some does not quite explain the actual buying; nor does the combination of Jimmy entertaining the eating of chocolate and believing that by buying some he would be able to. On the other hand, the combination of Jimmy's belief and desire does explain the behavior, so citing entertaining as a third component would be explanatorily pointless.

We might be able to cite entertaining in the explanation of how Jimmy came to form the desire: perhaps he entertained eating chocolate, considered that this is quite a good idea, and thence came to desire to eat chocolate. Likewise, entertaining might play a role in the explanation of Jimmy's belief's formation: perhaps Jimmy entertained a number of ways of satisfying his desire for chocolate – buying some, stealing some, making some – and came to think that the buying option is best, thus forming the belief. However, this does not quite cast entertaining as 'on a par' with belief and desire. For in this model entertaining is causally twice removed from the action it helps explain, so that its explanatory role is not quite as direct as that of belief and desire. (This is so even if it is not immediately obvious how to unpack 'direct.') Now, one could certainly quarrel about all of these claims. But it seems to me that something like them underlies the absence of entertaining in the fundamental taxonomy of mental states implicit in contemporary philosophy of mind.

In the background, it would seem, is something like the following taxonomic principle: we should classify mental states according to their explanatory role vis-à-vis action. A 'fundamental classification' of mental states would cite the states appearing in the 'direct' explanation of action; less fundamental types of mental state are those which explain directly not action but the mental states that explain action; and so on. This is in contradistinction to Brentano's taxonomic principle, which appeals instead to modes of intentionality or *ways of presenting*. Indeed, for all we have said here, everybody could in principle agree on the following: (a) *if* we classify mental states by explanatory role, then belief and desire are the only fundamental propositional attitudes; (b) *if* we classify mental states by modes of intentionality, then belief and desire must be complemented with entertaining. The disagreement, at bottom, is on how we should go about the taxonomic business.

Recall from §1 that, in Brentano, the fact that mode of intentionality is the principle of classification is connected to the fact that intentionality is the principle of demarcation. It stands to reason that mental states should be differentiated by mode of intentionality if what makes them mental in the first place is that they exhibit intentionality at all. A similar link may be supposed within the framework of action explanation: if mental states are classified by the kind of role they play in explaining action, it is because having a role in explaining action at all is what makes them mental states in the first place. And indeed, one gets the impression that explaining action is the 'mark of the mental' implicit in much contemporary analytic philosophy of mind.

To appreciate the plausibility of this mark claim, it is crucial to distinguish action from *movement, motor activity*, and so on (Dretske 1988). Imagine two identical leg movements, resulting in the same worldly state of affairs, but produced by two different causes: one is produced by the person's intention to kick a ball, the other by a dog bumping into the person's leg (which happens to adjoin a ball). Intuitively, we have here type-identical movements, but not type-identical actions. In fact, intuitively the dog-caused movement may not be an action at all, whereas the intention-produced movement clearly is. Clearly, then, there is more to action than movement. It is the explanation of action, and not of movement, that is proper to *mental* phenomena. Many neurophysiological phenomena that we would not consider mental (e.g., cerebral hormone secretions) are relevant to the explanation of movement and motor activity, but do not seem to have the same relevance to the explanation of action as such.

❧

Arguably, then, the gap between Brentano's taxonomy and ours lies, at bottom, in a different conception of what makes a given phenomenon mental in the first place: we today think of mental phenomena as those relevant to the explanation of action; Brentano thinks of them as those exhibiting intentionality. This conflict may, however, be more apparent than real. For recall that Brentano takes all mental states to be conscious, and accordingly is better understood as holding that intentionality is the mark of the *conscious*. Indeed, as we have seen in Chap. 2, it is a specific kind of intentionality – a felt quality of endogenous directedness which we called phenomenal intentionality – that serves as the mark of the conscious. Now, it is perfectly coherent to hold that what makes a state mental is that it is suitably relevant to the explanation of action, but what makes it conscious is that it exhibits phenomenal intentionality. Brentano himself would reject this, precisely because he sees no daylight between the mental and the conscious, but as I have argued in Chap. 1, this is probably the least plausible part of his philosophy of mind. A plausible yet largely Brentanian philosophy of mind, I suggest, would embrace the picture just articulated: action-explanation as the mark of the mental, endogenous directedness as the mark of the conscious.

This picture recommends two parallel taxonomies: a classification of *mental* states by kind of role played in action explanation, and another classification of *conscious* states by kind of endogenous directedness. From this perspective, it is natural to regard entertaining as a third fundamental type of *conscious* propositional attitude, on a par with conscious belief (judgment) and conscious desire (interest). Certainly Brentano himself considered the judgment/presentation distinction to be experientially manifest:

> ... inner experience (*Erfahrung*) directly reveals/shows (*zeigt*) the difference in the reference to their content that we assert of presentation and judgment.   (1874: II, 70 [225])[26]

What Brentano has in mind, I suspect, is that once we grasp the idea of presenting-as-F, and become inner-perceptually sensitive, for instance, to the difference between presenting-as-true and presenting-as-good, we can also become sensitive (in inner perception) to the difference between presenting-as-true and merely-presenting. When we inner-perceive side by side, so to speak, an imagined episode of consciously believing that *p* and an imagined episode of merely entertaining that *p*, we detect a difference in the manner in which each presents p. Thus these episodes are different not just qua mental states, but also *qua experienced conscious states*. So even if entertaining is not a *mental* state on a par with (i.e., at the same taxonomic level as) belief and desire, insofar as it does not play a similarly direct role in the explanation of action, it may nonetheless be a *conscious* state on a par with conscious believing and conscious desiring, insofar as it embodies a distinctive and equally fundamental way of being endogenously directed.

In contemporary philosophy of mind, not everybody is comfortable speaking of *conscious* belief. Belief, we are sometimes told, is essentially a standing state, rather than a conscious occurrence (Crane 2001). But even those who reject the notion of conscious belief often accept a conscious occurrence whose intentional profile is akin to that of belief (Crane 2013). They accept, for example, conscious occurrences with a mind-to-world direction of fit. Or better yet, they accept a conscious occurrence that presents-as-true. Consider this passage from L.J. Cohen:

Feeling it true that p may thus be compared with feeling it good that p. All credal feelings, whether weak or strong, share the distinctive feature of constituting some kind of orientation on the 'True or false?' issue in relation to their propositional objects, whereas affective mental feelings, like those of anger or desire, constitute some kind of orientation on the 'Good or bad?' issue.   (Cohen 1992: 11)

Cohen's outlook is extraordinarily similar to Brentano's. Feeling it true that p is a conscious occurrence directed at p in a distinctive, truth-committal manner, while feeling it good that p is a conscious occurrence directed at p in a distinctive, goodness-committal manner. Brentano would accept all this but insist that there is also a kind of felt conscious occurrence of simply apprehending p, where we neither feel it true that p nor feel it good that p, but just experientially grasp p.

In conclusion, despite the appearance of tension between Brentano's system of mental classification and ours, the two can be held together as long as we keep in mind one thing: that Brentano's is really tailored for the conscious domain, and is presented as targeting the mental domain only because of Brentano's (problematic) view that conscious states exhaust mentality.

Conclusion

The classification of conscious states by intentional mode is not only fundamental in Brentano's philosophy of mind, it is *foundational* for his entire philosophical system. As I will try to show in Parts II and III of this book, Brentano's accounts of the true, the good, and the beautiful are largely based on his accounts of judgment, interest, and presentation. Already in the *Psychology*, he writes:

We see that...the triad of ideals, the beautiful, the true, and the good, can well be explicated in terms of the system of mental faculties [presentation, judgment, and interest]. Indeed, this is *the only way in which it becomes fully intelligible (erklären)*...

(Brentano 1874: II, 122 [263]; my italics)

In the *Psychology*, Brentano only sketches the grounding of truth, goodness, and beauty in judgment, interest, and presentation – and sketches an early version of the idea that was to give way to a more sophisticated version. Parts II and III of the present book lay out the more sophisticated version. Part II focuses on Brentano's theory of judgment and the manner in which it grounds his metaphysics. Part III focuses on Brentano's theory of interest and the manner in which it grounds his value theory (both moral and aesthetic). Although presentation has an important role to play in Brentano's account of aesthetic value, it is less central to the system than judgment and interest – except insofar as both are asymmetrically dependent upon it. Accordingly, we have focused on it in the second half of the present chapter, instead of dedicating to it a chapter of its own.

Regardless of the specifics of Brentano's grounding of the true, the good, and the beautiful in judgment, interest, and presentation, it is an intriguing gambit to attempt to construct one's philosophical system around one's theory of mind. The gambit casts philosophy of mind in the role of *first philosophy*, the philosophical discipline that all others presuppose. For much of its history, analytic philosophy has taken philosophy of *language* as first philosophy, while early modern philosophy – certainly Descartes, the British empiricists, and Kant – reserved that role for epistemology. Brentano's tenure offers us a historical window in which philosophy of mind held this pride of place. And when we remember that Brentano's philosophy of mind is forsooth just a philosophy of consciousness, we realize that Brentano's system offers a unique opportunity to consider how a philosophy of consciousness can ground a comprehensive philosophical system in the traditional sense.[27]

Notes to Chapter 3

1. Chap. 5 of the *Psychology* offers a survey of traditional classifications of mental phenomena. Chap. 6 lays out Brentano's alternative scheme. Brentano considers that his classification diverges from the tradition in two important respects; the goals of chaps. 7 and 8 is to make the case for each divergence.
2. This parallelism between judgment and interest, the understanding and the will, is noted already in Brentano's doctoral dissertation, published when he was just 24: 'Just as the good is that at which the will aims, so the understanding aims at the true as its goal' (Brentano 1862: 29 [19]).
3. Clearly, the terms 'love' and 'hate' are used in a wide sense here. I love my wife, but I also love ice cream. It is the second, less demanding sense of 'love' that Brentano has in mind (1874: II, 36 [199]).
4. Brentano's 'Vorstellung' has been variously translated as presentation, representation, apprehension, idea, thought, and contemplation. In this book, I stick to the English term closest to *Vorstellung* in everyday non-philosophical talk – 'presentation.'
5. A word on supposition may be in order here. When one supposes that *p*, one is not thereby committed to the truth of *p*. There is a sense in which in supposing that *p*, one presents *p* to oneself under the guise of truth. Nonetheless, one is not genuinely *committed* to the truth of *p*. For Brentano, this lack of commitment to truth lands supposition in the category of

presentation. His student Meinong argued that in fact suppositions (*Annahmen*) share one essential characteristic with presentations but another with judgments, and so constituted a sui generis category (Meinong 1902). Brentano argues against this in several places, for example Brentano 1911: 149–50 [284–6] (see also manuscript XPs5).

6. Such attitudinal properties as presenting-as-true and presenting-as-good are in an important sense still *intentional* properties, and that is certainly how Brentano treats them. Presenting-as-F some *a* and presenting some *a* as F both cast *a* as F, so if the latter is regarded as an intentional property, so should the former. The difference goes back to where the F-information is encoded, in the content or the attitude. Both are *informative*, however.

7. The books were never published, and to my knowledge only a draft of the third – on presentation – exists (manuscript XPs53, 277 sheets' worth). But many relevant ideas exist in dispersed manuscripts. Incidentally, Book VI of the planned *Psychology* was supposed to concern the soul and its immortality: while all other envisaged books concerned mental *accidents*, the final one was to concern the mental *substance*.

8. Intentional action is treated here as a mental phenomenon, because what intentional action a person has performed – as opposed to what movements her body has undergone – is partially a matter of the intentions the person had in moving her body as she did.

9. In addition, conscious occurrent beliefs must have more to them than dispositional properties, since they are precisely *occurrent*. From this perspective, the fact that Brentano takes *all* mental states to be conscious and occurrent closes the functionalist avenue to him.

10. It is sometimes claimed that something other than truth is the norm of belief – for example, that knowledge is the norm of belief (Sutton 2007). But in any case, most everybody agrees that truth is *a* norm of belief, and those who are attracted by a normative approach to the nature of belief tend to take this norm as capturing the essence of belief.

11. Brentano stresses this when highlighting the systematic differences between judgment and presentation (as we will see in §3.3).

12. I am assuming here, with Brentano, that belief and disbelief are occurrent states with an inner-perceived experiential character. Obviously, this does not sit well with contemporary functionalist approaches to belief, which typically construe it as a standing state with no notable experiential dimension. This discrepancy will be taken up in §4.

13. It might be objected that in the case of pleasure and displeasure, there is a *phenomenal* difference between the two kinds of acts. But for Brentano, there is also a phenomenal difference between belief and disbelief, at least in the sense that they appear differently to inner perception (which is the only sense of 'phenomenal difference' Brentano would accept).

14. Such oppositional models were apparently commonplace in the surrounding culture of the Austro-Hungarian empire: the intellectual historian William Johnston, whose *The Austrian Mind* is a classic in the field, speaks of 'certain attitudes that have permeated Austrian thought, such as hostility to technology and delight in polar opposites' (Johnston 1972: 1).

15. This may be resisted on the grounds that we sometimes have a perceptual experience as of an object in whose existence we do not believe, say a centaur hologram. According to Brentano, however, this is just a case of having conflicting commitments: we are perceptually committed to the holographic centaur's existence and doxastically committed to its nonexistence simultaneously – just as we can sometimes want ice cream (it is tasty) and not want it (it fattens) at once (see Brentano 1982: 87 [93]).

16. There is also the important distinction between intrinsic and instrumental varieties of interests (Brentano 1907a: 149 [144]). We love happiness for its own sake, but dental health for the sake of something else. It is unclear to me, however, whether Brentano takes this distinction to pertain to the mode of presentation (attitude) or to the object presented (content).

17. The same applies to interest and its distinctive mode of presenting-as-good/bad.

18. In fact, according to Brentano the attitudinal distinction between perception and episodic memory in terms of temporal orientation derives ultimately from the distinction between oblique and direct presentations. His reasons for claiming that it is originally a distinction between kinds of presentation, rather than kinds of judgment (as perception and memory are) is that differences in temporal orientation apply equally to states of judgment and interest (Brentano 1928: 49 [36]). His reason for claiming that the distinction derives from the oblique/direct distinction has to do with his presentism (Brentano 1933: 18 [24]): he wants to say that 'Jesus died two thousand years ago' is directly about the present time and obliquely about Jesus' death, so that all *modus-recto* reference is to the present. For critical discussion, see Simons 1990.

19. One advantage of my proposed attitudinal approach to the sensory/intellectual distinction, from a Brentanian perspective, is that it falls out of it that perceptual experience is a *species* of judgment (since presenting-as-existent-here-and-now is a species of presenting-as-existent).

20. Part of the issue may be that (as we will see in Chap. 6) Brentano is a nominalist who does not believe in *mere* intelligibles, that is, entities which can be apprehended in principle only intellectually.

21. This is ultimately to be paraphrased in terms of propositions describing one's execution of the action-type j, since unwillingness too must be construed as a propositional attitude in this framework.

22. Obviously, for this to be the case, there must be such a thing as entertaining. Some psychologists and philosophers have denied this (Gilbert 1991, Mandelbaum 2013). Here I am going to assume that they are wrong; I offer an argument to that effect in Kriegel 2015: chap. 3.

23. One might object that the predicative/prepredicative distinction is not the only possible content distinction. Another is the distinction between presenting p as actually obtaining versus presenting it as merely (logically) possible. On this view, entertaining that p is just believing that $\Diamond p$ – which casts entertaining as a species of belief. One problem with this, however, is that arguably one can entertain even propositions one believes to be (logically-) necessarily false. For example, I might entertain Frege's set theory, or perhaps just its axiom of comprehension, even though, being familiar with Russell's Paradox, I believe it to be incoherent.

24. What motivates this picture is the observation that when we engage in the process of weighing the evidence for p and $\sim p$ and finally come down on the issue, the act of coming down – the act of *making the judgment* – seems to involve a certain feeling of finality or absoluteness. At the instant one makes the judgment, one effectively decides to bring one's 'inquiry' as to whether p to an end. This sense of finality or absoluteness attaches to *all* judgment-making, however confident. To accommodate this phenomenal feature of judging, while doing justice to the evident fact that beliefs can vary in degree of conviction, we might think that the state of conviction or confidence must lie outside the judgment proper.

25. To repeat, the present discussion indulges the currently orthodox supposition that such states as belief and desire have at bottom a propositional content; this is denied by Brentano, but is worth accepting for the sake of argument, to show that the rejection of belief-desire psychology does not presuppose Brentano's heterodox account of belief.

26. In the heading of §1 of Brentano 1874: II, chap. 7, Brentano refers to the judgment/presentation difference as provided by the 'testimony of inner experience.'

27. For comments on a previous draft of this chapter, I am grateful to Anna Giustina, Franz Knappik, Zdenek Lenner, Lylian Paquet, and Mikaël Quesseveur. I have also benefited from presenting materials from this chapter at École Normale Supérieure, King's College London, Northwestern University, and the University of Salzburg. I am grateful to the audiences there, in particular Mathilde Berger-Perrin, Johannes Brandl, Géraldine Carranante, Tim Crane, Daniel Harris, Colin Johnson, Sonia Kamińska, Sandra Lapointe, Olivier Massin, Ion Tanasescu, Mark Textor, and Alberto Voltolini. In addition, I have benefited from exchanges with Arnaud Dewalque and Denis Seron.

PART II
Being

4

Judgment

We already encountered two aspects of Brentano's account of judgment in Chap. 3. First, Brentano offers an *attitudinal* account of judgment, according to which what makes a given mental state a judgment is that it employs a certain mode of intentional directedness, the mode of *presenting-as-true* (or presenting-as-false). Secondly, Brentano uses the term 'judgment' idiosyncratically, to denote not just conceptual thoughts but all conscious states with mind-to-world direction of fit, including perceptual experiences. These were the aspects of Brentano's account of judgment that mattered for his classification of mental phenomena. But there is one aspect of Brentano's theory of judgment that is much more crucial for his ontology and metaontology, and which has not surfaced yet. This is Brentano's astonishing claim that judgment is *not a propositional attitude*, but an objectual attitude. In this chapter, I offer an exposition of this highly heterodox theory (§1), discuss the case for it (§2), and consider some objections (§3). In the following two chapters, we will see the theory's implications for metaontology and ultimately ontology.

1. The Belief-in Theory of Judgment

The core of Brentano's theory of judgment can be represented as the conjunction of two theses. The first is that *all judgments are existential*, the second that the existence-commitment involved in existential judgments is an *attitudinal property* of theirs. That is:

EXISTENTIAL: For any judgment J, J is an existential judgment.
ATTITUDINAL: For any existential Judgment E, E's existence-commitment is an attitudinal property of E.

In this section, I offer a preliminary explanation and motivation of the two theses. The remainder of the chapter will consider the case for them in more detail.

According to EXISTENTIAL, every judgment is in the business of affirming or denying the existence of something. Thus the judgments that there are marine mammals and that there are no flying dogs are paradigmatic. We are accustomed to think that not all judgments are like this – some are in the business of doing more than just affirming or denying the existence of something. Many, it is natural to think, involve an element of *predication*: rather than commenting on what there is, they make a claim about what something is *like*, what *properties* it has. Thus, the judgment that all dogs are cute predicates cuteness of dogs, thereby 'claiming' that dogs have a certain property, not (just) that they exist. Brentano, however, insists that predication is an accident of language that does not reflect the psychological reality of judgments. (More on that in §3.) In reality, judging that all dogs are cute is just judging that *there is no non-cute dog*. It thus comments on what there is after all.

To show that this generalizes, Brentano systematically goes over the four types of categorical statement in Aristotle's square of opposition (A, E, I, and O) and shows that they are all reducible or 'traceable back' (*rückführbar*) to existential statements (Brentano 1874: II, 56–7 [213–14], 1956: 121):

(A)   <All dogs are cute> is traceable to <There is not a non-cute dog>.
(E)   <No dogs are cute> is traceable to <There is not a cute dog>.
(I)   <Some dogs are cute> is traceable to <There is a cute dog>.
(O)   <Some dogs are not cute> is traceable to <There is a non-cute dog>.[1]

Brentano's talk of statements 'being traceable back' to other statements suggests he has something like *paraphrase* in mind: 'All dogs are cute' is paraphraseable into 'There is not a non-cute dog.' Such statements can *express* judgments, or they can be embedded into corresponding statements that *report* judgments: 'S judges that all dogs are cute' is paraphraseable into 'S judges that there is no non-cute dog.'

This is, at least, Brentano's treatment of Aristotle's four types of categorical statement *for most of his career*. In the final decade of his life, he seems to have complicated the account considerably, adopting his so-called double-judgment theory (see especially Appendix IX of the *Psychology*, as well as Brentano 1956: §30). We are not as yet in a position to understand the double-judgment theory. I will revert to it when we are. For now let me only point out that the double-judgment theory has two main parts, one of which will make no difference to our concerns here, while the other will.

Once all categorical statements are shown to paraphrase into existential ones, it is easy to show that hypotheticals follow suit (Brentano 1874: II, 59–60 [218]).[2] For example:

(H)   <If some dog is three-legged, then it is cute> is traceable back to <There is not a non-cute three-legged dog>.

Conclusion:

The reducibility/traceability (*Rückführbarkeit*) of categorical statements (*Sätze*), indeed the reducibility of all statements which express a judgment, to existential judgments is therefore indubitable.   (Brentano 1874: II, 60 [218])

More cautiously, all statements used *in Aristotelian logic* turn out to be disguised existentials. We will have to consider other types of statement in §2.

According to EXISTENTIAL, then, all acts of judging are forms of mentally committing to something's existence or nonexistence. According to ATTITUDINAL, now, the existence-commitment which existential judgments carry is an aspect of their *attitude* rather than *content*. On this view, mental commitment to the existence of *x* is not an aspect of *what* the judgment presents but of *how* it does the presenting. In other words: an existential judgment's commitment to the existence of *x* is not a matter of presenting *x* as existent, but a matter of presenting-as-existent *x*. Thus, to judge that some dogs are cute is to perform a mental act that presents-as-existent cute dogs, that is, presents cute dogs in an existence-affirming *manner*.[3]

The attitudinal account of mental existence-commitment is unsurprising given that, for Brentano, what characterizes judgment in the first instance is the attitudinal property of presenting-as-true. If all positive judgments present-as-true and all truth is existential, it stands to reason that positive judgments should turn out to be characterized by presenting-as-*existent*.

When it comes to simple *negative* existential judgments, such as that no dog can fly, Brentano's view is that these present-as-*non*existent some object, in this case a flying dog. Here we can start understanding Brentano's reluctance to reduce disbelief that *p* to belief that ~*p* (noted in Chap. 3). One *could* have the view that the judgment that there are no flying dogs presents-as-existent the absence of a flying dog, but this might embroil one in an ontology of absences. Construing that judgment as a mental state that presents-as-*non*existent a flying dog swiftly avoids this potential can of worms.

If the commitment to something's existence or nonexistence does not show up in judgments' content, then that content is exhausted by the individual item whose existence is affirmed or denied. If a judgment that a three-legged dog exists simply presents-as-existent a three-legged dog, then *what* is presented is exhausted by a certain kind of individual object: a three-legged dog. It follows that judgment is an *objectual* rather than *propositional* attitude.[4] Paradigmatic objectual attitudes include love and fear: I love my wife, not (only) *that* my wife is thus or so; I fear death, not (only) *that* death would preclude such and such.[5] Brentano's theory of judgment casts judgment as continuous with love and fear in being equally objectual: judgments are always directed at some sort of individual object, but present-as-existent/nonexistent that object.[6] The object at which one's judgment is directed can be quite complicated – a cute dog, a cute flying dog, a three-legged non-cute flying dog, etc. – but in any case what is presented by the judgment is always some kind of individual object. It is never any entity of a different ontological category, such as a proposition or a state of affairs (Brentano 1930: 122 [108]). This has momentous consequences for Brentano's metaphysics, as we will see in Chaps. 5–6.

It might seem odd to posit a *cognitive* attitude directed at objects and not propositions or states of affairs. Love and fear are *emotional* attitudes, and the suspicion may arise that the objectual structure is special to such attitudes. But in fact, we do speak not only of belief-that but also of belief-*in* – as in 'Jimmy believes in Santa Claus.' Belief-in is clearly a *cognitive objectual attitude*: the content of Jimmy's state is exhausted by some individual object, Santa Claus, the commitment to whose existence comes in at the level of attitude, through the attitude of believing-in.[7] So essentially, Brentano's theory of judgment can be summarized thus:

> BIT: All positive judgments are *occurrent acts of believing-in*; all negative judgments are occurrent acts of *dis*believing-in.[8]

Judging that some dogs are cute is just performing a mental act that presents-as-existent a cute dog, that is, occurrently believing in a cute dog; judging that no dogs can fly is just performing a mental act that presents-as-nonexistent a flying dog, that is, occurrently disbelieving in a flying dog.

To be sure, because of a long philosophical tradition of treating propositional attitudes as fundamental in cognition, it is natural for us today to think of 'S believes in x' as shorthand for 'S believes that x exists.'[9] For Brentano, this gets the order of analysis exactly wrong. The more fundamental notion is belief-in, precisely because it captures correctly the psychological structure of judgments, in particular the locus of existence-commitment in the attitude rather than content. Accordingly, Brentano would propose to take 'S believes in x' as fundamental and consider 'S believes that x exists' a cumbersome and misleading way of saying the same thing. This allows us to paraphrase the reports of Aristotelian categorical and hypothetical judgments more straightforwardly:

(A) 'S judges that all dogs are cute' ⇔ 'S disbelieves in a non-cute dog'
(E) 'S judges that no dogs are cute' ⇔ 'S disbelieves in a cute dog'
(I) 'S judges that some dogs are cute' ⇔ 'S believes in a cute dog'
(O) 'S judges that some dogs are not cute' ⇔ 'S believes in a non-cute dog'
(H) 'S judges that if a dog is three-legged then he is cute' ⇔ 'S disbelieves in a three-legged non-cute dog'

Here, '⇔' just means 'can be paraphrased into.' The arrow is bidirectional because paraphraseability is a symmetric relation: if '*p*' is a good paraphrase of '*q*,' then '*q*' is an equally good paraphrase of '*p*.' It is the philosophical *substance* of Brentano's theory of judgment that in each case it is the right-hand-side report that captures correctly the structure of judgment, even though it is the left-hand-side report that is more common in everyday speak.

I call Brentano's theory of judgment the *Belief-In Theory*, or BIT for short.[10] According to BIT, all judgments are conscious acts of (dis)believing in something (some kind of individual object). Brentano's terminology is different, of course. He calls the cognitive objectual attitude that embodies mental commitment to something's existence 'acceptance' or 'acknowledgement' (*Anerkennung*) and the cognitive objectual attitude embodying commitment to nonexistence 'rejection' or 'denial' (*Verwerfung*). However, the associated verbs ('accepting,' 'acknowledging,' 'rejecting,' 'denying') can perfectly grammatically take propositional complements. 'Believing in' and 'disbelieving in' have this advantage, that they can only take objectual complements. They are thus better for expressing Brentano's theory.[11]

Whatever the terminology, a crucial aspect of BIT is that judgment is an objectual attitude:

OBJECTUAL: All judgments are objectual attitudes.

OBJECTUAL follows from EXISTENTIAL and ATTITUDINAL given that (dis)belief-in is an objectual attitude. We may formulate the master argument as follows:

1) All token beliefs are existential (EXISTENTIAL);
2) All existential beliefs are beliefs-in (ATTITUDINAL);
3) All beliefs-in are objectual attitudes; therefore,
4) All token beliefs are objectual attitudes (OBJECTUAL).

On the emerging view, the sole business of cognition is to manage one's belief in some objects and disbelief in others. Obviously, this is an extremely heterodox view of cognition, which would require a very good argument indeed. I now turn to consider the case for it.

2. The Case for the Belief-in Theory

In the *Psychology*, Brentano spends considerable time and effort arguing that judgment is not essentially predicative. For example, he argues that since perception is a kind of judgment, and perception is not essentially predicative (sometimes we just perceive *a thing*), judgment need not be predicative (Brentano 1874: II, 50 [209]). However, these arguments establish, at most, that *some* judgments are not predicative (and therefore potentially non-propositional). They cannot establish that *all* judgments are objectual rather than propositional attitudes, as OBJECTUAL requires. As far as I can tell, there is no direct argument for OBJECTUAL in the *Psychology*. Nonetheless, in some of Brentano's (posthumously published) letters, dictations, and lecture notes, one can identify a case for EXISTENTIAL and ATTITUDINAL, hence for OBJECTUAL.

The starting point of Brentano's argument is a simple dispensability consideration. In a 1906 letter to his student Anton Marty, he writes:

...every assertion affirming your *entia rationis* [notably, propositions] has its equivalent in an assertion having only *realia* [i.e., concrete individual objects] as objects...Not only are your judgments equivalent to judgments about concrete objects (*reale Gegenstände*), the latter are always available [for paraphrasing the former]. Hence the *entia rationis* are entirely unnecessary/superfluous (*unnütz*) and contrary to the economy of nature.

(Brentano 1930: 93 [84]; see also Brentano 1956: §17)

The argument proceeds in two steps. First: every indicative statement that expresses a judgment can be paraphrased into an existential, meaning that indicatives ostensibly expressing beliefs-that can be paraphrased into ones ostensibly expressing beliefs-in. Second: the ontological commitments associated with a belief-in are always more economical than those associated with its corresponding belief-that; for propositions and the like *entia rationis* are more ontologically extravagant than concrete objects and the like *entia realia*. Accordingly, positing beliefs-in to the exclusion of beliefs-that is both feasible and commendable: feasible in virtue of the availability of paraphrase, commendable in virtue of ontological parsimony. The upshot can be summarized thus: the conjunction of EXISTENTIAL and ATTITUDINAL delivers significant onto-logical economies, and should be adopted on that basis. In what follows, I consider first the feasibility claim (§2.1), then the commendability claim (§2.2).

2.1. Dispensing with beliefs-that is feasible

In Brentano, the first step of the argument relies on producing the paraphrases for cat-egorical and hypothetical statements in Aristotelian logic (as seen in §1.1). One may wonder whether paraphrases will be available when we move to modern logic. I now turn to consider some (though not all) particularly hard cases: singular statements, relational statements, 'molecular' or 'compound' statements, and modal statements. I will argue that all admit of reasonably plausible existential paraphrases, with the potential exception of certain molecular statements.

2.1.1. SINGULAR JUDGMENTS

Start with such singular statements as 'Beyoncé is famous.' These have the form '*a* is F,' which does not immediately fit into any of A, E, I, or O. Leibniz, who also rejected the separation of subject and predicate (Leibniz 1686: §8), construed singulars as having the A form. So, 'Beyoncé is famous' is analyzed as 'All Beyoncés are famous,' which in Brentano's hands amounts to 'There is not a non-famous Beyoncé.' Sometimes Brentano sounds like a Leibnizian on this, but on other occasions he seems to treat singulars rather as having the I form.[12] This analyzes 'Beyoncé is famous' as 'Some Beyoncé is famous,' and ultimately as 'There is a famous Beyoncé.' In this second approach, unlike the Leibnizian one, '*a* is F' commits to the *existence* of something rather than to the *nonexistence* of something. If we follow Russell (1905a) in taking the existence of *a* to be a precondition for the truth of '*a* is F,' the Brentanian tack should appeal to us more than the Leibnizian.[13]

But what does 'There is a famous Beyoncé' exactly mean? A traditional descriptivist about names would take 'Beyoncé' to pick out whichever individual satisfies a descrip-tion that lists certain central properties of Beyoncé's. Call an individual that instanti-ates all the relevant properties *Beyoncésque*.[14] Within the descriptivist framework, then, 'There is a famous Beyoncé' means 'There is a famous Beyoncésque individual.' Within a direct-reference approach, however, 'Beyoncé' does not refer by courtesy of any description. Rather, it picks out whatever object is appropriately related to it by 'natural,' broadly causal relations.[15] In that framework, it is more natural to understand 'There is a famous Beyoncé' as meaning something like 'There is famous-Beyoncé,' or 'Famous-Beyoncé exists,' where 'famous-Beyoncé' is used as a name. Here the statement is used to simply affirm the existence of someone.[16] The burning question is of course what the name 'Famous-Beyoncé' refers to. Who is this person famous-Beyoncé?! This question takes center stage in Chap. 6.[17]

A particularly difficult variety of singular judgment is presented by demonstrative judgments, such as 'This dog is cute.' On the direct-reference view, if 'this dog' happens to refer to Julius, for instance, then 'This dog is cute' is equivalent to 'There is cute-Julius.' On a descriptivist view, it is equivalent rather to something like 'There is a cute dog-being-referred-to-herewith.'

This treatment of demonstratives gives us, by the way, the tools to understand the first part of Brentano's later double-judgment theory. Late in his life, Brentano came to think that 'Some dogs are not cute' expresses *two* judgments: (i) a judgment committing to the existence of certain dogs, and (ii) a judgment to the effect that the dogs referred to in (i) are not cute. The existential paraphrase is therefore something like: 'There is a dog & There is not a cute dog-being-referred-to-in-the-previous-conjunct.' Interestingly, Brentano thinks that the same double-judgment structure occurs in the judgment 'Some dogs *are* cute': we have here first (i) a belief in a dog and then (ii) a belief in the cuteness of *that* dog. We can see the point of this by comparing 'Some brown dogs are cute' and 'Some cute dogs are brown.' Intuitively, these say different things. Yet the original account would paraphrase them into 'There is a cute brown dog' and 'There is a brown cute dog,' respectively, which seem to say the same thing (unless we are willing to distinguish in our ontology between a brown-cute-dog and a cute-brown-dog).[18] The double-judgment theory provides distinct paraphrases: 'There is a brown dog & There is not a cute brown-dog-being-referred-to-in-the-previous-conjunct' and 'There is a cute dog & There is not a brown cute-dog-being-referred-to-in-the-previous-conjunct.'

2.1.2. RELATIONAL JUDGMENTS

I conclude that singulars are amenable to existential paraphrase, pending trouble in ultimately understanding what such names as 'Famous-Beyoncé' refer to. What about relational statements, such as 'Beyoncé and Jay-Z are in love'? Brentano seems to propose that this could be paraphrased into something like 'There is an in-love sum of Beyoncé and Jay-Z.' In a 1908 dictation on 'Ontological Questions,' he writes:

Thus if one part of an egg is red and another blue, then 'being multicolored' (*buntfarbig*) befits the whole. It comes to the same whether I say that the egg is multicolored or that the relevant individual parts differ in color. Wherefore it can be seen that with relations we are dealing with so to speak collective determinations. We are dealing with a plurality of things which are united (*vereinigt*) into one thing, and where a certain determination befits the whole in virtue of (*vermöge*) its various parts.   (Brentano 1933: 57–8 [50])

Here relational statements are paraphrased into structural ones: to say that Beyoncé and Jay-Z are in love is to say that the mereological sum of Beyoncé and Jay-Z has a certain intrinsic structural property, namely, that property an object has when it has two proper parts each of which loves the other (and does not have any proper part that does not overlap those two). More generally, every relational statement aRb is paraphraseable into a statement of the form $Sa+b$, where S is a structural property of the sum $a+b$. That is, 'Relation R holds between a and b' is always paraphraseable into 'There is an S-structured sum of a and b.'[19]

One problem is that this strategy cannot extend to antisymmetric relations, such as being-the-mother-of. One cannot paraphrase 'Beyoncé is the mother of Blue Ivy' into 'There is a motherly-structured sum of Beyoncé and Blue Ivy,' because the latter is compatible with Blue Ivy being the mother of Beyoncé. The source of the problem is that while there is such a thing as an *ordered set*, there is no such thing as an *ordered sum* – this is one of the key differences between the grouping operation and the summing operation. (This is why the symmetry of composition is another axiom of both Classical and Brentano's Mereology.) It might be suggested that statements ostensibly about antisymmetric relations could be paraphrased into statements about relational properties, for example if 'Beyoncé is the mother of Blue Ivy' could be paraphrased into 'There is a Blue-Ivy-mothering Beyoncé.' However, as Whitehead and Russell (1913) already showed in the *Principia*, the paraphrase fails: 'Beyoncé is the mother of Blue Ivy' entails 'Blue Ivy exists,' whereas 'There is a Blue-Ivy-mothering Beyoncé' does not. Nonetheless, if this is the only problem with the analysis of relations into relational properties, one wonders whether 'Beyoncé is the mother of Blue Ivy' could not simply be paraphrased into the conjunctive 'Beyoncé is the mother of Blue Ivy & Blue Ivy exists.' The latter certainly does entail that Blue Ivy exists!

This does require that we understand an ostensibly atomic judgment as a disguised compound judgment. That is perhaps not a major liability – provided we have suitable existential paraphrases for compound judgments.

2.1.3. COMPOUND JUDGMENTS

So far, I have considered only atomic statements, that is, statements no proper parts of which are statements. But what about compound or molecular statements? Since every binary truth-function is definable in terms of conjunction and negation, the task is really just to handle those two – and their combinations.

In separation, they are quite easy to handle. When it comes to straightforward conjunctions of the form p & q, such as 'Some cat is white and some dog is brown,' at least two options are open. One paraphrases them into atomic existentials about mereological sums, such as 'There is a sum of a white cat and a brown dog.' The judgment expressed here is a belief in the relevant sum. The other option is to treat conjunctions as expressing a plurality of simultaneous (atomic) judgments. On this approach, in truth we do not make *one* judgment expressed by 'Some cat is white and some dog is brown.' Instead, we simultaneously perform *two* judgments – an occurrent belief in a white cat and an occurrent belief in a brown dog – and we use conjunctive statements to express such multiplicity of judgments. In a way, the first option appeals to belief in a mereological sum, the second to a mereological sum of beliefs-in.

As for simple negation, in the Aristotelian system there are two separate cases: the E form ('No dogs are cute') and the O form ('Some dogs are not cute'). As we have seen, the former Brentano handles through the attitude of disbelief, which – recall from Chap. 3 – he takes to be a sui generis attitude irreducible to belief. This nonreductive treatment of disbelief allows Brentano to paraphrase 'S believes that no dogs are cute' into 'S disbelieves in a cute dog.' (Indeed, one senses that it is precisely the potential for accommodating such negations that *motivates* the nonreductive account of disbelief to Brentano.) As for such negations as 'Some dogs are not cute,' we have seen that Brentano construes them as expressing a special kind of positive judgment, in our case a belief in an uncute dog.

However, the wide-scope negation can also be treated in another way, indeed is so treated in Brentano's aforementioned double-judgment theory. Brentano proposes that 'No dogs are cute' really means 'It is not the case that some dogs are cute.' And to cast this as an existential, he claims that 'It is not the case that some dogs are cute' amounts to asserting that anyone who judges that some dogs are cute is judging incorrectly. The basic point may be put as follows: 'No dog is cute' is ultimately to be paraphrased into 'There is not a correct (*richtige*) belief in a cute dog.'[20] Here the 'double judgment' is not a matter of combination of two judgments, but of a single second-order judgment. This alternative treatment of wide-scope negation may be only optional at this point, given the availability of 'There is not a cute dog' as a legitimate (and simpler!) existential paraphrase of 'No dogs are cute.' But as we will soon see, this device is necessary for handling certain compound judgments that involve *both* negation *and* conjunction.

There are several ways to combine conjunction and negation operators in a single statement. Consider first statements of the form p & $\sim q$, such as 'Some cat is cute and no dog can fly.' If one were sufficiently ontologically lax, one could understand such a statement as expressing a belief in a cute cat and *the absence of a flying dog*. But Brentano is not laid-back enough to admit absences – or as he puts it, *negativa* – in his ontology (Brentano 1930: 81 [71], a fragment from 1905). If there are no absences, then a fortiori there are no mereological sums of cats and absences – and yet the belief expressed by 'Some cat is cute and no dog can fly' is true. It would seem, then, that Brentano's only live option is to take 'Some cat is cute and no dog can fly' to express a sum of two separate judgments, the belief in a cute cat and the disbelief in a flying dog.

Unfortunately, the opposite happens with statements of the form $\sim(p$ & $q)$, such as 'It is not the case that some cat is cute and some dog can fly.' Here there is only one judgment that can be said to be expressed. That judgment is a disbelief in the mereological sum of a cute cat and a flying dog. The unpalatable result here is that Brentano has no unified account of p & $\sim q$ and $\sim(p$ & $q)$. He must trot out different treatments for different combinations of conjunction and negation. That is something of an embarrassment.

Worse, neither account can handle a statement of the form $\sim(p$ & $\sim q)$, such as 'It is not the case that there are flying dogs but no cute cats.' On the one hand, it would be implausible to take such a statement to express a disbelief in the mereological sum of (a) a flying dog and (b) the absence of a cute cat. For then its negation would have to be taken to express a *belief* in that sum, and hence in an absence (which would commit the believer to the reality of absences). On the other hand, nor does 'It is not the case that there are flying dogs but no cute cats' seem to express a disbelief in the co-occurrence of two separate judgments, a belief in a cute cat and a disbelief in a flying dog. For what the subject rejects are not beliefs themselves. (For all she knows the beliefs may well exist!) To that extent, statements of the form $\sim(p \mathbin{\&} \sim q)$ can be handled neither by the '(dis)belief in sums' strategy nor by the 'sum of (dis) beliefs' strategy.

It is here that the introduction of second-order paraphrases for wide-scope negations becomes indispensable. Brentano's idea is to paraphrase 'It is not the case that there are flying dogs but no cute cats' into 'There is no sum of a correct belief in a flying dog and a correct disbelief in a cute cat.' This expresses a disbelief in such a sum of correct judgments. The point is that no one could *correctly* both (a) believe in a flying dog and (b) disbelieve in a cute cat – and this is what statements of the form $\sim(p \mathbin{\&} \sim q)$ really express.

One might reasonably complain that we are left here with a distressingly balkanized treatment of negation: we have seen different devices for handling $\sim p$, $p \mathbin{\&} \sim q$, $\sim(p \mathbin{\&} q)$, and $\sim(p \mathbin{\&} \sim q)$. These devices are: a sui generis attitude of disbelief, single statements expressing sums of different judgments, single judgments about mereological sums of objects, and second-order judgments about correct first-order judgments. This level of disunity looks like a major cost of Brentano's theory of judgment, the complaint might be.

However, it would seem that once we have introduced the device of second-order judgment about correct first-order judgment, it can be applied retrospectively to handle uniformly all four cases: $\sim p$ can be understood as expressing a disbelief in a correct judgment that p; $p \mathbin{\&} \sim q$ can be understood as expressing a judgment that p and a disbelief in a correct judgment that q; and $\sim(p \mathbin{\&} q)$ can be understood as a disbelief in a sum of correct judgments that p and that q.[21]

There is, however, another objection to which Brentano's account of negation *is* susceptible. Recall that Brentano's paraphrases are not intended as technical moves facilitating the regimentation of a formal language. They are intended to capture the deep psychological reality of our cognitive life. Arguably, however, it is psychologically unrealistic to think that 'No dogs are purple' actually expresses the second-order judgment that there is no correct belief in a purple dog. For harboring such a second-order judgment would seem to require the possession of such concepts as BELIEF and CORRECTNESS, yet a child may well believe that no dogs are purple without possessing those concepts. Furthermore, certain beliefs that appear simple enough that a child could have them are cast as extraordinarily complex in Brentano's theory, again making the theory psychologically unrealistic.

A good example is disjunctive judgments, such as would be expressed by 'Some cat is white or some dog is brown'. Chisholm (1976: 92) suggested on Brentano's behalf that we posit *disjunctiva*, in this case the individual which is either a white cat or a brown dog, and say that 'Some cat is white or some dog is brown' expresses an occurrent belief in this disjunctivum. However, Brentano himself would likely frown on disjunctiva just as much as on negtiva/absences. Instead, he exploits the definability of disjunction in terms of negation and conjunction:

> …anyone who says 'There is an A or there is a B or there is a C' expresses the following: in contemplating that A is not and B is not and C is not, he considers such a combination of thoughts incorrect.   (Brentano 1930: 80 [70])

We know that '$p \lor q$' is equivalent to '$\sim(\sim p \ \& \sim q)$'. So we can paraphrase 'Some cat is white or some dog is brown' into 'It is not the case that no cat is white and no dog is brown,' and then into 'There is no mereological sum of a correct disbelief in a white cat and a correct disbelief in a brown dog.'[22] However, it is quite plausible that a child could grasp the notion that some cat is white or some dog is brown well before she has the cognitive resources to grasp the idea of a mereological sum of correct disbeliefs.

2.1.4. MODAL JUDGMENTS

Finally, let us consider *modal* statements. These come in two varieties. The easy case is statements about possibilities pertaining to actual objects, for example 'There could be flying dogs.' Such statements can plausibly be paraphrased into 'There is a possibly-flying dog.' The latter attributes to something that exists, dogs, a special kind of property (a 'modal' property), that of possibly-flying. In general, where *a* is actual, 'Possibly, *a* is F' can be paraphrased into 'There is a possibly-F *a*.' However, this strategy has two costs. First, it requires accepting irreducibly modal ways a thing could be. Secondly, it does not work for modal statements about nonactual objects that nonetheless *could* exist, for example 'Unicorns are possible.' An industrial-strength modal realist in Lewis' (1986) vein might extend the strategy so as to paraphrase 'Unicorns are possible' into 'There is a possible-unicorn.' But the paraphrase implies that mere possibilia really exist. And Brentano explicitly rejects such modal realism (e.g., Brentano 1930: 81 [71]).

Brentano's own strategy for paraphrasing modal statements, including statements ostensibly about mere possibilia, relies instead on the introduction of new attitudinal features of judgments. Recall that for Brentano, judgments divide into acceptances (occurrent acts of belief-in) and rejections (occurrent acts of disbelief-in). These exhibit (respectively) the attitudinal properties of presenting-as-existent and presenting-as-nonexistent. But Brentano also holds that judgments divide into *apodictic* and *assertoric*, where these are two new attitudinal features: apodictic judgments exhibit the property of presenting-as-*necessary*, assertoric ones that of presenting-as-*contingent*. The two distinctions crosscut, producing four types of judgment (see Table 4.1).

Table 4.1. Modal character of judgments

	Acceptance	Rejection
Apodictic	present-as-necessarily-existent	present-as-necessarily-nonexistent
Assertoric	present-as-contingently-existent	present-as-contingently-nonexistent

With these distinctions in place, Brentano has the resources to articulate the following paraphrase strategy for modal statements (in a dictation from 1916):

Nouns such as 'non-being,' 'impossibility,' 'possibility,' and the like, as well as whole sentences, are often used as grammatical subjects and predicates, as though they were labels/designators (*Bezeichnungen*) for objects and named something…But philosophers would never have arrived at such absurd notions if they had kept in mind that these are fictions and so had not neglected to produce a paraphrase (*Rückübersetzung*). Then they would not have affirmed such things as the eternal subsistence of the impossibility of a round square, instead replacing this apparent affirmative with the negative judgment whereby a round square is apodictically rejected.   (Brentano 1933: 19–20 [25]; see also manuscript XPs12, dated 1909, and Brentano 1930: 78 [68], which is from 1904)

Thus, to say that a round square is impossible is *not* to assert 'There is an impossible round square,' whose grammar suggests that there is something, a round square, which has the unfortunate property of being impossible. Rather, it is to deny the existence of something but deny it in a modally beefed-up manner. It is to express *apodictic* disbelief in a round square, that is, a mental act that presents-as-necessarily-nonexistent a round square. To capture this in language, we might introduce an *apodictic quantifier*, 'There is-necessarily,' and paraphrase 'A round square is impossible' into 'There is-necessarily not a round square.'

What about possibility statements? Here Brentano appeals again to second-order negation:

…if I say that a thing is possible, I do not thereby accept the relevant thing, but rather only deny that anyone who *apodictically* rejects the thing judges correctly.
(Brentano 1930: 138 [121], my italics; see also 1930: 114–15 [101])

This again uses the device of appealing to second-order judgments about correct judgments: 'There could be unicorns' is paraphrased into 'There is no correct apodictic disbelief in a unicorn.' On this view, judging that unicorns are possible amounts to denying the existence of *correct* apodictic rejection of unicorns. It is to disbelieve in a correct apodictic rejection of a unicorn. Attractively, this account of modal truths does not require truthmakers from outside the actual world. Possibility statements are about *our* world: namely, that it does not contain certain (correct apodictic negative) judgments.

This account does face, however, the objection that some of these paraphrases are psychologically unrealistic. Thus, judging that unicorns are possible seems like a fairly simple affair, something a small child could do, whereas disbelieving in a correct apodictic disbelief in a unicorn is much more complicated, potentially requiring the application of concepts children are unlikely to possess.

There is a simpler paraphrase strategy, however, which Brentano does not consider but perhaps should have. This is to treat statements ostensibly about mere possibilia as really about modal properties of the actual world as a whole. Thus, 'There could be unicorns' may be understood to mean 'The actual world could contain unicorns,' which in turn paraphrases neatly into 'There is a possibly-unicorn-containing actual world.' Here the actual world is ascribed an unusual kind of property, that of possibly having a unicorny part so to speak. The only object whose existence is genuinely asserted here is the world as a whole, which does of course exist.

A limitation of this strategy is that it cannot allow us to paraphrase statements about merely possible worlds. Thus, 'There is a possible world with unicorns in it' must be treated as strictly speaking false. But it is not clear that this is a significant limitation. Arguably, when we contemplate a merely possible world, what we are really doing is just imagining ways the actual world could be. The objection would have teeth only if there were truths ostensibly about merely possible worlds that resisted paraphrase into statements about how the actual world might be. I would contend there are none.

The real cost of the strategy is the acceptance of irreducibly modal ways things could be. I suspect that it is the reason Brentano does not consider it seriously. For him, something about the ways things actually are must ground the truth of modal truths. His attitudinal approach using the apodictic quantifier delivers this.

In conclusion, although Brentano himself rests his case for the paraphraseability of all statements into existentials mainly on consideration of categorical and hypothetical statements, he has some reasonable options for existential paraphrases of singular, relational, compound, and modal statements as well. The paraphrases may not always be elegant, and sometimes entrain real costs, notably the contrast between the relative simplicity of believing (e.g.) that some baby or some dog is cute and the evident complexity of disbelieving in a mereological sum of a correct disbelief in a cute baby and a correct disbelief in a cute dog. Still, it is already remarkable that an existential paraphrase appears to be always *available*. It would therefore not be unreasonable to indulge Brentano and grant him the first step of his argument: dispensing with belief-that is *feasible*.

2.2. Dispensing with beliefs-that is commendable

Paraphraseability is a symmetric relation: if 'blah' paraphrases into 'bleh,' then equally 'bleh' paraphrases into 'blah.' Accordingly, in showing that all predicative statements paraphrase into existential ones, we would also be showing that all the relevant existentials paraphrase into predicatives. So the paraphrase by itself does not demonstrate that all seemingly predicative judgments are in fact existential. It could be equally well taken to suggest that the relevant seemingly existential judgments are in fact predicative.

Someone might respond, on Brentano's behalf, that interpreting the paraphraseability as showing that all judgments are existential brings with it increased theoretical unity; the opposite interpretation does not. In one version, the claim would be that although all predicatives paraphrase into existentials, there are also some extra existentials for which no predicative paraphrase is available. In another version, the claim might be that existentials as a class are simply more homogeneous than predicatives. However, both claims are suspect. On the one hand, it is doubtful that there are existentials that cannot be put in predicative form, given the availability of such first-order predicates as 'exists,' 'is existent,' and 'is real.' As for the claim that existentials are inherently more homogeneous than predicatives, it is hard to evaluate such claims in the absence of explicit measures of the relevant homogeneity. At the very least, the envisaged argument would require supplementation in the form of (i) providing a measure of class homogeneity for statements and (ii) showing that, as a class, existentials score higher on this measure than predicatives.

Brentano's own argument, in the above-quoted 1906 letter to Marty, is not from unity but parsimony ('the economy of nature'). The idea seems to be that if some judgments are predicative, then (i) their contents are propositional, which would require us to embrace propositions in our ontology, and (ii) their truthmakers are states of affairs, which would require us to embrace states of affairs as well. In contrast, Brentano seems to claim, existential judgments do not require a propositional content, and their truthmakers can be individual objects.

The notion that judgments may not require propositions as content is potentially greatly advantageous, given the force of worries about the 'unity of the proposition' prominent in recent philosophy of mind and language (King 2007). But the parsimony Brentano pursues most vigorously concerns truthmakers. The truthmaker of a belief that some dogs are cute, it is natural to say, is the *fact* (or the *obtaining state of affairs*) that some dogs are cute. In contrast, the truthmakers of the belief *in* cute dogs are simply the cute dogs. Each and every cute dog out there makes true the belief *in* cute dogs.[23] Thus the truthmakers of beliefs-in are individual objects rather than facts or states of affairs. Other things being equal, then, the thesis that *all* beliefs are beliefs-in paves the way to a nominalist ontology that dispenses with facts and states of affairs. This too is greatly advantageous, given worries about so-called Bradley's regress attending a state-of-affairs ontology.[24]

And indeed, as we will see in Chap. 6, Brentano will employ his heterodox theory of judgment to underwrite a nominalist ontology that recognizes only concrete particulars. What the 1906 letter to Marty suggests, I claim, is that that nominalist ontology is the *motivation* for the BIT theory of judgment.

The key to delivering nominalism is the notion that beliefs-in are made true by individual objects, not by *existential states of affairs* (of which such objects are constituents). It might be objected that the belief in dogs is made true not by each dog, but rather by each dog's *existence* – where a dog's existence is a state of affairs (the fact that the dog exists). But Brentano explicitly rejects this in the same letter to Marty:

[T]he being of A need not be produced in order for the judgment 'A is' to be...correct; all that is needed is A.   (Brentano 1930: 95 [85])

It is the object, and not (the fact of) the object's existence, that makes true the relevant existential. In a slogan: the truthmakers of (positive) existentials are not existences but existents.[25]

What is the reason to take the object itself, rather than its existence, to make true the existential judgment? One reason is parsimony of course. But Brentano also adduces a separate argument. It is an argument from infinite regress, presented in that letter to Marty (Brentano 1930: 95–6 [85–6]) and a subsequent letter to Hugo Bergman (Bergmann 1946: 84), as well as in a 1914 dictation (Brentano 1930: 122 [108]). Suppose for reductio that belief in my dog Julius is made true not by Julius, but by Julius' existence. Then in addition to Julius, we must add to our ontology the state of affairs of Julius existing. In adding this state of affairs to our ontology, now, we are clearly committing ourselves to its existence. And committing to the existence of the state of affairs of Julius existing is a matter of believing *in* that state of affairs. The question arises then of what makes this new belief true. One view is that it is made true by the state of affairs of Julius existing itself. The other view is that it is made true not by the state of affairs of Julius existing, but by *the existence of* that state of affairs (that is, by the state of affairs of the state of affairs of Julius existing existing!). If we take the former view, then we allow beliefs in certain items to be made true by those items themselves, rather than by their existences; so we might as well allow already the belief in Julius to be made true by Julius himself, rather than by Julius' existence. If, however, we take the belief in the state of affairs of Julius existing to be made true by *the existence* of that state of affairs, then we are including in our ontology a new, second-order state of affairs, namely, that of Julius' existence existing. This ontological commitment of ours requires us to *believe in* that second-order state of affairs – and we are off on a vicious regress. The only *non-arbitrary* way to avoid the regress is to recognize dogs themselves as the truthmakers of first-order beliefs in dogs.

In summary, the BIT theory of judgment has the advantage of dispensing with states of affairs as the kind of entities our judgments are answerable to. More precisely, what we have here is a dispensability argument to the effect that the conjunction of EXISTENTIAL and ATTITUDINAL results in a doubly parsimony-enabling theory of judgment: there is (i) no need to posit propositions to account for the structure of judgments, and (ii) no need to posit facts and/or states of affairs to account for the truth of (true) judgments.

༄༅

The argument is that we should adopt the conjunction of ATTITUDINAL and EXISTENTIAL because doing so will provide downstream benefits. The argument is powerful, but has two limitations. First, it offers no motivation for either ATTITUDINAL or EXISTENTIAL in separation from the other, and second, it presents no upstream considerations offering independent support for either ATTITUDINAL or EXISTENTIAL.

Now, in the entire Brentano corpus I do not believe there is any independent argument of the sort for EXISTENTIAL. But for ATTITUDINAL there are at least two.

The more explicit argument appears, to my knowledge, only in Brentano's lecture notes from his logic courses in Vienna at 1878–9 and 1884–5 (Brentano 1956: §15). Those who maintain that an existential judgment's existence-commitment is an aspect of content, Brentano reasons, have the following picture in mind. When you judge that the pope is wise, you put together the concept of pope and the concept of wisdom. Likewise, when you judge that there is a pope, or that the pope exists, you put together the concept of pope and the concept of existence. But note, says Brentano, that you cannot judge that the pope is wise without acknowledging (*anerkennen*) the pope, that is, presenting-as-existent the pope. By the same token, you cannot judge that the pope *exists* without acknowledging the pope. But once one has acknowledged the pope, there is no point in *additionally* judging that the pope exists – there is nothing in the latter not already in the former. Since the commitment to the pope's existence is already built into the acknowledging, that commitment is merely replicated in the act's content.

One objection might be that acknowledgement is not built into positive judgment the way Brentano claims. For example, one may judge that Alyosha Karamazov is emotionally wise without acknowledging Alyosha in the relevant sense. However, recall from Chap. 2 that for Brentano such statements as 'Alyosha Karamazov is emotionally wise' are elliptical for hypotheticals such as 'If Alyosha Karamazov existed, he would be emotionally wise.' This in turn expresses only a negative judgment, namely, that there is not a non-emotionally-wise Alyosha. Such negative judgments are irrelevant to Brentano's argument, since negative existentials do not commit to anything's existence (obviously: they rather involve commitment to nonexistence).

Another objection might be that acknowledgement only *appears* to be a distinctive attitude. In truth, to acknowledge something amounts to judging that the thing has the property of existing. In other words, just as Brentano claims that belief-that reports should be paraphrased into belief-in reports, the present objector claims we should do the inverse. What this objection shows, I think, is that deeper (nonlinguistic) considerations are called for to show that existence-commitment is an attitudinal rather than content property.

Brentano's *main* argument for this is implicit in the *Psychology*. The basic point is that acts of judging and acts of contemplating or entertaining can have the same content (Brentano 1874: II, 44–5 [205]). Yet the judging commits the subject to the reality of what is judged, while the contemplating does not commit to the reality of what is contemplated. Therefore, the existence-commitment cannot come from the content, which is shared. It must come from some other difference between judging and contemplating. The best candidate, says Brentano (1874: II, 64–5 [221–2]), is an attitudinal difference: the judging presents the judged in a way that the contemplating does not present the contemplated. It is that *way* of presenting that encodes (if you please) commitment to the relevant object's existence.

To my mind, this more implicit argument of Brentano's is cogent, and demonstrates that existence-commitment is indeed not a content property, but likely an attitudinal property.[26] It is worth mentioning, though, that there is another argument for ATTITUDINAL close to the surface in the *Psychology*. Consider the Kantian claim that 'existence is not a property,' which Brentano cites approvingly:

In his critique of the ontological argument for the existence of God, Kant made the pertinent remark that in an existential statement, i.e. in a statement of the form 'A exists,' existence 'is not a real predicate, i.e. a concept of something that can be superposed (*hinzukommen*) on the concept of a thing.' 'It is,' he said, 'only the positing of a thing or of certain determinations [read: properties], as existing in themselves.'   (Brentano 1874: II, 53 [211])

If there is no such thing as a property of existence, any attribution of existence to something would be attribution of a property that nothing has. Accordingly, any existential belief that attributed existence to something would perforce be *mis*attributing and therefore mistaken. But in fact not all existential beliefs are mistaken: it is correct, for example, to believe in ducks. So (correct) commitment to something's existence cannot involve attribution of a property of existence. If commitment to Fs' existence is not a matter of attributing existence to Fs, it must instead be built into the very nature of the attitude taken *toward* Fs. This is the attitude of *believing-in*, an attitude whose very *nature* is to present-as-existent.

One final consideration supports ATTITUDINAL as well. It seems that infants and animals can mentally commit to the existence of something even though, plausibly, they do not possess the concept of existence. A kitten may believe that there is food in her bowl – or rather, believe *in* enbowled-food – before she has had the time to acquire the concept of being or existence. If existence-commitment were an aspect of belief content, however, we would expect the relevant constituent of the content to be the concept of existence. By contrast, no such expectation arises if existence-commitment is an aspect of attitude. Similarly for an infant's belief that there is food in her plate. Furthermore: it would be odd to suppose that having started as an attitudinal aspect of this infant's food beliefs, the existence-commitment later migrates into the content once the child acquires the concept of existence.

I conclude that the case for both EXISTENTIAL and ATTITUDINAL is stronger than one might initially suspect. As noted, together they entail OBJECTUAL. And all three theses together constitute BIT, Brentano's Belief-In Theory of judgment. The theory is very unusual, but apparently more defensible than may initially appear. Its greatest cost, it seems to me, is the gap between the apparent simplicity of certain (notably compound) judgments and the evident complexity Brentano's theory attributes to them.

3. Objections and Replies

Given how unusual Brentano's view is, it is surprising that the case for it should be as solid as it is. Nonetheless, a number of objections suggest themselves. Let us consider the more pressing.

Clearly, Brentano's theory goes against our intuitions as twenty-first-century philosophers 'brought up' on a certain conception of the structure of judgment and belief: as having a subject-predicate structure akin to the structure of the sentences used to express them. But just as clearly, Brentano would reply that these intuitions of ours lie *downstream* of theorizing and therefore cannot be used to *support* the theory. We philosophers have the intuition because we have accepted the theory, not the other way round. We should reject the intuition along with the theory. The objector may insist, however, that the intuition does not come *only* from philosophical theory, but also from the structure of language, as used well before exposure to any theory. It is the subject-predicate structure of indicatives that suggests a similar psychological structure in the judgments they express.

This is a reasonable claim, to which Brentano responds by trying to explain why linguistic expressions of judgments have the structure they do (despite judgments having a completely different structure).[27] Ultimately, the explanation is that language and judgment have different *functions*: the primary, original function of language, he claims, is to facilitate communication (Brentano 1956: 25–6), whereas the primary function of thought and reasoning is the acquisition and management of knowledge. The problem is that if language were structured in a way that reflects accurately the structure of the thought it expresses and the reality it presents, it would be unable to perform its function – it would be 'an entirely new and most unwieldy language' (Brentano 1917a: 275 [367]). Insofar as structures derive over time from functions, there is no reason to expect the latter to converge where the former diverge.

The objector may press that certain systematicity phenomena could not be explained within the Brentanian framework. If the structure of language and thought mirror each other, we can understand why no person is in a position to judge that Mary loves John without being in a position to judge that John loves Mary (Fodor 1975). Brentano, in contrast, has no resources to explain this – he must treat as miraculous the simultaneous emergence of the capacities to make both judgments. For the belief in a Mary-loving John and the belief in a John-loving Mary have strictly *nothing* in common in their contents.[28]

This is indeed a very serious problem for Brentano, but perhaps he could respond as follows. As we have already seen, the fact that an intentional state is non-propositional does not mean that it does not mobilize concepts. Thus, even though fear is an objectual attitude, what a subject can fear depends on the concepts in the subject's possession: if S_1 possesses the concept of a Rottweiler while S_2 only possesses the coarser-grained concept of a big dog, their fears of the same object might be type-different intentional states. This is because S_1 will apply the concept of a Rottweiler to the object he fears while S_2 will apply the concept of a big dog. Now, we can imagine a subject who possesses both concepts, but in whom the two are disconnected in such a way that the subject is unaware that Rottweilers are dogs. In most subjects who possess both concepts, however, the two are linked in such a way that it is impossible for the subject to fear a Rottweiler without *ipso facto* fearing a dog. The Brentanian might hope to produce a similar explanation of why every normal human subject in a position to contemplate a Mary-loving John is also in a position to contemplate a John-loving

Mary. It is far from clear how the explanation would go, but it is not inconceivable that some story could be devised. Still, as long as no actual story is proffered, it remains an outstanding theoretical debt of BIT to show that it can recover the phenomena of systematicity.

A related objection is that BIT is false to the phenomenology of making a judgment: what it is like to judge that there are cheetahs and what it is like to judge that all cheetahs are fast is different – there are type-distinct feels associated with these. It is natural to explain this felt difference by invoking something like a 'phenomenology of predication' present in one and absent in the other.[29]

Claims of this sort are notoriously hard to evaluate,[30] but in any case Brentano *can* accommodate the alleged felt differences. In the case of the judgments that there are cheetahs and that all cheetahs are fast, Brentano can readily recognize a felt difference between a positive and a negative judgment: the occurrent belief in cheetahs and the occurrent *dis*belief in non-fast cheetahs. Admittedly, this response would not work in other cases. Judging that there are cheetahs and judging that *some* cheetahs are fast feel different, but in both cases they involve believing in something – a cheetah in the first case, a fast cheetah in the second. Here, however, Brentano could suggest that the difference comes from the intentional object – it is the difference between present-ing-as-existent a cheetah in one case and a fast cheetah in the other. The crucial point is that Brentano can offer an account of the felt difference that does not appeal to a phe-nomenology of predication. For the objection to be probing, we would need a case where felt differences persist when the contents and the positive/negative orientation are the same. If there were felt differences between occurrently believing that some cheetahs are fast and occurrently believing in fast cheetahs, for example, that would do the trick. At this point, however, it is *extremely* hard to make the case for a genuinely *felt* difference.[31]

The objector may press that even if BIT is not false to the phenomenology of *atomic* judgments, it certainly is to that of *compound* judgments. As we have seen, Brentano recasts an ostensibly first-order positive judgment that either some cat is white or some dog is brown as a complex affair involving the second-order disbelief in the sum of correct disbeliefs in a white cat and in a brown dog. It might be claimed that the judg-ment that either a cat is white or a dog is brown *feels* much simpler than how it would if Brentano's theory were accurate. Or perhaps that making the judgment feels *easier* than making the complex second-order negative judgment Brentano adduces. Brentano might deny that there is a feel associated with a judgment's complexity or hardness, but this is problematic. There is a clear sense in which making the judgment that $14 + 17 = 31$ feels easier (to most of us) than making the judgment that if $a \leq 1$ then $2 - 2a \geq 0$. In the same sense, it feels easier (to most of us) to judge that some cat is white or some dog is brown than to make the complex second-order judgment Brentano claims we are making.

To my mind, this is a genuine liability of Brentano's account. There are some possible approaches to it, but none terribly satisfying. One is to hide behind the notion that phenomenological claims are too methodologically problematic to warrant rejecting a view for; but this would be odd for a philosopher whose central project was 'descriptive psychology,' the descriptive study of phenomenal experience.[32] Another option is to retreat to the claim that the existential paraphrases are not *intended* to capture the psychological reality of judgment, but to perform a more subtle theoretical task; but then the account would be much better presented as concerning sentences than as concerning judgments (whereas Brentano does the opposite). A third option is to revert to Chisholm's suggestion that disjunctive judgments are occurrent beliefs in disjunctiva; unfortunately, it is unclear that this fares any better on the phenomenological front (does the judgment really feel directed at a single thing which is either a white cat or a brown dog?). A fourth option might be to deny the existence of disjunctive judgments and replace them with disjunctions of judgments (just as conjunctive judgments are replaced with conjunctions of judgments); this may be the most satisfying option in the area. Perhaps the view could be framed in terms of credence distributions: one does not really have .9 credence in <there is a white cat or a brown dog>, but rather $.n_1$ credence in <there is a white cat> and $.n_2$ credence in <there is a brown dog> such that $n_1 + n_2 = 9$. With the right background story about the phenomenological interpretation of credence talk, this may be workable. Still, the resulting account is bound to be somewhat revisionary and may run into further problems. This is why I consider this issue a genuine liability for Brentano's theory of judgment.

A completely different objection is that BIT is *pragmatically* problematic, perhaps because its acceptance would complicate the conduct of inquiry. More specifically, it might be claimed that predicate logic has worked very well for us to formalize large tracts of science, but with BIT, predicate logic would have to be renounced wholesale. This objection is important, but all it shows is that Brentano owes us a predicate-free formal logic to go along with his predication-free theory of judgment. As it happens, Brentano did start on this project (Brentano 1956), which was further developed by his student Franz Hillebrand (Hillebrand 1891). Suppose a subject judges both that (i) there is a party and that (ii) if there is a party then there is booze, which leads her to judge that (iii) there is booze. The validity of her reasoning is captured in traditional *modus ponens*. Within the Brentanian framework, the reasoning is recast as follows: the subject both believes in a party and disbelieves in a boozeless party, which leads her to believe in booze. The task, then, is to reformulate the familiar laws of logic, in this case *modus ponens*, so that this reasoning is ratified as valid. What has been proposed by various logicians is to replace the traditional:

$$\frac{p \rightarrow q \quad p}{p}$$

with:

$$\frac{Na^-b \quad Ea}{Eb}$$

This reads: *a* is not without *b* (there is not a boozeless party); *a* is (there is a party); therefore, *b* is (there is booze). With this law in place, we can readily explain why the subject's reasoning to the conclusion that there is booze is valid. Similarly for other logical laws. Now, while I have no competence to affirm that Hillebrand's system works, I have all the competence needed to report that Peter Simons thinks it does (see Simons 1987b).

Conclusion

I personally think that Brentano's theory of judgment is a masterpiece of philosophical creativity. Against the overwhelmingly common philosophical treatment of judgment and belief as propositional attitudes with an internal structure mimicking that of sentences, out of the blue comes Brentano and argues that these are rather objectual attitudes whose only function is to acknowledge or deny existence, or more accurately, present-as-existent or present-as-nonexistent some individual object. Given its considerable originality, I find the case for Brentano's theory surprisingly solid. Real liabilities loom around the issues of systematicity and the phenomenology of compound judgments. Still, the ontological benefits accruing to this kind of theory – in particular, the dismissal of propositions and non-concrete truthmakers – will surely appeal to many. These benefits will take center stage in Chap. 6. There we will see how the theory underwrites a nominalist ontology that manages to avoid the liabilities and loose ends attending more modern forms of nominalism. That ontology relies on a certain metaontology suggested by Brentano's theory of judgment. It is to this metaontology that we turn next.[33]

Notes to Chapter 4

1. It is worth noting that Brentano's existentials do not have the form 'There is an *x*, such that *x* is F', but rather the simple form 'There is an F'. The whole point of the paraphrase, for Brentano, is to show that judgments do not have a predicative structure: 'We have shown that the combination of subject and predicate and other similar connections in no way go to the essence of judgment. We based this claim on consideration of affirmative as well as negative existential statements; we confirmed this...by means of the reduction/tracing back (*Rückführung*) of categorical and, indeed all types of assertion, to existential statements.' (Brentano 1874: II, 64 [222])

2. Brentano writes: 'The statement (*Satz*) "If a man behaves badly, he harms himself" is a hypothetical statement. As far as its meaning is concerned, it is like the categorical statement "All badly-behaving men harm themselves." And this, in turn, has no other meaning than that of the existential statement "A badly-behaving man who does not harm himself does not exist," or to use a more felicitous expression, "There is no badly-behaving man who does not harm himself"'. (Brentano 1874: II, 59–60 [218])

3. Brentano nowhere states the attitudinal account of existence-commitment as explicitly as one might wish. But he comes close at various points. For example: 'The most natural

expression is "A is," not "A is existent," where "existent" appears as a predicate... [But such an existential statement] means rather "If anyone should think of A in a positive way, his thought is fitting (*entsprechend*)".' (Brentano 1930: 79 [69]) The commitment to A's existence is an aspect of the *way* (or mode) in which the thinking is done.

4. To my knowledge, the expression 'objectual attitude' comes from Forbes 2000; and the expression 'propositional attitude' from Russell 1904. But the concepts far predate the expressions.

5. The existence of such objectual attitudes is defended by Forbes 2000 and Montague 2007 among others.

6. In fact, for Brentano *all* mental states are objectual in this way – this is why he writes that 'All mental references refer to things' (1911: 158 [291]). Here 'thing' is used to refer to an individual object or concrete particular, and 'mental reference' is another term for intentionality.

7. There are uses of 'belief in' that may denote non-cognitive attitude, as in 'believe in yourself!' or 'we believe in the future' (which seem to denote emotional attitudes such as confidence and hope). But there is also the cognitive usage highlighted in the main text.

8. To endorse this formulation, one has to accept that there is such a thing as occurrent believing-in. If one takes believing-in to be always dispositional, then Brentano's view would have to be formulated more cumbersomely: all judgments are occurrent manifestations of believings-in. For the sake of smooth exposition more than anything else, I am here treating belief-in as a state that *can* be occurrent.

9. Two exceptions are Szabó (2003) and Textor (2007), who reject the analysis of 'S believes in x' in terms of 'S believes that x exists,' though on grounds other from Brentano's.

10. The name is suboptimal, insofar as belief-in captures only one half of the span of judgments – disbelief-in captures the other half. But BIT has the advantage of being cute, and I trust the reader to keep in mind the relevance of disbelief-in.

11. It might be objected, to my interpretation of Brentano's *Anerkennung* as belief-in, that Brentano was adamant that there are no degrees of acceptance, whereas belief-in may very well vary in confidence (constituting a kind of objectual credence). However, it is possible to account for the degree of confidence associated with a belief-in not as an aspect of the belief-in itself, but as a kind of second-order state directed at the likely truth of the first-order belief-in. In itself, then, the belief-in would be absolute in its existence-commitment.

12. One place where Brentano sounds non-Leibnizian is in his discussion of mereological relations among colored spots in Brentano 1982: chap. 2. One place in which he mentions the Leibnizian paraphrase in a sympathetic tone of voice is in his discussion of Kant's classification of utterances in Brentano 1956: §28.

13. For background, see Russell's disagreement with Strawson discussed in Chap. 2.

14. What happens if there is more than one individual with those properties? Several avenues are open to descriptivists – divided reference, reference failure, and more – but the issues surrounding this possibility have nothing specifically to do with Brentano's project, so I will set them aside here.

15. In Kripke's (1972) causal theory of reference, for example, there is a relation of nondeviant causal chain between a current use of the name and a baptismal event in which the name is introduced in the presence of the named. One may of course reject this view, while still

do justice to most of Kripke's insights, for example by holding a kind of causal descriptivism (Kroon 1987), according to which a name refers to whatever object satisfies the token-reflexive description 'the object suitably causally linked to this very use of the name.' On this view, 'Beyoncé is famous' means the same as 'The object suitably causally linked to this very use of "Beyoncé" is famous.' This would allow for the standard Brentanian paraphrase.

16. Statements of the form 'There is N' (where 'N' ranges over proper names) are awkward, but ultimately they mean the same as 'N exists,' which is not awkward. So the idea is essentially to paraphrase 'Beyoncé is famous' into 'Famous-Beyoncé exists.'

17. The short answer is that for Brentano Beyoncé and Famous-Beyoncé are two numerically distinct but spatiotemporally coinciding objects. More on this in Chap. 6!

18. I thank Géraldine Carranante for presenting me with the problem of distinguishing 'Some brown dogs are cute' and 'Some cute dogs are brown'; before she did I never managed to understand the importance of the double-judgment theory.

19. To be general, this paraphrase strategy requires there to be a mereological sum for every pair of related individuals. That is, it requires Classical Mereology's axiom of unrestricted composition. As we saw in Chap. 1, this axiom is clearly adopted in Brentano's mereology (Brentano 1933: 11 [19]). So this treatment of relational statements seems indeed available to Brentano.

20. By the same token, by the way, 'Every dog is cute' is to be paraphrased into 'There is not correct belief in a non-cute dog.' Brentano's notion of a correct judgment will be expanded upon in Chap. 5.

21. The only kind of negative judgment for which it might seem that this device is irrelevant is that expressed by 'Some dogs are not cute.' As we have seen, however, on the double-judgment theory this amounts to 'There is a dog & There is not a cute dog-being-referred-to-by-the-previous-conjunct.' This could now be seen to express actually two simultaneous judgments: a belief in a dog and disbelief in a correct belief in a cute dog-being-referred-to-by-the-other-judgment.

22. A similar strategy can be extended to material conditionals, since $p \to q$ is equivalent to $\sim p$ $\lor$ q, hence to $\sim(p \,\&\, \sim q)$. It might be objected that disbelief in sums of correct judgments is too weak to capture the content of disjunctive and conditional judgments. The claim is not just that nobody has *in fact* made the relevant correct judgments. It is rather that if anyone did make those judgments, they could not do so correctly. This latter claim has a modal depth to it entirely missing from the simple rejection of two correct judgments co-occurring. This objection smells right to me, but it just invites discussion of Brentano's treatment of modality, which is our next topic.

23. There might be something odd about talk of truthmakers for beliefs *in*. Perhaps it might be thought ungrammatical to say that the belief in ducks is true; it is certainly more natural to say that such a belief is *correct*. In that case, we should speak rather of the worldly correctnessmakers of beliefs-in. I am sympathetic to all this, but will stick with the word 'truthmaker' for simplicity. On this, see Textor 2007: 78–9.

24. In the present context, by 'state-of-affairs ontology' I mean any ontology that admits such entities as states of affairs. Any such ontology faces Bradley's regress (Bradley 1893). The problem is how to understand the 'metaphysical glue' that joins an individual and a property when together they compose a state of affairs. The fact (obtaining state of affairs) that Alec the electron is negatively charged is more than just the sum of the two facts that

(i) Alec exists and (ii) being negatively-charged is instantiated. It involves also some kind of 'metaphysical glue' that 'brings together' Alec and being negatively-charged. If we try to understand this 'glue' in terms of a *relation* between Alec and being negatively-charged – 'exemplification' or 'instantiation,' say – then we would require something to glue Alec, being negatively-charged, and that relation. Appealing to a second-order metaphysical glue would only launch us on a regress – Bradley's regress.

25. There is a question of how to handle the truthmaking of negative existentials. This is something Brentano had nothing to say about. Perhaps this is because for him the issue is not really one of truthmaking, but of the ontological commitment that positive existentials involve. Since negative existentials involve no ontological commitment, the same issue does not arise for them.

26. I write 'likely' because other candidate explanations of the difference between contemplating and judging have to be ruled out (other than the content candidate) before we can more confidently assert that the difference is attitudinal. Much of the issue overlaps with the question of the irreducibility of presentation to judgment, discussed in the previous chapter.

27. In general, Brentano takes the structure of language to be a poor guide to the structure of our mental life. This is stated unequivocally in a short 1905 fragment titled 'Language' (Brentano 1930: 81 [71]) and can be found in various places in the aforementioned logic courses (e.g., Brentano 1956: §12).

28. Thanks to Marie Guillot for pressing on me this objection.

29. This objection presupposes that there is a phenomenology of making a judgment, a so-called cognitive phenomenology (Pitt 2004). This could be rejected, but since neither Brentano nor I would do so, I do not call into question this presupposition.

30. It is noteworthy that Brentano virtually never rests his case for a thesis on a phenomenological claim, or as he would put it, the testimony of inner perception. One gets the sense that his theses are sometimes *motivated* by the testimony of his inner perception, and when they are he tends not to be shy about asserting that that is the testimony of inner perception. But he always adds further arguments, and gives the testimony of inner perception only a supporting role.

31. Another option for the objector is to claim that differences in intentional objects (what is judged) cannot by themselves account for phenomenal differences – only differences in attitude and in the *structure* of content can. But this seems like a difficult argument to carry through. Certainly it is the objector's burden to do so.

32. Brentano distinguished between two kinds of psychology, *genetic* and *descriptive*. The former provides causal explanation of the genesis of mental phenomena; the latter merely describes the phenomena. That is, the former answers questions of the form 'How did it come to be?,' the latter questions of the form 'What *is* it?' For Brentano, importantly, descriptive psychology is prior in the order of understanding to genetic psychology: in an ideal reconstruction of science, we would presumably proceed first by describing the phenomena in need of explanation and only then offering an explanation of them. Without knowing what 'it' *is*, it is hard to see how we might be able to explain how 'it' came to be. For more on this, (see Seron 2017).

33. For comments on a previous draft, I am grateful to Géraldine Carranante, Anna Giustina, Alex Gzrankowski, Franz Knappik, Michelle Montague, and Kevin Mulligan. I also

benefited from presenting related materials at the Australian National University, Columbia University, École Normale Supérieure, the University of Girona, and at IHPST and IJN in Paris; I am grateful to the audiences there, in particular Damiano Costa, Imogen Dickie, Nemira Gasiunas, Thibaut Giraud, Anna Giustina, Vincent Grandjean, Erick Llamas, Myrto Milopoulos, Michael Murez, Ben Phillips, David Pineda, Maria van der Schaar, Benjamin Schnieder, Moritz Schultz, Robert Stalnaker, Daniel Stoljar, Eric Tremault, Agustín Vicente, and especially Marie Guillot.

5

Metaontology
Existence

Brentano's theory of judgment serves as a springboard for his conception of reality, indeed for his ontology. It does so, indirectly, by inspiring a very specific *meta*ontology. To a first approximation, ontology is concerned with what exists, metaontology with what it means to say that something exists. So understood, metaontology has been dominated by three views: (i) existence as a substantive first-order property that some things have and some do not, (ii) existence as a formal first-order property that everything has, and (iii) existence as a second-order property of existents' distinctive properties. Brentano offers a fourth and completely different approach to existence talk, however, one which falls naturally out of his theory of judgment. The purpose of this chapter is to present and motivate Brentano's approach.

1. Introduction: Metaontology and Existence Talk

Moral philosophy is usefully divided into ethics and metaethics. Oversimplifying considerably, the distinction is this: ethics is concerned with what is good, metaethics with what it means to say that something is good. The goal of ethics is to produce a comprehensive list of goods. Metaethics concerns a more fundamental question: when we say that *x* is good, what exactly are we saying? In a way, ethics is concerned with the *extension* of the concept GOOD, metaethics with its *intension*.

This is an oversimplification in at least two ways. First, ethics and metaethics are concerned with other normative concepts, such as RIGHT, VIRTUE, and REASONS. Secondly, metaethics deals with other issues, such as moral epistemology – how we can come to know which things are good. Still, there is a clear sense in which answering the question of what exactly we are doing when we say that something is good lies at the heart of metaethics.

A similar division of labor may be applied to ontology and metaontology. Again oversimplifying, ontology is concerned with what exists, metaontology with what it means to say that something exists. The goal of ontology is to produce a comprehensive list of existents; that of metaontology is to answer the question of what exactly we are saying when we say that *x* exists. To that extent, ontology is concerned with the extension of the concept EXISTENCE, metaontology with its intension.

One way in which this oversimplifies is that ontology may well be concerned with other concepts, such as GROUNDING, FUNDAMENTALITY, or ESSENCE.[1] Another is that metaontology is also concerned with other issues, notably the methodology of ontology.[2] Nonetheless, there is a sense in which at the heart of metaontology lies the question 'when we say that *x* exists, what exactly are we saying?' We may think of this as the *organizing question* of metaontology.

To this question, there are three prominent answers in the extant literature. According to the first, to say that *x* exists is to attribute to *x* a substantive, discriminating first-order property that some things have and some do not (Meinong 1904, Parsons 1980). According to the second, it is to attribute a second-order property of existents' distinctive properties or of the concept designed to pick them out (Frege 1884, Russell 1905b). According to the third, more popular in recent discussions, to say that *x* exists is to attribute to *x* a formal, *un*discriminating first-order property that everything has (Williamson 2002, van Inwagen 2003). Each of these has met with strong resistance and faces extraordinary objections, but each has also been admirably defended. Just by way of motivating the search for an alternative approach such as Brentano's, I now present a brief survey of the three familiar views and some of their immediate difficulties.

The simplest view is that to say that *x* exists is to attribute a substantive property to *x*. When I say that Leo Messi is brilliant, I attribute to Messi a certain property, the property of being brilliant. Some players have that property and some do not. In exactly the same manner, when I say that Messi exists, I attribute to him a property, this time the property of existing. Brilliant, existent, short, Argentinean – those are all Messi-esque attributes on a par. Accordingly, existential claims are at bottom of a kind with predicative claims: 'ducks are cute' and 'there are ducks' *look* different, but the latter is just an unhelpful rendering of 'ducks are existent.'

Dissatisfaction with this approach is rife. There are technical problems to do with negative existentials and existential generalization. From 'Jimmy is not Argentinean' I can infer 'There is a non-Argentinean.' If existential claims work just like predicative ones, from 'Shrek does not exist' I should be able to infer 'There is a nonexistent.' But this requires a distinction between 'there is' and 'exists' that many find odious (Quine 1948), including Brentano (1930: 127–8 [112], 1933: 29–31 [32–3]). Proponents of the view are of course well aware that their position requires a distinction between 'there is' and 'exists' and embrace it unflinchingly. It remains that *natural language* does not seem to draw such a distinction – 'There are ghosts' and 'Ghosts exist' seem to say the same thing – so this view of existence talk cannot quite be right for existence talk *in natural language*. There are also nontechnical problems: as Hume (1739: I, II, vi) noted, the idea of existence adds nothing to the idea of an object. The idea of a cute duck is different from the idea of a duck, which means that the idea of cuteness contributes something to the idea of a cute duck. But the idea of an existing duck is nowise different from the idea of a duck; so it is unclear what the idea of existence is supposed to contribute.

Perhaps the most dominant view in twentieth-century philosophy has been that, in saying that x exists, we are attributing a property not to x, but either (i) to x's distinctive, individuating *properties* or (ii) to the *concept* of x. In the first case, we attribute the property of being (co-)instantiated; in the second, that of (successfully) referring. In both versions, existence is construed as a *second-order* property, since it is not a property of x itself but of some properties of x or the concept of x. Thus, when I say that Messi exists, what I am doing is attributing to the properties that individuate Messi (whatever they are) the property of being (co-)instantiated, or else attributing to the concept MESSI the property of (successfully) referring. Likewise, when I say that dragons do not exist, I am saying that nothing co-instantiates all the properties definitive of dragons, or else that the concept DRAGON is empty.

This approach raises its own set of difficulties. Some are technical and pertain to its application to singular existentials. The approach seems to suggest that the proper name 'Messi' is semantically associated with certain properties. For example, if the truth of 'Messi exists' requires that the property of being the only five-time Ballon d'Or winner be instantiated, then it seems that 'Messi' refers partly via the description 'the only five-time Ballon d'Or winner.' Likewise, if the truth of 'Messi exists' requires that the concept of Messi refer, then it seems that 'Messi' refers partly in virtue of expressing that concept. But many philosophers deny that 'Messi' is associated with *any* properties, descriptions, or concepts; they maintain that it refers *directly* to the individual himself, without any such mediators (Kripke 1972). There are also nontechnical problems with the approach: it implies that in saying that Messi exists, we are not saying anything *about Messi*; in fact, we are not speaking of Messi at all, but of some different (though associated) entity. What we are speaking of is not even a concrete particular, but a property cluster or a concept. This feels wrong: saying that x exists feels like a comment on x, not on something else suitably related to x.[3] When we exclaim excitedly that the Higgs boson exists, it is the discovery of the boson itself that excites us. Perhaps most problematically, 'Messi exists' can be true even if there are no such things as properties and concepts, as some nominalists maintain, whereas 'The Messirific properties are co-instantiated' and 'The concept MESSI refers' cannot.[4] The problem here is *not* that such nominalism is so plausible that its rejection is an unwelcome commitment of the second-order property view; rather, it is that metaontological views should not have *any* first-order ontological commitments – they should not prejudge, or be beholden to, first-order questions. (Compare a metaethical theory whose account of what we do when we say that something is good has any chance of working only if consequentialism is false!)

A view gathering momentum in recent metaontology is that existence is a first-order property of things, but not a substantive, discriminating one that divides entities into two subsets, those which have the property and those which do not. Rather, it is a formal or 'pleonastic' property that everything has. Other logical or formal properties are like that as well: the property of being self-identical does not divide entities into two subsets either.

One problem for this view concerns intuitively true singular negative existentials, such as 'Robin Hood did not exist.' On some (popular!) views, proper names such as 'Robin Hood,' at least if they were not explicitly introduced as shorthand for certain descriptions, are *directly referential*. This means that their referent is the only contribution they make to the meaning of sentences in which they appear. On this view, 'Santa Claus is coming to town' is meaningless rather than false, because there is no proposition it expresses. If we accept this view, as many do, then it is unclear how someone who holds that *everything* exits can obtain the result that 'Robin Hood does not exist' is true. If Robin Hood is part of this 'everything,' then 'Robin Hood exists' is true, and so (on most logics) 'Robin Hood does not exist' is false. If, on the other hand, Robin Hood is not part of everything, then 'Robin Hood does not exist' is as meaningless as 'Santa Claus is coming to town.' This presents the proponent of the view that existence is a property that everything has with some tough choices: either she adopts a descriptivist view of proper names, or she embraces the consequence that 'Robin Hood does not exist' is untrue.

To be sure, proponents of each view have offered various responses to these and other problems. I do not wish to dwell on these matters here. My principal aim here is to articulate and motivate Brentano's alternative approach. Brentano worked on this in two main periods of his life. His doctoral dissertation was on the notion of existence in Aristotle (Brentano 1862), but he returned to the topic forty years later, composing and dictating a number of important essays and notes (see Brentano 1930, 1933). The basic idea is quite original, and flows nicely from his account of judgment. However, the resulting view has received essentially no attention outside the circles of Brentano scholarship. My goal here is to motivate it to a wider audience and show that it merits serious consideration.

2. Mental Existence-Commitment: Brentano's Attitudinal Account

To say that *x* exists is to perform a certain linguistic act. The performance of this act commits the performer to *x*'s existence. To that extent, we may think of the act of saying that *x* exists as *linguistic existence-commitment*. Saying '*x* exists' is of course only one form of linguistic existence-commitment. Others include asserting 'there is an *x*,' 'there exist *x* s,' '*x* is,' 'the *x*s are existent,' and so on.

It is, of course, possible to commit oneself to the existence of *x* without saying anything. I may think to myself that *x* exists and keep the thought to myself. This would also be a form of existence-commitment, but not *linguistic* existence-commitment. Rather, it would be *mental* existence-commitment. Mental existence-commitment is commitment to something's existence *in thought*, whereas linguistic existence-commitment is commitment to something's existence *in language*. Like many modern philosophers of mind, Brentano presupposes the priority of the mental over the linguistic, taking linguistic representation to derive from mental representation (see esp. Brentano 1956). Accordingly, he starts from an account of mental existence-commitment, and devises his account of linguistic existence-commitment on its basis.

When I think to myself that Messi exists, I mentally commit to the existence of Messi. The three familiar views share the assumption that in doing so, I attribute a property to something. (They differ on what property is attributed and what it is attributed to, but they agree that some property is attributed to something.) Underlying this is an even deeper assumption: that the commitment to Messi's existence is an aspect of the relevant thought's *content*. The property attributed is a constituent of the content of my thought. On the first-order views, the content may be represented as <Existence, Messi>; on the second-order one, as <Instantiatedness, Messirific properties> or <Referentiality, MESSI>. Either way, some existence-related property figures in the content of existence-committing mental acts.

Brentano rejects this, as we saw in Chap. 4. For him, mental commitment to something's existence is not an aspect of the relevant mental state's content, but of its attitude. When you mentally commit to Messi's existence, your mental state is that of belief in Messi, not that of belief in Messi's existence. Messi by himself exhausts the content of your belief in Messi – no property is invoked in the content. (That is why belief-in is an *objectual* attitude.) The existential commitment is encoded in the very attitude of believing-in, and neither needs nor can be replicated within the content. In this Brentano's approach to mental existence-commitment is fundamentally different from the three more familiar views.

Obviously, not all attitudes are existence-committal. Among attitudes that do not incorporate commitment to *x*'s existence, some expressly involve the opposite commitment, namely to *x*'s *nonexistence*; others are 'existentially silent.' I would love to have a gold-coated private jet; my desire for such a jet, and my contemplation of it, commit me neither to the jet's existence nor to its nonexistence. They are noncommittal on the question of the gold-coated jet's existence. By contrast, my disbelief in Shrek is not neutral in this way. It *takes a stand* on Shrek's existence – a negative stand. It encodes mental *nonexistence*-commitment.

Brentano's attitudinal account of mental existence-commitment does raise a problem. If mental existence-commitment is an aspect of existence-committing acts' *content*, then linguistic existence-commitment can be construed in terms of linguistic acts with the very same content. But this cannot work if mental existence-commitment is an aspect of mental acts' *attitude*. A structurally similar account of linguistic existence-commitment would still be possible if there were an existence-committing *force* in language to parallel the existence-committing *attitude* in thought. But no such force appears to exist. Perhaps the force characteristic of *assertion* could be thought of as a kind of linguistic representing-as-*true*. But that is not quite yet representing-as-existent.

If there were a special tone of voice, such that uttering 'Messi' in it would convey the utterer's commitment to Messi's existence, or a special punctuation symbol, a kind of 'existence stroke' akin to Frege's 'judgment stroke,' such that prefacing a noun phrase with it conveyed the author's commitment to the existence of the object denoted by the phrase, then that tone or symbol could underpin an account of linguistic existence-commitment structurally similar to Brentano's account of mental linguistic-commitment. But in fact there are no such linguistic devices, and it is instructive that at the linguistic level existence-commitment appears always to be achieved through an aspect of content, with the aid of precisely such words as 'exists.' So what exactly are we doing when we add the word 'exists' after 'Messi,' as though we have added a verb like 'kicks' or 'scores,' if in reality there is no *activity* or *state* denoted by 'exists' (as Brentano maintains)? Answering this question is crucial for providing an answer to what I described above as the organizing question of metaontology: when we say that *x* exists, what exactly are we saying? That is after all a question about *saying*, so it concerns linguistic existence-commitment, existence-commitment in the representational medium in which the community of ontologists conducts its inquiry.

3. Linguistic Existence-Commitment: Brentano's Fitting Belief-in Account

For Brentano, in asserting '*x* exists,' we are not saying that *x* has the property of existing, nor that some *x*-distinctive properties are instantiated. What we are saying is this: that *x* is a suitable object of acceptance, that is, an appropriate intentional object of belief-in. We are saying that belief-in would be the correct attitude to take toward *x* – that the right attitude to take toward *x* is that of believing in it. If *x* is to be an intentional object of belief-in or disbelief-in, it ought to be the object of belief-in.

By the same token, when we say that *y* does *not* exist, what we are saying is that if *y* is to be an intentional object of belief-in or disbelief-in, it ought to be the object of *disbe-lief-in*. The correct attitude to take toward *y* is that of disbelieving in it. In that sense, *y* is a suitable (intentional) object of rejection or disbelief-in. Disbelief is appropriate to it. The general picture, then, is this:

Let us call the area for which affirmative judgment is fitting/appropriate (*passende*) the area of the existent (*Existierenden*)…and the area for which the negative judgment is fitting/appropriate the area of the nonexistent.   (Brentano 1930: 24 [21])

This passage, from an 1889 lecture to the Vienna Philosophical Society, states the view in terms of fittingness. Fifteen years later, in a 1904 essay, Brentano puts the view in terms of correctness:

'The existent' (*Existerendes*), in the proper sense, is not a name that names something, but rather amounts to 'something correctly affirmatively thought-of' (*richtig positiv Gedachtes*), 'something correctly accepted' (*richtig Anerkanntes*).   (Brentano 1930: 79 [68])

In general, *richtig* ('correct') is Brentano's favorite term in these contexts. However, in at least one place he explicitly offers as synonyms *konvenient*, *passend*, and *entsprechend* – more or less interchangeably translatable as 'appropriate', 'suitable', or 'fitting' (Brentano 1889: 76 [74]).

This account of existence talk may be summarized, or sloganized, with what I will call *Brentano's Dictum*:

(BD)   To be is to be a fitting object of belief-in.

Although I formulate Brentano's Dictum in the material mode of speech, it is intended in the first instance not as an account of what existence itself consists in, but as an account of what existence talk comes down to. It cannot be an account of the nature of the property of existing, of course, since Brentano disbelieves in such a property. More generally, there is no way to generate an account of the nature of existence itself, or of what existence consists in. There is no way to 'get underneath existence', as Jonathan Schaffer once put it to me. All we can do is explicate what we do when we engage in linguistic existence-commitment. That is what BD is *really* trying to do.[5] Note well: in BD, 'object' means *intentional object*, not *entity* or *concrete particular*. In this sense of 'object', the Eiffel Tower is an object of my acceptance in the same sense my wife is the object of my affection.

The way I understand BD, it is *only* an account of what we do when we make an existence claim. Accordingly, it is not intended to help us go about actually discovering what exists. That is, it is not a *guide* to ontological commitment. (More on this in §5.2.) In addition, BD is not intended as a substantive account of existence. It is not an attempt to capture the intrinsic nature of a property of existence. That is, the idea is *not* that existence is the property whose nature is being-fittingly-acceptable. Indeed, *there is no such property as existence* – though there are of course existents. Following Kant, Brentano puts this point by saying that existence is not a 'real predicate':

> In calling an object good, we do not thereby give it a material/real (*sachliches*) predicate, somewhat as we do when we call something red or round or warm or thinking. The expressions good and bad work in this respect like existent and nonexistent. We do not seek with these to add a further determination to the relevant thing; rather, we want to say that whoever accepts [believes in] a certain thing, and rejects [disbelieves in] another, judges truly.
>
> (Brentano 1952: 144 [90])

There is no material predicate of existence, that is, a nonformal, discriminating predicate that separates objects into two groups, those that satisfy it and those that do not. This is precisely why existence-commitment cannot be part of the content of a mental state. There is not some aspect of the world, or of things in it, that we are trying to capture with our concept EXISTENT. And yet existence talk is perfectly meaningful, and existence claims are often true. It is true that ducks exist. The only way to make sense of the notion that it is true that ducks exist, without saying what makes it true is the fact that ducks have the property of existing, is to say that what is true is the fact that belief in ducks is fitting.

To see this, suppose that mental commitment to the existence of x were a content feature, say a matter of the belief that x exists. Then it would be natural to hold that linguistic existence-commitment is a matter of asserting the kind of sentence that expressed that belief and thus shared the same *content* as it. But if mental commitment to the existence of x is attitudinally encoded in the existence-committal state, then uttering a sentence with the same content as that state accomplishes nothing. To replicate the intentional structure of the relevant mental state in a linguistic utterance, there would have to exist an existence-committal force, so that one could simply utter 'x' with that force. Since no such force exists, committing linguistically to x's existence must rather take the form of commenting on the kind of mental attitude it would be appropriate or correct to take toward x.

It is useful, in this context, to distinguish two explicitly contrastive readings of BD:

(BD$_1$)   To be is to be a fitting *rather than unfitting* object of belief-in.

(BD$_2$)   To be is to be a fitting object of belief-in *rather than disbelief-in (or contemplation)*.

BD$_1$ is true, insofar as all existents are fitting rather than unfitting objects of belief-in. But BD$_1$ does not *explain* existence talk. It does not *account* for what it means to say that something exists. What explains that is BD$_2$, the thought that to say that x exists is to take a stand on which attitude it would be correct to take toward x, which attitude is *appropriate* for x.

To that extent, Brentano's account of existence talk can be thought of as a sort of *fitting-attitude account*. Such accounts have recently proliferated in the metaethical literature (Jacobson 2011). The basic idea is that for x to be good is for it to be a fitting object of approval or the like pro attitude; for x to be bad is for it to be a fitting object of disapproval or the like con attitude. As we will see in Chap. 8, Brentano is quite clearly a fitting-attitude theorist *of value*, indeed may well be the first such. And as we will see in Chaps. 8 and 10, his accounts of the existent and of the good are *supposed* to be structurally symmetrical, something he is quite explicit on in several places (see Seron 2008). Accordingly, we would be quite justified to consider Brentano's approach, as captured in BD$_2$, a fitting-attitude account of linguistic existence-commitment.[6]

Brentano's account faces an immediate challenge: what does it mean for belief-in to be fitting or correct? The most natural answer is of course unavailable to Brentano. The most natural answer is that it is fitting or correct to believe in x just when x really exists. (Compare: it is appropriate for us to believe that p just when p is true.) Adopting this answer would result in immediate circularity, however: what it is for a belief in x to be fitting is just for x to exist, but what it is for x to exist is for it to be fitting to believe in x. Upshot: Brentano must have some other, less obvious account of belief fittingness.

4. Further Developments: What Is Belief Fittingness?

Brentano's account of belief fittingness proceeds in two steps. The first is an analysis of belief fittingness in terms of self-evidence (*Evidenz*). The second is a primitivist account of self-evidence. I take these up in reverse order. I will then raise a leftover circularity concern and address it on Brentano's behalf.

4.1. The nature of self-evidence

Brentano's approach to self-evidence remained more or less constant throughout his career. From the first extended discussion in *Psychology* II (Chap. 3, §§2–4) to a series of dictations on the topic in the second week of July 1915 (twenty months before he died), Brentano's views both on what *is* self-evident and what it is to be self-evident changed little. Recall from Chap. 1 that inner perception is self-evident. Since perception is for him a species of judgment, we can say that inner-perceptual states constitute one kind of self-evident judgment. The only other kind is constituted by certain a priori judgments, notably logical and mathematical (see, e.g., Brentano 1930: 148 [130]). These judgments' status as self-evident *entrains* a number of enviable features: infallibility, certainty, immediacy, and so on. But these features are not what self-evidence *amounts* to. On the contrary, self-evidence is more basic than them and *underlies* them:

What is self-evident cannot be in error. And where something is self-evident there cannot be doubt. But neither freedom from error nor freedom from doubt makes a judgment a self-evident judgment... (Brentano 1930: 144 [126])

Inner perception is infallible *because* it is self-evident. Belief in the law of contradiction is certain *because* it is self-evident. But their being self-evident goes deeper than their infallibility and certainty.

If self-evidence is not *just* infallibility, certainty, immediacy, and so on, but something deeper that underlies and explains these, then what is it? According to Brentano, the notion of self-evidence is primitive and unanalyzable. In consequence, we cannot come to grasp what self-evidence is by digesting the right philosophical theory of it. Nonetheless, there are certain intellectual exercises we can perform that enable us to grasp *directly* the nature of self-evidence.[7]

To see how this works, consider the 'revelation theory' of color (Johnston 1992). According to it, it is a mistake to try to appreciate the nature of colors by articulating the right philosophical theory (whether in terms of objective reflection/refraction properties, dispositions to elicit color experiences, categorical bases of such dispositions, or anything else). To appreciate the nature of green, says the revelation theorist, we just need *to look*. When we look at a paradigmatically green apple, the nature of greenness *reveals* itself to us. Regardless of whether we ultimately wish to subscribe to a revelation theory, the notion that a property may be such that its nature can be appreciated through direct awareness, rather than through a philosophical theory, is rather plausible. Brentano's view is that this is exactly the case with the property of self-evidence – and also, as it happens, with the property of greenness.

Now, the reader might be forgiven if s/he feels that there is a certain disanalogy between the cases of greenness and self-evidence. In the former, when we are told that we will grasp directly the nature of greenness just by looking, we know immediately what to do, and whether we have succeeded in capturing that which we were promised we would grasp simply by looking. In the case of self-evidence, however, it is not immediately obvious what we are supposed to do and what would count as having successfully done that. This may raise a suspicion about a revelation theory of self-evidence: if self-evidence *reveals* its nature, should it not be *immediately obvious* that – and how – it does?

Brentano is aware of this objection and responds, somewhat underwhelmingly, that self-evidence revealed itself in an immediately obvious way to certain philosophers, notably Aristotle (Brentano 1952: 157 [98]). But there is a deeper point to be made here. Arguably, the immediate plausibility of the notion that colors 'reveal' their nature is not due entirely to our visually witnessing the *intrinsic nature* of the colors. Rather, it is due in part to the rife and sharp *contrasts* that we witness among different colors in our environment. Imagine a planet – call it Green-Earth – much like ours but for two differences: (i) all objects there are shades of black and white and (ii) all are naturally illuminated by green light (perhaps because of the special properties of Green-Earth's sun), instead of the standard white sunlight we are used to here on Earth (so-called D65).[8] Importantly, the visual apparatus of Green-Earthlings, from sensory transducers to high visual cortex, is identical to ours. We can compare normal visual experiences of objects on Earth and on Green-Earth by considering the two scenes portrayed on this book's cover.[9]

Consider now pairs of Green-Earthly and green Earthly objects that reflect exactly the same light (and, *ex hypothesi*, are processed by the exact same apparatus). Let us stipulate that the the two second doors to the left on the cover answer to this description. It seems to me that although Earthlings may well grasp directly the nature of green just by looking at the relevant green Earthly objects, Green-Earthlings are ill positioned to grasp the nature of green just by looking at the relevant Green-Earthly objects (despite the identity of physical reflection and refraction properties and of 'opponent processing' apparatus).[10] More precisely, perhaps, Green-Earthlings cannot grasp the nature of green *as such*, that is, the determinable of which all specific green shades are determinates. What is missing on Green-Earth, it would seem, is the proper contrast: since everything is green-tinged, there are no objects (surfaces, volumes, films) completely 'free of green.'[11]

If this is right, then direct grasp of F's nature requires the right kind of contrast. Sometimes the world is set up so that the contrast occurs naturally (as is the case with colors on Earth), but sometimes it is the philosopher's task to adduce the contrast. This is done by dwelling on certain examples of pairs of phenomena, whether real or thought-experimental, with the goal of 'helping' one's interlocutor to grasp the nature of F for herself. The result is a kind of 'assisted revelation' account of the nature of F.

Brentano's approach to the direct grasp of self-evidence is precisely of this 'assisted revelation' variety:

> The correct method is one that we use in many other cases where we are concerned with a *simple* mark or characteristic. We will have to solve the problem by considering a multiplicity of judgments which are self-evident and then *juxtaposing and contrasting (vergleichend gegenüber stellen)* them with other judgments which lack this distinguishing characteristic. This is what we do, after all, when we make clear to ourselves what is red or not red...
>
> (Brentano 1930: 143 [125], my italics; see also Brentano 1928: 3 [4])

'Simple' here is meant as the antonym of 'composite': a simple characteristic is one that cannot be accounted for in terms of more elemental constituents. Brentano's contention is that self-evidence – like other incomposite, primitive features – can only be appreciated through suitable contrasts (Brentano 1956: 111). In particular, although self-evident beliefs involve a *feeling of strong confidence*, indeed of being *compelled to believe*, that feeling can attach to other beliefs as a result of habit, indoctrination, wishful thinking, or prejudice. When we hold in memory or imagination a *self-evident* confident belief and a *non-self-evident* confident belief, and contrast the two, we can directly grasp the feature present only in the former:

> Descartes' example of [self-evidence] is the knowledge we possess when we are aware of thinking, seeing, hearing, wanting or feeling something. No matter how far I go with my doubt, he said, I still cannot doubt that I doubt. And he did not mean by this that I just have an incontrovertible urge (*unüberwindlichen Drang*) to believe in my thinking, but rather that I perceive with complete certainty the fact of my thinking. A comparison with a deep-rooted prejudice brings out the characteristic that contrasts [the inner-perceptual judgment] with a case of blind urge to believe; be the urge as powerful as you like, something is still missing here that shows up there [in the inner-perceptual judgment], and that is simply what we label self-evidence.
>
> (Brentano 1928: 3 [4])

A college student may feel equal confidence in 'I think, therefore I am,' which he learned yesterday, as in 'Shaving makes the hair grow back thicker,' which his father imparted on him upon his sixteenth birthday. Nonetheless, when we as theoreticians consider these two beliefs side by side, as it were, we 'see' that although they are similar insofar as they both exhibit an acute feeling of certainty, they are also crucially different. More precisely, in juxtaposing the two in thought we become directly acquainted with a dimension along which they differ. That dimension we label 'self-evidence.' As theoreticians, we focus our mind on the right incomposite feature by imagining ourselves thinking 'I think, therefore I am,' imagining ourselves thinking 'Shaving makes the hair grow back thicker,' and comparing and contrasting these two imagined judgments. There is no other way for us to truly grasp what self-evidence is.

4.2. Self-evidence and belief fittingness

So much, then, for Brentano's primitivist account of self-evidence. For Brentano, the fittingness or correctness of a belief can be analyzed in terms of self-evidence:

Truth belongs to the judgments of the correct/fitting judger – to the judgments, therefore, of someone who judges in the way he who made his judgments on the matter with self-evidence would.   (Brentano 1930: 139 [122])

This passage combines two ideas. The first, which does not directly concern us, is that a judgment's truth comes down to its correctness/fittingness. The other, which does concern us, is that a token judgment's correctness/fittingness is a matter of its conforming to a type-identical judgment that is self-evident.

More precisely, the view is this. A person may make a judgment regarding x's existence – that is, decide to believe or disbelieve in x – in one of two ways: *with* or *without* self-evidence. If she makes the judgment with self-evidence, then whatever she ends up deciding, her judgment is fitting. For example, if she decides to believe in x, then since she judged the matter with self-evidence, her belief in x is self-evident and a fortiori fitting. Now, if the person makes the judgment *without* self-evidence, then for her resulting judgment to be fitting, a certain counterfactual must hold: namely, that *if* she judged with self-evidence, she *would* end up making the same judgment – or more exactly, that if *anyone* judged with self-evidence, s/he would end up making that judgment. For example, if she decides to believe in x, then her belief is fitting iff were any subject S to judge on x's existence with self-evidence, S would come to believe in x.

Suppose I believe that my wife is sad now (or rather believe *in* my wife's current sadness). My wife herself may know with self-evidence that she is sad, since she can inner-perceive her sadness, and inner perception is self-evident. My own belief in her sadness, however, is not self-evident, since I *cannot* inner-perceive her sadness. Still, the following counterfactual is still true: if my wife were to judge on whether she is sad or not, she would come to self-evidently believe in her sadness. It is because this counterfactual is true, claims Brentano, that *my* belief in my wife's sadness is fitting.

It is a consequence of this account that one cannot truly appreciate the nature of belief fittingness without grasping the nature of self-evidence, since fittingness is analyzed in terms of self-evidence. Therefore, it is also a consequence that one cannot appreciate the nature of belief fittingness without encountering in inner perception the contrast between self-evident and non-self-evident beliefs-in (Brentano 1952: 141–2 [88]).

This account of belief fittingness faces an immediate difficulty, raised by Chisholm (1986: 39), but apparently aired already by Ehrenfels (Bacigalupo 2015: 56). It is that in some cases it may be impossible for *anyone* to make a judgment on whether x exists with self-evidence. Indeed, given that for Brentano self-evidence extends only to inner perception and certain a priori beliefs, there seem to be large tracts of our a posteriori knowledge for which self-evidence is simply not in the cards. Belief in ducks, for example, seems eminently fitting, yet nobody can hope to have this belief with self-evidence.[12]

Chisholm himself deems that Brentano's only option here is to resort to God's a priori insight into all things (Chisholm 1986: 39). The reason my belief in ducks is fitting, on this view, is that God self-evidently believes in ducks. Insofar as this response makes

Brentano's analysis beholden to theism, however, it is not particularly satisfactory –
though one might suggest that the analysis does not quite commit to God's existence,
but only to her conceivability. Now, Brentano himself was of course a theist (see
Brentano 1929), but in general he seems not to appreciate the move of parachuting
God into the dialectic to solve otherwise insurmountable philosophical problems.
And as we will see in Chap. 8, he explicitly opposes the appeal to God in a parallel
dialectical setting to do with the nature of goodness.

It might be suggested that appeal to God is not Brentano's only option here. Another
option is to appeal to *counterpossibles*, that is, counterfactuals whose antecedents are
necessarily rather than contingently false. Consider the claim that if, *per impossibile*, I
formed a judgment on the matter of ducks' existence with self-evidence, the judgment
I would form is that of believing in ducks. For all Brentano might care, one might
suggest, the analysis of belief fittingness could invoke such counterpossibles. The
idea would be that when we say that belief in x is fitting, what we are saying is that if,
perhaps *per impossibile*, someone judged with self-evidence on x's existence, s/he
would believe in x.[13]

The main problem with this is that it is unclear how we are supposed to evaluate the
plausibility of such counterpossibles. When we plug the emerging view of belief
fittingness into the fitting belief-in account, we obtain the following: to say that x exists
is to say that belief-in is the attitude that would be adopted toward x by someone who,
perhaps *per impossibile*, judged the matter of x's existence with self-evidence. Thus, to
say that ducks exist is to say that if, *per impossibile*, anyone could make a judgment on
the existence of ducks with self-evidence, then the attitude she would take toward
ducks is that of belief-in (rather than disbelief-in). To evaluate the claim that ducks
exist, then, it would seem that we must first evaluate the claim that the relevant impossible subject would have a self-evident belief in ducks. But how are we supposed to
know what attitude this impossible subject would take toward ducks? If we suppose
that she would believe in ducks on the grounds that *it is true that there are ducks*, then
we fall into circularity again.

It might be suggested that Brentano would have done better to account for fittingness without reference to self-evidence, appealing instead to obligation, the 'epistemic
ought,' evidence, or related epistemic notions (see Sosa 2009 and McHugh 2014). The
idea might be, say, that it is fitting to believe in ducks because the weight of evidence
recommends such a belief. The obvious problem here, however, is that nothing prevents (i) the existence of things we have insufficient evidence to believe in, nor (ii) our
having substantial evidence for the existence of things which do not in fact exist. If a
belief's fittingness were a matter of its being supported by evidence, then (i) would
involve existents in which it is not fitting to believe and (ii) would involve fitting beliefs
in nonexistent. It is perhaps natural to embrace such possibilities, but not if one *also*
wants to hold that to be is to be a fitting object of belief-in.

Consider an example. It is perfectly possible that the world doubled in size instantaneously last night at midnight. If this event of instantaneous cosmic doubling did

occur, and existence is to be accounted for in terms of fitting belief-in, then Brentano would have to say that it is fitting to believe in that event. However, given that the event would entail the instantaneous doubling of our measuring instruments, the meter in Paris, and so on, it is in principle impossible to produce any evidence for its occurrence. In that scenario, then, it would be fitting to believe in an event for which no evidence is possible. It is probably because of such limitations on the appeal to evidence and similar epistemic notions that Brentano instead appealed to *self*-evidence, which, recall, ensures infallibility. As we have seen, however, analyzing fittingness in terms of self-evidence creates a problem in cases where self-evidence is not in the cards for us, as in the belief in ducks.

What to do? In my opinion, Brentano's best move here is to go primitivist about belief-fittingness *directly* and construe self-evidence as just a particularly acute or manifest instance of fittingness. On this view, the only way to grasp the nature of belief fittingness is to contemplate side by side fitting and unfitting beliefs in things, and this is easiest to do with the most starkly fitting beliefs, namely, the self-evident ones. To be clear, fittingness itself does not come in degrees – a belief in x is either fitting or unfitting. But how *manifest* a belief's fittingness is does come in degrees. The most manifestly fitting beliefs are the self-evident ones. Our college student's belief in his own existence is fitting in an inner-perceptibly manifest way in which his belief in hair growing back thicker after shaving is not. By contemplating the contrast between these two beliefs, and other belief pairs like them, we grasp directly the nature of manifestly fitting belief. We then understand a fitting belief as one which is like the manifestly fitting ones in the relevant respect but is not manifestly such (or better: as one which is like a *highly* manifestly fitting belief in the relevant respect but is *less* manifest).

This kind of fittingness primitivism is not ideal, insofar as it leaves the extrapolation from manifestly fitting (i.e., self-evident) judgments to merely fitting ones somewhat opaque. The resulting account of existence talk would certainly benefit from an elaboration on the nature of this extrapolation. It does seem to me, however, a more promising route than appeal to either God or counterpossibles. In any case, Brentano would profit here from stating that his is not an account of how *we come to know* that something exists, but of *what we are saying* when we say that something exists. In reality, my sense is that Brentano's account of existence talk is actually intended to pave the way to a kind of classical foundationalism about existential *knowledge* (see Brentano 1928).[14] All the same, the account of existence talk may well be more plausible than the corresponding account of existential knowledge.

4.3. Existence and the nature of belief-in

I have attempted to show that Brentano's account of existence talk in terms of fitting belief-in need not fall prey to circularity. So far, however, all I have shown is (at most!) that there is no circularity hidden in the requirement that beliefs-in be *fitting*. There might still be some circularity hidden in the requirement that the fitting state be the objectual attitude of *belief-in*. After all, in Chaps. 3–4 we have characterized belief-in as the state whose distinctive, essential feature is the attitudinal property of presenting-as-*existent*. If we plug this into what I have called Brentano's Dictum, we obtain: to be is to be a fitting object of presentation-as-existent. Brentano's fitting belief-in account, then, might be circular after all. For its answer to the organizing question of metaontology seems to be this: when we say that x exists, what we are saying is that the correct attitude to take toward x is that attitude which presents-as-existent x.

The response *must* be that 'existent' is not really a constituent of 'presenting-as-existent'. As in Chap. 2, we must read this locution as syntactically simple, with 'existent' appearing in it as a morphological but not syntactic part. The expression 'presenting-as-existent' is useful as a 'philosophical wink' of sort, to give a sense of the property we are trying to point at. But strictly speaking, 'presenting-as-existent' is just a label, picking out the relevant property directly, not by mediation of a description such as (the non-hyphenated!) 'presenting as existent'.

This response may work, but only if the compositional understanding of 'presenting-as-existent' is not the *only* way we have of understanding which property is meant. There must be some other way for us to understand 'presenting-as-existent'. And indeed, Brentano does offer us such a way. In fact, Brentano himself never characterizes the attitudinal property essential to judgment in terms of presenting-as-existent – or for that matter, in any other terms. For him, that property is another primitive we can only grasp directly, using the same contrastive method we use to grasp the nature of self-evidence:

…judgment is an irreducible (*irreduzibler*) act, directed at an object, that cannot be further analyzed. In other words, a judgment consists in a specific relation to the object whose nature can be elucidated only by examples and which can be expressed by 'accepting' and 'rejecting'.
(Brentano 1956: 100)

It is by inner-perceiving judgments and other (nonjudicative) conscious states, then 'recreating' both types of state in episodic memory and attending to the difference between them, that we come to grasp the distinctive nature of judgment. Someone who has never judged cannot grasp the nature of judgment – not by understanding the expression 'present-as-existent' and not otherwise.[15]

In conclusion, Brentano's gambit is to account for existence talk in terms of fitting belief-in, and then claim that both the notion of fittingness and the notion of belief-in can be understood without prior understanding of what existence is. The notion of fittingness can be understood in terms of self-evidence, which is grasped directly, and the notion of belief-in is grasped directly as well. Both self-evidence and belief-in are primitive notions we can understand, ultimately, only thanks to inner-perceptual encounter. This is why already in the *Psychology* Brentano promises, somewhat cryptically, that an empiricist treatment of the concept EXISTENCE as ultimately acquired by perception, albeit inner, is workable:

Some have held that this concept [EXISTENCE] cannot be derived from experience… [But] we will find that this concept undoubtedly is derived from experience, but from *inner experience*, and we acquire it *with regard to judgment.*   (Brentano 1874: II, 52 [210]; my italics; see also Brentano 1952 §40)

Brentano does not develop the idea any further in the *Psychology*. Against the background of this section's discussion, what he has in mind should be clear though: inner perception of judgments, especially self-evident ones, is the ultimate basis on which we acquire our concept of existence.

If we use boldface to mark primitive notions, graspable only via direct encounter (against appropriate contrasts), Brentano's fully explicit account of existence talk can be put as follows: to say that *x* exists is to say that **belief-in** is the attitude that would be adopted toward *x* by someone who judged the matter with **self-evidence**. I have recommended, however, that Brentano retreat to the thesis that to say that *x* exists is to say that **belief-in** is the attitude it would be **fitting** to adopt toward *x*, with self-evidence entering the picture only heuristically, as a particularly stark instance of inner-perceptible fittingness.

5. Advantages and Disadvantages of the Fitting Belief-in Account

Brentano's account is very different from the three more standard approaches to existence. For one thing, at least two of those standard approaches offer theories of the nature of *existence itself*, whereas Brentano's fitting-attitude account is primarily a theory of existence *talk*. What it says about existence itself is, first, that there is no property of existence, and second, that although there are existents, there is nothing that *makes* them existents – they just exist. Accordingly, there is no way to 'get underneath' existence, and all we can hope to obtain in this area is illumination of existence thought and discourse – that is, of the nature of mental and linguistic commitment to existence. Furthermore, Brentano's account differs substantially from the three standard approaches also specifically on the nature of such existence-commitment. Most notably, for Brentano mental existence-commitment does not involve attribution of a property to anything. There is a sense in which linguistic existence-commitment does: when we assert that *x* exists, we implicitly attribute the property of fittingness to the belief in *x*; indeed, *x* itself is attributed the property of being a suitable object for belief-in. At the same time, this is very different from the property-attribution involved in the more standard accounts of existence talk, insofar as the property attributed is not ostensibly ontological (it is not a property such as existing or being instantiated). In this section, I consider the potential advantages (§5.1) and disadvantages (§5.2) of Brentano's account.

5.1. *Avoiding the problems of traditional accounts*

Brentano's unusual approach avoids many of the central problems bedeviling the three better-known approaches discussed in §1. To be sure, there may be other solutions to these problems – the literature on this is enormous. But it is remarkable that many of these problems do not even *arise* within Brentano's fitting belief-in framework.

Two issues were raised in §1 with the first view, existence as a substantive first-order property. The first concerned the treatment of negative existentials, such as 'There are no dragons.' The view under consideration interprets this to mean something like 'Dragons have the property of not existing.' The latter, however, entails, by simple existential generalization, the incoherent-sounding 'There is an *x*, such that *x* has the property of not existing.' There may be ways around this, notably by devising formal systems in which existential generalization is not an automatically valid inference. It is noteworthy, though, that the problem does not even arise in the Brentanian framework. For Brentano interprets 'There are no dragons' as meaning something like 'It is appropriate to disbelieve in dragons.' The latter does *not* entail 'There is an *x*, such that it is appropriate to disbelieve in *x*.' For the expression 'appropriate to disbelieve in' creates an intensional context, certainly a context where existential generalization is not supported.[16] Accordingly, negative existentials do not yield the aforementioned incoherent-sounding result.[17]

The second problem for the 'substantive first-order predicate view' was Hume's observation that the idea of existence 'adds nothing': asked to contemplate not just a duck, but an existent duck, we end up contemplating the same thing we did before – a duck. This militates against the notion that EXISTENCE picks out anything substantive. It is clear that Brentano's fitting belief-in account respects Hume's observation. Indeed, the notion that existence is not a *content feature* of existence-committal mental states can *explain* the fact that there is no *content difference* between the ideas of a duck and of an existent duck.

The second view mentioned in §1, existence as a second-order property, raised two issues as well. The first concerned its compatibility with direct-reference accounts of proper names. We noted, for example, that if 'Messi exists' simply means 'The property of being the only five-time Ballon d'Or winner is instantiated,' then 'Messi' would seem to refer partly via the description 'the only five-time Ballon d'Or winner' – contrary to the most popular view of nominal reference. (If 'Messi exists' means rather the same as a much more complicated statement of the form 'The properties of being $F_1, \ldots, F_n$ are co-instantiated,' this would suggest that 'Messi' refers through the corresponding much more complex description.) In contrast, there is nothing about the fitting belief-in account that requires one to take any position on how 'Messi' refers. Suppose 'Messi' refers thanks to a causal chain leading to a baptismal event taking place in 1987 in Rosario. Then 'Messi exists' can still mean the same as 'It is fitting to believe in Messi.'

The second problem with the second-order view was that it cast 'Messi exists' as not about Messi, but about his Messirific properties or the concept MESSI. Here it is less *immediately* clear that Brentano's account fares meaningfully better. For in construing 'Messi exists' as meaning 'It is fitting to believe in Messi,' it casts the former as primarily about a certain belief, not a certain footballer. One might try to defend Brentano by noting that 'Messi' still *appears* in 'It is fitting to believe in Messi' (whereas it does not in 'The Messirific properties are co-instantiated'). To that extent, we may say that the statement is still *secondarily* about Messi (Brentano would say that it is 'obliquely' about Messi), which is perhaps an advantage over the second-order property view.[18] A more important advantage, arguably, is that all this concerns only *linguistic* existence-commitment. As far as *mental* existence-commitment is concerned, it is clear that the *belief in* Messi involves mental reference to Messi himself, not to any associated entities. Since linguistic existence-commitment derives from mental existence-commitment, this means that the fundamental, nonderivative form of existence-commitment does refer to Messi himself; the proponent of the second-order property view cannot boast the same.

As for the third view mentioned in §1, existence as a *formal* first-order property, I have argued that it is hard to see how it could explain the acquisition of the concept of existence. The model of differential perceptual interaction with existents and nonexistents is a nonstarter, while the genus-et-differentia model cannot designate any relevant genus (that is, any genus of which existence, construed as a formal property that everything has, is a species). As we have seen in §4, however, Brentano *can* offer a compositional story about EXISTENCE in terms of *genus et differentia*: the genus is (potential) belief-in, the 'differentium' is simply fittingness. Ultimately, all the relevant notions are understood in terms of logical vocabulary plus two primitive concepts, belief-in and self-evidence, which *are* acquired by differential perceptual interaction, namely, inner-perceptual interaction with (i) beliefs-in and other mental states (for the concept BELIEF-IN) and (ii) self-evident (dis)beliefs and non-self-evident ones (for SELF-EVIDENCE).

5.2. Objections and replies

At bottom, though, what motivates the fitting belief-in account of linguistic existence-commitment is not just the problems facing other views in the area. It is also the attitudinal account of *mental* existence-commitment. As noted in §3, if mental commitment to the existence of x is attitudinally encoded, then linguistic commitment to x's existence must take the form of commenting on the kind of mental attitude it would be fitting to take toward x.

Brentano's account does face certain difficulties of its own, however. Paralleling the thought that 'Messi exists' should be about Messi and not some associated entities, for example, is the thought that 'Messi exists' should be construed as a descriptive rather than normative statement. It comments on how things are, not how they ought to be. Construing it as a claim about the kind of attitudes we *ought* to take – plainly a normative statement – seems to that extent false to the phenomenology of making existential pronouncements.

I take this to be a genuine liability for the Brentanian account. Its force is somewhat blunted by the fact that the fundamental form of existence-commitment in Brentano's account is *mental* existence-commitment, and the latter is still entirely descriptive. Belief-in has a mind-to-world rather than world-to-mind direction of fit. Still, it would clearly be preferable, all things considered, to have an account of existence *talk* that cast it as descriptive talk.

Another potential worry is that Brentano's Dictum is a rather shallow precept, nowise illuminating or facilitating the conduct of ontological inquiry. Consider Quine's Dictum: to be is to be the value of a variable (Quine 1948). Its formulation has been extraordinarily useful for the field of ontology in the second half of the twentieth century, as it allowed tractable formulations of many debates which were previously hard to pin down. The question of whether there are numbers, for example, became greatly sharpened when recast as the question of whether quantification over numbers would be indispensable in our final theory of the world. The latter question is a more concretely tractable question that has given rise to technically sophisticated debates. It is a question on which progress can more straightforwardly be claimed.[19] It is unclear how Brentano's Dictum could be similarly helpful. Told that to be is to be a suitable object of belief-in, we can recast the question of numbers as the question of whether it would be fitting to adopt the attitude of believing in numbers. But this moves us forward not one inch from the initial question. Indeed, when we consider whether it would be fitting for us to believe in numbers, we simply consider the arguments for and against the existence of numbers! To that extent, Brentano's Dictum provides us with no methodological guidance in the conduct of ontological inquiry.

There are two possible and somewhat conflicting responses to this objection. The first rejects the notion that methodological fecundity of the sort Quine's Dictum boasts is a desirable feature of a metaontological position, insisting that what we really want from our metaontology is *total neutrality*: we want our metaontology to avoid prejudging any first-order ontological questions. These two desiderata seem to be in tension. Consider that Quine (1948) himself took his quantificational approach to pave the way for an argument that numbers must in fact be included in our ontology. Granted, Quine's Dictum does not quite *deliver* a pro-numeric ontology. But nor is it exactly *neutral* on the question, as it reshapes the dialectic in a way that turns out to favor numbers. Brentano's Dictum on its own, in contrast, does not affect the dialectic in any way. The dialectical landscape remains pristinely untouched after we adopt the fitting belief-in account of existence talk, and this may be seen as a plus.

The second possible response to the worry under discussion is that Brentano's metaontology is in fact far from neutral, and paves the way to its own first-order onto-logical gains, though ones different from Quine's. In particular, the fact that the funda-mental form of existence-commitment involves an objectual rather than propositional attitude paves the way, within Brentano's framework, to a nominalist ontology in which only individual objects are admitted. Propositions and states of affairs, almost auto-matically needed to account for *propositional* attitudes and their truth, are peremptor-ily avoided when the only attitudes we need to account for are objectual. We have encountered some of these considerations in Chap. 4, and will develop them in more detail in Chap. 6.

✌️ॐ

Perhaps more deeply than these specific objections, what might give pause to some is the fact that the fitting belief-in account is directly inspired, and motivated, by Brentano's thoroughly heterodox theory of judgment. The notions that all beliefs are existential, and that no beliefs have propositional content, are, all said and done, quite hard to swallow. If, all said and done, one chooses to stick with a more traditional conception of cognition, how attractive does the fitting belief-in account of existence talk look?

The answer, it seems to me, is 'very attractive.' It is true that the fitting belief-in account is inspired by, and meshes very nicely with, the peculiarities of Brentano's theory of judgment. But in no way does the former *logically depend* upon the latter. The only thing it depends on is the claim that belief-in is irreducible to existential belief-that. For as long as belief-in is a real and distinctive kind of state in our psychological repertoire, one can still maintain that to say that *x* exists is to say that the right attitude to take toward *x* is that of believing in it. That is, the view is still available to one, and still exhibits all the aforementioned advantages, even if one has no truck with (the rest of) Brentano's theory of judgment. The fitting belief-in account simply does not need the claim that *all* beliefs are beliefs-in, as long as *some* beliefs are. Interestingly, some philosophers have indeed argued that belief-in does not reduce to existential belief-that without making any claim about converse reduction (Szabó 2003).[20]

There is another commitment of Brentano's that seems entirely superfluous to his fundamental approach – so much so that up till now I saw no need to mention it. Brentano takes tense at face value: for him, it is inappropriate to believe that there are dinosaurs, though it is perfectly appropriate to believe that there *were* dinosaurs. As we saw in Chap. 3, temporal modality is for Brentano an attitudinal affair just as much as ontological status:

> …we must designate temporal differences as modes of [intentionality]. Anyone who considered past, present, and future as differences in objects would be just as mistaken as someone who looked upon existence and nonexistence as real attributes. (Brentano 1911: 143 [279]; see also Brentano 1976: 128 [107])

Just as mental existence-commitment and nonexistence-commitment are a matter of distinct mental states presenting-as-existent and presenting-as-nonexistent their objects, so temporal orientation must be a matter of distinct mental states presenting-as-past, presenting-as-present, or presenting-as-future theirs. From this perspective, there is no difference in *what* one believes when one believes that there *are* dinosaurs or one believes that there *were* dinosaurs. The difference is *not* that between believing in present-dinosaurs and believing in past-dinosaurs. Rather, it is an entirely attitudinal difference (Brentano 1933: 9 [18]), a matter of presenting-as-presently-existing a dinosaur versus presenting-as-pastly-existing a dinosaur. As Brentano puts it, the former is a 'judgment in the *modus praesens*' whereas the latter is a judgment in the preterite mode.

I belabor this point because Brentano's *real* dictum is actually this: to be is to be a fitting object of *modus-praesens* belief-in. Thus we find the following in a 1914 dictation:

If we ask, 'What, then, *is* there in the strict sense of the word?', the answer must be: 'That which is correctly (*mit Recht*) accepted in the *modus praesens*.'   (Brentano 1933: 18 [24])

Brentano's full answer to the 'organizing question' of metaontology, then, is this: to say that *x* exists is to say that it would be fitting to believe in *x* in the *modus praesens*.[21] This excludes attitudinally past-directed and future-directed beliefs-in from the scope of attitudes the fittingness of taking which captures existence.

This twist on Brentano's Dictum seems to pave the way to *presentism*, the thesis that only present beings should be included in our ontology. And eternalists, who maintain that past and future objects can have the exact same ontological status as present ones, may object to it. However, this is why I introduced the topic of Brentano's presentist twist as another completely superfluous commitment of his metaontology, something which Brentano happened to be attracted to but which does not go to the core of the general approach of understanding existence talk in terms of fitting belief-in. An eternalist could readily adopt the fitting belief-in approach to existence talk, and simply resist the presentist twist in Brentano's own version of the view.

Conclusion

Once we rid Brentano's metaontology of some inessential baggage – the presentist twist and the thesis that *all* judgments are beliefs-in – we obtain a view of existence talk that ought to be attractive to any fair-minded observer. Two main liabilities still attach to it, to my mind. The first is that it casts what seem like existential *assertions* as disguised normative claims, claims about what attitudes we ought to have; this is counterintuitive and contrary to the phenomenology of engaging in existence talk. The second is its account of fitting belief-in in terms of what a person who judged with self-evidence would believe, which is problematic in contexts where self-evidence is impossible for us.

Nonetheless, the more familiar theories in this area are not without their problems and liabilities. As in most philosophical areas, the logical space seems exhausted by positions which contain at least one hard-to-swallow component. So these problems attending Brentano's fitting belief-in account should not be taken as disqualifying. As the old French adage says: when you analyze it's upsetting, when you compare it's consoling.

What is most striking to me in Brentano's metaontology is, *again*, how extraordinarily original it is. Like his mereology and his theory of judgment, it seems to come out of nowhere – it is, as far as I can tell, presaged by nothing in the history of philosophy. And yet upon close examination the case for it is no weaker than standard fare in the area. The view is no less believable than its more familiar competitors.

In previous chapters, we have seen several recurring philosophical devices in Brentano's theorizing, notably the appeal to mereological notions to elucidate intricate structures and the use of resources provided by attitudinal properties to illuminate the nature of fundamental mental phenomena. In this chapter came to the fore another recurring Brentanian theme, namely, that the most fundamental notions of a philo-sophical system cannot be grasped through appreciation of the right philosophical theory; instead, they must be treated as primitives which can only be grasped through direct encounter. In practice, this means they must be experienced by oneself and brought into sharper relief through appropriate contrasts.

In Chap. 2, we saw a remark to this effect by Brentano regarding the notion of inten-tionality (recall – or reconsult – the quotation from Brentano 1966: 339). In this chapter, we saw even more developed primitivist accounts of self-evidence and of judgment. We will see further instances of this in later chapters. The general idea is expressed clearly by Brentano already in his 1889 lecture on truth. He closes the lecture with three general morals, the final of which is this:

Many believe that…elucidation (*Verdeutlichung*) [of a concept] always requires some general determination [i.e., definition by *genus et differentia*], and they forget that the ultimate and most effective means of elucidation must always consist in appeal to the individual's intuition…What would be the use of trying to elucidate the concepts of red and blue if I could not present one with something red or with something blue?   (Brentano 1930: 29 [24–5])

Twenty-seven years later, just a year before his death, Brentano distills the basic point as follows:

The basis for understanding any discourse consists not in explication (*Erklärung*) through words but in explication through the objects themselves, provided these objects are presented for comparison and thus for grasping a common general concept.   (Brentano 1933: 205 [150])

The basic point is that grasping things themselves, rather than words or concepts for them, must ultimately ground our conceptual scheme, hence be the foundation for any genuine understanding of reality. As it happens, for Brentano it is only through inner perception that we can grasp things themselves – because of the constitutive connection between inner perception and its objects that we encountered in Chap. 1. Accordingly, genuine understanding of truth, goodness, and beauty must all be traced back, ultim-ately, to some inner-perceptual encounter with corresponding phenomena. In the case of truth, we can theorize truth in terms of existence, existence in terms of fitting belief-in, and the fittingness of a belief in terms of self-evidence; but for the whole theoretical edifice to be intelligible, we must also grasp directly the natures of self-evidence and of believing-in.[22]

Notes to Chapter 5

1. See Schaffer 2009 for a view of ontology as concerned primarily (perhaps even exclusively) with grounding and fundamentality rather than existence, and Lowe 2008 for the view that essence is a central part of what ontology is about.

2. Thus, debates over Quine's (1948) quantificational method vs. Armstrong's (2004) truthmaker method belong within the sphere of metaontology.

3. See Frege 1884: 67 for the explicit claim that 'x exists' is not about x, and Thomasson 2015: chap. 2 for criticism of it.

4. Thanks to Kevin Mulligan for pointing out this particular difficulty.

5. I use the material mode to parallel 'Quine's Dictum' (to be is to be the value of a variable) and 'Alexander's Dictum' (to be is to be causally efficacious) (more on that in §5).

6. It might be suggested that Brentano's account is rather a form of 'metaontological expressivism,' since it casts linguistic existence-commitment as a matter of expressing an attitude rather than describing a state of affairs. However, this would be very different from expressivism as standardly conceived (in metaethics and elsewhere), since the attitude expressed, believing-in, is *cognitive* rather than conative or emotive.

7. In modern analytic philosophy, there is another philosophical technique commonly thought to be capable of illuminating primitive notions. This is to fully specify its theoretical role within our theory of the relevant phenomena. This is the technique regimented through so-called Ramsey sentences (see Lewis 1972). Brentano himself does not consider this option, but although I do not have the space to properly delve into this issue here, there are arguments in the extant literature that characterization via theoretical role cannot be the *only* technique for characterizing primitives, and direct grasp or acquaintance must always be appealed to at some point (see Newman 1928). To that extent, it is an advantage of Brentano's primitivism that it appeals to this latter technique.

8. In saying that all objects on Green Earth *are* black and white, I am presupposing (merely for sake of exposition) an objectivist conception of color. If one rejects such a conception, the correct way to describe Green Earth would be to say that the objects there would be black and white on Earth, or something of that sort.

9. It might be that our visual system is so designed that it would quickly 'edit out' all greenness from the awareness of Green-Earthly objects. If so, the thought experiment would have to include the further condition that Green-Earthlings' visual system is unlike ours in that respect. More directly, we might just stipulate that Green-Earthlings' visual experience is suffused with a green tinge. Whether Green-Earthlings, so conceived, are nomologically possible is immaterial to the thought experiment.

10. Observe the distribution of hyphens in this sentence!

11. Thus we can more easily imagine how Green-Earthlings may directly grasp the nature of the darker-than and lighter-than *color relations* than to imagine how they directly grasp the nature of the color *property* green.

12. Furthermore, as far as assertoric as opposed to apodictic judgment is concerned, self-evidence shows up only in inner perception, and inner perception produces only *positive* judgments (you cannot inner-perceive what is not taking place in your mind). Accordingly, self-evidence is not in the cards for *any* assertoric negative judgment! (Thanks to Géraldine Carranante for pointing this out to me.)

13. Less dramatically, one might suggest appealing to logical as opposed to nomic counter-factuals, claiming that even though it is nomically impossible for us to judge on the existence of ducks with self-evidence, it *is* logically possible (this seems to be suggested by Bacigalupo 2015: 56–7). Recall from Chap. 1, however, that, according to Brentano, the only reason inner perception is self-evident is that there is a constitutive connection between the perceiving and the perceived. If so, the laws of nature have little to do with the possibility of self-evident a posteriori belief. What makes that possible is rather a metaphysical relation between belief and believed in certain cases. For us to have self-evident beliefs in ducks, then, the same metaphysical relation would have to hold. That is, we would have to undergo perceptual experiences of which ducks are merely distinguishable parts. Setting aside phenomenal externalism (e.g., Dretske 1996), which is very contrary to the spirit of Brentano's philosophy of mind, it is an open question whether it is *logically* possible for us to have ducks as constituents of our conscious states.

14. Brentano's foundationalism is not explicitly billed as foundationalism about specifically existential knowledge, but since for Brentano all judgment is existential and knowledge is a kind of judgment, it follows that for him all knowledge is existential anyway.

15. Perhaps more accurately: someone could understand the notion of judgment as the notion of a mental state which is either a belief-in (acceptance) or a disbelief-in (rejection). But the notions of belief-in and disbelief-in can be understood only thanks to 'assisted revelation.'

16. It is not immediately clear to me whether it also fails to support *salva veritate* substitution. Consider the following inference: it is appropriate to disbelieve in Shrek; Shrek = Jimmy's favorite animated character; therefore, it is appropriate to disbelieve in Jimmy's favorite animated character. At first glance, this seems like a valid inference. Certainly its 'positive' counterpart is. Thus, the following inference seems valid: it is appropriate to believe in Phosphorus; Phosphorus = Hesperus; therefore, it is appropriate to believe in Hesperus. It remains that, at least in the 'negative' case, existential generalizations is clearly failed.

17. Note that, interestingly, 'appropriate to *believe* in' is extensional, and certainly does support existential generalization. From 'It is appropriate to believe in Santa Claus' it seems intuitively permissible to infer 'There is an *x*, such that it is appropriate to believe in *x*.'

18. Relatedly, 'It is fitting to believe in Messi' has a close neighbor which is *primarily* about Messi, namely, 'Messi is a fitting object of belief-in.' It would probably be unwise, though, to construe 'Messi exists' as meaning the same as 'Messi is a fitting object of belief-in.' For then 'Shrek does not exist' would have to mean the same as 'Shrek is a fitting object of disbelief-in,' which seems to quantify over Shrek, thus yielding again the results entrained by the first-order substantive view that we tried to avoid.

19. Similar remarks apply to 'Alexander's Dictum': to be is to be causally efficacious (Kim 1992). This principle has allowed progress in particular in the ontology of properties, but has been invoked (sometimes under the name 'the eleatic principle') also in discussions of individuals, events, and so on.

20. If belief-in reduces to existential belief-that, then saying that *x* exists iff it is fitting to believe in *x* just means that *x* exists iff it is fitting to believe in the existence of *x*, which seems to appeal to the notion of existence in elucidating that very notion.

21. If we use, for the sake of convenience, the eternalist's 'exists,' we may say that first presents-as-presently-nonexistent a dinosaur, whereas the second presents-as-pastly-existent a

dinosaur. Of course, Brentano would reject this way of describing the attitudinal properties in question, since he thinks that 'pastly-existent' is nonsense.

22. For comments on previous drafts, I am grateful to David Chalmers, Anna Giustina, Vincent Grandjean, Jonathan Schaffer, Jack Spencer, Amie Thomasson, and Alberto Voltolini. I have also benefited from presenting this paper at École Normale Supérieure, the Jean Nicod Institute, the University of Rennes-1, the University of Liège, and LOGOS in Barcelona. I would like to thank audiences there, in particular Géraldine Carranante, Samuele Chilovi, Arnaud Dewalque, Filipe Drapeau-Vieira-Contim, Manuel García-Carpintero, Baptiste Le Bihan, Valentin Lewandowski, Mikaël Quesseveur, Sven Rosenkranz, Denis Seron, and Mark Textor. Some of the material in this chapter overlaps with my article 'How to Speak of Existence,' published by Brill in a collection entitled *Themes from Ontology, Mind, and Logic: Essays in Honor of Peter Simons*; I am grateful to the publisher for allowing me to reuse this material.

6

Ontology
The Existents

As we have seen, Brentano's formal answer to the question 'What is there?' is simply: that which it is fitting to believe in. But in what *is* it fitting to believe? Brentano's considered answer to *that* question is decidedly nominalist, accepting only concrete particulars, such as Socrates, Beyoncé, and the Eiffel Tower in his ontology. However, Brentano's specific version of nominalism is very different from versions familiar from current-day debates, and involves also very unusual concrete particulars, such as wise-Socrates, famous-Beyoncé, and tall-Eiffel-Tower. The purpose of this chapter is to try to make the contemporary reader see what kind of ontology Brentano had in mind and what drew him to it. I will not quite *defend* Brentano's ontology, but I will argue that it is considerably more attractive than may initially appear.

1. Introduction: Reism and Nominalism

At least starting September 1904, Brentano maintained that 'there is nothing other than things (*Reales*)' (Brentano 1930: 79 [68]), where 'things' is supposed to exclude propositions, states of affairs, abstracta, possibilia, ficta, merely intentional objects, and more.[1] Brentano scholars refer to this ontological theory as *reism* ('thingism'). The term was coined by Brentano's *Enkelschüler* ('grand-student') Tadeusz Kotarbiński, who retroactively applied it to Brentano (Kotarbiński 1966).[2]

One might wonder whether 'reism' is just an odd name for what we know today as nominalism (see Bergman 1966: 366). To some extent, it is. But there is also a good reason to preserve the name. The term 'nominalism' is commonly used in two relatively independent areas of philosophy (Rodriguez-Pereyra 2011). It is used in the philosophy-of-mathematics literature to designate the rejection of abstract objects such as numbers. In the literature on the metaphysics of properties, meanwhile, it is used to designate the rejection of universals. We should therefore distinguish three views that go by 'nominalism': rejecting abstracta, rejecting universals, and rejecting both.

A nice way to appreciate this is through Donald Williams' (1953) scheme for a four-way classification of putative entities. The scheme is the product of two crosscutting distinctions: between particulars and universals and between concreta and abstracta. These yield a matrix of four ontological categories: concrete particulars, abstract universals, abstract particulars, and concrete universals (see Table 6.1). Concrete

Table 6.1. Williams' categorization

	Concrete	Abstract
Particular	Kant	Kant's-being-wise
Universal	Kant-ness	wisdom

particulars are unrepeatable individual objects such as Beyoncé and my laptop. Abstract universals are entities that can be wholly present in more than one place at one time, notably properties such as fame and grayness. Abstract particulars are entities such as individual events, states of affairs, and property-instances (e.g., Beyoncé's-fame and my-laptop's-being-gray) – unrepeatable entities that tend to cohabit in large droves. Finally, concrete universals are haecceities or 'individual essences,' for example Beyoncé-ness.

How to draw the concrete/abstract and particular/universal distinctions in a principled but extensionally adequate manner is a controversial matter we need not resolve here. What matters for our purposes is that Williams' fourfold categorization allows us to divide nominalistic ontologies into three types. The first is *anti-universals nominalism*:

(N₁) There are only particulars (concrete and abstract).

The second *anti-abstracta nominalism*:

(N₂) There are only concreta (particular and universal).

Finally, we may call *strict nominalism* the view that frowns on both universals and abstracta:

(N₃) There are only concrete particulars.

Brentano's term 'thing' is intended to capture Williams' concrete particulars. His is thus a *strict* nominalism.

Barry Smith (2006: §14) has argued that Brentano's notion of a thing is actually a completely formal one, intended to cover anything that can be the object of a presentation. If this is right, then in claiming that 'there is nothing other than things,' Brentano is not advocating nominalism at all. However, although Brentano does stress that only things can be objects of presentation, he takes this to be a substantive rather than definitional claim, something that requires argument and does not simply fall out of the meaning of words.[3] More importantly, even where Brentano takes the concept of a *Reales* to be the most generic concept, as in the following 1905 fragment, he also adds that its extension is exhausted by individuals:

Everything that is is a *Reales*, or – what comes to the same – an entity (*Wesen*)...Here we have the most general/generic (*allgemeinste*) concept. Yet to it correspond only individual entities (*Einzelwesen*). (Brentano 1930: 82 [72])

It is a substantive claim, it would seem, that all *Wesen* are *Einzelwesen*. Thus the multitude of terms used by Brentano with slightly different inflections certainly creates confusion; but there is no doubt that he was a strict nominalist in the substantive sense. We can see this very clearly by considering his remarks on the three other categories of putative entity in Williams' fourfold division.

Brentano's distaste for abstract universals is evident already in a 1901 letter to Marty:

> In the things (*Dingen*) nothing is universal. The so-called universal, as such, is only in the thinker...I know full well that [this] is far-reaching, for now all abstracta join the class of delusions/phantasms (*Wahngebilde*).   (Brentano 1930: 74 [64])

As for abstract particulars, Brentano discusses mostly states of affairs, which he finds multiply problematic (1930: 92 [82–3], 122–5 [108–10] *inter alia* – see §4 for details) and accordingly rejects:

> ...we should always paraphrase (*substituieren*) a statement accepting something as a state of affairs (*Tatsache*) into an equivalent statement in which a thing (*Ding*) in the proper (*eigentlich*) sense is accepted or rejected.   (Brentano 1917b: 234–5 [337])[4]

Meanwhile, he dismisses tropes, or particularized properties, as 'curious intermediates (*Mitteldinge*) between the absurd universals and the real individuals' (Brentano 1933: 60 [52]). It is true that he sometimes discusses 'individual accidents,' which he does accept in his ontology, but as we will see in §3, these are *not* tropes, but rather a special kind of concrete particulars. As for concrete universals, Brentano virtually never discusses them. Still, in one undated dictation on the concept of substance, he speaks of 'the wholly imaginary fiction of an haecceity' (Brentano 1933: 147 [112]). Clearly, then, in claiming that 'there is nothing other than things,' Brentano restricts his ontology to concrete particulars.

As we will see, Brentano's version of strict nominalism is thoroughly heterodox. Yet his case for it is driven by remarkably modern considerations. Earlier commentators have often pinned Brentano's case for his reism on a single argument, to do with the univocality of 'something' in such statements as 'S thinks of something' – an argument that has been dismissed as inconclusive (Woleński 1994, 2012) and even 'extraordinarily bad' (Simons 2006: 89). However, this 'argument' merely makes a move at a relatively advanced stage of the dialectic.[5] To properly understand the source of Brentano's attraction to reism, we must start from much more basic considerations pertaining to the ontological import of simple declarative sentences.

2. Nominalism, Truthmakers, and Paraphrase

A traditional and rather commonsense ontology admits not only things (in the sense of concrete particulars), but also (i) properties and (ii) states of affairs comprising things and properties. Such an ontology is straightforwardly suggested by our language and thought. This can be appreciated through the demand for *truthmakers*. Consider the following truth:

(T$_1$)   Beyoncé is famous.

Since T_1 is true, something in the world must *make* it true; it must have a truth*maker*. The truthmaker, it is natural to suppose, is the *state of affairs* of Beyoncé being famous. This state of affairs is a structured entity, involving as constituents a particular thing, Beyoncé, and a property, fame, connected in a specially intimate way ('instantiation' or 'exemplification'). Although intimately connected in this state of affairs, the two constituents can come apart and combine with other entities to compose different states of affairs. Consider the following truth:

(T_2)   Beyoncé is two-legged.

Its truthmaker appears to be the state of affairs comprised of the particular Beyoncé and the property of two-leggedness (intimately connected). It is the same Beyoncé from the truthmaker of T_1 but intimately connected to a different property. Or consider the following truth:

(T_3)   Chalmers is famous.

Here the truthmaker appears to be the state of affairs comprised of Chalmers and fame, again intimately connected. Thus the selfsame fame appears to be a constituent of two different states of affairs. It is in this sense a universal. Following Armstrong (1978), most contemporary ontologists would prefer theorizing it as an Aristotelian *in re* universal rather than a Platonic *ante rem* universal, but still as a universal.[6]

This kind of ontology, admitting not only particular things but also (*in re*) universals and states of affairs, has become quite popular over the past three decades. Truthmaker considerations have been essential in the case for it (see Armstrong 1997, 2004). Thus strict nominalism has been strongly undermined by what we may call the *truthmaker challenge*: the challenge of identifying truthmakers featuring concrete particulars exclusively for such truths as T_1–T_3.

What strategies are available to the strict nominalist in trying to meet the truthmaker challenge? In the modern literature, two broad strategies can be discerned; we may call them *ostrich nominalism* and *paraphrase nominalism*.

According to ostrich nominalism (Devitt 1980), in a standard subject-predicate sentence only the subject term is ontologically committing; predicates are not. (This is supposed to fall directly out of Quine's quantificational criterion of ontological commitment.[7]) Consequently, the truth of T_1 and T_2 does not require positing anything beyond Beyoncé, and the truth of T_3 anything beyond Chalmers. There is no need to posit further entities, such as fame, which would be shared by Beyoncé and Chalmers (nor states of affairs that have these further entities as constituents).

It is not immediately clear how the ostrich nominalist proposes to address the truthmaker challenge. She might claim either (a) that truths such as T_1 do not *require* truthmakers, or (b) that they have concrete particulars such as Beyoncé as truthmakers. The problem is that both are highly implausible.

Consider first (a). It has sometimes been claimed that certain special truths – notably negative existentials – require no truthmakers. For example, 'There are no dragons' is true but nothing *makes* it true.[8] It is questionable whether this is ultimately acceptable. It would be much harder, in any case, to accept that such simple positive truths as T_1–T_3 have no truthmakers. For that would mean that the truth of even the simplest positive claims is inexplicable, brute, and groundless. On this view, we are to smile on T_1 and frown on ~T_1, but there is no *reason why*; some sequences of symbols are true and some are false, and nothing explains why the ones are favored and the other disfavored. This is hard to believe.

Consider next (b), the view that T_1 is made true by Beyoncé herself. This is triply problematic. First, it is unclear why Beyoncé herself, independently of her properties, would make true 'Beyoncé is famous' rather than 'Beyoncé is unfamous'; the subject term is the same in both sentences, after all. Secondly, when presented with a truth-maker, one expects to be able to infer a truth. Presented with rain, I can infer that 'It rains' is true. Likewise, when presented with Beyoncé, I can infer that 'Beyoncé exists' is true. However, I *cannot* infer that 'Beyoncé is famous' is true. Thirdly, (b) has the unto-ward consequence that T_1, T_2, and all other Beyoncé truths have the same truthmaker.

Let me expand somewhat on this last problem. It has sometimes been held that different truths can have the same truthmaker, in particular when one is more funda-mental than the other. For example, 'Beyoncé is famous' and 'Beyoncé is famous or eight-foot-tall' are both made true by Beyoncé's being famous; 'Beyoncé is a homo sapiens' and 'Beyoncé is a mammal' are both made true by Beyoncé being a homo sapi-ens; and so on. Arguably, however, at the fundamental level each atomic truth should have its own distinct truthmaker.[9] Consider three truths about Tony the lepton: 'Tony has mass m,' 'Tony has electric charge C,' and 'Tony exists.' It is implausible to hold that all three have the same truthmaker. After all, they say different things about the world, so we should expect different aspects of the world to make them true. One way to think of this is in terms of the connection between a statement's truthmaker and its truth-conditional content. To a first approximation, and at least as restricted to fundamental truths, one would expect the following connection: if entity E is the truthmaker of (true) statement T, then T's truth-condition is the condition that E exist. Insofar as T's content or meaning is captured by its truth-condition, then, T's content is given by the condition that E exist. Likewise, at least as restricted to atomic fundamental truths without co-referential terms, when T_1 and T_2 have *different* contents, they have different truth-conditions. That is, there are different entities E_1 and E_2, such that E_1's existence is T_1's truth-condition and E_2's existence is T_2's truth-condition. Therefore, E_1 should be T_1's truthmaker and E_2 should be T_2's. Thus we should expect T_1 and T_2 to have different truthmakers. Yet on the view under consideration, 'Tony has mass m,' 'Tony has electric charge C,' and 'Tony exists' all have the same truthmaker – Tony.

❧

Most nominalists have adopted a more flexible strategy with respect to truthmakers, whereby truths such as T_1 are *paraphrased* into statements whose truthmakers are manifestly comprised entirely of concrete particulars. Perhaps the best-known version of this is *class nominalism* (see Lewis 1983). Call the class of all famous things 'Jimmy.' Then T_1 can be paraphrased into:

(P$_1$)   Beyoncé is a member of Jimmy.

What this means is that T_1's truthmaker consists in Beyoncé's membership in the set of all famous concrete particulars.[10] Another version of this strategy is *mereological nominalism* (Quine 1950). Call the mereological fusion of all famous concrete particulars 'Johnny.' Then T_1 can be paraphrased into:

(P$_2$)   Beyoncé is a part of Johnny.

A third version is *resemblance nominalism* (Rodriguez-Pereyra 2002). Consider Chalmers, Obama, the Eiffel Tower, and every other famous concrete particular. According to this view, the truthmaker of T_1 is just Beyoncé's resemblance to all these things. That is, T_1 can be paraphrased into:

(P$_3$)   Beyoncé resembles Chalmers, Obama, the Eiffel Tower, ...

The full sentence here would have to be closed with the complete list of metaphysical celebrities. The basic idea is to invert the intuitive direction of constitution between Beyoncé's fame and her resemblance to other famous things: it is not that she resembles them because she too is famous, but rather she is famous precisely insofar as she resembles them.

Each of these paraphrases faces its own special difficulties, but there is also one (arguably insurmountable) difficulty they all share. This is that they fail to deliver truthmakers that genuinely do away with universals and abstracta. In particular, there is always a *relation* that figures in their truthmakers. Thus, P$_1$ invokes not only Beyoncé and Jimmy, but also a membership relation between them;[11] P$_2$ invokes not only Beyoncé and Johnny, but also a parthood relation between them;[12] P$_3$ invokes not only all famous things, but also a resemblance relation among them. On the face of it, these relations would appear to be universals, fully present in different places at the same time. For example, the membership relation holds not only between Beyoncé and Jimmy, but also between Chalmers and Jimmy, Obama and Jimmy, and so on. Similarly for the parthood relation. As for the resemblance relation, it holds not only among all famous things, but also among all two-legged things, all long-haired things, and so on.

The nominalist has some moves available for handling these relations, but they are all unsatisfying. One move is to go struthious with respect to just the one relation she needs; but it is unclear why it is so much better to be struthious with respect to just one apparent universal than with respect to many. Another option is to recursively apply the same paraphrase strategy to the relevant relation, for example reconstrue the membership relation as the set of all ordered pairs whose first item is a member of the second; but this would appear to involve infinite regress, without the explanation ever bottoming out. There may be other moves, but it is hard to imagine that any might be very plausible.

The upshot is that nominalism has a real problem with such positive atomic truths as T_1 and T_2. It would be nice if we could have different truthmakers for these two truths, but ones that involved no illicit relations. This is where Brentano's work becomes interesting: the combination of his reism and his theory of judgment, discussed in Chap. 4, paves the way to a fourth and genuinely relation-free paraphrase strategy.

3. Brentano's Reism: The Coincidence Model

In this section, I present Brentano's reism as though it were a response to the truth-maker challenge. I start with the ingenious paraphrase strategy that Brentano's theory of judgment allows him to field, which meets the truthmaker challenge but admittedly involves several bizarre-sounding claims (§3.1). I then present a model that makes sense of Brentano's reism (§3.2) and show how the model illuminates and motivates Brentano's bizarre-sounding claims (§3.3). The upshot is that the nominalist has in her arsenal an all-things-considered plausible view that seems to overcome the truth-maker challenge. (I will consider objections in §4.)

3.1. Brentano's reistic paraphrases

Sentences such as T_1 lend themselves to state-of-affairs truthmakers mainly because of their subject-predicate structure: it is natural to think that the subject term refers to a concrete particular, the predicate term to a universal, and the copula to the intimate connection between them. As we have seen in Chap. 4, however, for Brentano this subject-predicate structure is an accident of public language. Ultimately, such indicatives derive their meaning from the judgments they express, and those do *not* have a subject-predicate structure. They do not involve predication at all, and are in fact objectual rather than propositional attitudes. Indeed, as we have seen in Chap. 4, a sentence such as 'Beyoncé is famous' simply expresses a belief in a famous Beyoncé. That is, T_1 should be paraphrased into:

(P$_4$)   There is a famous-Beyoncé.

Some other renderings may be more expressive: 'There is a famous Beyoncé-thing,' 'There is a famous Beyoncésque concrete particular,' and so on. But the point is that P_4 seems to simply assert the existence of a certain individual, though a somewhat strange one (more on that momentarily). Importantly, P_4 offers an alternative paraphrase strategy to the standard modern nominalist paraphrases P_1–P_3. And the strategy generalizes: given that for Brentano *every* categorical is paraphraseable into an existential, a paraphrase of P_4's form is available for *every* indicative with a subject-predicate surface structure.

Now, Brentano himself would never state his ontological project in terms of providing truthmakers for such truths. As we saw in Chap. 5, for Brentano truth is a matter of correctness and correctness a matter of actual or counterfactual self-evidence. So to the question 'What makes truth T true?,' his answer will be 'The self-evidence that attaches, or would attach, to the judgment expressed by T.' At the same time, there is a sense in which Brentano thinks that a certain ontology can be read off from the statements we assent to, so these statements must be *ontologically responsible*. This is the only way to make sense of the considerable efforts he puts into paraphrasing so many kinds of statement we unreflectively assent to in everyday life. Indeed, this is why Brentano insists on paraphrasing 'Beyoncé is famous' into 'famous-Beyoncé is' – he is worried that the former in some way commits to an ontology of entities corresponding to predicates. So although Brentano would not put his project in terms of truthmaking, the underlying ontological anxiety motivating his project is very similar to that fueling standard truthmaker nominalism. In what follows, then, I will speak freely as though Brentano addresses himself to the truthmaker challenge – even though, strictly speaking, he does not.

Brentano's approach to the challenge, then, is to claim that the truthmakers of our judgments are always individual objects, namely, the putative individual objects that the relevant beliefs are beliefs *in*. What makes a belief in famous-Beyoncé true, or correct, is that which this belief-in is about – the individual famous-Beyoncé. In virtue of being the truth/correctness-maker of this belief-in, famous-Beyoncé is also the truthmaker of T_1. So on Brentano's view, there is a certain individual, famous-Beyoncé, that makes true 'Beyoncé is famous.'

The advantages of Brentano's paraphrase should be evident. Clearly, no illicit relation even *appears* to be involved. No membership, parthood, or resemblance is invoked – just an unusual concrete particular called famous-Beyoncé! Furthermore, it is clear why this concrete particular makes true T_1 and not $\sim T_1$. The latter would be made true, if anything, by *un*famous-Beyoncé. Moreover, T_1's is a different truthmaker from T_2's: the latter's is two-legged-Beyoncé, which is a concrete particular numerically distinct from both Beyoncé and famous-Beyoncé (more on this in §3.2). Thus the problems attending modern forms of paraphrase nominalism are entirely avoided by Brentano's reistic paraphrase.

The question that arises immediately is this: What kind of entity is famous-Beyoncé, and how is it related to Beyoncé (and to two-legged-Beyoncé)? On this, Brentano says some very strange things indeed. They may be summarized through two 'surprising' claims:

(C_1)   Beyoncé is a substance whereas famous-Beyoncé is an accident, though both are concrete particulars.

(C_2)   Beyoncé is a proper part of famous-Beyoncé, though an unsupplemented proper part.

The traditional view is that Beyoncé is a substance and fame is one of her accidents. Brentano is happy to preserve the substance/accident terminology, but recasts the accident as famous-Beyoncé, an individual on a par with Beyoncé. In a 1908 essay, he writes:

Plato took the concept of thing (*Ding*) to be unitary, surely correctly, whereas Aristotle was misled by his view of accidents to reject the unity of the concept of thing. An accident, he said, is not a thing in the same sense as a substance…For our part, we designate accident and substance a thing in the same sense…   (Brentano 1933: 53–5 [48])

Given that accidents are individuals just like substances, Brentano plumps for a peculiar mereological relation between them:

Every accident contains its substance as a part, but does not add to it a second part, something entirely new.   (Brentano 1933: 11 [19])

Thus every connection between a substance and an accident is a counterexample to the axiom of supplementation of Classical Mereology. Recall from Chap. 1 that according to that axiom, if *x* is a proper part of *y*, then there is a *z*, such that (i) *z* does not overlap *x* and (ii) *z* is a proper part of *y*. Since the table-leg is a proper part of the table, the table must have some other, distinct proper part that supplements the table-leg and 'makes whole' the table. The table itself, however, is for Brentano a proper part of the brown-table, and yet there is no brownness that supplements the table and makes the brown-table whole. Or so Brentano claims. What to make of all this?

3.2. *The coincidence model*

As noted, on Brentano's view famous-Beyoncé is a thing in the very same sense in which Beyoncé is a thing. This means that famous-Beyoncé is a *fully determinate concrete particular*, one that has two legs, long curly hair, is a singer, is from Houston, has a daughter named Blue Ivy, and so on.

Every existent (*Seiendes*) is fully determinate, but we think a thing in multiple ways, without thinking the totality of its determinations.   (Brentano 1933: 15 [22])

Since an accident such as famous-Beyoncé is an existent, in itself it is as fully determinate as a substance such as Beyoncé; indeterminacy attaches only to the way we think of famous-Beyoncé, not to famous-Beyoncé herself. (Note that famous-Beyoncé is a woman, just like Beyoncé!) Both Beyoncé and famous-Beyoncé extend in all three spatial dimensions. In that respect and others, famous-Beyoncé is very unlike a trope or abstract particular such as Beyoncé's-fame. You can bump into famous-Beyoncé, but not into Beyoncé's-fame; the former has two legs and long hair, the latter is legless and hairless; and so on.

Indeed, speaking carelessly for the sake of exposition, we might say that *famous-Beyoncé has all the same properties as Beyoncé*. This is doubly careless. First, strictly speaking there are no properties according to the reist, since there are only things. So any claim about properties must be understood metaphorically or fictionalistically, or as a ladder to be thrown away after its use. (Perhaps talk of 'determinations' can be understood as an attempt to express similar ideas without mentioning properties.) Secondly, even within the property fiction, it would be inaccurate to say that Beyoncé and famous-Beyoncé share *all* their properties. Rather, Beyoncé and famous-Beyoncé share all their *non-modal* and *non-temporal* properties, but differ in their modal and temporal properties. Thus, Beyoncé has the property of being *possibly-unfamous*, whereas famous-Beyoncé does not. Likewise, Beyoncé has the property of existing in 1986, whereas famous-Beyoncé does not. But for any non-modal, non-temporal property F, Beyoncé has it iff famous-Beyoncé does. (The reason to except modal and temporal properties is that they interact with the identity and existence conditions of their bearers in ways that other properties generally do not. We can see this from the way identity talk often leads to talk of identity *across worlds* and *across times*.)

Suppose for the sake of exposition that the essential properties (or determinations) of people are their biological origins (Kripke 1972). What, on this view, are Beyoncé's essential properties? Call the relevant sperm Mathew and the relevant egg Tina. Then Beyoncé's only essential properties are (i) originating-from-Mathew and (ii) originating-from-Tina. Beyoncé could not fail to have these properties without failing to be altogether. Now, Beyoncé *also* has the property of being famous, but she has it *accidentally*: she could become utterly unknown without ceasing to exist. On the model I want to propose, this is the crucial difference between Beyoncé and famous-Beyoncé in Brentano's ontology. Unlike Beyoncé, famous-Beyoncé could not cease to be famous without ceasing altogether. So famous-Beyoncé has *three* essential properties: (i) originating-from-Mathew, (ii) originating-from-Tina, and (iii) being famous.

Obviously, it may well be that, *pace* Kripke, biological origins are not essential to human beings. Perhaps some other (potentially conjunctive) property F is, such that F determines Beyoncé's identity and persistence conditions. We would then say that, on Brentano's view (when expressed using the property fiction), Beyoncé's essential property is being F whereas famous-Beyoncé's essential properties are (i) being F and (ii) being famous. Likewise, two-legged-Beyoncé's essential properties are (i) being F and (ii) being two-legged; famous-two-legged-Beyoncé's essential properties are (i) being F, (ii) being famous, and (iii) being two-legged; and so on. I will continue to conduct the discussion assuming the essentiality of origins, but do so merely for ease of exposition. We will shed this assumption in §3.3.

On this way of understanding the relation between Beyoncé and famous-Beyoncé, the two are simply *coincident objects*, somewhat as the statue and the clay are often claimed to be.[13] A minority of philosophers holds that the statue and the lump of clay are numerically identical; this is 'one-thingism.' But most philosophers are 'two-thingists,' holding that the statue and the clay happen to be collocated but are nonetheless distinct entities. Typically, this is motivated precisely by their differences in modal (or temporal) properties: the statue could not (or will not) survive shuttering to pieces, but the clay could (or will) (see Baker 1997). My suggestion is that we understand Brentano's theory of substance and accident on the model of the statue and the clay. Call this the *coincidence model*. In a way, Brentano's reism can be seen as a sort of 'many-thingism' that posits a great multitude of coinciding concrete particulars. It recognizes not only the statue and the clay, but also the shapely-statue, the beige-statue, the hard-clay, and so on. Still speaking metaphorically, or within the property fiction, we may say that these many things coincide and have the same non-modal and non-temporal properties, but differ in their modal and temporal ones.

∝⃛

To repeat, this talk of difference in properties is merely instrumental in the statement of the coincidence model. Strictly speaking, on this view there are no properties. Accordingly, Beyoncé and famous-Beyoncé are simply brutely numerically different things. Ultimately, there is nothing *in virtue of which* they are different, nothing that *accounts for* their difference. More generally, Brentano takes the individuation of things as an inexplicable fundamental: things are just different, nothing *makes* them different.

This may seem initially puzzling, but of course every ontology must take *something* as fundamental. For *each* candidate 'something,' we naturally prefer some metaphysical explanation over fundamentalism. Yet we cannot give a metaphysical explanation for *all* of them. Somewhere in our ontology we must accept inexplicable fundamentals. Brentano's is the individuation of concrete particulars – they are primitively different, without anything *making* them different.

Upon reflection, the identity and difference of concrete particulars is a perfectly reasonable place to go fundamentalist. For it may well be independently plausible. It is commonly thought that *properties* are not powerful enough to individuate particulars: there could be a world with relativistic space in which there is nothing but two qualitatively indistinguishable spheres floating about (Black 1952). This has motivated some to posit *haecceities* to account for the individuation of particulars. But it is hard to see what this buys us. The idea is that John and Mary are different because (i) John's-haecceity and Mary's-haecceity are different and (ii) the difference between John's-haecceity and Mary's-haecceity is brute and inexplicable. But how is saying that the difference between John's-haecceity and Mary's-haecceity is brute and inexplicable better than saying that the difference between John and Mary is brute and inexplicable? Brute individuation of haecceities is no less brutal than brute individuation of concrete particulars. And given that we have no independent handle on what haecceities actually *are*, we might as well go fundamentalist at the level of concrete particulars. (Perhaps this is why Brentano dismissed haecceities, as we have seen, as 'wholly imaginary fictions.') Thus brute individuation of concrete particulars may well be independently motivated (see also Hazlett 2010).[14]

It might be objected that the analogy with the statue/clay case is too weak to render intelligible the present interpretation of Brentano's reism. In the statue/clay case, there is an asymmetry between the two things, insofar as the clay *constitutes* the statue (but the statue does not constitute the clay). Coincidence is a symmetric relation, observes the objector, but we can make sense of it only in conjunction with constitution, which is asymmetric. There are no cases of coincidence without constitution. In contrast, Brentano's reism involves many coincident things with no asymmetric relation between them: famous-Beyoncé, two-legged-Beyoncé, long-haired-Beyoncé, etc. are all on a par, with no constitution relations obtaining between them.

My response is twofold. First, coincidence without constitution is nowise *excluded* by the statue/clay case. Suppose Sculp and Tor are sculptors commissioned by City Hall to collaborate on a new clay statue for the city square. Through a misunderstanding, Sculp is under the impression that they are to sculpt a duck, while Tor is under the impression that they are to sculpt a rabbit. Improbably, the misunderstanding is never discovered and their collaboration results in a duck-rabbit contraption. On the reasonable assumption that sculpture individuation is sensitive to sculptor intentions, it is not implausible to hold that the city square ends up hosting *three* coincident objects: the clay, the duck sculpture, and the rabbit sculpture. Although the clay asymmetrically constitutes both the duck sculpture and the rabbit sculpture, the coincidence relation between the two sculptures is perfectly symmetric. At the very least, then, we can use the relationship between Sculp's and Tor's sculptures as a model for famous-Beyoncé and two-legged-Beyoncé.

Admittedly, in this case both sculptures individually depend asymmetrically on a third item, in that neither could exist without the clay but the clay could exist without either. But we find this feature in Brentano's reism as well: famous-Beyoncé, two-legged-Beyoncé, long-haired-Beyoncé, and the like all depend asymmetrically on Beyoncé: none of the former could exist without the latter but the latter could exist without any of the former. It is for this reason, in fact, that Brentano considers Beyoncé a *substance* and famous-Beyoncé, two-legged-Beyoncé, and long-haired-Beyoncé mere *accidents*.

3.3. The coincidence model and Brentano's theory of substance and accident

Recall (C_1): Beyoncé is a substance whereas famous-Beyoncé is an accident, though both are concrete particulars. The coincidence model makes sense of this surprising claim. The traditional notion of a substance is that of an entity enjoying independent existence; an accident is an entity whose existence depends on another's. To say that famous-Beyoncé is an accident of Beyoncé whereas Beyoncé herself is a substance, then, is to say that famous-Beyoncé's existence depends on Beyoncé's whereas Beyoncé's existence does not depend on anything else's. The first part of this falls out of the coincidence model straightforwardly. In the model, Beyoncé and famous-Beyoncé have all the same (non-modal, non-temporal) properties, but different subsets of these are essential. For Beyoncé, the essential subset is:

S_2: {originating-from-Mathew, originating-from-Tina}.

For famous-Beyoncé, it is:

S_3: {originating-from-Mathew, originating-from-Tina, being famous}.

Note that every member of S_2 is also a member of S_3, whereas not every member of S_3 is a member of S_2. It follows that there is a possible circumstance in which all members of S_2 are co-instantiated but not all members of S_3 are, namely, the circumstance in which Beyoncé exists but is not famous; but there is no possible circumstance in which all members of S_3 are co-instantiated but not all members of S_2 are. The instantiation of all

S_2's members is thus a *precondition* for the instantiation of all S_3's members (but not vice versa). Within the coincidence model, this means that Beyoncé's existence is a precondition for famous-Beyoncé's (but not vice versa). That is, famous-Beyoncé's existence depends asymmetrically on Beyoncé's. So the former is an accident of the latter. More generally, we may say that for any concrete particulars x and y, x is an *accident of y* iff the set of y's essential properties is a proper subset of the set of x's essential properties.[15] We may then say that x is a *substance* iff there is no y such that x is an accident of y.

Since S_3 is not a proper subset of S_2, Beyoncé is not an accident of famous-Beyoncé. But this does not yet guarantee Beyoncé the status of a substance. For Beyoncé to be a substance, there must be no *other* thing Beyoncé is an accident of. Now, one might claim that there clearly does exist proper subsets of S_2, for example:

S_1:   {originating-from-Mathew}.

This appears to imply that Beyoncé, whose essential subset of properties is S_2, is an accident of the thing whose essential subset is S_1 – call it 'Mathew-originating-Beyoncé.' If Beyoncé is an accident of Mathew-originating-Beyoncé, then Beyoncé is not a substance after all. Intuitively, this is an uncomfortable consequence: Beyoncé is the substance and Mathew-originating-Beyoncé the accident.

However, this apparent problem is an artifact of imposing on Brentano a doctrine not his, namely the essentiality of origins. Brentano's own view, as we saw above, is that things individuate *brutely* – not in virtue of their origins and not in virtue of anything else. There are no specific *characteristics* in virtue of which Beyoncé is the thing she is; she just is what she is and that is all there is to it. On this view, there is a difference between the truthmakers of the following two truths:

(T$_4$)   Beyoncé originates from Mathew and Tina.
(T$_5$)   Beyoncé exists.

Only the truthmaker of T$_5$ is Beyoncé herself. If anything, a better approximation of Brentano's view (still within the property fiction) would cite in the essential subset of Beyoncé's properties only her individual essence (the right concrete universal):

S_0:   {Beyoncé-ness}.

Clearly, S_0 has no proper subset. Therefore, there is no thing of which Beyoncé is an accident, so Beyoncé comes out a substance. In truth, however, even S_0 cannot really be assigned to Beyoncé, since she individuates brutely, without the aid of *any* characteristics.[16]

Brentano's use the term 'accident' to denote concrete particulars might still seem odd. But if the crucial feature of accidents is that, unlike substances, they are incapable of independent existence, then it is perfectly reasonable within a reistic framework to call concrete particulars incapable of independent existence 'accidents.' Insofar as famous-Beyoncé's existence depends on other existents', then, famous-Beyoncé is an accident – despite being a concrete particular. Beyoncé is a substance not simply because she is a concrete particular, but because she is a concrete particular whose existence depends on no other's. This appears to entitle Brentano to say that there is only one substance in one place at one time, thus respecting the old *impenetrability principle*, the notion that 'no two substances can interpenetrate (*durchdringen*) spatially' (Brentano 1933: 212 [154]). There may be many concrete particulars in the same place at the same time, but only one substance in a place at a time.

୶৶

Recall next C_2: Beyoncé is a proper part of famous-Beyoncé, but an unsupplemented proper part. The first part of this makes perfect sense within the coincidence model. Suppose again that Beyoncé's essential properties are S_2 and famous-Beyoncé's are S_3. Since S_2 and S_3 as *sets* of properties, we may note that the former is a proper *subset* of the latter. But if we think of the *sums* of properties corresponding to S_2 and S_3, we can say that the former is a proper *part* of the latter. Now, since in the reistic framework there are forsooth no properties, literally we can only speak directly of the objects, saying that Beyoncé is (primitively) a proper part of famous-Beyoncé. This is what Brentano does. But the metaphor or fiction of essential properties is helpful for seeing why we should say this.

Brentano's most perplexing claim is doubtless that although Beyoncé is a *proper* part of famous-Beyoncé, famous-Beyoncé has no *other* part that 'makes whole' Beyoncé. More generally, every substance is an unsupplemented proper part of each of its accidents. This is an extremely bizarre claim, and it is natural to dismiss it as straightforwardly incoherent (Simons 2006: 92); certainly it is incoherent if we take the axiom of supplementation to be definitional of parthood. However, although Brentano could have chosen a more judicious way of putting things, the idea is not unmotivated, and the coincidence model can help us see why.

Let us revert to indulging the supposition that in Beyoncé's location, there is one thing whose essence is originating-from-Mathew&Tina and a second thing whose essence is originating-from-Mathew&Tina + being-famous. For there to be something that supplements the first thing and makes whole the second, there would have to exist, in the same location, also a thing whose essence is *just* being-famous. This would be a thing with all the same (non-modal, non-temporal) properties as Beyoncé, but whose only essential property is being famous. We may call this putative thing 'The Famous.' If The Famous existed, then it could supplement Beyoncé and make whole famous-Beyoncé. But Brentano evidently thinks there simply is no such thing as The Famous.

Why not? Brentano's argument for this is presented in this quite difficult passage from 1912 or 1913:

Suppose an atom were capable of thinking: then the thinking atom would be a whole which, if the atom ceased to think, would be reduced to one of its parts. But one could nowise say that this thinking (*Denkens*) could survive if the atom ceased to exist…If another atom were to think the same thing, it would differ from the first not only qua atom but also qua thinker (*Denkendes*), in that the second thinker would be individuated qua thinker through the individuality of the atom.   (Brentano 1933: 152 [115])

The curious focus on a thinking atom is intended to purge the thought-experiment of any distracting features: we are to imagine a partless entity – an atom in the mereological sense – engaging in the simple activity of thinking. Brentano's starting point is that this atom, Bobby, is a proper part of thinking-Bobby. For Bobby to be supplemented within thinking-Bobby, the supplementer would have to be a third object, The Thinker, such that thinking-Bobby = Bobby + The Thinker. We may represent Brentano's argument as a dilemma. Either The Thinker is a substance or it is an accident. But on the one hand, it cannot be a substance. For the thinking would not survive the destruction of Bobby. If Bobby goes out of existence, not only thinking-Bobby does, but the thinking does as well. So the thinking does not have the kind of independent existence characteristic of a substance. So The Thinker could only be an accident. If it is an accident, however, then it depends for its existence on some substance, which therefore must be a proper part of it: 'just as absolutely no whole can subsist (*bestehen*) without one of its parts, no real [accident] can exist without its substance' (Brentano 1925: 29).[17] But if The Thinker has some proper part, the same question arises again: is there something else that supplements that proper part within The Thinker? The ensuing regress of questions will bottom out, presumably, in *some* substance involved in the supplementation of Bobby within thinking-Bobby. Yet as we have seen, there can be no such further substantive part of thinking-Bobby, since all such parts cannot survive the destruction of Bobby.

The argument is difficult, but strikes me as cogent: there is simply no such substance as The Famous that might supplement Beyoncé within famous-Beyoncé. In addition, two further arguments line up on Brentano's side. First, if there were such an entity as The Famous, it would have to be something that could in principle be a famous singer one moment, a famous rock the next, and a famous concept a moment later. That is an odd entity to welcome into one's ontology. Secondly, consider that if there *were* such an entity as The Famous, it would have to reappear elsewhere in the world to make up the difference between Chalmers and famous-Chalmers, Messi and famous-Messi, and so on. At that point, however, The Famous would no longer be an irrepeatable concrete particular. It would be a recurring universal. So there could be no place for The Famous within Brentano's reistic framework.

The upshot is that since The Famous does not exist, it cannot supplement Beyoncé and 'make whole' famous-Beyoncé. Accordingly, Beyoncé is an unsupplemented proper part of famous-Beyoncé. In this way, the coincidence model helps us see how Brentano ends up with unsupplemented proper parts. His terminological choice may have been infelicitous. Chisholm, in an exemplary exercise of interpretive charity, tries to defend Brentano by suggesting that he simply 'takes the term "part" somewhat more widely than it is ordinarily taken' (Chisholm 1978: 202). Nonetheless, it might have been wiser to devise a new term for the wider relation – Chisholm himself proposes 'constituency' (Chisholm 1978: 202) – and reserve the term 'parthood' for the relation that obeys the axiom of supplementation. We might then say that in Brentano's ontology, Beyoncé is a constituent of famous-Beyoncé but (still surprisingly) famous-Beyoncé has no *additional* constituent. If Beyoncé and famous-Beyoncé are coinciding individuals which simply have (within the property fiction) different essential properties, we can see why that would be: because the additional constituent would have to have only fame as its essential property, and that, as we have seen, is multiply implausible.

4. Objections and Replies

I close the discussion of Brentano's reism by considering four objections to it: that it is unintuitive, that it is unparsimonious, that it has untoward consequences, and that it is unmotivated.

The first objection to consider is that Brentano's reism is unacceptably counterintuitive: it contravenes the intuitions that (i) it is rare to have more than one concrete particular in one place at one time and that (ii) there are entities shared among different concrete particulars – universals. However, Brentano can readily *explain away* these conflicts with intuition.

The intuitive pull of (i) is largely inherited from the impenetrability principle, the notion that there can be only one substance in one place at the same time. This principle is frequently (and, for Brentano, mistakenly) conjoined with the idea that only substances are concrete particulars – itself a philosophical dogma rather than a folk intuition. Once we reject this second idea, we see that impenetrability can be respected without commitment to (i): although there are many concrete particulars in a place at a time, only one of them is a substance. Furthermore, Brentano is not alone in feeling the need to posit such curious coincident particulars as famous-Beyoncé and two-legged-Beyoncé; he fits squarely in an Aristotelian tradition stretching from Aristotle's own discussion of the relationship between the man and the musical man (in *Physics* I.7) to Kit Fine's more recent discussion of 'qua objects' (Fine 1982) such as the man-qua-musical and Beyoncé-qua-famous.

Meanwhile, the explanation for (ii) is that although the psychological reality of judgments is such that they are all existential, public-language sentences have a subject-predicate surface grammar that misleads us into 'parsing' the world into entities that correspond to subject terms and entities that correspond to predicates (namely, universals). As noted in Chap. 4, Brentano holds that the original function of language is to facilitate communication, a task success at which need not involve accurate representation of the structure of reality (Brentano 1956: 25–6). Once we realize the real structure of *judgments*, and tailor our ontology to provide truthmakers to them rather than to public-language *sentences*, the pull to universals ought to dissipate.

It may be objected that positing so many things in Beyoncé's spacetime is not only unintuitive but also egregiously unparsimonious. There might well be infinitely many Beyoncé truths, in which case Brentano would have to posit infinitely many concrete particulars sharing Beyoncé's spacetime – a crowded ontology indeed.

However, Brentano's ontology cannot be worse off here than the currently popular 'Armstrongian' ontology discussed in §2. After all, that ontology faces just as many truths, to which it too wishes to provide truthmakers. It is just that *its* truthmakers tend to be states of affairs rather than concrete particulars. Still, they are entities/quantifia-bilia/ontoids all the same.[18]

Admittedly, Armstrong (2004: 10) makes a number of moves that allow for economy in truthmakers, mostly using his 'entailment principle': if entity E makes true p, and p entails q, then E makes true q. However, nothing prevents Brentano from adopting the entailment principle (but with E ranging over concrete particulars rather than states of affairs). He would thereby incorporate parallel economies into his reism. Just as Armstrong rejects the state of affairs of Beyoncé-being-famous-or-eight-foot-tall and lets Beyoncé-being-famous make true 'Beyoncé is famous or eight foot tall,' Brentano could reject the concrete particular famous-or-eight-foot-tall-Beyoncé and let famous-Beyoncé make true 'Beyoncé is famous or eight foot tall.'[19] In this way, Brentano would guarantee his reism will be just as parsimonious as Armstrong's ontology. The only difference, to repeat, is that it appeals to unusual concrete particulars to do a job that Armstrong assigns to states of affairs.

The objector might press that all this shows, at most, that Brentano does *no worse*, parsimony-wise, than Armstrong; it does not show that he does any *better*. If the two do equally well, and Armstrong has the advantage (such as it is) of appealing to entities whose structure reflects the structure of sentences, perhaps we should prefer his ontology after all.

In reality, Armstrong's ontology is in fact at a disadvantage relative to Brentano's. Although it posits the exact same number of *token* entities as Brentano's, in the process it invokes a *greater* number of *types* of entity. It posits not only concrete particulars, but also states of affairs, as well as such constituents of states of affairs as properties and relations. By contrast, reism posits only concrete particulars. So however it scores on token-parsimony, reism certainly outscores the Armstrongian ontology on type-parsimony. This is especially significant if, as some philosophers have argued (Lewis 1973), only type-parsimony matters in philosophy. (On this view, two ontologists can sens-ibly argue over whether there are ducks or only particles arranged duck-wise, but how many token ducks there are is the zoologist's rather than ontologist's business.[20]) But even if *both* type- and token-parsimony are relevant to the assessment of ontological theories, Brentano's fares better than Armstrong's: it wins on type-parsimony and ties on token-parsimony!

One way to curtail Brentano's advantage in the type-parsimony department is to deny that states of affairs have concrete particulars and properties/relations as con-stituents. According to Skyrms' (1981) 'factualism,' for example, states of affairs are simple, unstructured entities with no parts or constituents. Indeed, Skyrms attempts to assay individuals and properties in terms of different types of state-of-affairs collection: Beyoncé is nothing but the collection of all Beyoncé facts (Beyoncé's-being-famous, Beyoncé's-being-two-legged, etc.); fame is nothing but the collection of all fame facts

(Beyoncé's-being-famous, Chalmers'-being-famous, etc.), and so on. Such 'factualism' would *not* be at a type-parsimony disadvantage relative to reism. In a way, it parallels reism very closely but simply replaces truthmakers such as famous-Beyoncé and thinking-Bobby with truthmakers such as Beyoncé's-being-famous and Bobby's-thinking (that is, Bobby's-being-in-the-process-of-thinking).

Brentano does have an 'explosion argument' against a state-of-affairs ontology. Here it is:

> If where A is, there also were (in the full sense of the word), as something distinct from A, the being of A, as well as the being of that being of A, and so forth, the endless complication and proliferation would already be disconcerting.   (Brentano 1930: 122 [108])

Consider the truth 'The Higgs boson exists.' What is its truthmaker? For Brentano, it is the boson itself.[21] The factualist, however, would cite the state of affairs of the *Higgs-boson's-existence* as the truthmaker of 'The Higgs boson exists.' But then the following would also be a truth in need of truthmaker: 'The state of affairs of the Higgs-boson's-existence exists.' *Its* truthmaker would presumably be the state of affairs of the Higgs-boson's-existence's-existence; this would in turn underlie a new truth: 'The state of affairs of the Higgs-boson's-existence's-existence exists'; and so on ad infinitum.[22]

If there are harmful objections to Brentano's reism, then, they probably target the specifics of the theory rather than general issues of intuitiveness and parsimony. Let me now consider two objections to the effect that the theory has embarrassing consequences. Although I will argue that the first objection can be overcome, I think the second one represents a genuine problem for Brentano.

The first objection is that it is not only the individuation of concrete particulars that must be brutal in Brentano's reism; their similarity and dissimilarity will be as well. Intuitively, for instance, famous-Beyoncé resembles Beyoncé more than she does Messi. Also intuitively, there is *an explanation* of this. The standard explanation is that famous-Beyoncé shares more properties with Beyoncé than she does with Messi. This explanation is obviously unavailable to a strict nominalist like Brentano, who does not countenance properties. So it would seem Brentano must also countenance brutal resemblance in his ontology.

In truth, this problem is not special to Brentano. Any strict nominalist must provide a truthmaker for such truths as 'The Eiffel Tower resembles the Empire State Building more than it resembles the moon.' The case of 'Famous-Beyoncé resembles Beyoncé more than she does Messi' is special to Brentano's theory, but it does not involve a new and distinct difficulty. The real question, then, is how to provide a truthmaker for such resemblance truths without citing a relational universal of resemblance.

According to Rodriguez-Pereyra (2002: chap. 6), the only serious option for the nominalist is to hold that the truthmaker of such resemblance truths is simply the plurality of the individuals involved. Thus, 'The Eiffel Tower resembles the Empire

State Building more than it resembles the moon' is made true by the Eiffel Tower, the Empire State Building, and the moon – end of story. This suggestion raises many difficulties, however, not least of which the difficulty of understanding how 'The Eiffel Tower resembles the Empire State Building more than it resembles the moon' manages to say more than 'The Eiffel Tower, the Empire State Building, and the moon exist,' given that their truthmaker is one and the same.

However, it seems to me that Brentano can offer an alternative and more satisfying truthmaker for 'The Eiffel Tower resembles the Empire State Building more than it resembles the moon,' namely, that strange concrete particular we might call the resembling-the-Empire-State-building-more-than-the-moon Eiffel Tower – a concrete particular collocated with, but numerically distinct from, the Eiffel Tower. By the same token, Brentano's truthmaker for 'Famous-Beyoncé resembles Beyoncé more than she does Messi' would be resembling-Beyoncé-more-than-Messi Famous-Beyoncé. The strategy here is to deploy the paraphrase of asymmetric-relational truths proposed in Chap. 4 to 'translate' resemblance claims into existential claims about single individuals, then identify the relevant unusual individual in Brentano's ontology that makes those claims true.[23]

A different objection is that Brentano's notion of unilateral dependence cannot account for the substance/accident distinction. Recall that on Brentano's account, x is an accident of y iff x depends for its existence on y (and x is a substance if there is no y such that x depends for its existence on y). The problem is that there seem to be pairs of entities $\{E_1, E_2\}$, such that intuitively E_1 is not an accident of E_2, but E_1 does depend for its existence on E_2. Consider my old car Mia, and the following two truths about it:

(T$_5$)   Mia exists.
(T$_6$)   Mia is spatially extended.

Within Brentano's framework, T$_5$ is made true by Mia, while T$_6$ is made true by spatially-extended-Mia. These are two numerically distinct things. It is also independently plausible, now, that Mia cannot exist without extended-Mia existing: a car is incapable of disembodied, extensionless existence. To that extent, Mia's existence depends on extended-Mia's. If so, Mia is *not* a substance, since her existence depends on something else's. The same reasoning can be repeated with obviously fundamental truths, such as 'Tony the lepton exists' and 'Tony the lepton has mass.' Presumably, Tony cannot exist without massy-Tony, but intuitively Tony is the substance and massy-Tony the accident.

To my knowledge, Brentano nowhere addresses this issue. There are several options open to him, but none is entirely comfortable. One is to accept that Mia and Tony are not substances, offering the status of a substance to fewer things than expected. The cost here is that he may well end up with no substances at all, as this kind of example reproduces quite easily. A second option is to hold that, appearances to the contrary, Tony and massy-Tony are one and the same thing (as are Mia and extended-Mia). The cost here is that we end up assigning the same truthmaker to different fundamental truths, opening Brentano up to a *tu quoque* from the ostrich nominalist. A third option is to modify the account so a substance's existence is allowed to depend on another thing's existence, provided the dependence is not unilateral. Thus, since extended-Mia's existence depends on Mia's just as much as Mia's does on extended-Mia's, Mia comes out a substance after all. The cost here is that extended-Mia seems to come out a substance as well (as does massy-Tony); this is a problem insofar as it violates the impenetrability principle. A fourth option is to allow that Mia is not essentially a car, in fact could still be the very same Mia and yet be altogether an aspatial entity. The cost here is simply the admission of entities so strange. A fifth option is to simply rid reism of the substance/accident distinction and give all concrete particulars equal status. The emerging view is still strictly nominalist, though there is a sense that the resulting leaves out an important metaphysical distinction: Beyoncé and Tony certainly *seem* in some sense ontologically prior to famous-Beyoncé and massy-Tony. A final option is to decree that it is a brute fact that massy-Tony is an accident of Tony and not the other way round, just as it is a brute fact that Tony has just the mass m it does. The cost here is the brutality. That contingent facts at the fundamental level of reality are brute is understandable; but intuitively, massy-Tony is an accident of Tony in *every* possible world in which both exist, so this is not a *contingent* fundamental truth.

A completely different kind of complaint is that Brentano nowhere tells us clearly why we should *want* to be reists. Even if his reism were *the best* version of strict nominalism, what motivates strict nominalism to begin with?

According to Kraus, Brentano's basic motivation has to do with the ultimate intelligibility of putative entities. In his final footnote to Brentano's 1889 lecture on truth, Kraus writes:

> It is the principle that any conceptual investigation must ultimately go back to intuition [i.e., direct grasp] that finally led Brentano to the critique and withdrawal of the doctrine of *irrealia*.
> (Brentano 1930: 176 [154])

As we have seen in previous chapters, for Brentano appreciating the nature of a putative type of entity requires that it would either (i) be directly graspable or (ii) admit assay in terms of *something* which is directly graspable. This is a fundamental working principle throughout Brentano's philosophy, so it is not a bad hypothesis that Brentano reached his reism through application of this principle.

At the same time, it is not clear that the principle really delivers strict nominalism. Russell (1912) claimed that we have direct acquaintance with universals (see also Chudnoff 2013). Campbell (1990) argued that tropes are precisely what perceptual experience presents us with. Looking up, you see the sky's blueness, that is, the 'sky-based' individual blueness-instance. The factualist could make a similar claim, suggesting that what you directly perceive is the *sky's being blue* – and what you directly *inner*-perceive is *your experience's being as of blue*.

More importantly, it is not clear that concrete particulars are better candidates for direct grasp (or assay in terms thereof) than abstract particulars, such as tropes and facts. Consider that for Brentano, only *inner* perception enables direct grasp. But do we really inner-perceive concrete particulars? Given Brentano's subjectist account of intentionality (see Chap. 2), inner perception of immanent intentional objects is not in the cards. The only concrete particular inner perception is in a position to acquaint us with is *the self*. Now, Brentano does think that inner perception presents you with your self. But he insists that it never presents you with the naked self, so to speak. It only presents the self *as in some particular mental state*:

…when we grasp ourselves as thinker, we do not grasp our substance on its own (*für sich allein*), but rather with an accident, which in its manifold changes our substance sometimes exhibits and sometimes not.   (Brentano 1933: 155 [117])

Thus the phenomena, as Brentano himself conceives of them, seem friendlier to the notion that in inner perception we grasp directly individual facts (of the form our-substance-having-a-temporary-accident) than concrete particulars (such as our substance). It is true, of course, that ultimately Brentano takes accidents to be concrete particulars as well; but we are looking for something to *motivate* precisely this view. It is hard to see how the direct-grasp principle, by itself, could motivate a strict-nominalist ontology.

As a rival hypothesis, I would suggest that Brentano's reism is motivated simply by the fact that, once the belief-in theory of judgment is in place, it becomes *possible* to rid one's ontology of all entities but concrete particulars. For it becomes *possible* to paraphrase every truth into a statement about concrete particulars only, and *possible* to take every true judgment to require for its truth only the existence of some concrete particular. I suspect in the background is an assumption shared by many ontologists: that *if* it is possible to have a monocategorial ontology, then we should certainly go for it. That is, if we can bring ultimate unity to our ontology, by assaying all reality in terms of a single category of existent, then we should do so. From this perspective, philosophers who end up with pluricategorial ontologies do so only because they take monocategorial ontologies to be unworkable. What the belief-in theory of judgment buys us, then, is the *viability* of monocategorial ontology. More specifically, it shows how one monocategorial ontology – Brentano's – *could* provide truthmakers for all and only truths.

If this is how we think of the basic motivation for reism, then at bottom it simply has to do with a premium on parsimony (and unity). A monocategorial ontology is elusive, but is an ontological ideal: if a monocategorial ontology can be shown to be adequate to the phenomena (that is, provide truthmakers for all truths), no further justification is needed for adopting it. To the question 'What would it be fitting to believe in?,' it answers: this concrete particular, that concrete particular, and so on.

Obviously, Brentano's reism is not the only coherent monocategorial ontology. There are also class nominalism, mereological nominalism, resemblance nominalism, Skyrms' aforementioned factualism, the kind of trope theory that assays all reality in terms of tropes (Williams 1953), and more. Presumably, what Brentano thinks is that these monocategorial ontologies face independent problems that makes them *incapable* of producing a truthmaker for all and only truths. In other words, reism is the only monocategorial ontology *adequate to the phenomena.*

To my mind, this is quite a compelling motivation for reism. Even if it were not Brentano's after all, it would be a strong motivation *for us* to consider positively Brentano's ontology.[24] It is a separate question whether there might be independent liabilities accruing to reism. As we have seen, reism faces some tough decisions when it comes to the substance/accident distinction (think of Tony's dependence on massy-Tony), ones that are sure to render the view ultimately less attractive. In addition, *all* forms of strict nominalism are equally vulnerable to certain general objections (see, notably, Jackson 1977b). And as we have seen in Chap. 4, the belief-in theory of judgment that underlies the reistic paraphrases has its own issues. Still, reism appears to be a viable fourth option for truthmaker nominalism, worth considering.

5. From Reism to Monism

Suppose the motivation for reism is that it is an adequate monocategorial ontology. Can the push for parsimony be taken any further? Clearly, it is not possible to have fewer categories of existent than one! Still, it might be possible to have fewer elements within the relevant category. Consider Horgan and Potrč's view – known as 'blobjec-tivism' or 'existence monism' – according to which there is only one concrete particular, the cosmos (Horgan and Potrč 2000, 2006, 2008). On this view, the universe exists, but it has no parts. It is the *only* concrete particular in existence. If one combined this view with reism, one would probably reach the most parsimonious ontology possible (setting aside Gorgias' view that *nothing* exists!).

Brentano never held quite this view. For one thing, his acceptance of a multitude of world-accidents collocated with the world-substance would preclude it. For another, as a substance dualist he took each of us to have a distinct soul, which is a concrete particular in its own right.[25] However, Brentano could still hold consistently with all this that *there is only one physical substance* – the material universe as a whole. And indeed, at least for one heady afternoon, on 30 January 1915, Brentano seems to have adopted precisely this view. In this final section, I present Brentano's view as expounded in the relevant text (§5.1) and his argument for it (§5.2). I should note that this section is entirely 'optional,' in that it is not needed for an understanding of Brentano's overall system. (It is hard to know, in fact, how seriously Brentano took his monist ruminations, and what credence he placed in them over the final twenty-six months of his life.)

5.1. Brentano's one-day monism

To my knowledge, the dictation from 30 January 1915 is the only place in the Brentano corpus where (material-substance) monism is floated.[26] The manuscript is archived at

Harvard's Houghton Library under the title 'The Lorentz-Einstein Question' (Brentano MS N7). Kastil showed remarkable insight in including his edited version of the piece, retitled 'The Nature of the Physical World in Light of the Theory of Categories,' as an appendix in the *Kategorienlehre* (Brentano 1933: 296–301 [208–11]).[27]

Brentano's very first statement of his monism is this:

…one might go as far as to conjecture that the totality of physical matter (*Gesamtheit des Körpliches*) constitutes a single stationary physical substance (*einzige ruhende Körpersubstanz*), which would be littered (*da und dort behaftet*) with certain particular accidents… [O]ur mechanical laws, as well as everything physics, chemistry, and physiology have established, would pertain to these accidents and their changes and mutual interactions. (Brentano 1933: 298 [209])

Imagine a big, quivering, translucent ball, under the surface of which appear, disappear, and reappear various vaguely glowing color patches. If the color appearances evolve in sufficiently systematic ways, we might be tempted to posit colorful 'things' or entities that 'travel' just below the ball's surface, 'bump into' each other, change directions, and so on. And we might wish to formulate the natural laws that govern these patches' behavior and interactions. But for all that, there may be no 'things' under there – there may just be undifferentiated *stuff* that exhibits different colors in different places at different times. We could study the laws that govern changes in the colors exhibited, but we should resist the temptation to think of these as laws describing the persistence and interaction of a multitude of independent entities. Brentano's universe is of course very different from this ball: it does not quiver, but is strictly immobile, and it is probably not spherical, but has some arbitrary, brutely contingent shape (Brentano 1933: 301 [211]). Nonetheless, like this ball it does not host any independent things or objects, but instead seems to be a single unitary 'blobject' that simply exhibits a certain (spatial and temporal) qualitative *structure*.

In some respects, the picture Brentano presents very much reminds of Horgan and Potrč's blobjectivism. On the other hand, in accounting for the world's qualitative heterogeneity, Brentano avails himself quite insouciantly of locations and indeed parts:

In place of the ether there would be the stationary, unitary substance (*ruhende, einheitliche Substanz*). In place of what had formerly been regarded as the substances of physical matter, there would be accidents inhering in (*haftend an*) the [stationary unitary] substance, which would be transmitted from one part (*Teil*) of it to another. The laws of mechanics would pertain to the interchange and persistence of these accidents. (Brentano 1933: 298 [209])

Here Brentano speaks explicitly of the universe's parts. In another passage, he speaks of the universe's portions/parcels (*Parzellen*) (Brentano 1933: 299–300 [209–10]; quoted in §5.2). But if the universe has parts, strictly speaking it cannot be the *only* material object, as blobjectivism requires.[28] Instead, we appear to have on our hands the kind of so-called *priority monism* defended by Jonathan Schaffer (2010a, 2010b). According to Schaffer, the world does have parts, but is nonetheless ontologically prior to them. Schaffer is thus a pluralist about material objects; he is only a monist about the number of *fundamental* material objects.

This may well be Brentano's ultimate view. After all, he is a monist only about material *substance*. He is perfectly happy to accept a plurality of material objects, as long as only one of them is a substance. The others are *accidents*. As Brentano writes in the passage just quoted, instead of 'the substances of physical matter, there would be accidents inhering in the [cosmos], which would be transmitted from one part of it to another.' Here a substance's accidents are still construed as concrete particulars, but ones which need not be perfectly collocated with the relevant substance; instead, they may be *proper parts* of that substance. In any case, since for Brentano accidents depend ontologically on their substances, a substance is always ontologically prior to its accidents. So the view really does resemble priority monism more than existence monism. Perhaps we could summarize the view by saying that it combines priority monism about (physical) concrete particulars and existence monism about (physical) substance.

There is another question to consider, though, regarding what exactly 'the (material) cosmos' is supposed to be. Three main approaches present themselves: (i) the cosmos as spacetime; (ii) the cosmos as the totality of matter filling up spacetime; (iii) spacetime *plus* the matter filling it up. Schaffer, for example, seems to support the first option (Schaffer 2009). Brentano, though, would presumably go for the second option, given that he treats 'empty space' as a syncrategorematic (pseudo-referential) expression akin to 'the hole in the wall' and 'lack of enthusiasm.' In a 1915 dictation, he writes: 'An empty space needs to be something positive just as little as does the absence of a sound when a sound is skipped in playing a scale' (Brentano 1976: 178 [150]; see also Brentano 1930: 79 [68]) – a remark he repeats in different variations throughout the piece. If our ontology can countenance only regions of space filled with matter, it would seem that it is really only the relevant 'material filling' that is real.

Brentano's monism about the physical world can thus be characterized through the conjunction of the following three theses: (1) There exists only one material substance, the cosmos as a whole; (2) this substance is just the totality of physical matter ('*Gesamtheit des Körpliches*'); (3) it has parts, which however (i) are not themselves substances and (ii) depend for their existence on the one material substance.

5.2. Brentano's argument for monism

Interestingly, just as modern monism is motivated by considerations drawn from physics – more specifically, the phenomenon of quantum entanglement (see Schaffer 2010a: 50–5, Calosi 2014) – Brentano motivates monism by appeal to one of the burning questions of the physics of his day, the null result of the Michelson-Morely experiment. Let me explain the result, then Brentano's inference from it.

Suppose you sit in a small room and watch your friend tap dancing. If all the air is instantaneously sucked out of the room, you will no longer be able to hear those taps. The reason is that without the air, the sound waves bringing the sound to your ears will be unable to travel. Sound waves are waves *of* or *in* something – in this case air (hence 'airwaves'). Sound does not need air to travel through, it can also travel through water, helium, and so forth. But it does need *some* kind of medium – some substance must be undulating if sound waves are to occur.

This might be thought to raise a question: how can light travel from faraway stars and reach our eyes *through empty space*? Do light waves not need some undulating medium of their own? Many nineteenth-century physicists thought so, arguing that the space between us and those faraway stars cannot be real vacuum; instead, it must be filled with some unusually unimposing substance, a kind of pervasive foam-stuff, through which light waves travel.

On this picture, the earth does not revolve in a void, but rather 'swims' through this foam-stuff. Now, just as when you swim in otherwise motionless water, you create a current around you, one would expect the earth to produce its own extraordinarily light 'current' as it swims through the foam-stuff. And in the normal go of things, this should mean that light waves would travel faster 'downstream' than 'upstream,' that is, against the earth's motion than along it. This speed difference is precisely what the 1887 Michelson-Morely experiment failed to find. Try it any way you like, it seems light travels through the foam equally fast in all directions, regardless of what and how bodies are moving in it.

Toward the end of the nineteenth century, physicists were preoccupied with trying to explain this striking null result. Michelson himself thought it showed that the foam – better known as *ether* – was not actually stationary, but was 'dragged along' by bodies as they moved about space (a hypothesis aired already in the 1840s by George Stokes). Lorentz insisted that the foam was stationary, conjecturing that as bodies swam through it they contracted in the direction of their movement, thus producing a weaker current behind them than they would otherwise – exactly as much weaker, in fact, as would be needed to perfectly cancel out the speeding up of light's downstream travel! Einstein's special relativity, however, made room for the simplest explanation of the null result – the explanation that there simply *is* no ether, so naturally it has no effect on the behavior of light. Einstein reverted to Newton's old idea that light does not travel in waves at all, and thus does not depend on the existence of an undulating substance or medium. Instead, light is corpuscular – there are tiny particles of light that move through empty space in just the same way, say, the Earth does. These light particles are of course the photons. As is well known, ultimately photons (and soon thereafter electrons) came to be thought of as something in-between particles and waves, exhibiting properties of both.

It is in this context, of trying to explain the Michelson-Morely null result, that Brentano offers up his monist hypothesis. He writes:

I believe that only through such a [monist] recasting (*Umbildung*) of our conception of the physical world (*Körperwelt*) do certain paradoxes, which face our physicists [Lorentz and Einstein] due to the results of Michelson's and related experiments, resolve themselves easiest. This recasting would pave the way to a somewhat deeper grasp of the physical world; the notion of the unitary substance (*einheitlichen Substanz*) taking the ether's place would make much more sense than what we have been taught about the ether's peculiarities (*Eigenheiten*), especially its impenetrability, and would also cast so-called Matter (*Materie*) in a totally new light.[29]

(Brentano 1933: 299–300 [210])

How does monism help with Michelson-Morely? Brentano is a tad telegraphic on that; the only comment of relevance seems to be this:

As for light and electricity radiation, it is not impossible to conjure up a plausible story (*gee-ignet Vorstellungen bilden*) that bears some analogy to both the [particle] emission theory and the [wave] undulation theory, which would do justice to the phenomena just as well as them, if not better. It would not be concerned with oscillations or relocations of parts of the substance underlying the rays...but only with the relocation of qualities, which may be thought of as dividing into very small parcels/portions (*Parzellen*). In this way everything remains in essence unaltered...   (Brentano 1933: 299–300 [209–10])

The idea seems to be this. Light radiates neither in waves nor in corpuscles. In fact, there *are* neither waves nor corpuscles – there is no undulating medium like Lorentz's ether and there are no light particles like Einstein's photons. Instead, there is a single, immobile substance with undifferentiated, homogeneous constitution that simply exhibits different properties in different places. That is, there is qualitative variation in the world, but no quantitative variety. Accordingly, the transmission of light from A to B involves neither traveling particles nor an undulating medium; it is just a matter of the universe exhibiting the relevant light properties in A at one time and in B at a later time. The laws of mechanics describe the regularities governing such changes in properties across the single substance that is the universe, not some processes that might involve the interaction of separate objects. The Michelson-Morely null result simply tells us something about what these regularity laws are; it raises no deep puzzle once we stop expecting there to be an undulating medium through which light travels.

It is doubtful that Brentano's argument is a cogent reason to go monist. Presumably there are other ways to accommodate the Michelson-Morely result, notably Einstein's special relativity (see Einstein 1920: §16). At the same time, it is striking that Brentano suggested that the underlying physical reality is more fundamental than either particles or waves a decade before de Broglie hypothesized essentially the same (which earned him the 1929 Nobel Prize). Perhaps the deep thrust of Brentano's argument for (material-substance) monism is this idea: only if the cosmos is in reality a single unitary substance can we make sense of the idea that matter is neither fully corpuscular nor fully wavy.

Conclusion

In a 1914 dictation, Brentano succinctly presents his considered ontological inventory:

An existent (*Seiendes*) in the proper sense is not only any substance, any plurality (*Mehrheit*) of substances, and any part of a substance, but also any accident.   (Brentano 1933: 11 [19])

In a way, existents come in four varieties: substances, accidents, substance-parts, and substance-pluralities. However:

... every plurality of things and every part of a thing is itself a thing.   (Brentano 1933: 11 [19])

Since we have already seen that accidents are also things, it turns out that all existents are things, that is, concrete particulars. This is what I have called strict nominalism. Brentano's specific version is reism – strict nominalism with a special strategy for paraphrasing simple positive truths about our world that do not *seem* to cite only concrete particulars.

I have not argued that Brentano's reism is *the one true ontological theory*, but rather for the following more nuanced thesis: *if* one is antecedently attracted by (i) a nominalist ontology and (ii) a truthmaker approach to ontological theorizing, *then* whereas the current literature showcases three theoretical options to choose among, Brentano's reism represents a fourth viable option – no less plausible, upon consideration, than the other three.

In addition, I have considered favorably a late attempt by Brentano to produce further economies in his ontology by admitting in it only one material substance – the cosmos as a whole. This leaves of course many other concrete particulars, including every part and every accident of the cosmos, as well as every soul in it. Nonetheless, one would be hard pressed to find a more parsimonious ontology in the history of Western philosophy. Consider that while Horgan and Potrč admit in their ontology only one concrete particular, they also require properties as a second ontological category. Schaffer may posit only one concrete particular at the fundamental level, but supplements it there with fundamental tropes and resemblance (and spatiotemporal) relations (Schaffer 2001: 247). Importantly, Brentano's substance dualism is logically independent of his reism and limited monism. A materialist could therefore adopt Brentano's reism and monism – and obtain a monocategorial, monosubstantival ontology on which there is only one ontologically independent existent: the world.[30]

Notes to Chapter 6

1. According to Sauer (2017), Brentano came to adopt reism sometime between January and September 1903. In September 1903, Brentano writes to Marty that he 'is making a new attempt to understand all *entia rationis* as fictions, that is, to deny that they are' (Brentano 1966: 108). My own sense is that Brentano's 'new attempt' is not the first one, but reflects a long-held wish to be able to adopt a nominalist ontology with a clear conscience.
2. Kotarbiński was a student of Kazimierz Twardowski's in Lvov, after the latter returned from Vienna, where he worked with Brentano from 1885 to 1889. Kotarbiński was apparently unaware of Brentano's ontological views until Twardowski wrote to him a letter about them *after* Kotarbiński had published his main reistic work (Kotarbiński 1929).
3. For example, in a 1914 letter to Kraus he announces: 'I shall begin at once, today, by bringing forward a proof, in what I believe is a very simple and rigorous manner, that nothing other than things can at all be objects of our presenting and therefore of our thinking...' (Brentano 1930: 105–6 [94]).

4. The reason a statement *accepting* a state of affairs may need to be paraphrased into a statement *rejecting* a particular thing is that there ostensibly are *negative* states of affairs (but no *negative particulars*). For example, acceptance of the state of affairs of there being no dragons would have to be replaced by rejection of a dragon.

5. Moreover, the argument is clearly accompanied by two further arguments (Brentano 1930: 122 [108]) which are supposed to address the same stage in the dialectic. It is true, however, that several letters to Kraus from the same period highlight the argument from univocality.

6. An *in re* universal is an immanent universal, one that inheres in the particulars that instantiate it. What makes it a universal, then, is not the fact that it is 'outside spacetime' (as an *ante rem*, transcendent universal is), but the fact that it is *fully* present at different places at the same time. My green car is fully present in a single place at a time; the state of Hawaii is present in different places (different islands) at the same time, but is only *partially* present in each distinct place; the *in re* universal Greenness, by contrast, is present at the same time in all places occupied by green things, and moreover is *fully* present in each such place.

7. According to Quine's criterion, an assertion '*a* is F' ontologically commits to *a* because it is a law of logic that from '*a* is F' we can infer 'There is an *x*, such that *x* is F,' which is an explicitly existential assertion. It is not a law of logic, however, that from '*a* is F' we can infer 'There is an X, such that *a* is X,' so asserting '*a* is F' does not commit us ontologically to the existence of something that is picked out by 'F.'

8. See Mulligan et al. 1984, Simons 2000, 2008, and Lewis 2001. A friend of states of affairs or facts might posit 'absence facts,' such as the fact that there are no dragons. It would then be the presence of an absence that makes true truths of the form 'there are no Fs.' But many ontologists understandably find it distasteful to posit presences of absences as genuine chunks of the world.

9. An atomic truth is a truth no part of which is a truth. It is a separate question how to best characterize the ideas of one truth being more fundamental than another and of a truth being fundamental *tout court* (that is, having no other truth more fundamental than it). This issue is actively debated in current ontology (see Williams 2010 for recent discussion). Here I will assume that even if we do not yet have any consensus on the nature of truth-fundamentality, typically we know it when we see it.

10. To make the example more precise, we might replace reference to the property of being famous with reference to a much more precise property, such as being heard of by 55% of humans over the age of 6.

11. In addition, Jimmy seems to be an abstract object (insofar as classes generally are), hence ruled out by strict nominalism.

12. In addition, it is controversial whether the mereological fusion of all famous things exists. Mereological universalists (Lewis 1991, Van Cleve 2007) think so, but many do not, including mereological nominalists (Rosen and Dorr 2002, Sider 2013), mereological restrictivists (Markosian 1998, Smith 2005), and existence monists (Horgan and Potrč 2008).

13. What is coincidence? When the coincident concrete particulars are material, coincidence amounts to collocation. But the notion of coincidence must be wider than that of collocation: in Brentano's ontology, there are also a-spatial concrete particulars – mental substances – and those would coincide, but would not be collocated, with their mental accidents.

14. Furthermore, even if it were not so plausible, and represented a cost, it would not be a pointless cost. For it buys us a fourth option for a strictly nominalist ontology. Arguably,

this cost is not special to Brentano's reism, but must be accrued by any ontology that buys us a strictly nominalist ontology *without* illicit relations and *with* distinct truthmakers for distinct fundamental truths. For if there are no illicit relations and properties posited, then we cannot appeal to such properties and relations to *characterize* concrete particulars and thereby account for their difference in terms of their different characteristics. It then becomes hard to see what else we could appeal to in order to explain their difference.

15. This implies that two-legged-famous-Beyoncé is an accident of famous-Beyoncé, hence an accident of an accident. This may be thought implausible. Brentano, however, is nowise perturbed by this implication and insists on it on many occasions: e.g., '…just as a substance may be the subject of an absolute [i.e., non-relational or intrinsic] accident, so too an absolute accident may be the subject of another absolute accident' (Brentano 1933: 122 [95]). And indeed it is hard to see here a major liability for the view: just as ontologists are generally comfortable with higher-order properties (e.g., the property of being Jimmy's favorite property), they should be comfortable with higher-order accidents.

16. In any case, recall that Brentano's strict nominalism commits him to denying the existence of such concrete universals as Beyoncé-ness. We are speaking here of citing Beyoncé-ness only within the property fiction. Doing so is the best approximation of Brentano's view, I claim, but is still not quite his view, even within the property fiction. The literal view is that there is nothing we can cite as essential to Beyoncé – she is just herself and that is all there is to it. This is brutal individuation in action. It may be worth noting that already in his 1866 habilitation defense, Brentano claims explicitly (in his seventeenth thesis) that a substance cannot be defined (Brentano 1866: 139).

17. A quick reminder on the structure of the dialectic: we are assuming here Brentano's framework, and our question is whether such a thing as The Thinker could be admitted within that framework. The question is *not* whether the existence of such a thing is independently plausible (except insofar as that second question affects charity considerations).

18. To regard an ontology as more extravagant only because its posits are concrete particulars rather than states of affairs would be to regard concrete particulars as somehow 'more real' than states of affairs. But even if we could make sense of the expression 'more real,' it would be quite ironic for the opponent of nominalism to rely on the greater reality of concrete particulars!

19. Note also that if reism shuns 'disjunctiva,' it becomes exceedingly unlikely that it would need to posit *infinitely* many concrete particulars in Beyoncé's location.

20. Personally, I am somewhat skeptical of Lewis' view here. It seems to me that reism's proliferation of concrete particulars, though limited to one type of entity, is nonetheless driven by philosophical rather than empirical considerations, and therefore is very much the philosopher's business (see Nolan 1997). However, it is still worth noting that *if* one holds the view that only type-parsimony matters, this certainly casts reism as greatly superior to its more traditional competitor.

21. Recall the 1906 letter to Marty mentioned in Chap. 4: 'The being of A need not be produced in order for the judgment "A is" to be…correct; all that is needed is A' (Brentano 1930: 95 [85]).

22. Skyrms might respond by suggesting to stop the regress at the second step, letting the Higgs-boson's-existence make true both 'The Higgs boson exists' and 'The Higgs-boson's-existence exists.' But in addition to being ad hoc and inelegant, this move puts factualism in the same tension with truth-conditional semantics that we encountered with ostrich

nominalism. Perhaps the better option would be for Skyrms to simply bite the bullet and accept infinitely many states of affairs implicated in the very existence of each object. The cost here is evident.

23. One might press further, asking why there should be such an individual as the resembling-the-Empire-State-building-more-than-the-moon Eiffel Tower. But I think this kind of question is misplaced. One might as well ask why the Eiffel Tower exists. There are of course *causal* answers to this question, but in wanting an explanation of resemblance truths, we are not seeking a *causal* or explanation; we seek a *metaphysical* explanation. And while it is an important question what metaphysical explanation is, that is not the topic here. It is clear that the friend of universals provides such a metaphysical explanation when she claims that what makes true '*a* resembles *b*' is the fact that there are sufficiently many universals which inhere in both *a* and *b*. What I have claimed is that Brentano has his own truthmaker to offer for '*a* resembles *b*,' namely, the *b*-resembling *a*. And while there are *causal* explanations for this individual's existence, there are no *metaphysical* explanations to be had for *any* individual's existence.

24. I confess to having no evidence that this line of thought was operative in Brentano's original pull to reism. In his 1901 letter to Marty, which seems to be the first place where Brentano voices his account of the substance/accident distinction (see Brentano 1930: 74–5 [64]), the attraction is presented as emanating from technical problems with Brentano's previous view rather than with the application of some general principle (that is, as flowing from the bottom up rather than from the top down, from the phenomena themselves rather than from an independently attractive theory). Nonetheless, the phenomena produce pressure toward a certain theoretical account only against the background of a certain conception of what counts as adequately accounting for the phenomena. In the present case, the technical problem Marty presented to Brentano had to do with a certain lack of symmetry in the model Brentano's previous account offered (Brentano 1930: 73 [63]). It would seem, then, that in Brentano's eyes such symmetry is crucial for the adequacy of the account. This need for symmetry clearly does not come from the phenomena themselves.

25. However, although Brentano's monism is restricted to physical substance, it has been argued that it creeps up again in the mental domain, namely, as a theory of the unity of consciousness at a time. According to Giustina (2017), Brentano was a monist in this area as well, holding that the whole conscious state of a person at a time is ontologically prior to the various parts (visual, auditory, mnemonic, intellectual, etc.).

26. Although Brentano does not develop the idea anywhere else, it often seems to constrain, and sometimes to irrigate, his speculations on space and matter in the last two years of his life (see Brentano 1976).

27. As was his style, Kastil took considerable liberties in editing Brentano's original text. Having inspected the manuscript, I can say that in this instance Kastil's 'creative' editing did not involve any misunderstanding or misrepresentation of Brentano's thought. In any case, I am indebted to Laurent Iglesias for making me appreciate the significance of this dictation (see Iglesias 2015).

28. Clearly, Brentano *needs* the world to have parts in order to account for its qualitative structure. Blobjectivism denies that the world has parts, but it can avail itself of *properties* in accounting for the world's structure. These must be special properties, exhibited only by the world – properties of the form being-F-in-L-at-t – but pending special difficulties with

such properties, it is legitimate for the blobjectivist to appeal to them. Brentano, however, rejects properties, so he must account for the world's qualitative structure in terms of concrete particulars, which would presumably be parts of the world.

29. It should be noted that the first sentence of this passage is rather heavily edited by Kastil. Large parts of Brentano's text are modified or ignored, while other parts are introduced, though often imported from other parts of the manuscript, skipped over elsewhere in Kastil's 'transcription.' However, I do not find that Kastil's 'creative editing' has changed the meaning of Brentano's original text in this instance.

30. For comments on previous drafts of some or all of this material, I am grateful to Géraldine Carranante, Anna Giustina, Ghislain Guigon, Mikaël Quesseveur, Jonathan Schaffer, and Mark Textor. I have also benefited from presenting the paper at the Universities of Aix-en-Provence, Liège, Miami, and Turin, as well as at École Normale Supérieure and the Jean Nicod Institute in Paris; I am grateful to the audiences at all these places, in particular Guido Bonino, Guillaume Bucchioni, Otavio Bueno, Eli Chudnoff, Simon Evnine, Denis Fisette, Vincent Grandjean, Ghislain Guigon, Laurent Iglesias, Keith Lehrer, Peter Lewis, Alice Martin, Gianmarco Brunialti Masera, Jean-Maurice Monnoyer, Alejandro Perez, Venanzio Raspa, Elizabetta Sacci, Alessadro Salice, Nick Stang, Amie Thomasson, Giuliano Torrengo, and Alberto Voltolini. Some of the material in this chapter overlaps with my article 'Thought and Thing: Brentano's Reism as Truthmaker Nominalism,' published in *Philosophy and Phenomenological Research*; I am grateful to the publisher, Wiley, for allowing me to reuse this material. The final section of the chapter appeared almost verbatim in *Brentano Studien* under the title 'Brentano's Latter-Day Monism'; I am grateful to the publisher, J.H. Röll, for permission to integrate the material in this chapter.

PART III
Value

7

Will and Emotion

As we saw in Chap. 3, Brentano divides conscious states into three fundamental categories: 'presentation,' 'judgment,' and 'interest.' We have discussed the nature of presentation in Chap. 3 and the nature of judgment in Chap. 4. The present chapter is dedicated to the nature of interest.

Brentano's theory of interest offers a unified account of will, emotion, and pleasure/pain. In contemporary philosophy of mind, the theory of emotion and the theory of pleasure/pain are contentious areas featuring a bewildering variety of competing theories. The account Brentano offers, however, is not properly represented in either literature, and here I will try to make the case for its plausibility. Interestingly, the will, in particular desire, is *not* nearly as contentious in current philosophy of mind, and the account many accept, however implicitly, seems to be precisely Brentano's. Accordingly, I will try to leverage the evident plausibility of Brentano's account of will (§1) to claim similar plausibility for his parallel accounts of emotion (§2) and pleasure and pain (§3).

1. The Will

In contemporary analytic philosophy of mind, discussion of the will focuses on the nature of desire, intention, and action. But the most prominent of these notions is by far desire (see under: 'belief-desire psychology'). Accordingly, I start this section with a presentation of leading accounts of desire in the relevant literature (§1.1). I then discuss Brentano's account as a particularly well-developed version of one of them (§1.2).

1.1. Desire in contemporary philosophy of mind

A common account of desire in current philosophy of mind characterizes it in terms of its *functional role* within the overall economy of mind. The idea is that desire and belief are complementary states that together causally explain the occurrence of observable behavior. For example, if Aristide goes to the kitchen, opens the fridge, and takes out a beer, we can causally explain this piece of behavior by citing (i) Aristide's desire for beer and (ii) his belief that by going through this sequence of actions he will obtain beer

(Davidson 1963). Within this picture, belief and desire are characterized in terms of complementary clusters of causal dispositions. Robert Stalnaker puts the picture crisply:

> Belief and desire... are correlative dispositional states of a potentially rational agent. To desire that P is to be disposed to act in ways that would tend to bring it about that P in a world in which one's beliefs, whatever they are, were true. To believe that P is to be disposed to act in ways that would tend to satisfy one's desires, whatever they are, in a world in which P (together with one's other beliefs) were true.   (Stalnaker 1984: 15)

On this picture, desire is nothing but a cluster of distinctly motivational dispositions.

From a Brentanian perspective, this kind of functionalist account is a nonstarter, since, as we saw in Chap. 1, Brentano rejects the existence of dispositional mental states. He accepts that we have the kind of tacit dispositions commonly attributed to subjects, but insists that 'these are not mental phenomena' (Brentano 1874: I, 86 [60]) but merely (neuro)physiological phenomena.[1] Even if one accepts the existence of dispositional states, however, it is natural to suppose that the relevant dispositional profiles are grounded in mental states' occurrent, categorical properties.

There is also a deeper reason why Brentano would completely reject a Stalnaker-style functionalist account. To regard desires and beliefs as clusters of (potentially dormant) dispositions is to treat them as *unobservable theoretical entities*, posited only for the purpose of explaining observable action. For Brentano, however, the phenomena of the will, including desire, are not in the first instance explanatory posits, a hidden explanans of a perceived explanandum. Rather, they are (inner-)perceived types of conscious experience. Indeed, desire is one of descriptive psychology's explananda, in addition to whatever role it plays as an explanans in genetic psychology.[2] This is not unreasonable: even blindfolded, I can know immediately and noninferentially that I *desire* to eat ice cream rather than *believe* I eat ice cream. The notion that knowledge that I want ice cream is *always* based on inference from observation of my ice-cream-seeking behavior seems absurd. Brentano's view is that it is (at least sometimes) based on direct inner perception of the desire itself. If so, theorizing about the nature of desire should not be driven entirely by considerations of action explanation. It should first seek an explicit and precise description of that which inner perception presents in an unarticulated and 'blurry' fashion.

Another approach to desire in contemporary philosophy of mind construes it as the paradigmatic state with a world-to-mind direction of fit: whereas belief is the kind of state that is supposed to fit the way the world is, desire is the kind of state that the world is supposed to fit.[3]

From a Brentanian point of view, however, this approach to desire faces a number of problems. First, it is far from clear what direction of fit *means*; it is a suggestive metaphor, but unpacking it literally proves difficult (Zangwill 1998). Secondly, the most natural accounts of direction of fit construe it as a matter of functional role (e.g., Smith 1994); but as we have just seen, Brentano cannot accept a dispositional account of desire. Thirdly, even if we grant that belief is supposed to fit the world, whereas desire is such that the world is supposed to fit it, these do not seem like brute, inexplicable facts. It seems that something must explain them: there must be something about belief – some psychological feature of it – that makes it supposed to fit the world, and something about desire that makes it such that the world is supposed to fit it. Facts about supposed fit seem too 'normative' to be psychological bedrock. One is naturally led to surmise that such facts are rather grounded in more straightforwardly psychological characteristics of the relevant mental states.

There is also a third approach to desire one finds in modern philosophy of mind, which approach dovetails much better with Brentano's thinking. This is the notion that desire is an *essentially evaluative* state: it represents what it does *as good* (in a suitably generic sense). When you desire chocolate, there is a palpable sense in which your desire casts the chocolate in a positive light. Thus philosophers working out the distinction between belief and desire within the framework of 'belief-desire psychology' have sometimes highlighted the following idea: while a belief that p and a desire that p represent the same thing (have the same content), the former represents p 'under the guise of the true' whereas the latter represents p 'under the guise of the good' (Velleman 1992). Here is how Dennis Stampe puts it in his classic 'The Authority of Desire':

[W]hile the belief and the desire that p have the same propositional content and represent the same state of affairs, there is a difference in the *way* it is represented in the two states of mind. In belief it is represented *as obtaining*, whereas in desire, it is represented as a state of affairs *the obtaining of which would be good*. This *modal* difference explains why a desire that p is a reason to make it true that p, while the belief that p is not.   (Stampe 1987: 355; italics original)

We may put the idea by saying that desire is *goodness-committal*: it commits to the goodness of its intentional object. (By this I mean that desire itself is committed to the object's goodness, not that the desire commits *the subject* to the object's goodness.[4]) Sergio Tenenbaum calls this the 'Scholastic view' – which he formulates as follows:

... just as theoretical attitudes such as belief express what the agent holds to be true even when the belief is false, the scholastic view claims that practical attitudes, such as intending [and desiring] express what the agent holds to be good.   (Tenenbaum 2009: 96; see also Tenenbaum 2007: 9)

In a similar vein, Graham Oddie writes: 'The desire that P is P's seeming good (or P's being experienced as good)' (Oddie 2005: 42).

Interestingly, the dispositional account, the direction of fit account, and the evaluative account do not seem to be regarded as competitors in the contemporary literature. They are treated rather as different facets of a single comprehensive picture of the nature of desire. And indeed, at one level there is no reason to choose among them, insofar as desire may well exhibit all three characteristics: a distinctive functional role, a distinctive direction of fit, and a distinctively evaluative character. At the same time, one of these characteristics may turn out to be more explanatorily fundamental than the other two: the latter may be mere symptoms of the former, or the possession of the former may underlie and explain the possession of the latter. This is particularly plausible, in fact, in the present case. As we have seen, dispositional facts about desire's functional role are plausibly grounded in more fundamental categorical facts about desire, and normative facts about desire's supposed-fit relation to the world are grounded in more fundamental 'descriptive' facts about desire's psychological properties. Only desire's evaluative character does not invite inquiring about further underlying properties.

Interestingly, the evaluative character is also well positioned to *explain* desire's dispositional and normative properties. More specifically, I would claim that (i) desire's direction of fit is explained by its functional role and (ii) its functional role is explained by its evaluative character – its goodness-commitment. On the one hand, the *reason* 'success' (or 'fulfillment') for desires involves the world changing so as to come into accord with the mind is precisely that desire, by its very nature, motivates the subject to act on the world and try to mold it in a certain way. But in a second stage, it is also natural to think that my desire for chocolate motivates me to mold the world so that I obtain chocolate precisely *because* it presents it as *good* that I should have chocolate. That is, the desire for chocolate has the functional role it does because it evaluates the chocolate the way it does. In this way, evaluative character underlies functional role, which in turn underlies direction of fit. This casts desire's evaluative character as the most fundamental of its three distinctive characteristics.

From a Brentanian perspective, it is also noteworthy that nothing prevents desire's goodness-commitment from being an occurrent, inner-perceptible feature. This allows us to do justice to the fact that desire is something we are familiar with from our personal experience, not merely a theoretical posit experientially opaque to us.

All this suggests that desire's goodness-commitment is plausibly regarded – certainly from a Brentanian perspective – as the *essential* feature of desire, what *makes* it a desire. On this picture, desire's characteristic motivational role and direction of fit *flow from* its evaluative character; it is the evaluative character that constitutes desire's deep nature.

1.2. Brentano's evaluative-attitudinal account of desire and will

Brentano himself does not discuss the will primarily in terms of desire. Nonetheless, I will conduct the discussion as though he does, for the sake of continuity; we will revisit the relationship between will and desire with a more critical mindset in §2.2.

Brentano clearly has an evaluative account of will/desire: 'every [desire] takes an object to be good or bad' (Brentano 1874: II, 36 [199]). However, there is an important difference between Brentano's view and, say, Stampe's or Oddie's. Stampe and Oddie maintain that desire is *perception* of the good. Brentano rejects this, just as he rejects the notion that desire is *belief in goodness*: to desire ice cream is *not* to believe in the ice cream's goodness, and nor is it to perceive the ice cream as good. Instead, it is a *sui generis* way of positively evaluating the ice cream, irreducible to perceptual and belief-like ways of doing so:

I do not believe that anyone will understand me to mean that [desires] are cognitive acts (*Erkenntnisakte*) by which the goodness or badness, value or disvalue, of certain objects are *perceived* (*wahrgenommen*); indeed I note explicitly, in order to make such an interpretation completely impossible, that this would be a complete misunderstanding of my real view. First, that would mean that I viewed these phenomena as judgments; but in fact I set them apart as a special class.   (Brentano 1874: II, 89 [239])

The question is how to characterize the sui generis way desire presents goodness.

As we saw in Chap. 4, Brentano takes the essential characteristic of judgment to be its distinctive mode of presenting: its existence-commitment. As a mode of presenting, existence-commitment is an *attitudinal* feature of judgments. A belief in ghosts, we said, does not present ghosts as existent, but rather presents-as-existent ghosts. In saying that desire presents the good, but in its own sui generis way, Brentano suggests that he envisages a similarly attitudinal account of desire's goodness-commitment. My desire's commitment to the goodness of chocolate should be understood not as a matter of presenting chocolate-as-good, but of presenting-as-good chocolate. And indeed, Brentano explicitly says:

The essence of will consists in approval or disapproval, hence in a taking-as-good (*ein Gutfinden*) or taking-as-bad (*Schlechtfinden*)...   (Brentano 1874: II, 91 [241])

That is, a volitional state (e.g., desire) concerned with chocolate is directed at the chocolate through the presenting-as-good relation, a distinctive way of intentionally relating to an object.

The attitudinal approach recommends itself very strongly in the case of desire. For clearly, in desiring chocolate one does not desire *that the chocolate be good* (nor desires *the chocolate's goodness*). One simply desires the chocolate. More precisely, while one *can* desire the goodness of a chocolate, or the enjoyableness of a jog in the park, or the pleasantness of a holiday in Greece, ordinarily one simply desires chocolate, a jog in the park, or a holiday in Greece. The fact that we do not need to mention goodness of any sort in specifying the content of an ordinary desire, and yet the desire commits to the chocolate's goodness (in a suitably generic sense of the term, recall), suggests that goodness shows up as an aspect of the desire's *attitude*, of *how* the desire presents what it does, rather than as an aspect of its content, of *what* the desire presents. We might say that the desire casts chocolate in a positive light rather than casts light on positive chocolate. This is just the idea that the desire does not present chocolate-as-good but presents-as-good chocolate. The goodness is a modification of how the desire does the presenting. Accordingly, to desire *x* is to adopt an attitude that somehow *favors x*, is *pro x*. In this respect, the modern notion of 'pro attitude' is very apt here: for Brentano, desires, indeed volitional states more generally, do not just *happen* to be pro attitudes – it is their essential characteristic.[5]

We can appreciate the point by contrasting a desire for chocolate with a belief in or perception of chocolate's goodness. In the latter, goodness appears precisely as part of the state's content; in the former, it is merely attitudinal. Compare the intentional structure of the following four putative states:

Belief that chocolate is good::	present-as-true <chocolate is good>
Belief in chocolate's goodness::	present-as-existent <chocolate's goodness>
Perception of chocolate's goodness::	present-as-existent <chocolate's goodness>
Desire for chocolate::	present-as-good <chocolate>

In this representation, angle brackets are used to capture a state's content and pre-senting-as-F designates the state's distinctive attitudinal character. Notice that the attitudinal characters of perception and belief-in are cast as identical (consistently with Brentano's account of judgment – see Chaps. 3–4). We can see in this representation that the element of goodness shows up in the *content* of evaluative belief and evaluative perception.[6] Only in desire does it show up in the *attitude*. It is in this sense that desire involves essentially a sui generis *mode* of presenting the intentional object.

This is something that many modern proponents of the evaluative account of desire seem to have missed. In the above quotation, Stampe refers to the evaluative dimension of desire as 'modal' – presumably in the sense of being attitudinal. Nonetheless, he strug-gles with the difference between desire and evaluative belief, worrying that in these two cases 'one and the same state of affairs is represented "in the same way," that is, as having the same property' (Stampe 1987: 356). And that leads him to suggest that desire, unlike evaluative belief, is direct *perception* of value. But Stampe's supposed problem rests on a mistake. As we have just seen, desire and evaluative belief *do not* present the same object: the belief presents chocolate's being good, the desire just chocolate.

It might be objected that the content of desire is never simply an object, such as chocolate, but is always a kind of action, such as *eating* chocolate. The canonical logical form of desire ascription is thus 'S desires to φ' and not 'S desires x.' When we use the latter form in everyday speak we rely on context to make evident which proposition of the former form we are trying to convey (what can you want with chocolate other than to eat it?!). This objection raises important issues but in the present dialectical context it is a non sequitur. For even if what you want is strictly speaking not just chocolate, but your eating of the chocolate, it is still not the case that what you want is the *goodness* of your eating the chocolate. Thus the full specification of the desire's content does not need to mention goodness, regardless of whether it needs to mention some action.

In the contemporary literature, only two accounts of desire appear to converge with Brentano's, namely, Sergio Tenenbaum's (2007) and Karl Schafer's (2013). At the same time, important differences persist.

For Tenenbaum, the attitudinal nature of desiderative evaluation seems to bottom out in the fact that desire *aims* at the good in the same sense belief *aims* at the true. But even if 'aim' talk can be understood literally, one would expect here, too, that there be something about desire that *makes* it aim at the good. Aim facts, like supposed-fit facts, do not look like psychological bedrock. Brentano would say that such facts are grounded in the distinctive attitudinal character of each type of mental state. A desire aims at the good precisely *because* it presents-as-good. It is this latter property that is the most fundamental in Brentano's account of desire, grounding desire's characteristic aim, direction of fit, and functional role.

Meanwhile, Schafer's theoretical goals are importantly different from Brentano's. His primary goal is not to capture the nature or essence of desire, but rather to explain the fact that what it is rational for one to do often depends on what one desires. Schafer's claim is that the best explanation of this fact is that desire is characterized by a special 'imperatival force,' where any 'state that presents A with imperatival force to me presents A to me as something that I ought to do' (Schafer 2013: 277). This diverges from Brentano's account in two main ways. First, Schafer's designated attitudinal property is something like presenting-as-to-be-done, as opposed to presenting-as-good. Secondly, while Schafer asserts that a desire always employs this kind of attitudinal property, he does not assert that this property is essential to its status as a desire.

Brentano's account of desire can be captured in the following pair of theses:

EVALUATIVE-D::   Any desire D for an object O essentially commits to the goodness of O.

ATTITUDINAL-D::   A desire D's commitment to the goodness of an object O is an attitudinal property of D.

Being a nominalist, Brentano would not put things in terms of properties, of course, but in terms of special kinds of concrete particular (as we saw in the previous chapter). He might say, for example, that a desirer is nothing but a presenting-as-good subject. For expediency, here I put things in terms of properties. Note that EVALUATIVE-D ascribes more specifically an *essential* property. It is an essentiality claim, not just a universal or even modal one. It *implies* that all desires are necessarily goodness-committal, but that can be accepted by functional-role accounts of desire as well. Where it goes beyond the functional-role accounts is in claiming that it is of the essence of desire to commit to its object's goodness – that is part of what it is for something to be a desire. At the same time, EVALUATIVE-D is compatible with accounts of desire that build the evaluation into its content. A belief in the goodness of world peace is also goodness-committal, but through its content. This is what is ruled out by ATTITUDINAL-D. The upshot is an account of desire that construes desire as essentially goodness-committal in virtue of an attitudinal feature; call this the *evaluative-attitudinal account*.

To repeat, I present this as Brentano's account of desire, but in truth it is his account of volitional states in general, that is, of all states of a person's *will*. I focus on desire only for the sake of continuity with contemporary philosophy of mind, which has tended to take desire as the paradigmatic mental state with world-to-mind direction of fit.

What is Brentano's *argument* for the evaluative-attitudinal account? The answer, I am afraid, is that he has no direct argument. He dedicates §3 of chapter 8 of *Psychology* II to defending the view, but the defense simply appeals to authority: Lotze, Kant, Mendelssohn, Aristotle, and Aquinas all shared the view, we are told, so the view 'can be regarded as generally accepted (*anerkannt*)' (Brentano 1874: II, 90 [241]). One gets the impression, however, that for Brentano, central to the view's attraction is the way it fits into an elegant bigger picture. In particular, the symmetry between an account of desire in terms of presenting-as-good and an account of belief in terms of presenting-as-true indirectly recommends both. Such 'top-down' considerations rarely play a role in current philosophy of mind, but are highly operative in Brentano's thinking.

Our discussion has raised, however, certain independent considerations in support of Brentano's account. And the extant literature provides further considerations. These considerations can be divided into those that motivate the evaluative approach in general and those that support the attitudinal version more specifically.

What motivates evaluativism in general is the way it avoids the problems attending rival approaches, in particular the functional-role and direction-of-fit approaches. Indeed, as we have seen there are good reasons to think that desire's evaluative character underlies and explains its distinctively motivational functional role and its distinctively world-to-mind direction of fit.

In addition, however, it should be noted that in the contemporary literature a powerful argument for the 'guise of the good' thesis has been developed, which argument readily adapts for EVALUATIVE-D. The main idea is that unless desires are goodness-committal, the behaviors they bring about are doomed to be unintelligible. We can see this, claims Anscombe (1963) for example, by the fact that others' actions are entirely mystifying to us as long as we are unable to understand the good they hope their actions will bring about. The point is nicely articulated in this passage by Philip Clark:

Suppose, for example, that you notice me spray painting my shoe. You ask why I am doing that, and I reply that this way my left shoe will weigh a little more than my right. You ask why I want the left shoe to weigh a little more. Now suppose I just look at you blankly and say, 'That's it.' I seem not to understand your puzzlement. You grasp for straws. 'Is this some sort of performance art, on the theme of asymmetry?' 'No.' 'Is someone going to weigh your shoes as part of some game?' 'No. Why do you ask?'   (Clark 2010: 234–5)

The argument may be put as follows: 1) desires rationalize, or render intelligible, the actions they bring about; 2) if desires were not inherently goodness-committal, they would not rationalize, or render intelligible, the actions they bring about; therefore, 3) desires are inherently goodness-committal. The argument might be resisted, of course, but we can see the kind of initial motivation it provides for evaluativism.

As for the attitudinal approach to desiderative evaluation, as we have seen it is supported by the simple observation that in desiring chocolate one is not ordinarily desiring that chocolate be good, but only desires the chocolate. Given that the desire nonetheless commits to the chocolate's goodness, the only way to accommodate this simple observation is to build desire's goodness-commitment into its distinctive attitude. In addition, the attitudinal view shows us how to handle alleged counter-examples to the guise of the good thesis. For it is often objected to the thesis that desire cannot be essentially goodness-committal, since we routinely desire what we know full well to be bad (Stocker 1979, Velleman 1992). One may want the boss to be embarrassed, even though one takes such embarrassment to be bad morally, prudentially, and otherwise. In response, however, I would claim that such cases involve conflicting evaluations. The desire still presents-as-good boss-embarrassment, but is accompanied by an evaluative *belief* that presents-as-true that boss-embarrassment is bad. The occurrence of a state presents-as-good *x* is perfectly compatible, in a psychological sense, with the occurrence of another state that presents-as-true that *x* is *not* good – in fact such 'internal conflicts' are tragically pervasive in our mental life!

2. Emotion

In addition to an evaluative-attitudinal account of the will, Brentano also presents an evaluative-attitudinal account of emotion (§2.1). This does raise the question of how to account for the evident *difference* between will and emotion – something Brentano has very interesting things to say about (§2.2).

2.1. Brentano's evaluative-attitudinal account of emotion

The philosophy-of-mind literature on emotion is much larger than that on desire. But here too, a stubborn strand casts emotional states as essentially evaluative. Indeed, the evaluative approach to emotion has gained considerable traction toward the end of the twentieth century. Consider this encyclopedic assessment:

Most recent accounts of the structure of emotion, despite their differences, agree that emotions (somehow) present the world to us as having certain *value-laden features*. Following their lead, we will say that emotions involve *evaluative presentations*.   (D'Arms and Jacobson 2000: 66; my italics)

Admiring Shakespeare, respecting one's colleague, and loving one's child are all emotional states that evaluate their objects positively; resenting the boss, abhorring Donald Trump, and being indignant about police killings of unarmed African-Americans evaluate their objects negatively. The claim of the evaluative account is that emotions involve such evaluations universally, necessarily, and indeed essentially.

  Brentano too adopts an evaluative account of emotion. We can see this from the fact that he considers 'emotion' (*Gemüt*) one appropriate name for the category of mental state for which he offers the evaluative account. This category covers clearly volitional states, such as desire, decision, and intention, but also emotional states. In one place Brentano writes:

A single appropriate expression is lacking most of all for the third fundamental class [of mental states], whose phenomena we designated as *emotions/affects* (*Gemüthsbewegungen*), as phenomena of *interest*, or as phenomena of *love*…Everybody would call anger, anxiety, and passionate desire (*heftige Begierde*) emotions/affects; but in the general way in which we use the word, it also applies to every wish, every resolution/decision (*Entschluss*), and every intention.

(Brentano 1874: II, 35 [199]; emphasis original)

Thus phenomena of the will belong in a single category with emotional states. And the evaluative account is supposed to apply to both equally:

Just as every judgment takes an object as true or false, so in an analogous way every phenomenon belonging to this third class takes an object as good or bad.   (Brentano 1874: II, 36 [199])

It would seem, then, that Brentano's evaluative account of desire is intended to apply to emotion as well.

The more recent evaluative accounts typically come in two varieties. One casts emotions as evaluative *judgments* (Solomon 1976): to admire Shakespeare is to judge him admirable, where admirability is a species of goodness (being admirable is a way of being good, in a suitably generic sense of 'good'). The other casts emotions as evaluative *perceptions* (de Sousa 1987): to abhor Donald Trump is to perceive him as abhorrent (where being abhorrent is a way of being bad). As we have seen, however, Brentano does not take mental states belonging to the relevant category to be evaluative judgments or perceptions, but to constitute a sui generis category characterized by a distinctive presentational mode. For him, then, the evaluative dimension of emotion cannot consist in emotion presenting 'value-laden features' or indeed any normative entities. It must be rather a matter of emotions *normatively presenting* 'regular' entities. As he puts it:

the expressions which we use here [to designate the evaluative character of emotion] do not mean that, in the phenomena of this class, goodness is *ascribed* to something which is agreeable as good, and badness is *ascribed* to something which is disagreeable as bad; rather, they too denote a particular *way* in which mental activity refers to a content.   (Brentano 1874: II, 90 [240]; my italics)

My admiration does not present Shakespeare as good but rather presents-as-good Shakespeare. My resentment does not present the boss as bad, but presents-as-bad the boss.[7]

Accordingly, we may formulate Brentano's account of emotion on the pattern of his account of the will. The parallel account would look like this:

EVALUATIVE-E::   Any positive (negative) emotion E about an object O essentially commits to the goodness (badness) of O.

ATTITUDINAL-E::   An emotion E's commitment to the goodness (badness) of an object O is an attitudinal property of E.

We may call this the evaluative-attitudinal account of emotion. Although evaluative approaches to emotion are common in contemporary analytic philosophy of mind, their attitudinal version is less so. Indeed, to my knowledge the only contemporary theory of emotion committed to both EVALUATIVE-E and ATTITUDINAL-E is Julien Deonna and Fabrice Teroni's (see especially Deonna and Teroni 2012: chap. 7, 2015). However, in Deonna and Teroni's account the bodily feelings associated with emotions play a crucial role – the evaluative attitudes of emotions seem to be somehow 'embodied', to be stances taken *by the body* in some sense. This is very different from what Brentano has in mind. For Brentano, all the combination of EVALUATIVE-E and ATTITUDINAL-E means is that the essential property of emotions is an attitudinal property, the property in virtue of which they are emotions, is the property of presenting-as-good (or presenting-as-bad). Any link to the body is merely causal, not constitutive.

Obviously, if one adopts both an evaluative-attitudinal account of emotion and an evaluative-attitudinal account of will, one faces the immediate question of what (if anything) *distinguishes* will and emotion. This question is the topic of §2.2.[8]

The main motivation for the attitudinal twist on the evaluative theory of emotion is, again, that the value is not part of *what* is presented in emotion, what the subject emotes *about*. When you admire Shakespeare, it is just Shakespeare that you admire. It is not Shakespeare's admirability that you admire, and more generally not his goodness that you emote about. Perhaps you admire Shakespeare *in virtue* of his (relevant type of) goodness. That would mean that Shakespeare's goodness is the *cause* or *reason* of your admiration. All the same, Shakespeare's goodness is not the *object* of your admiration. The object of your admiration is just Shakespeare. Accordingly, any evaluation of Shakespeare involved in admiring him cannot come from the content of the admiration. It must be built into the admiring attitude. To admire Shakespeare is thus not to be in a mental state that presents Shakespeare-as-admirable, but in one that presents-as-admirable Shakespeare. The property of presenting-as-admirable is an attitudinal property. It is related to the property of presenting-as-good as species to genus: presenting-as-admirable is *eo ipso* presenting-as-good in the same sense being a cat is *eo ipso* being a mammal. Just as admirability itself is a species of goodness, presenting-as-admirable is a species of presenting-as-good.

The same applies to negative emotions. When one is afraid of a dog, one experiences the dog as dangerous. But one's fear is not a fear *that the dog be dangerous*, nor a fear of *the dog's dangerousness*. No, it is simply a fear *of the dog*. Here too, the fact that danger need not be explicitly cited in a full specification of the fear's content – that which is feared – suggests that the element of danger must be attitudinal: one's fear presents-as-dangerous the dog (where presenting-as-dangerous is a species of presenting-as-bad).

It should be noted that in speaking of 'positive' and 'negative' emotions here, we use the adjectives 'positive' and 'negative' to signal the kinds of *evaluation* encoded in the emotion, not the kinds of *affect* the emotion involves (whether it is pleasant or unpleasant). Positive-affect emotions do often evaluate positively (love feels mostly good, and evaluates positively the loved) and negative-affect emotions typically evaluate negatively (anger feels bad, and evaluates negatively the angering). But the correlation is not universal. Thus, on the face of it the experience of yearning for more tenderness in one's life presents-as-good such tenderness but is painful rather than pleasant. More subtly, nostalgia for one's senior year in college presents-as-good that period of one's life, but involves an unmistakable melancholic streak. Now, it is possible that some philosophical moves could reestablish the coextension between positive-evaluation and positive-affect in emotion; but regardless of how that shakes out, what matters for Brentano's division of emotions into positive and negative is the evaluative rather than affective dimension.[9]

2.2. Distinguishing emotion and will

Having defended an evaluative-attitudinal account both of will and of emotion, Brentano faces the problem of how to *distinguish* the two. Since they have the same underlying nature, he takes them to belong to a single 'fundamental class.' We might put this by saying that there is a single 'natural kind' that counts both emotional and volitional states among its members. It remains that there seems to be some real difference between emotion and volition, and this difference needs accounting for. The problem is that finding a satisfactory way to distinguish the two within the Brentanian framework is not straightforward.

2.2.1. UNSATISFACTORY DISTINCTIONS

It might be suggested that the ultimate difference between will and emotion is simply *primitive*: there is a feature F that volitional states exhibit and emotional states do not, and F can be appreciated through direct grasp in inner perception, but cannot be articulated in a theoretically informative way.

Some passages in the Brentano corpus actually appear to recommend this interpretation. Consider:

> A man may have exercised his faculties of loving and hating [i.e., his emotional faculties] with great frequency; nonetheless, if he had never willed anything, the distinctive nature of the phenomenon of will would not become fully clear to him from the analysis given here.
>
> (Brentano 1952: 220 [138])

No analysis of what must be added to a state that presents-as-good in order for it to qualify as a volitional state can make someone grasp the nature of willing who has never experienced willing for herself.

At the same time, the passage just quoted makes clear toward the end that Brentano does offer an *analysis* of the will ('the analysis given here'). Perhaps the idea is that an analysis is possible, though not one that would help a will-less person grasp the nature of the will. Still, those of us who have experienced both will and emotion – both volitional and emotional states – are in a position to articulate the key difference between the two, thus providing an informative account of the difference. The question is what that account ought to be.

One suggestion might be that while emotional states come in both a positive and a negative variety, volitional states can only be positive. For example, it would be a mistake to think that a desire for avoiding vodka presents-as-bad vodka; rather, it presents-as-good vodka-avoidance. (We can see this from the fact that avoidance has to be mentioned in the specification of the content of the desire. What the desire is *for* is: avoiding vodka.) All desires necessarily present-as-good. But some emotions present-as-bad, and this might be taken to mark the difference between will and emotion.

There are at least two problems with this suggestion. First of all, there might be volitional states other than desire that essentially present-as-bad. If aversion is a volitional state, for instance, it surely constitutes a 'negative volition': aversion to vodka certainly presents-as-bad vodka. More importantly, the present suggestion could not serve as a principled distinction between will and emotion, since for every given *positive* interest state, we still want to know whether it is a volitional state or a positive emotion. Thus an acceptable distinction between will and emotion should identify a feature F that *all* emotional states exhibit and *no* volitional state exhibits or that *no* emotional state exhibits but *all* volitional states do.

(For the same reason, we cannot use the fact that emotions, such as regret and disappointment, can be directed at the past, whereas the will is only directed at the future and present, to draw the will/emotion distinction. For this too offers no help when we want to determine whether a given future-directed interest state is volitional or emotional, given that some emotional states, such as hope, are certainly future-directed. And likewise we cannot say that the content of volitional states is necessarily an action whereas that of emotional states is not. For some emotional states do have actions in their content, as when one is glad that one is writing a book on Brentano.)

A different suggestion might be that we appeal to the presence of bodily feelings to distinguish emotional from volitional states. Brentano himself points out that 'the emotions (*Gemüthsbewegungen*) are usually taken to cover only affects (*Affecte*) connected with noticeable physical agitation/arousal (*Aufregung*)' (1874: II, 35 [199]).

At the same time, Brentano's tone suggests that he sees this manner of separating out the emotions as superficial, a piece of folklore more than a deliverance of descriptive psychology. One may reasonably speculate that, ultimately, he considers bodily arousal accidental to, rather than constitutive of, emotion. What is essential to emotional states on Brentano's view is their evaluative-attitudinal character, but arguably, bodily arousal plays no role in such attitudinally encoded evaluation, even if it accompanies it with complete regularity.

One might push back, suggesting that emotions involve essentially a kind of bodily evaluations – they are 'felt bodily stances' (Deonna and Teroni 2015: 293; see also Deonna and Teroni 2012: 78–9). Anger *feels bad*, in that the bodily feelings involved in being angry are unpleasant ones. The suggestion under consideration is that it is *because* anger at x feels bad that it presents-as-bad x. Moreover, the specific way in which anger at x presents-as-bad x differs from the specific way in which frustration with x presents-as-bad x, and the difference comes down to the slightly different ways in which anger and frustration *feel bad*. In any case, all emotional experiences exhibit the attitudinal property *bodily-presenting-as-good/bad*. This is in contrast to volitional states, which rather exhibit *nonbodily*-presenting-as-good/bad.

This suggestion faces a number of serious challenges, however. First, there might be some relatively refined emotions – some occurrences of mild indignation, or aesthetic delight, perhaps – that involve no noticeable bodily arousal. Secondly, as we have seen, in some cases yearning for x feels bad but presents-as-good x. So positive emotional evaluation appears to sometimes go with negative bodily feeling. Thirdly, even if positive bodily feeling and positive emotional evaluation covaried perfectly, it is unclear what grounds what here: it may well be that in some cases a bodily feeling is experienced as positive only because it embodies positive emotional evaluation. The sensation in one's stomach when an elevator lifts up briskly and brusquely is not all that different, qua visceral feeling, from the nervous 'butterflies in the stomach' – but in the elevator it feels rather nice! So we may surmise that the butterflies in the stomach are experienced as unpleasant precisely *because of their association with nervousness*, which presents-as-bad the unnerving object. Fourthly, some token volitional states may well involve their own felt bodily stances. Paul Ricœur writes: 'when I have decided to make a delicate move, I feel myself somehow charged, in the way a battery is charged' (Ricœur 1950: 62); the description resonates for at least some token decisions, and evokes a familiar, if subtle, kind of *bodily* feeling.

৵৵৵

A different suggestion, which Brentano seems to support more fully, is that the crucial distinction between will and emotion has something to do with *action*. Brentano writes:

Every willing (*Wollen*) has to do with a doing (*Tun*) we *believe to lie in our power*, with a good which is expected to result from the willing itself.   (1874: II, 103 [249]; my italics)

A volitional state 'has to do with' (*geht auf*) the achievability of the good targeted (see also Brentano 1952: 219 [137]).

If the idea, however, is that emotional and volitional states differ in that the latter imply a belief the former do not, then it is probably only a symptom of a deeper, more essential distinction. For note that it is a *cognitive* difference, whereas in their intrinsic natures volitional and emotional states are *non*cognitive states. Accordingly, the relevant beliefs must be mere accompaniments of volitional or emotional states.[10] Distinguishing volitional from emotional states in terms of these accompaniments would be a distinction in terms of *extrinsic* properties. Yet surely there is some *intrinsic* difference between the two – a difference grounded in their *natures* rather than in their *accompaniments*.

Chisholm has proposed that Brentano draw the will/emotion distinction in terms of a link to action as well, but action showing up in the content of pro attitudes, not beliefs. He writes:

In the case of an act of will, we have not only a desire for a certain thing, but the desire *that that desire bring about that thing*... An act of will has as part of its object something that the agent *does*.   (Chisholm 1986: 22–3)

Chisholm probably does not have in mind here that a desire for *x*, unlike an emotion about *x*, is always accompanied by a higher-order desire that *x* be obtained by the first-order desire. For that would be to explain desire in terms of second-order desire, which would not be terribly explanatory and would launch one on a regress. So what Chisholm must have in mind is that a desire for *x*, unlike an emotion about *x*, has as part of its content its own causal efficacy in bringing about the obtaining of *x*. That is, desires, and volitional states more generally, are *token-reflexive*: they are partly about themselves. A volitional state V presents not just *x*, but something like *x*-because-V (compare Searle 1983: chap. 3). When you *hope* to drink beer, the content of your hope is fully specified by <drinking beer>; but when you *intend* to drink beer, the content of your intention is fully specified only by <drinking beer as a result of this very intention> (observe: 'this very' is the *locus* of token-reflexivity).

It is somewhat problematic to attribute to Brentano a content-based way of distinguishing will from emotion. But perhaps Chisholm is not trying to get Brentano exactly right, but is rather free-styling within a broadly Brentanian approach. Still, his suggestion faces substantive difficulties. Even if one grants (the very strong claim) that all volitional states are token-reflexive in the way indicated, it is unclear why one could not emote about one's causal efficacy in bringing about certain results. A new-age enthusiast might, for example, hope not only that world peace obtain, but also that it obtain partly in virtue of that very own hope. He does not hope that lasting world peace come to pass for any old reason – say, as the outcome of 'a war to end all wars' – but rather hopes specifically that it issue from the peaceful hopefulness of so many human individuals, himself among them. His is a token-reflexive hope, then. Such token-reflexive emotions are rarities, but they *can* occur. And when they do, they do not cease to be emotions and suddenly become volitions. So something else must be constitutive of a mental state's status as emotional or volitional. This 'something else' may well explain why token-reflexivity tends to characterize volitional states much more centrally than emotional states, but it is a separate, deeper feature of the relevant states.

The discussion so far lays certain expectations from Brentano's account of the will/emotion distinction. In particular, we should expect it to be (i) a noncognitive rather than belief-based distinction and (ii) an attitudinal rather than content-based distinction. At the same time, it should *explain* the evident fact that volitional states are more intimately connected to action than emotional states. (Thus, although both volitional and emotional states present-as-good their objects, only volitional states tend to entrain beliefs to the effect that these objects are achievable by one.)

One idea might be that volitional states do not present their objects just under the guise of the good, but more specifically under the guise of the *achievable* good, or the guise of the *actionable* good, or something like that. On this view, while my being happy about writing a book on Brentano involves presenting-as-good the writing of the book, my *intending* to write a book on Brentano presents-as-*actionably*-good the writing of the book. A related idea might incorporate Schafer's aforementioned account of desire in terms of presenting-as-to-be-done into an account of the distinction between will and emotion as two kinds of interest state. Perhaps a volitional state frames its object not just as a good, but as a *good to be done*. In fact, I think Brentano went for a third option – in the same general neighborhood, but importantly different.

2.2.2. BRENTANO'S DISTINCTION

In Brentano's lecture notes for his Vienna practical philosophy course, which he wrote up originally in 1876 and refined and developed until 1894, Brentano writes:

> I can love [i.e., have a positive emotion toward] things that are incompatible (*unvereinbar*) with one another, for example doing sums and writing. The one [positive emotion] does not preclude/rule out (*schließt aus*) the other. In contrast, in any particular case I can decide on (*mich entscheiden*) one of the two. These decisional acts (*Entscheidungakte*) are not compatible with one another.   (Brentano 1952: 218–19 [137])

In a 1907 piece titled 'On Loving and Hating,' Brentano writes this:

> There are things which are incompatible (*unverträglich*) with others, as when for example it is impossible for the selfsame material object to be at once round and square, at rest and in motion, liquid and solid, red and blue. Whoever *wants* or *wishes* (*will oder wünscht*) that an object be one of these things cannot at the same time reasonably (*vernünftiger Weise*) want or wish that it be one of the others. But he *can* at the same time *find pleasure* in it being round and in it being square etc.   (Brentano 1907a: 156 [150]; my italics)

It is in these passages, I contend, that we get a glimpse into Brentano's ultimate account of the will/emotion distinction; other passages giving voice to the same approach include Brentano 1889: 78 [114], a letter dated 1908, and Brentano 1911: 156–7 [290]. Here is how I understand the account.

Suppose you have to choose a wine to accompany your meal. You do not like rosé, but would be happy with either white or red. Suppose, however, that the restaurant does not allow 'mixing' and that you much prefer red to white. You are *happy* with white wine, in the sense that you would be perfectly *satisfied* with it, but *decide* on red. Both your happiness (satisfaction) with the white and decision on red present-as-good their respective objects. However, while you can be both happy (or satisfied) with white and happy (satisfied) with red, even on the assumption that you cannot get both, you cannot both decide on white and decide on red in such circumstances. (Likewise, you cannot both *intend* to get the white and intend to get the red.) An emotional attitude such as happiness or satisfaction with x can be rationally directed at incompatible objects, but a volitional attitude such as deciding or intending can be rationally directed at most at one among incompatible objects. The general idea, then, is that conflicting emotional states can rationally coexist, but conflicting volitional states cannot – and this is what distinguishes the two kinds of state. That is:

> DISTINCTION$_1$::   For any interest state S, S is an *emotional state* iff there is a pair of objects x and y, such that (i) x and y cannot coexist and (ii) it is possible to rationally bear S both to x and to y; S is a *volitional state* iff there is no such pair.

Here 'object' covers any intentional object (anything we may present), not only concrete particulars; actions, events, and states of affairs are all potential intentional objects. Also, although incompatibility is interpreted here as incompossibility, in truth a subtler story is probably called for, where relations of probabilifcation and improbabilifcation play a role.[11]

It might be objected that a person may have both a volitional *and* an emotional attitude toward *x* – say both intend to, and be happy about, donating one's old blanket to charity – but that DISTINCTION₁ does not provide for this (either donating the blanket is compatible with some other action or it is not!). But this is wrong. All DISTINCTION₁ rules out is the existence of a *single mental state* which is both volitional and emotional. A person may certainly bear two separate attitudes toward a single object *x*, one of which it is irrational to hold *also* toward an incompatible *y* and one of which it is perfectly rational to. The person who both intends to, and is happy about, donating her old blanket bears two attitudes toward the donation: the intention-attitude she cannot rationally bear also toward keeping the blanket, but the happiness-attitude she can.

Two aspects of DISTINCTION₁ are not very Brentanian in spirit, however. First, DISTINCTION₁ does not seem to draw the will/emotion distinction in *attitudinal* terms. Indeed, it reads naturally as drawing a content-based distinction. Secondly, it does not seem to cite an *intrinsic* difference between emotional and volitional states: to decide whether a mental state is emotional or volitional, we must determine whether it is rationally compatible with some other state.

✍∾

Perhaps, however, there is a way to build the distinction pointed to in DISTINCTION₁ into specific attitudes intrinsic to emotional and volitional states.

In contemporary moral philosophy, there is a familiar distinction between prima facie and all-things-considered normativity. Against certain critics of deontological theories, W.D. Ross (1930) argued that we do have a duty not to harm others, for example, but it is a prima facie rather than all-things-considered duty. Thus if harming a terrorist might save a thousand innocent civilians, the prima facie duty not to harm others does not proscribe harming the terrorist. In that scenario, harming the terrorist would be prima facie wrong but ultima facie (all-things-considered) right. Conversely, helping an old lady cross the street is prima facie good, but if it slows traffic to the point that an ambulance arrives to hospital too late to save someone, then it is ultima facie bad.[12]

Now, one way to unpack the prima facie/ultima facie distinction is in terms of compatibility. Thus, to say that helping the old lady cross the street is *prima facie* good is to say that it is good in a sense of 'good' that makes it conceptually possible for some incompatible state of affairs to be good as well – for example the state of affairs of the ambulance arriving to the hospital on time. To say that helping the old lady cross the street is not *ultima facie* good is to say that it is not good in any sense of 'good' that rules out the goodness of other, incompatible states of affairs. Thus there is a straightforward conceptual connection between the kinds of compatibility relations exploited in DISTINCTION₁ and the distinction between prima facie and ultima facie normativity.

I suggest we use this conceptual connection to formulate succinctly Brentano's distinction between will and emotion in attitudinal terms. The idea is that positive emotions cast their objects in a *prima-facie*-positive light, since positive emotions evaluate their object positively in a way that allows a positive evaluation of incompatible objects; but acts of the will cast their objects in an *all-things-considered*-positive light, since their positive evaluations of their objects rule out a similar evaluation of incompatible objects.

Let us go back to the accompanying-wine dilemma. We may now say that in being happy with white wine, you experience white wine as prima facie good, but in deciding on red wine, you treat red wine as ultima facie good. (Note well: you may still change your mind and decide on white wine, for whatever reason. But the decision and intention to get red wine cannot survive this kind of change of mind – they must go out of existence when incompatible decisions and intentions come into existence. In this they differ from positive emotions toward either wine.) Thus although both volitional and positive-emotional states are goodness-committal, the goodness in question is ultima facie in the case of deciding on red wine but prima facie in the case of being happy with red wine.

Recall, now, that all these states are still presentations-as-good of the wine, not presentations of the-wine-as-good. Accordingly, we might say that while your happiness (an emotional state) presents-as-good$_{PF}$ (for 'prima facie good') white wine, your decision (a volitional state) presents-as-good$_{UF}$ (for 'ultima facie good') red wine.[13] All positive interest states generically present-as-good their intentional objects, but some specifically present-as-good$_{PF}$ their objects while others present-as-good$_{UF}$ theirs. The former are positive emotions, the latter states of the will. In other words:

> DISTINCTION$_2$:: For any interest state S toward object x, S is an emotional state iff S presents-as-good$_{PF}$ x (or presents-as-bad$_{PF}$ x); S is a volitional state iff S presents-as-good$_{UF}$ x.

In DISTINCTION$_2$, we have an *attitudinal* way of distinguishing will from emotion, one that draws the distinction in terms of the essential nature of will and emotion as evaluative states. Relatedly, it draws the distinction in terms of intrinsic properties of these states, rather than in terms of extrinsic properties that ultimately refer to merely accompanying states. At the same time, it explains the intimate connection of volitional states to action: once an intentional object has been not just presented-as-good, but presented-as-*ultima-facie*-good, hence as better than all alternatives, it remains only to *pursue* it.[14] In all these ways, DISTINCTION$_2$ has the 'look' of a bona fide Brentanian thesis.

2.2.3. A DIFFICULTY

Our Brentanian account of the distinction faces an important difficulty, however. In addition to cases of conflicting emotions, we are all familiar with cases of conflicting *desires*. Indeed, there are cases where (i) two of our desires conflict, (ii) we are aware that they conflict, but (iii) it is rational to hold on to both. After all, this is how *moral dilemmas* arise. Consider Sartre's renowned student, who faces the choice between leaving Paris to fight the Nazis and staying in Paris to look after his ailing mother

(Sartre 1946). Both the desire to fight the Nazis and the desire to tend to his mother are commendable, but they are incompatible. The decision which one to pursue is not an easy one, and at least for a while, the student can *reasonably* desire both. If so, both desires merely present-as-good$_{PF}$ their respective objects. By DISTINCTION$_2$, they would qualify as emotional rather than volitional states. This looks like an unwelcome consequence of DISTINCTION$_2$.

At the same time, there seems to be an important insight in Brentano's appeal to the prima facie/all-things-considered distinction in drawing the emotion/will distinction. Certainly it is true that our pro attitudes divide into two importantly different groups, depending on whether they cast their objects as prima facie or all-things-considered good. When it comes time to try and implement his pro attitudes in the world, Sartre's student *must* choose between the two options, thus entering a fundamentally new kind of mental state that surpasses his conflicting desires and paves the way to action. Entering that mental state is the beginning of mobilizing the will.

How are we to resolve these tensions? I think Brentano's best bet here is to boldly deny that desire is a volitional state and argue that, upon reflection, it is better classified as an emotional state. The question is how to make this sound non-ad-hoc.

For starters, note that although in analytic philosophy of mind desire has often been taken as the paradigmatic state with world-to-mind direction of fit, other philosophical traditions, notably the phenomenological tradition, have opted for other paradigms. According to Paul Ricœur, for example, the paradigmatic volitional state is *decision*, not desire (Ricœur 1950). The reason is that desire involves only a *hypothetical* pull to action, whereas decision's commitment to action is *categorical* (Ricœur 1950: 70). It is essential to my desire for red wine that *if* no other considerations outweigh it, it would lead to my trying to get red wine. Thus in desire the connection to action is conditional or hypothetical: the desire presents the action as to be performed *pending countervailing considerations*. In contrast, a decision's connection to action is categorical: in making the decision to get red wine, I commit to trying to get it, *period*. The commitment is unconditional.[15] The kinship between Ricœur's picture and Brentano's is evident (compare hypothetical/categorical to prima facie/ultima facie). But my point here is just that the tendency to treat desire as a paradigmatically volitional state may be specific to the philosophical tradition of analytic philosophy of mind. It does not reflect some deeper consensus.

More importantly, observe that, all said and done, desire is a *passion* rather than an action – something we find ourselves with rather than something that issues from the exercise of our will. In contrast, when we take a decision, say, we precisely *exercise* our will; to that extent, it is a phenomenon of the will *par excellence*. There is thus a bright line between the two phenomena. As Wallace puts it:

… intentions, decisions, and choices are things we do, primitive examples of the phenomenon of agency itself. It is one thing to find that one wants some chocolate cake very much, … quite another to resolve [or decide] to eat a piece. The difference, I would suggest, marks a line of fundamental importance, the line between the passive and the active in our psychological lives.

(Wallace 1999: 637)

It is therefore reasonable to hold that the most important line of division within the realm of mental states that present their objects under the guise of the good is one that divides them as follows: it places on one side passive states with hypothetical pull to action (i.e., ones that present-as-good$_{PF}$), and on the other side active or agentive states with a categorical pull to action (i.e., ones that present-as-good$_{UF}$).[16] We may consider this line a division of interest states into emotional and volitional, or find some other names for the two subclasses. But however we call things, it would seem desire falls on the side of this line in which emotional states belong rather than on the side in which such paradigmatic volitional states as decision and intention do.[17]

Is there any reason to think that Brentano himself would look favorably on such a reclassification of desire? I think so. Recall Brentano's claim that volitional states imply the belief that their intentional objects 'lie in our power' (1874: II, 103 [249]). In several places, Brentano is explicit that *wanting* need not imply any such belief. For example:

It is nowise built into wish or want (*Will*) that I believe it to be something which is in my power to realize/accomplish (*realisieren*). I can *wish*, but cannot *choose*, that the weather be good tomorrow.   (Brentano 1907a: 157 [151])

In analytic philosophy of mind, 'want' and 'desire' are typically taken to denote the same mental state. But in any case, Brentano makes a similar claim directly in terms of desire (*Begehrung*):

Kant indeed defined the faculty of desire simply as 'the capacity to bring into existence the objects of one's presentations through those presentations.'... This is why we find in Kant that curious claim that any wish, even if it were recognized to be impossible, such as the wish to have wings for example, is an attempt to obtain what is wished for and contains a presentation of our desire's causal efficacy.   (Brentano 1874: II, 117 [259])

Such passages appear to commit Brentano to the first two premises of the following straightforward argument: 1) for any subject S and object x, if S has a volitional state directed at x, then S believes that S can obtain x; 2) for some subject S and object x, S wants/desires x and S believes that S cannot obtain x; therefore, 3) wanting/desiring is not a volitional state. Brentano tends to make the point with emphasis on wishing, which is more antecedently amenable to reclassification as an emotion than wanting or desiring; but clearly, he plans to extend the same treatment to the latter two as well.[18]

In conclusion, the Brentanian account of will and emotion falls within the 'scholastic conception' treating these as mental states whose essence is to present their intentional objects under the guise of the good. However, Brentano's account stands out in building this into the attitudinal character of emotional and volitional states: their essence is to present-as-good their intentional objects. And his elegant approach to the *difference* between emotion and will is to identify two distinct species of the relevant attitudinal character: emotional states present-as-prima-facie-good, whereas volitional states present-as-ultima-facie-good. In addition to its considerable elegance, this picture's various components are, I have argued, quite plausible. The picture does imply that desire is an emotional rather than volitional state, contrary to the way it is typically treated in mainstream analytic philosophy of mind. Upon reflection, however, I suspect this consequence is eminently defensible.

3. Pleasure and Pain

This final section extends Brentano's evaluative-attitudinal account to the algedonic feelings of pleasure and pain. I first present Brentano's account (§3.1), then discuss the relationship between algedonic feelings and will and emotion (§3.2).

3.1. Brentano's evaluative-attitudinal theory

As we saw in Chap. 2, Brentano holds that pleasure and pain are *intentional* states, ones that present something. When we are in pain, we are pained *by something* (and not *only* in the causal sense of 'by'); when we have a pleasure, we are pleased *with something*. This is controversial, of course, but Brentano asserts it unambiguously:

> [Pleasure] always has an object, is necessarily a pleasure in something, what we perceive or apprehend (*vorstellen*). For example, sensory pleasure has a certain localized sensible quality (*Sinnesqualität*) for object.   (Brentano 1952: 179 [113])

Specifically, pain and pleasure present certain sui generis secondary qualities.[19]

For most of the twentieth century, the notion that pleasure and pain may be intentional states was taken as a nonstarter. Instead, it was assumed that such algedonic feelings are characterized by monadic phenomenal properties admitting of no further analysis – 'sensations.' In current philosophy of mind, however, intentionalism about pleasure and pain is very much a live view. According to intentionalism, not only do algedonic feelings *have* intentional properties, their specific intentional properties are what makes them (i) the algedonic feelings they are and (ii) algedonic feelings at all.

The big question, within this framework, is how to characterize the distinctive intentional properties of algedonic feelings. An early intentionalist account of pain identified its distinctive intentional properties with the tracking of tissue damage:

> Now *what* I experience or feel, in having a pain in a leg, is that there is some disorder in the leg, some damage that is painful or hurts. So, a pain in a leg, I suggest, is a token sensory experience which represents that something in the leg is damaged . . .   (Tye 1990: 228; italics original)

This account faces a number of difficulties. For starters, it is unclear how the account might be extended to pleasure. What does bodily pleasure track? Certainly not tissue *flourishing*, but what then?! (Massin 2013). More deeply, while the tracking of tissue damage in the leg might explain the fact that the pain is felt in the knee, it does not explain why the pain is so *unpleasant* (Aydede 2005). The point can be made by considering such unusual experiences as so-called morphine pain and pain asymbolia (see Grahek 2007), where subjects report that they are detecting a pain sensation but are entirely unbothered by it. Paradigmatic pain is of course very different from this, and involves a manifest *badness* of the pain. This additional aspect of pain experience remains unexplained by the original intentionalist account. In a slogan: it accounts for the sensory dimension of sensory pain, but not for the painfulness dimension of sensory pain.

The natural fix here is to suggest that pain also has an *evaluative* content: a knee-pain experience presents not only a specific event in the knee, but also presents the badness of that event. David Bain summarizes the view as follows:

A subject's being in unpleasant pain consists in his (i) undergoing an experience (the pain) that represents a disturbance of a certain sort, and (ii) that same experience additionally representing the disturbance as *bad* for him in the bodily sense.   (Bain 2013: 82; italics original)

This account has the advantage of extending straightforwardly to pleasure: an orgasm does present something *good* down there! It even extends naturally to Brentano's 'mental' pleasures: the sublime pleasure of hearing BWV 565 presents, among other things, the piece's goodness.

Brentano certainly adopted an evaluative conception of algedonic feelings, since he took them to belong in the same category of mental state as will and emotion (this is what chapter 8 of Book II of *Psychology* is mostly about). But given that for him the evaluative dimension of will and emotion are attitudinally encoded, we may see him as offering an evaluative-attitudinal account of algedonic feelings as well.[20] This distinguishes Brentano's view from Bain's and other contemporary evaluativists'. Labeling pleasure the positive algedonic feeling and pain the negative one, we may put Brentano's view as follows:

EVALUATIVE-F::   Any positive (or negative) algedonic feeling F about an object O essentially commits to the goodness (or badness) of O.

ATTITUDINAL-F::   An algedonic feeling F's commitment to the goodness (or badness) of an object O is an attitudinal property of F.

A toothache presents-as-bad the relevant buccal event, an orgasm presents-as-good the salient genital event.[21]

Arguing for this view is the mandate of §4 of chapter 8 of *Psychology* II, which opens as follows:

Let us now turn to the other phenomena at issue, namely pleasure (*Lust*) and displeasure (*Unlust*), which are the ones most commonly separated, as feelings, from the will. Is it true that here, too, inner experience reveals (*erkennen läßt*) with clarity this distinctive manner of reference to a content – this 'agreeableness (*Genehmsein*) as good' or 'disagreeableness as bad' – as the fundamental character of the phenomena? . . . As far as I am concerned, this seems no less obvious in this case than in the case of desire.   (Brentano 1874: II, 92–3 [242])

Brentano offers in that section three considerations in support of the evaluative-attitudinal view of algedonic feelings. The first, manifest in the passage just quoted, is that inner perception *reveals* the shared essence of algedonic feelings and states of the will (1874: II,

84 [235], 93 [242]). The second is that respectable authorities (Aristotle and Kant, but also Aquinas, Moses Mendelssohn, William Hamilton, Hermann Lotze, and Herbert Spencer) have maintained the view (1874: II, 93–8 [242–5]). The final consideration pertains to ordinary language and the way it mixes talk of pleasure, will, and love in a way that suggests they somehow belong together (1874: II, 98–100 [245–7]).

None of these is particularly probing. Nonetheless, the view itself has much to recommend it. On the one hand, it is clear that pleasure in a hazelnut ice cream casts the ice cream in a favorable light, and to that extent commits to its goodness. Theories of algedonic feelings that make no allowance for this evaluative dimension, such as the aforementioned early intentionalist theories, seem to leave out a central dimension of algedonic feelings. At the same time, the ice cream's value does not seem to be part of what the pleasure is directed *at*. They do not show up in the pleasure's content. To see this, ask yourself, which aspects of the ice cream are you aware of in this distinctively pleasurable way? The answer is probably: the sweet, hazelnutty *flavor* of the ice cream, its smooth texture, and perhaps also its cold, refreshing quality. *That* is what your pleasure responds to. Goodness does not appear in this list, because the pleasure-awareness is not awareness of goodness, even if you take pleasure in the ice cream *because* of its goodness. Accordingly, evaluative theories of algedonic feelings that place the evaluation within the feelings' content appear false to our experience of pain and pleasure. On the face of it, then, the commitment to the ice cream's goodness is attitudinally encoded: the pleasure must present-as-good the hazelnut ice cream rather than present the ice cream as good.[22]

An immediate challenge the account faces is to provide a story about the distinctive way pleasure and pain present-as-good/bad compared to emotion and will. Clearly, there is a felt difference between being pleased with an ice cream, hoping for ice cream, wanting ice cream, and deciding on ice cream. Yet all four present-as-good ice cream. So to capture the nature of pleasure, as distinct from all those other interest states, something more must be said.

3.2. Distinguishing algedonic feelings from emotion and will

As far as the distinction between presenting-as-good$_{PF}$ and presenting-as-good$_{UF}$ is concerned, it is clear that pleasure aligns with emotion rather than will. You can take pleasure in the particular purplish hue of a fragment of an El Greco painting, even as you think that its brightness ruins the painting's composition and renders the painting weaker than it would have been, say, if El Greco had opted for a dull pink there. As far as your pleasure is concerned, so to speak, that bright purple is good, but there are incompatible options which would have been better. In other words, it presents-as-good$_{PF}$ the fragment's purple hue. This distinguishes pleasure from decision and other volitional states. There is still the question, however, of what distinguishes pleasure from positive emotion (and pain from negative emotion).

I am not familiar with a discussion of this question anywhere in the Brentano corpus. The planned Book V of the *Psychology* was supposed to be about the entire category of interest (Rollinger 2012). Presumably, it would be part of that book's agenda to separate different types of interest, including algedonic and emotional. Unfortunately, that book was never written. So we are left to speculate in a Brentanian vein on the algedonic/emotional distinction.

One view might be that there is no real difference here. The idea might be that since they are characterized by the same attitudinal feature, emotional and algedonic states share an underlying nature that makes them belong to a single 'natural kind.' Another version would suggest we treat pleasure as one (positive) emotion among others, on a par – or on a continuum – with joy, satisfaction, contentment, and happiness. We have already noted that different emotions aim at different species of goodness or badness. For example, admiration presents-as-admirable whereas satisfaction presents-as-satisfying, where being admirable and being satisfying are two different ways of being good. One might hold that being pleasant is also a way of being good, and that pleasure is simply that mental states that presents-as-pleasant its object. As such, it can be seen as one among the positive emotions, or just a member of the same natural kind that the positive emotions are members of.

Although the view just presented is quite elegant, there is something uncomfortable about throwing such a simple and one-dimensional mental state as pleasure in the same basket with emotions, which can be so complex, textured, and multidimensional. Feeling satisfaction about finishing a paper one likes may involve pleasure in the fact, but it involves so much more: an appreciation of the paper's *worth*, of personal responsibility for the existence of that worth, and so on. Likewise, grief involves pain, but goes far beyond it, involving also appreciation of loss, of irreparability, and more. Even if at some level of abstraction pain and grief belong in a single category of mental states, surely there is a finer-grained taxonomy that also sets them apart; ditto for pleasure and satisfaction. Our question is how to articulate that which separates algedonic from emotional feelings in a principled way (that coheres well with Brentano's approach to mental taxonomy).

One thought might be that pleasure/pain is simply a *part* or *component* of emotion, one that can also occur by itself. Consider the fact that emotions divide into positive-affect ones and negative-affect ones. The former are pleasant, the latter unpleasant. One might suggest that positive-affect emotions involve pleasure as component, while negative-affect ones involve pain as component. At the same time, this constant aspect of emotion – its affective valence – is one that can detach from emotions and occur on its own. When it does, we experience simple pleasure or pain. On this line of thought, the difference between pleasure and (positive) emotion is the difference between a simple feeling F and a complex feeling F* of which F is a proper part.

However, even if all this is true, it does not help us draw the distinction between pleasure and emotion. For being part of an emotion is neither sufficient nor necessary for being a pleasure. On the one hand, the fact that a mental state is a component of a positive emotion does not entail that it is a pleasure: plausibly, being happy that the weather is nice involves as part believing that the weather is nice, but a belief is not an algedonic feeling. (Indeed, some emotions also involve *other emotions* as parts: plausibly, anger is a component of indignation.) Conversely, as we saw pleasure can also occur outside any emotional constellation.

A different approach is to draw the pleasure/emotion distinction within the category of interest in a way that would parallel the perception/belief distinction within the category of judgment. As we saw in Chap. 3, for Brentano the perception/belief distinction is not one of attitude but of content: the intentional objects of perception are sensibles whereas those of belief are intelligibles (Brentano 1928: 58 [44–5]). If the pleasure/emotion distinction were parallel, it would be a content distinction: presumably, pleasure would be directed at sensibles, positive emotion at intelligibles.

However, the view is not really plausible: many emotional experiences are directed at sensible rather than intelligible objects, as when one is happy about one's new coffee-table; conversely, the 'mental pleasure' we take in *The Brothers Karamazov* would appear to have an intelligible rather than sensible object.

In Chap. 3, I rejected on parallel grounds Brentano's content-based distinction between perception and belief. And I also proposed on Brentano's behalf what I take to be a much better, *attitudinal* account of the perception/belief distinction. This was that while belief in *x* presents-as-existent *x*, perceptual experience of *x* presents-as-existent-here-and-now *x*. Belief-in aims at existents, perception aims at *present* existents (in both the spatial and the temporal sense of 'present'!). In similar fashion, we might hold that positive emotion aims at goods while pleasure aims at *present* goods. The difference between being glad about the new carpet and taking pleasure in the new carpet, on this view, is that the pleasure can be appropriately taken only in the *presence* of the carpet, whereas the gladness can be appropriately experienced anywhere, anytime. You can sit in your office and pleasurably contemplate your new carpet, but the result would be gladness about the carpet, not pleasure in it. It may involve pleasure in *the idea* of the carpet, or in the idea of having the carpet, but not pleasure in the carpet itself. One has to be in the presence of an object, be in some sensory contact with it, to experience pleasure in that object. To that extent, pleasure is like perception in presenting its objects 'in the flesh.' If so, we might try to distinguish emotional from algedonic states as follows:

DISTINCTION$_3$:: For any mental state S intentionally directed at *x*, (a) S is a positive emotion about *x* iff S presents-as-good$_{PF}$ *x*; (b) S is a pleasure in *x* iff S presents-as-good$_{PF}$-here-and-now; (c) S is a negative emotion about *x* iff S presents-as-good$_{PF}$ *x*; (d) S is a pleasure in *x* presents-as-good$_{PF}$-here-and-now *x*.

To be clear, I am not attributing DISTINCTION$_3$ to Brentano. Indeed, I suspect that Brentano would plump rather for the content-based distinction between sensible and intelligible intentional objects, or perhaps for the 'single natural kind' approach. All the same, I recommend that a Brentanian philosophy of mind adopt DISTINCTION$_3$ as the best option for its account of the realm of mental states that present under the guise of the good.[23] (Note well: the account does not rule out the possibility of experiencing emotions about the here-and-now; it is just that the here-and-now must show up in the *content* of such emotions, whereas it is built into the *attitude* of algedonic feelings.[24])

If this approach could be made to work, we would obtain a principled distinction between the algedonic and the emotional that parallels the principled distinction between the perceptual and the doxastic – and does so with a distinctly Brentanian flair, whether or not Brentano would assent to it. The approach portrays the realm of interest states as comprised of all and only states which present-as-good, and structures that realm by the different manners in which different interest states do so: volitional states present-as-ultima-facie-good, emotional states present-as-prima-facie-good, and algedonic states present-as-prima-facie-good-here-and-now!

For Brentano, whatever the *differences* between pleasure, pain, emotion, and will, their *commonality* goes much deeper, making them belong to a single 'fundamental class.' What makes the class fundamental is that the *intra*-class differences pale in comparison to the *inter*-class differences. There are differences between presenting-as-good$_{PF}$ and presenting-as-good$_{UF}$, and there are even deeper differences between presenting-as-good and presenting-as-bad. Yet the fact that all interest states frame their objects in terms of value sets them apart from mental states that either frame their objects in terms of existence or merely present them in a neutral fashion (Brentano 1874: II, 105 [250]).

In modern philosophy of mind, this deep commonality between will, emotion, and pleasure/pain has been by and large neglected. To my knowledge, the only exception is Bennett Helm, who argues for a unified account of these three types of phenomenon precisely as *felt evaluations* (Helm 2002). Helm's account is to that extent thoroughly (though unwittingly) Brentanian. At the same time, it is unclear that Helm's account insists on the *attitudinal* construal of felt evaluation.

Conclusion

In the philosophy of mind of the past quarter-century, the literatures on emotion and on pain have rarely intersected. In contrast, it is clear that Brentano's evident need for a systemic bird's-eye view, expressed in a series of symmetries and parallels, pushes him to recognize the fundamental commonality among the phenomena he calls 'interest' – and their categorical difference from the two other mental categories. The most fundamental parallelism in the whole of our mental edifice is probably this:

If something can become the content of a judgment in that it can be accepted as true or rejected as false, it can also become the object of a [state of interest] in that it can be agreeable (*genehm*) (in the broadest sense of the word) as something good, or disagreeable (*ungenehm*) as something bad.   (Brentano 1874: II, 88–9 [239])

Just as believing in ducks commits to the existence of ducks, loving chocolate commits to the goodness of chocolate, and just as disbelieving in ghosts commits to the nonexistence of ghosts, hating vegemite commits to the badness of vegemite. All four kinds of mental state, we saw in Chap. 3, rest on a fifth: sheer presenting.

Seeking this kind of symmetry appears to be a methodological heuristic in Brentano's theorizing about the mind. When one's account of interest phenomena turns out to exhibit the same internal structure as one's account of judgment, this should give one a sense that one is onto something. Lack of symmetry, meanwhile, should raise prima facie suspicion. Obviously, this kind of heuristic has by and large disappeared from modern philosophy of mind. One might speculate that this disappearance goes hand in hand with the fragmentation and specialization in modern philosophy discussed in the Introduction. In Brentano's time, however, the degree of specialization and fragmentation characteristic of today's philosophical world was absent. It was still possible for philosophers to have their 'finger in every pie' and do so with a respectable level of scholarship. Relatedly, considerations of system-wide symmetry played a much more central role.

It is an independent question whether such systematic thinking is an intellectual virtue or vice. Certainly it is not clear in what way symmetry and cohesion might be *truth-conducive*. That is, given two theories T and T*, such that T exhibits more symmetries (and generally greater cohesion) than T*, should we, other things being equal, expect T to be more likely to be true? To my knowledge, there exists no *argument* for a positive answer. And in the history of philosophy, certainly in the history of German idealism, systematic thinking has tended to come with a familiar intellectual vice, namely, that of reinterpreting the phenomena in light of one's big-picture theory, or 'denying the datum' in order to protect the stability of one's system. The danger here is a kind of increasing insulation from reality as one's system evolves. The rise of analytic philosophy in *fin-de-siècle* Cambridge was inspired in large part by British idealists' intemperance in this domain (see Moore 1899), and Hegel is certainly no improvement. A bottom-up approach that was deemed more intellectually honest and more respectful of the phenomena entrenched itself in analytic philosophy in the aftermath.

Importantly, however, Brentano himself does not tend to impose preconceived theory on the phenomena. When the phenomena themselves create asymmetries, he is quick to point this out. A case in point is the asymmetry between judgment and interest we pointed out in Chap. 3: Brentano highlights the fact that goodness comes in degrees (some things are better than others), whereas truth and existence do not (no existing thing is 'more existent' than any other). This forces him to posit a primitive comparative interest state, *preference*, matched by no parallel state in the domain of judgment (more on this in Chap. 8). In this and other instances, Brentano gives expression to his deep empiricist sensibilities (see especially Brentano 1925), with the pride of place they assign to the phenomena.[25] Brentano's philosophy is a living example, then, of peaceable cohabitation between, on the one hand, systematic, top-down thinking and, on the other hand, empirically responsible, bottom-up thinking in a single philosophical project.[26]

Notes to Chapter 7

1. This point applies also to more textured functionalist accounts of desire, which designate a more substantive set of causes and effects distinctive of desire. Consider Alan Goldman's account, which identifies five or six specific effects of a paradigmatic desire (and considers anything a desire which shares sufficiently many of these effects): 'A paradigm desire for *x*...disposes one to bring about *x*, produces pleasant thoughts of *x*, involves a positive evaluative judgment of *x*, a yearning sensation in its absence, a direction of attention to things related to *x*, and possibly produces other instrumental desires for means to satisfy it' (Goldman 2017: 335). This kind of account, too, would be unacceptable to Brentano, as long as some of the effects are ones desire is said to be only *disposed* to bring about.

2. Recall that *descriptive* psychology is for Brentano the project of describing the nature of the phenomena of consciousness, while *genetic* psychology is the project of offering causal explanations of their occurrence and development (genesis). Brentano seems to hold that the nature of states of the will, which makes them such, is manifest to inner perception (see Brentano 1874: II, 83 [235]).

3. For more on the notion of direction of fit, see Chap. 3.

4. That is, I do not mean to suggest that every desire commits *the desirer* to that goodness. It *may*, namely in case the desirer *endorses* her desire – but often we do not endorse our desires. So the point is that as far as the desire itself is concerned, the object is good. The point of using commitment talk here, as elsewhere, is to stay neutral for a time on the question of whether it is the state's content or attitude that ensures the casting of the object as good.

5. The only connotation of the term 'pro attitude' we must explicitly cancel here is that this is a *dispositional* state. As we saw in Chap. 1, Brentano rejects the existence of dispositional mental states. Accordingly, he takes desire and other interest states to be occurrent conscious states. They are occurrent pro attitudes, then.

6. I assume for the sake of exposition that there is such a thing as evaluative perception – since this is how Stampe understands desire. As we will see in Chap. 8, however, Brentano rejects this notion (Brentano 1952: 119–20 [74]).

7. This attitudinal twist is dialectically significant, because most arguments against evaluative accounts of emotion target the claim that values are presented by emotions (see, e.g., Dokic and Lemaire 2013). But Brentano's evaluative account does not claim that values are presented by emotions, so it is not vulnerable to arguments of this sort. Opponents of evaluative theories must therefore proffer some new argument against the attitudinal version of the evaluative account.

8. One option we will consider, in fact, is that desire *just is* a kind of emotion on Brentano's view. If so, EVALUATIVE-E and ATTITUDINAL-E in fact *entail* EVALUATIVE-D and ATTITUDINAL-D.

9. One might suggest, for example, that mixed-valence or 'bittersweet' emotions (see Massin 2011), such as nostalgia, are always composites involving a plurality of emotional elements and corresponding objects, some of which are presented-as-good and some are presented-as-bad. Perhaps nostalgia for one's senior year in college combines presenting-as-good one's lifestyle during that time and presenting-as-bad the irrecoverable loss of that lifestyle, or of youth itself. Thanks to Kate Pendoley for discussion on this point.

10. If volitional states were composite states with a cognitive component, this cognitive component could be a constitutive part of their nature. But Brentano seems to think that interest states do not have a cognitive component *essentially*.

11. If we introduce gradient incompatibility, whereby x's existence *probabilifies* y's nonexistence, we could also define a continuum of states between pure emotions and pure volitions. But this is not strictly forced on us: some bright line might be drawn somewhere along the envisaged continuum. In that case, the will/emotion distinction remains dichotomous.

12. By this I mean that the resulting state of affairs is ultima facie bad. This can be so even if the act leading to that state of affairs is not considered wrong, say because the person helping the lady was unaware of the ambulance.

13. Note well: since you are also *happy* with red wine, you also harbor a mental state that presents-as-good$_{PF}$ the red wine. It is perfectly rational for you to be both happy with white and happy with red. But a volitional state such as decision or intention you can bear only toward one of the two wines.

14. This may not quite amount to the kind of 'internal connection' demanded by so-called motivational internalism (see, originally, Falk 1945, and more recently, Smith 1994: chap. 3). But such an internal connection goes far beyond what Brentano needs here. All he needs is an intimate connection to action exhibited by volitional but not emotional states.

15. This does *not* mean that decisions cannot involve conditional commitment to action. It is just that when they do, the conditionality must be part of their *content*. I can certainly decide that I want the red wine unless it costs triple as much as the white wine. Here I enter a mental state with an unconditional attitudinal commitment to a conditional content. (This is to be distinguished from a case where I simply decide to get the red wine but am *later* told that it will cost triple as much as the white, whereupon I make a *new* decision. The latter is not a case of a conditional decision, but rather of a *change of mind* from one unconditional decision to another.)

16. There seems to be a close connection between the hypothetical/categorical pull distinction and the prima facie/ultima facie good distinction: if G is a *prima facie* good, then one ought to pursue G *unless* there are incompatible goods superior to it; but if G is an *ultima facie* good, one ought to pursue G, *period*.

17. A more nuanced version of this move would distinguish two notions of desire and place one in the emotional domain and the other in the volitional domain. Thus, in his book *Desire*, G.F. Schueler distinguishes between two notions of desire: 'In one sense of "desire," ... from the fact that an agent intentionally performed some action, it follows that he or she wanted to do whatever it was that action was supposed to achieve. But in the other perfectly good sense of "desire," there is nothing at all problematic or mysterious about people doing things they have no desire to do, things they don't *want* to do *at all.*' (Schueler 1995: 29; italics original) The first (arguably, more theoretical) notion of desire belongs in the will, but does not allow for conflicts of desire (since the agent cannot perform simultaneously conflicting actions). The second (more commonsensical) notion of desire, however, needs to be reclassified with the emotions.

18. It might be objected that even if the status of first-order desires as volitional is negotiable, that of second-order desires is much less so. Indeed, one view is that a person's will can be *identified* with what she desires to desire. (An approximation of this kind of view is developed in Frankfurt 1971.) However, arguably this sort of view is framed naturally in

terms of second-order *desires* partly because of the prominence of desire talk in current discussions of the will. But if the above considerations are cogent, perhaps this kind of approach would be better framed in terms not of desired desires but desired *decisions* (or indeed decisions toward which one has any pro attitude).

19. This applies not only to sensory pleasure, but also to 'mental' (*geistigen*) pleasure, such as the 'refined delight (*edle Freude*) we experience when listening to a Beethoven symphony or gazing at one of Raphael's madonnas' (Brentano 1952: 186 [118]).

20. It is perhaps worth noting that Crane (2009) supports an attitudinal account of pleasure and pain as well. But crucially, Crane does not offer an evaluative characterization of the relevant attitude. In fact, in Crane pleasure is claimed to present in a distinctive mode, but what that mode is remains unsaid. Brentano's account is in this respect considerably more developed: it tells us that pleasure's characteristic mode is that of presenting-as-good, pain's that of presenting-as-bad.

21. Likewise, an experience of 'refined delight' at one of Shakespeare's better soliloquies or one of Messi's better slaloms presents-as-good the soliloquy or slalom, while the deep pain of missing one's deceased grandfather presents-as-bad his absence.

22. Another theory of pain that has been gaining momentum in current philosophy of mind and has commonality with Brentano's is imperativism (Klein 2007, Martínez 2011). According to this, pain is characterized by an *imperative* content, something like 'Avoid tokens of this type of event!' What is special about imperatives is their *force*, which aligns on the side of attitude rather than content. In this respect, the view is similar to Brentano's. The main difference is that an imperative force is in essence an action-guiding feature rather than an evaluative feature. At the same time, the action-guiding and evaluation tend to go hand in hand. In a way, then, the difference between the two views is in what each takes to be more fundamental, and thus essential, to pains. Imperativism takes the action-guiding character of pain to be essential to it, and sees evaluation as something that comes along with action-guidance; Brentano takes pain's evaluative character to be essential and sees action-guiding-ness as something that falls out of this evaluative character.

23. It might be objected that DISTINCTION₃ cannot account for *mental* or *spiritual* pleasure, such as the pleasure taken in a powerful poem. But perhaps *that* type of pleasure could be safely classified as an emotion: it is at bottom just an experience of being happy about something. Relatedly, one might argue that even if DISTINCTION₃ is extensionally adequate for pleasures canonically picked by 'S takes pleasure *in*', it seems obviously extensionally inadequate for pleasures canonically picked out by 'S is pleased *that*' (as in 'Jimmy is pleased that Juventus lost'). But since Brentano rejects the existence of propositional mental states, he has to assay pleasure-that in terms of pleasure-in anyway (just as he assays belief-that in terms of belief-in).

24. The same applies to belief, of course. I may believe not just in a table, but in a (spatially and temporally) present table. And likewise, I can be happy about my son smiling, but I can also be happy about my son smiling here and now (happy about his present-and-current smile). In contrast, I am suggesting, it is in the nature of perception and pleasure to commit to the spatial and temporal proximity of their objects. That proximity is not part of *what* one perceives, and nor is it part of what one is pleased by.

25. Indeed, one might speculate about Brentano's historical role in putting the phenomena first in twentieth-century philosophy. A similar concern for starting from the phenomena

themselves can be found in Husserl's phenomenological method and its German and French practitioners, and as already noted Husserl was Brentano's student in Vienna from 1884 to 1886. At the same time, Brentano exercised immense influence on George Stout (witness Stout 1896), who was both Moore's and Russell's tutor at Cambridge. One may therefore surmise that Brentano's project of descriptive psychology – with its emphasis on starting from the phenomena – was an inspiration to both phenomenology and analytic philosophy.

26. For comments on a previous draft, I am grateful to Mathilde Berger-Perrin, Paul Boswell, Géraldine Carranante, Julien Deonna, Lionel Djadaojee, Guillaume Fréchette, Anna Giustina, Vincent Grandjean, Tricia Magalotti, Karl Schafer, Josh Shepherd, and Fabrice Teroni. I have also benefited from presenting drafts of this chapter at the University of Geneva, as well as to two different audiences at École Normale Supérieure. I am grateful to the audiences there, in particular Romain Bourdoncle, Maria Gyemant, Raluca Mocan, Lylian Paquet, and Justin Winzenrieth.

8

Metaethics
Goodness

In Chap. 5, we saw how Brentano develops a metaontology based on his account of judgment. In this chapter, we will see that he develops a structurally analogous metaethic on the basis of his account of interest phenomena (will, emotion, and pleasure/pain). The chapter presents, develops, and up to a point defends Brentano's account. In §1, I lay out a logical geography within which Brentano's theory can be usefully placed. In §2, I present Brentano's theory. §3 is dedicated to Brentano's *case* for his theory. In §4, I discuss a number of objections, both to the theory and to the argument for it – among them one which I do find devastating to Brentano. This will lead us to discuss Brentano's theory of *beauty* in §5.

1. Introduction: Theories of Value

The organizing question of metaethics, recall from Chap. 5, is 'What does it mean to say that something is good?' Answers to this question can be classified in any number of ways, but there are two deep divisions among such answers that run through the history of philosophy. The first is the division between naturalist and nonnaturalist answers; the second is between what I will call 'object-end' and 'subject-end' answers.[1] This section introduces these two distinctions.

At the broadest level, naturalism and nonnaturalism are distinguished by their take on the relation between fact and value. Nonnaturalists hold that there is a *dichotomy* or *categorical difference* between the two realms: matters of value are *irreducible* to matters of fact, and nothing in the latter can *account for* the former. Naturalists deny this, trying to reductively explain the domain of value in terms of the domain of facts.

It is far from obvious how to formulate such impressionistic characterizations as precise theses. To a first approximation, we may think of nonnaturalism as the following thesis: There are normative truths whose truthmakers have constituents which cannot be accounted for naturalistically. Thus, 'Genocide is wrong' is strictly true, and has as its truthmaker the state of affairs of genocide having the property of being wrong, where the property of being wrong cannot be accounted for by anything within the 'natural' or 'empirical' realm. This is still quite vague, but note that it allows for two distinct ways of being a naturalist: either by denying that there are normative truths, or by allowing such truths but insisting that their truthmakers are fully explicable in naturalistic terms. Both routes have been taken: 'expressivists' (Ayer 1936: chap. 6, Gibbard 1990), for example, deny the existence of normative truths, while 'Cornell realists' (Boyd 1988, Brink 1989) deny that normative truthmakers have naturalistically recalcitrant constituents.

Two questions still press: (i) what makes a truth 'normative'?; (ii) what makes an entity 'natural(istic)'? To bypass the first question, I propose that we simply focus on putative truths about goodness, which would be normative if anything is. As for the second question, three main strands can be discerned in discussions of (non)naturalism. All three are problematic as accounts of the *nature* of the natural, but make for reasonably reliable *symptoms* of naturalness.

The first and most dominant approach is to construe the natural as that which is invoked in the natural sciences – today's natural sciences in one version, the natural sciences at the 'end of inquiry' in another (Moore 1903a: 92). This leads to the following version of nonnaturalism:

(NN$_1$)   There is a statement S of the form 'x is good,' such that (i) S is true and (ii) at least one constituent of S's truthmaker is neither itself invoked in, nor reductively explicable in terms of entities invoked in, (end-of-inquiry) natural science.

The idea is that (end-of-inquiry) natural science will not mention goodness, and what it will mention will not be sufficient to reductively explain goodness.

The main problem with NN$_1$, as a formulation of nonnaturalism, is the following dilemma. Appealing to *today's* natural sciences probably rules out very natural phenomena that are yet to be recognized in our (presumably still incomplete) science. If we appeal instead to end-of-inquiry natural science, the ensuing thesis is somewhat vacuous, since we have no idea what might show up therein and how continuous it might be with our current picture of nature. Signing up on 'naturalism' without any clear grasp of what type of thing 'natural' might refer to only gives the *illusion* of having asserted something. One has no real sense of what one has committed to.[2]

A second strand in discussions of naturalism construes the natural as the spatiotemporal, or the causally-efficacious spatiotemporal (Armstrong 1997, Kim 2003). This suggests the following formulation of nonnaturalism:

(NN$_2$)   There is a statement S of the form 'x is good,' such that (i) S is true and (ii) at least one constituent of S's truthmaker is neither (causally-efficaciously) spatiotemporal nor reductively explicable in terms of (causally efficacious) spatio-temporal entities.[3]

Here the idea is that nature is a spatiotemporal system of causally interacting entities, and something is 'natural' just when it is suitably embedded in that system.

One problem here is that, intuitively, we take such things as ghosts and witches to be naturalistically unacceptable, yet *if* they existed they would be very much spatiotemporal and causally efficacious. A ghost might live in the castle attic (spatial) for two centuries (temporal) and make candlelights flicker (causal). A witch would live in Salem for a hundred years and would incite adultery. Yet part of what we want in wielding naturalism is to produce an interdiction on appeal to ghosts and witches in explaining flickers and betrayals.

A third approach construes the natural as that which can be empirically observed (Copp 2003). The resulting nonnaturalist thesis is:

(NN$_3$)   There is a statement S of the form 'x is good,' such that (i) S is true and (ii) at least one constituent of S's truthmaker is neither empirically observable nor reductively explicable in terms of empirically observable phenomena.

The goodness of generosity, on this view, is neither observable itself nor reductively explicable in terms of what is.

The fundamental problem here is that NN$_3$ provides an epistemological characterization of an ontological notion. Furthermore, the characterization seems too narrow: leptons too are neither observable (because too small) nor reductively explicable in terms of what is observable (because fundamental), yet are clearly natural phenomena.

All three characterizations face real difficulties, then.[4] Nonetheless, all three cite features that tend to be symptomatic of natural entities. Certainly an entity which were invoked both in current and end-of-inquiry science, were spatiotemporal and efficacious, and were empirically observable would qualify as natural. Thus we may take these three characterizations collectively as useful *guides* to 'the natural.'

We say that genocide is bad, but also that approval of genocide is bad; and that generosity is good, but also that approval of generosity is good. Such evaluations seem to go hand in hand: generosity is good iff generosity-approval is; genocide-approval is bad iff genocide is. (Also: generosity is good iff generosity-disapproval is bad, and genocide is bad iff genocide-disapproval is good.) This raises a Euthyphro-style question: is generosity-approval good because generosity is, or is generosity good, ultimately, precisely because approval of it is? Some ethical theories ground the value of generosity-approval in the value of generosity, others ground the value of generosity in that of its approval. Let us say that the former offer an *object-end* answer to our Euthyphro question, the latter a *subject-end* answer.[5]

The distinction between object-end and subject-end views applies both to naturalist and to nonnaturalist theories of value. The aforementioned Cornell realists, for example, are object-end naturalists: they ground the goodness of generosity-approval in the goodness of generosity, then the goodness of generosity in functional properties that acts of generosity exhibit. Meanwhile, some (though not all) response-dependent theorists of value are subject-end naturalists: they ground the goodness of generosity in the goodness of generosity-approval, then ground the goodness of generosity-approval in some purely psychological properties of the approval (Lewis 1989, Gert 2009).

Twentieth-century *non*naturalism has been dominated by the object-end approach expounded by Moore in *Principia Ethica* (Moore 1903a). This tradition has continued to be influential in twenty-first-century nonnaturalist thinking (Shafer-Landau 2003, Enoch 2011). But twenty-first-century metaethics has also seen an impressive rise in *fitting attitude* accounts of value (D'Arms and Jacobson 2000, Zimmerman 2001, Danielsson and Olson 2007, Way 2012, Chappell 2012, Kauppinen 2014, McHugh and Way 2016), which are paradigmatically subject-end.[6] We may formulate the fitting-attitude account of goodness as follows:

(FA$_1$)   For any good g, (i) it is fitting to take a pro attitude toward g, and (ii) g is good *because* (i).[7]

Some (though not all) fitting-attitude theorists are subject-end *non*naturalists: they ground the goodness of generosity in the fittingness of generosity-approval, but then deny that the fittingness of generosity-approval can be accounted for in any nonnormative terms.

The distinctions between naturalist and nonnaturalist theories of value, on the one hand, and object-and subject-end theories, on the other, produce a matrix of four positions on the nature of value: object-end naturalism, subject-end naturalism, object-end nonnaturalism, and subject-end nonnaturalism. Where does Brentano's theory of value fit in this matrix?

2. Brentano's Subject-end A-naturalism

Brentano does not comment on whether he is a naturalist or nonnaturalist. Furthermore, whether he is best interpreted as a naturalist or as a nonnaturalist depends on what symptom of naturalness we focus on. It is beyond question, however, that Brentano took a subject-end rather than object-end approach to value. Accordingly, I start with a presentation of the subject-end character of Brentano's account (§2.1), which I then fill in with some details (§2.2); I then take up the issue of naturalism (§2.3).

2.1. Brentano as fitting-attitude theorist

Brentano states his preference for the subject-end approach in many places. Here is one clear statement from an 1889 lecture before the Vienna Legal Society, a lecture which then became the basis for his main metaethical work, *The Origin of Our Knowledge of Right and Wrong*:[8]

We call something 'good' when the love concerned with it is correct/fitting (*richtig*). In the broadest sense of the word, the good is that which can be loved with a correct/fitting love – that which is love-worthy (*Liebwerte*).   (Brentano 1889: 19 [18])

Here is another, from a separate 1889 lecture:

…everything thinkable divides into two classes: one containing everything for which love is fitting (*passend*), the other everything for which hate is. Whatever belongs in the first class we call good, whatever is included in the other we call bad.   (Brentano 1930: 25 [21–2])

And a third, from the 1876–94 lecture notes on practical philosophy:

…when we call certain objects good, and others bad, we are saying thereby nothing more than that whoever loves the former and hates the latter has taken the right stand (*verhalte sich richtig*).   (Brentano 1952: 144 [90])

Two terminological reminders are in order. First, as we saw in Chap. 7, Brentano uses the terms 'love' and 'hate' to cover all pro and con attitudes (respectively). Secondly, Brentano's *richtig* is not supposed to mean anything like 'true' or 'veridical.' As noted in Chap. 5, in one footnote he offers *konvenient, passend,* and *entsprechend* as interchangeable with *richtig* (Brentano 1889: 60 [74]). This makes clear that what he has in mind is something like 'appropriate,' 'fitting,' or 'suitable.' When we take these two terminological clarifications into account, we see that Brentano is a straightforward fitting-attitude theorist: he grounds the goodness of any *x* in the fittingness of pro attitudes toward *x*.

Indeed, Brentano is plausibly the *first* fitting-attitude (FA) theorist. It is sometimes said that Sidgwick floated FA before Brentano's *Origin*, when he wrote that ultimate or final good is 'that of which we should desire the existence if our desire were in harmony with reason' (Sidgwick 1884: 108). But first, it is not clear that the 'should' in Sidgwick's formulation is normative; it appears to be rather the past subjunctive of 'shall.' And in any case, Brentano actually asserts his FA already in his 1866 habilitation (aged 28!):

…we call something good insofar as it is desire-worthy (*begehrenswert*).   (Brentano 1866: 141; see also 1874: II, 100 [247])

Thus Brentano has a good claim to the status of first fitting-attitude theorist.

It might be objected that Brentano could not possibly be a *subject*-end theorist, since in some places he stresses the independence of goodness from our mental life. Consider this striking passage:

The objective condition for any [pro attitude] being potentially correct/fitting lies in the goodness of the object at which it is directed. This says nothing, however, as to whether there is anyone who could harbor such a [pro attitude]. The analogy with the true in the sense of the existent will make this immediately clear. When we say that for something [to exist] means that it can be correctly/fittingly [believed in], we do not thereby say that there must be such [a belief]. What is would continue to exist even if nobody were to [believe in] it.   (Brentano 1952: 208 [131]; see also 1889: 24 [24])

This passage appears, if anything, to give priority to the goodness of objects over the fittingness of attitudes toward those objects. At the very least, it may motivate attributing to Brentano a 'no-priority view' of the sort McDowell (1985) seems to defend.

However, the suggestion that Brentano takes mind-independent goodness to be prior to fittingness runs against the veritable difficulty that Brentano does not seem to think there *is* such a thing as worldly goodness inhering in things themselves. In a 1909 letter to Oskar Kraus, he writes:

It is incomprehensible to me what you seek to gain here with your belief in the existence (*Bestehen*) of goodness with which the emotions are found to correspond (*in einer adäquatio gefunden*).   (Brentano 1966: 207; see also Brentano 1930: 81 [71])

It is hard to see how to square such a statement even with a no-priority view. It is much more plausible that, in stressing the independence of the good from our attitudes toward goods, Brentano is merely stressing the independence of what it is *fitting* to have a pro attitude toward from the attitudes we *actually* have. To say that it is fitting to have a pro attitude toward generosity is to assert a potentially-counterfactual conditional: *if* anyone should have a pro attitude toward *generosity*, that attitude would be fitting. This does not guarantee that anyone *will* have such a pro attitude. It is only this cleft between attitudes we have or will have and the attitudes it would be fitting for us to have, I suggest, that Brentano shines a light on in the passage that stresses the attitude-independence of goodness. There is no intimation here of any further cleft, between what it would be fitting for us to have a pro attitude toward and what is good.

Brentano is clearly an FAist, then. Recall that for him, the essential characteristic of pro attitudes is the attitudinal feature of presenting-as-good. So *his* FA comes to the following:

(FA$_2$)   For any good g, (i) it is fitting to have a mental state that presents-as-good g, and (ii) g is good because (i).

As in Chap. 5, any circularity here is merely apparent: 'presents-as-good' should be understood as a merely suggestive but syntactically unstructured expression ('good' is no more a syntactic part of 'presents-as-good' than 'cat' is a syntactic part of 'catastrophe'). What FA$_2$ asserts, perfectly coherently, is that fitting presenting-as-good is prior to goodness: we can understand what it is for something to be good only by understanding what it is to fittingly favor something.

More precisely, Brentano applies his fitting-attitude account to *intrinsic, noninstrumental* goodness – goodness 'in the proper sense,' as he puts it. We call a salad healthy, a jog healthy, and a body healthy. But only the body can be healthy in a proper, independent sense; the salad and the jog are healthy in a derivative sense, insofar as they are instrumental to the body's health. In a similar way, claims Brentano, some things are good only in a derivative sense, namely, the sense that they are instrumental in bringing about things which are good in and of themselves. The real question is what makes anything intrinsically good in this way, and it is to answer this question that he offers the fitting-attitude account. In other words, Brentano's overall account of value is better formulated as follows:

(FA$_3$)   For any good g, either (a) (i) it is fitting to have a mental state that presents-as-good g, and (ii) g is good because (i), or (b) there is a g^*, such that (iii) g is instrumental in bringing about g^*, (iv) it is fitting to have a mental state that presents-as-good g^*, and (v) g^* is good because (iv).

Here Clause (a) accounts for intrinsic or proper goodness and Clause (b) for instrumental or derivative goodness. Any thing is good that exhibits one or the other.

2.2. What is fittingness?

In its rather short modern career, FA has generated a sizable critical literature (Baldwin 1999, Rabinowicz and Rønnow-Rasmussen 2004, Heathwood 2008, Alfonso 2009, Bykvist 2009, Reisner 2009, *inter alia*). The ensuing debates have focused mostly on the advantages and disadvantages of FA. But whatever betides these debates, surely the deepest challenge facing FA is to explain what it means for an attitude to be *fitting* (or correct, or appropriate).[9] Thus FA's first order of business is to provide a compelling account of *the nature of fittingness*.

Brentano's account of attitude fittingness parallels closely his account of belief fittingness. Indeed, he develops the analogy explicitly virtually wherever he presents his FA. Thus, the essentials of the account are presented in the comparatively lengthy §27 of *Origin*, but Brentano prepares the way in §26 with a recapitulation of his account of belief fittingness (see also Brentano 1952: 134–47 [84–91]). The account of belief fittingness, recall from Chap. 5, proceeded in two steps: (i) an account of fittingness in terms of self-evidence and (ii) a primitivist account of self-evidence as graspable only through 'assisted revelation.' In like fashion, Brentano's account of pro/con-attitude fittingness involves a primitive phenomenon analogous to self-evidence, graspable only through inner perception against suitable contrasts; the fittingness of the attitudes is then understood in terms of this primitive phenomenon.[10]

To see what Brentano has in mind here, consider first an approximative example. Suppose you pay a cashier for your beers with a 10€ bill, but he gives you back change for 20€. You immediately register his mistake, whereupon two palpable forces instantly start swirling in your consciousness: (a) a desire to tell the cashier of his mistake, and (b) a desire to pocket the extra money. After the fact, you may construct various reasons for and against (a) and (b). But during the two-second interval in which this is all going down, there is something very simple that you just *experience*: you experience that (a) is right or fitting whereas (b) is wrong and unfitting. One could maintain that fittingness in the practical domain just is the feature that this experiential contrast highlights – the feature that (a) exhibits and (b) lacks.

The resulting moral theory would be inadmissibly naïve about the sources of our experiences of fittingness or rightness. Accordingly, Brentano's theory takes a similar but more nuanced form. (It is a separate question, to which we will revert in due course, whether his nuancing is sufficient to overcome this initial naïveté.) Recall that for Brentano, it is not belief fittingness itself which can only be grasped directly; it is self-evidence, a particularly acute kind of fittingness. Compare the judgment that I have hands and the judgment that *it seems to me* that I have hands (or the judgment that I have a visual experience *as of* having hands). Both judgments are fitting. Moreover, in both cases we feel an irresistible compulsion to endorse the judgment. Nonetheless, there is an important difference between the two, claims Brentano: the judgment that it seems to me that I have hands is self-evident, whereas the judgment that I actually do have hands is not. We have discussed Brentano's defense of this claim in Chap. 5. The claim that concerns us *here* is that some interest states exhibit an analogous feature, one that goes beyond their fittingness and their irresistibility; it is 'the analogue of self-evidence in the domain of judgment' (Brentano 1889: 22 [22]). We can say perhaps that in the same sense in which some judgments are self-evident, some pro or con attitudes are *self-imposing* (my label).[11] It is this feature, this self-imposingness, that Brentano takes to be primitive and unanalyzable, graspable only directly in inner perception.[12] And it is what serves as normative bedrock in his moral philosophy – all value talk is ultimately to be analyzed in terms of this notion.

৵৵

As in the case of Brentano's 'assisted revelation' account of self-evidence, contrast cases can help inner perception home in on, and grasp with greater clarity, self-imposition. Brentano proffers a contrast of the following form. Imagine creatures similar to us in every respect but two: (i) they find chocolate disgusting and mud delicious and (ii) they disapprove of kindness and approve of meanness.[13] These creatures have pro attitudes toward mud and meanness and con attitudes toward chocolate and kindness. Consider now *three* contrasts: (a) the contrast between our and their attitudes toward chocolate and mud; (b) the contrast between our and their attitudes toward kindness and meanness; (c) the contrast between (a) and (b). The feature which interests Brentano is that which comes through clearly in (c). In both (a) and (b), we feel irresistibly compelled toward our own attitude distribution. Nonetheless:

[In (a),] the compulsion (*Drang*) is an instinctive urge; [in (b),] the natural positive emotion (*Gefallen*) is a higher love [pro attitude] with the character of correctness (*als richtig charakter-isierte*). When we encounter in ourselves (*in uns finden*) such a love, we notice not only that its object is loved and loveable, and that its absence and contrary are hated and hateable, but also that the one is love-worthy (*liebenswert*) and the other hate-worthy... (Brentano 1889: 23 [22]; see also Brentano 1952: 145–6 [91])[14]

Clearly, we cannot shake an intense feeling of commitment to our own attitude distribution toward mud and chocolate; we feel strongly compelled to prefer chocolate. The same feeling of unshakable commitment to our own attitude distribution attends the contrast between our and their attitudes toward kindness and meanness; again we feel strongly compelled to prefer our own attitude distribution. But in this case, there is an *additional* difference we appreciate when we entertain and compare the two sets of attitude: ours feel *incontrovertibly justified*; they *impose themselves* on us all-overridingly.

Careful: such descriptors as 'all-overridingly self-imposing' and 'incontrovertibly justified' are supposed to be *helpful* in intimating the practical analogue of self-evidence. But the only way to *really* grasp that which they attempt to intimate is to hold before the mind clearly the feature which contrasts the two attitude distributions in (b) but not in (a). I labeled that feature 'self-imposition,' but we should not mistake a label for a description. Just like self-evidence, self-imposition *cannot* actually be described – it is primitive and graspable only in inner perception. In a way, the descriptive characterizations offered here tell us *where to look*, not *what we see* when we look where we should.

Once we grasp in inner perception the nature of self-imposition, fittingness is defined in terms of it in the same way belief fittingness was defined in terms of self-evidence. That is: a pro attitude is fitting iff either it is self-imposing or it is such that had the subject's attitude been self-imposing, it would be a pro rather than con attitude.[15] So, Brentano's FA could be formulated more fully as follows:

(FA$_4$)   For any good g, either (a) (i) any self-imposing interest state directed at g would present-as-good g, and (ii) g is good because (i), or (b) there is a g^*, such that (iii) g is instrumental in bringing about g^*, (iv) any self-imposing interest state directed at g^* would present-as-good g^*, and (v) g^* is good because (iv).

In Chap. 5 we encountered some difficulties for the parallel account of existence. There I recommended that Brentano treat self-evident beliefs as just specially acute or manifest cases of fitting belief, so that fitting beliefs are understood simply as beliefs which resemble manifestly fitting ones in relevant respects. A similar move is possible for attitude fittingness and self-imposingness: a self-imposing pro attitude could be seen as an attitude whose fittingness is manifest from the first-person perspective. It is with reference to such manifestly fitting pro attitudes that we can grasp directly the nature of fittingness, but once we grasp it we can imagine a fitting attitude whose fittingness is not manifest in the same way.[16]

2.3. Naturalism or nonnaturalism?

Brentano's theory of value reductively accounts for goodness in terms of fitting pro attitudes, then, and for attitude fittingness in terms of (actual or counterfactual) self-imposition. Is this a form or moral naturalism or nonnaturalism?

In discussing the formulation of moral (non)naturalism, we have distinguished three conceptions of the natural. The first identified the natural with what is (a) invoked by (current or future) natural science, or else (b) is reductively explicable in terms of what is. More specifically, it construed moral naturalism as the claim that there are no moral truths whose truthmakers have non-natural constituents by the lights of this 'natural science' criterion. On the face of it, this understanding of moral naturalism casts Brentano's account as rather *non*naturalist. Brentano does accept that there are moral truths. For him, the truthmaker of a moral truth such as 'Generosity is good' is the fact that it is fitting to have a pro attitude toward acts of generosity, and ultimately, the fact that anyone who adopted a *self-imposing* pro or con attitude toward acts of generosity would adopt a *pro* attitude.[17] In this ultimate truthmaker, such notions as 'pro attitude' and 'acts of generosity' are plausibly invoked in some natural sciences (notably psychology and sociology). The problem is self-imposition. As a normative notion, self-imposition does not seem like the kind to be invoked in any natural science. Certainly it is not invoked in any *current* natural science, but the problem seems principled, so that future natural science is unlikely to invoke self-imposition as well. It is furthermore clear that for Brentano, self-imposition cannot be reductively explained in terms of some notions that are or will be invoked by natural science, since it cannot be reductively explained at all – it is a primitive notion. So, by the lights of the 'natural science' criterion, Brentano's FA seems nonnaturalist.

On the other hand, perhaps Brentano would insist that there is at least one natural science that does invoke self-imposition, namely, descriptive psychology. After all, the contrastive procedure by which self-imposition comes into inner-perceptual relief is a bit of Brentanian descriptive psychology. On these grounds, some scholars have argued that Brentano is a naturalist after all (Olson 2017).

This is connected also to the third conception of the natural we have considered, that of 'empirical observability.' Recall that self-imposition is revealed by inner perception, and inner perception is the cornerstone of 'psychology from an *empirical* standpoint' (that is, *empirical* psychology). We may therefore say that self-imposition is empirically perceptible, and to that extent can be seen as a natural phenomenon. Indeed, its empirical perceptibility is what grounds its appearance in descriptive psychology, a natural science. So by these lights, Brentano's FA seems naturalist.

On the other hand, for Brentano empirical perceptibility is not quite empirical *observability*. The latter requires the capacity to *attend* to that which one perceives. The natural scientist does not just *see* things, she *looks at* them and *observes* them – this is part of what it means to *study* them. Now, typically what is perceptible is also observable. But as we saw in Chap. 1, the move from perception to observation is problematic in the mental domain, the domain of phenomena studied in descriptive psychology. What is outer-perceptible is typically also outer-observable at the time of its occurrence, but what is inner-perceptible is *not* also inner-observable at the time of its occurrence. This is because outer observation does not alter the character of the thing observed, whereas inner observation does. I am not defending any of these claims here, but am pointing them out as potential grounds for denying that, all said and done, Brentano takes self-imposition to be *observable* – observable the way it really is independently of its being observed, that is.

So far we have reached no decisive result regarding the naturalistic status of self-imposingness. Might a tiebreaker be provided by the conception of the natural as the spatiotemporal? Unclear. At one level, this conception does favor the attribution of nonnaturalism to Brentano. Recall, first of all, that Brentano rejects properties in his ontology. So *his* theory of value is not a theory about the status of the *property* of self-imposition. Instead, it concerns the status of certain special concrete particulars, of the sort discussed in Chap. 6. In addition to the substance Beyoncé and the 'accident' famous-Beyoncé, there are also the accidents generosity-approving-Beyoncé, fittingly-generosity-approving-Beyoncé, and self-imposingly-generosity-approving-Beyoncé.

Our question is whether self-imposingly-generosity-approving-Beyoncé is a spatiotemporal particular or not. And the answer, it seems, must be that it is temporal but *not* spatial. Because of his substance dualism, Brentano holds that Beyoncé herself is an *immaterial* substance (a soul). This seems to imply that such accidents as generosity-approving-Beyoncé and self-imposingly-generosity-approving-Beyoncé are immaterial accidents. For they coincide with Beyoncé, and it is hard to make sense of an immaterial concrete particular coinciding with a material one. So self-imposingly-generosity-approving-Beyoncé is probably an immaterial concrete particular in Brentano's ontology. This would appear to cast it as non-spatial:

> All physical phenomena, it is said, have extension and spatial location...The opposite applies, however, to mental phenomena; thinking, willing, etc. appear extensionless and without spatial location.   (Brentano 1874: I, 120 [85])[18]

It would seem, then, that self-imposingly attitudinizing persons are *not*, in Brentano's picture, spatial entities neatly embedded in the spatiotemporal manifold that current-day naturalists take to constitute the natural world. To that extent, Brentano seems like a nonnaturalist by the lights of the spatiotemporal criterion.

At the same time, part of the reason current-day naturalists take nature to be a spatiotemporal system is that they do not think of mental phenomena as aspatial. If they did, they might very well expand their conception of nature to include aspatial phenomena, perhaps insisting only that all natural phenomena must be (i) temporal and (ii) causally efficacious. (Self-imposition appears to be very much causally efficacious in Brentano's picture!) Thus to the extent that Brentano comes across as a nonnaturalist by the lights of the spatiotemporal criterion, this is not because of any special feature of his *metaethical* theory; it is only due to an ancillary position on the mind-body problem. (A reist of a materialist bent who accepted every detail of Brentano's FA could qualify as a naturalist about goodness.)

I conclude that none of the standard conceptions of the natural renders an unequivocal verdict on whether Brentano is a moral naturalist or nonnaturalist. At bottom, however, I think the reason it is hard to settle this question is Brentano's own fault. There is an internal tension in *his* conception of self-imposition that pulls us in different directions. On the one hand, he wants it to be an *inner-perceptible* feature and to that extent a *psychological* feature, a feature that shows up in a complete descriptive psychology. On the other hand, he wants it to be a genuinely *normative* feature, something that goes beyond what takes place and pertains to what *ought* to take place. Importantly, however, this is not part of a reductive project of accounting for normativity in nonnormative terms. As we will see in the next section, Brentano stresses the difference between the following two claims:

> (C$_1$) x is good because x elicits in us a pro attitude.
> (C$_2$) x is good because it is fitting for x to elicit in us a pro attitude.

Brentano argues, as we will see, that we must move beyond C$_1$ and adopt C$_2$. Accordingly, the facts that it is fitting to disapprove of genocide and that it is unfitting to approve of genocide are fully independent of what actually *happens* in the world. If it just so happened that nobody had ever actually enjoyed a self-imposing attitude, then a complete empirical description of the world would leave out the fact that it is fitting to disapprove of genocide. And yet, this would not make it any less the case that it is fitting to disapprove of genocide and unfitting to approve of genocide. So: there is no reductive project here, so self-imposition is an irreducibly normative property – and yet it is an inner-perceptible property, hence a psychological property.

In §4.3, I will discuss more critically this inner tension in Brentano's conception of self-imposition. The point I am making now is just that this Janus-faced character of self-imposition creates conflicting pressures to classify Brentano both as a naturalist and as a nonnaturalist. On the one hand, he seems like a naturalist insofar as he takes a certain *psychological* feature to be normative bedrock. But ultimately, we cannot seriously attribute to Brentano moral naturalism, given that he allows a complete description of the natural world to leave out the fact that it is fitting to disapprove of genocide (hence that genocide is bad) – and not because of any expressivism about what is thereby said. If this is naturalism, it is unlike any naturalism we are familiar with. So we cannot comfortably classify Brentano either as a naturalist or as a nonnaturalist. Moreover, this does not seem like a case of a perfectly stable view that simply defies traditional categories; it looks more like an unstable view that tries to eat a cake and have it too – in this case, to maintain irreducible normativity but have it submit to perceptual detection. (More on this in §4.3.)

For want of a better option, I hereby resolve to consider Brentano's a form of moral *a-naturalism*. What does 'a-naturalism' mean? Nothing more than a metaethical theory that cannot be comfortably classified as naturalist.

3. The Case for Subject-end A-naturalism

In *Origin*, Brentano offers no sustained argument for his a-naturalist fitting-attitude theory of value. There is a gesture toward a very patchy argument from elimination in §§8–10 and another gesture toward an argument from analogy (with the case of truth) in §§26–7. In his lecture notes, however, Brentano develops a more sustained version of both arguments. The argument from analogy probably captures Brentano's most basic motivation for his fitting-attitude theory, but it presupposes much Brentanian orthodoxy; accordingly, I leave discussion of it to the end of the section (§3.4). The bulk of this section is dedicated to Brentano's argument by elimination, which enjoys a more neutral starting point. Strikingly, the argument anticipates substantially Moore's well-known *open-question argument* (Moore 1903a: §27). I open with a presentation of Brentano's version of the open-question argument (§3.1), then raise and try to address two lacunas in Brentano's argument (§§3.2–3.3).

3.1. Brentano's open-question argument

Brentano's argument (1952: 114–33 [71–83]) proceeds in two steps. First, Brentano sets forth two constraints on the adequacy of any account of 'the right end,' that is, of what goals we ought to pursue. Second, he shows how these constraints cannot be satisfied by various competitors of his FA. The first constraint is:

If something is recognized as the right end (*Zweck*), no place remains for the question: 'Am I doing good (acting reasonably) if I pursue it?'... Thus we already have one [adequacy] criterion/standard (*Maßstab*) in the requirement that the concept of the right end should not be so formulated that such a question could still arise once something has been established to be that end.   (Brentano 1952: 114 [71])

The other is:

Another requirement is equally justified: the definition (*Bestimmung*) of the right end may not presuppose anything that does not exist.   (Brentano 1952: 114 [71])

The first adequacy constraint is that an account of value not be susceptible to an open-question argument. The second is that it be ontologically adequate, so to speak, availing itself only of what is real (thermodynamics, with its ideal gas laws, would not pass this test!).

Not unlike Moore, Brentano uses his first constraint to brush aside various broadly utilitarian accounts of the nature of the good, notably Mill's. He construes Mill's view as the claim that we should maximize desire-satisfaction, and objects to it as follows:

...the concept of 'most-desirable' (*Begehrbarste*) does not coincide with the concept of the right end. One must ask *why* ought one to desire the most desirable state of affairs.

(Brentano 1952: 132 [82]; emphasis original)

Here 'desirable' should be understood nonnormatively, as designating simply what satisfies our desires (Brentano speaks of *begehrbar*, not *begehrwert*). Brentano's objection is that such an account leaves open the question of why we should maximize desire-satisfaction. Various other forms of object-end naturalism are targeted by Brentano as well; he wields his ontological constraint against some of them, but the open-question constraint against all.[19]

The ontological constraint is more operative in Brentano's critique of subject-end naturalism, notably naturalist response-dependence theories. According to these, something is good just if it tends to elicit certain responses in normal subjects under normal conditions. Brentano divides such theories into two groups: those that identify the relevant responses as *perceptual* states, and those that identify them as *emotional* states.

The first hold that for something to be good is for it to elicit the right moral-perceptual experiences in the right subjects under the right conditions. Brentano objects:

There is just no such thing as a sensation/perception (*Empfindung*) having for an object a quality called moral goodness; it is an *ad hoc* invention. But even if there were such a sense directed at a moral quality, it would be questionable (as it is with colors and sounds) whether the objects of that sensory perception are reality or mere appearance. In other words, the goodness of a given pursuit could be a mere delusion/mirage (*vorgespiegelt sein*), [so] the question would be justified *why* we ought to pursue it.   (Brentano 1952: 119–20 [74]; emphasis original)

Brentano denies here the *existence* of moral perception, on the grounds that moral properties are not sensible (see McBrayer 2010). In addition, he points out that the resulting response-dependence theory leaves open the why-question: since perceptual experience is never guaranteed to be veridical, moral-perceptual experience may be nonveridical as well; it would then be very reasonable to ask why we should pursue what such experience presents as good. If so, what-we-should-pursue cannot be identified with what-we-perceive-as-good.

The second response-dependence account Brentano considers is the more familiar one that *x* is good just if it elicits a positive *emotion* in normal subjects under normal conditions. This is more ontologically acceptable, since there clearly *are* moral emotions. However, it does not close the why-question:

> Suppose other, perhaps higher, kinds of beings did not share these human feelings, but on the contrary disapproved of that which we like, having reason on their side? Or is it [i.e., reason] actually on ours? The question is well-placed, and that suffices for us to reject the definition.
>
> (Brentano 1952: 120 [75])

Since emotional reactions can vary, it will always be perfectly intelligible to ask which emotional reactions we should trust, and in particular whether it is our own that we should. Thus subject-end naturalism succumbs to the open-question argument as well.

It is noteworthy that Brentano does not offer, in the relevant lecture notes, any argument against object-end *non*naturalism such as Moore's. I suspect he thinks object-end nonnaturalism blatantly violates his ontological constraint: as we already saw, Brentano rejects the existence of worldly goodness (recall the 1909 letter to Kraus). Thus between the two of them, his constraints appear to rule out all major competitors. One wishes, of course, that Brentano had provided *an argument* against nonnatural worldly goodness; but to my knowledge he had not.

There are two kinds of competitor Brentano does not address, however. Probably they simply did not occur to him. One competitor accepts the entire argument, but points out that nothing about the argument forces us to account for fittingness in terms of self-imposingness. Alternatives include accounting for it in terms of *reasons* or in terms of *ideal observers*; we take up this lacuna in §3.2. Another competitor rejects the open-question constraint, arguing that goodness can be reductively accounted for in a way that does not make the why-question disappear. Many modern naturalists have taken this route, offering a Kripkean necessary but *a posteriori* identification of goodness with natural properties and insisting that this is consistent with the persistence of an open question (see Ball 1988); we take up this competitor in §3.3.

In addition, it would presumably strengthen Brentano's argument if he showed that *his* account, as captured in FA$_4$, satisfies his two constraints. Presumably he would not appeal to something he does not think actually exists in his account. But he could still try to show that the account closes the why-question. To my knowledge, he does not do so. Fortunately, in responding to Moore's version of the argument, A.C. Ewing (1939) fills in this gap:

What Moore is attacking is any attempt to define 'good' wholly in non-ethical terms, and in this I agree with him...What I shall suggest is a definition of 'good' partly in ethical and partly in psychological terms... [Specifically,] 'the good' means 'what it is fitting to bring into existence for its own sake,' or 'what ought to be brought into existence, other things being equal'; but the important point I think is that 'good' has been defined in terms of what Ross calls a pro-attitude. When something is good it is fitting that we should welcome it, rejoice in it if it exists, desire and seek it if it does not exist.   (Ewing 1939: 6, 8)

Regardless of whether one ultimately accepts it, FA indeed seems unsusceptible to the open-question argument. Suppose I ask you why I should favor an end to world hunger, and you reply that an end to world hunger is something that merits approval, something it would be fitting to approve of. I can then reasonably ask you why it merits approval, but I cannot reasonably ask you why I should favor something that merits approval. To ask why I should favor something it is fitting to favor is to betray a lack of mastery of the words I am using.[20] Contrary to Moore, then, goodness does submit to analysis – just not an analysis that does away with normative terms. What it submits to is a Brentanian analysis in terms of fittingness. This gives a certain initial attraction to Brentano's FA. Nonetheless, there are still the two kinds of competitor that need to be addressed.

3.2. Alternative accounts of fittingness

According to the buck-passing account *of goodness*, *x* is good just when there is a sufficient reason to have a pro attitude toward *x* (Scanlon 1998). This need not, but *can*, be factorized into two distinct ideas: a fitting-attitude account of goodness and a reasons-based account *of fittingness*. According to the latter, the fittingness status of an attitude is a resultant of all the reasons for and against adopting it (Schroeder 2010). When the balance of reasons favors adopting the attitude, doing so is fitting. In short: an attitude A is fitting iff there is sufficient reason to adopt A. Thus, it is fitting to approve of generosity because there are sufficient reasons to do so – the balance of reasons for and against approving of generosity favors approval. If one goes on to treat the notion of reason as unanalyzable and fundamental, one obtains a 'reasons first' approach to value.

The main problem for this approach is the much-discussed 'wrong kind of reasons' (WKR) problem (Crisp 2000, Rabinowicz and Rønnow-Rasmussen 2004). Suppose an omnipotent demon threatens to kill everybody unless I adopt a pro attitude toward him, say admire him or wish him well. Intuitively, this (a) gives me a sufficient reason to adopt the pro attitude toward the demon, but (b) does not make the demon good. The problem appears to apply mutatis mutandis to the reasons-based account of fittingness. For it is also intuitive that the demon's demand (a) gives me a sufficient reason to adopt a pro attitude toward the demon, but (b) does not make it fitting, in the pertinent sense, to do so.[21]

The literature is replete with attempts to overcome the WKR problem, and some may well succeed. But it is noteworthy that the problem cannot even arise if we adopt Brentano's primitivist account of fittingness. If the nature of fittingness, or at least manifest fittingness (i.e., self-imposition), is grasped directly through inner perception against appropriate contrasts, then far from being an embarrassment, the evil-demon scenario is a potential *tool* of the account. For it provides further contrast, hence further opportunity for homing in on the right feature in inner perception. In contemplating side by side, so to speak, (a) an admiration for a colleague of striking integrity and (b) an admiration for a person who threatens terrible consequences unless we admire her, we *grasp directly* an evident difference between the two. Something is missing in (b) that is present in (a), and that feature is what we have labeled fittingness.[22]

It might be objected that this is a cheap response to the WKR problem. *Of course* we can see intuitively that there is a difference between (a) and (b); nobody contests that. The problem is to *account* for this difference in a principled and noncircular manner. However, for Brentano there is no account of the difference to be had, principled or otherwise; all we can aspire to is inner-perceptual acquaintance with the right feature. Admittedly, underlying the objection under discussion is an understandable kind of intellectual disappointment: being told 'just look in this direction and pay close attention' does not offer material for reasoned consideration and debate, and in some sense does not advance our theoretical understanding of the phenomena. This, I suspect, is the substance of the complaint at hand. But although understandable, the relevant intellectual dissatisfaction is (for Brentano) something we must learn to live with. Every theory has its primitives, and the same stock complaint could be lodged against it when it confesses to its own primitives. The 'reasons first' approach will be in the exact same position when it comes to elucidating the notion of a reason.[23] The advantage of Brentano's account is that it involves a sophisticated, thought-out approach to the appreciation of primitives, namely, the assisted-revelation approach discussed in Chap. 5.

'Reasons first' is probably the most popular approach to fittingness. A more recent but perhaps more attractive approach may be called 'ideality first.' The idea is that a pro attitude is fitting just if an ideal observer would adopt it (Kauppinen 2014).[24] The reason it is fitting to approve of generosity is that an ideal subject would. When this is plugged into FA, we effectively obtain the ideal-observer account of value: *x* is good iff 'any ideal observer would react to *x* [with a pro attitude] under such and such conditions' (Firth 1952: 321).

Kauppinen motivates this view by noting that our instinctual, prereflective pro attitudes may lead to various practical problems: 'acting on just any desire may result in ill health, garish wallpaper, a broken marriage, or a distrustful community' (Kauppinen 2014: 580). To avoid these practical problems, we try to step back from our instinctual pro attitudes and form more sophisticated ones, ones that lead to fewer problems. Ideal observers are ones who form those pro attitudes which bring such problems to the minimum. Other things being equal, their reward is good health, tasteful wallpapers, lasting marriages, and widespread trust.[25]

Debates surrounding ideal-observer theories tend to center on the nature of the ideal observer (Brandt 1955), the motivation for idealizing (Enoch 2005), potential indeterminacy problems (Carson 1984), and epistemological concerns about non-ideal humans' access to ideal observers' attitudes (Sayre-McCord 1994). Here I want to present a *metaphysical* argument against 'ideality first,' arguing that it has implausible consequences for what is ontologically bedrock.

A major attraction of moral naturalism about value is the parsimonious picture of ontological bedrock it offers: it allows one to claim that only the microphysical is fundamental. Nonnaturalist approaches to value, in contrast, require that we add something of a normative character to our ontological bedrock. For Moore, that 'something' is simply the property of goodness. For Brentano, it is rather self-imposition, or more accurately self-imposingly-attitudinizing-subjects. In an 'ideality first' framework, meanwhile, what must be added to our ontological bedrock are *ideal observers*. What I want to argue in the remainder of this section is that ideal observers are not the right sorts of thing to serve as ontological bedrock.

As noted, there is disagreement about what constitutes an ideal observer. A natural view construes the ideal observer as (i) a perfect reasoner who (ii) knows all the relevant facts. One could then say that it is fitting for S to approve of x just if a perfect reasoner who knew all the (nonnormative) x-relevant facts would approve of x; that is, just if someone with (i) complete knowledge of the nonnormative facts and (ii) the disposition to perform all and only epistemically justified inferences would approve of x. The immediate problem with this is that there probably *are* no such subjects in the actual world. (Who among us knows *all* the nonnormative facts pertaining to, say, whether Brazil ought to negotiate a trade agreement with Singapore?) Accordingly, all ideal observers *reside in other possible worlds*. This is a problem for the claim that ideal observers are *fundamental*. For it entails that certain fundamental entities are not actually present in our world. They occur only in nonactual worlds. What is mysterious is how the ontological bedrock of *this world*'s beings can include *other worlds'* entities. How are *actual* facts about fittingness and goodness supposed to be undergirded by 'facts' about ideal observers which are *nonactual*?

The basis of the objection is the thought that while we resort to modal notions routinely in philosophy, it is highly controversial to do so *at the fundamental level*. We expect the ungrounded grounders of reality, so to speak, to be part of the actual world. This is why metaphysicians make enormous efforts to find actual truthmakers for modal truths (see Armstrong 1997: chap. 10 for discussion). Modulo Lewis' (1986) industrial-strength realism about concrete possible worlds, it is a challenge to identify an element of *reality* (read: the actual world) that makes true 'Possibly, there are seven-foot tall butterflies.' Likewise, it should be a challenge to find an element of reality that makes true 'In possible world W_{17}, Jimmy (an all-informed perfect reasoner) approves of a trade deal between Brazil and Singapore.' But note that if we did identify some such actual-world truthmaker for this claim, then presumably that truthmaker would preempt ideal observers as fundamental.

It would represent only minor progress to trade modality for dispositions here. It might be suggested that we idealize not the observers themselves, but the triggering conditions of their dispositional states. The claim would be that if *ordinary* subjects are disposed to approve of x upon (i) learning all the relevant facts and (ii) performing all and only justified inferences of relevance, then it is fitting to approve of x.[26] In this picture, it is fitting to approve of generosity because *ordinary* subjects are disposed to do so under *ideal* triggering conditions. The problem, obviously, is that most philosophers reject the notion of dispositions at the fundamental level of reality. It is typically assumed that dispositions must be grounded in some categorical bases.

A theist 'ideality first' theorist might of course claim that God is an actual-world all-knowing perfect reasoner. So it is fitting to approve of generosity because God does. This is not quite a divine *command* theory but a 'divine example' or 'divine guidance' theory (see Jordan 2013) – the sort encapsulated in 'What would Jesus do?' This view brings the ideal observer into the actual world, making appeal to fundamental modality (or dispositions) unnecessary. One obvious problem with it, however, is that it would work only for theists. In any case, Brentano himself would reject this, despite his theism, on the grounds that a divine command/guidance theory is susceptible to the open-question argument: 'If divine revelation is appealed to, the question of whether God's word is worthy of belief remains open...' (Brentano 1952: 30 [19]; see also 1952: 115 [72]).

One might suggest instead that we simply lower our expectations from so-called ideal observers, lower them sufficiently as to welcome some such into our actual world. Thus, in his critique of Firth's ideal-observer theory, Brandt (1955) argues that the ideal observer must be recognizably human to be ethically relevant, and therefore should meet only two kinds of requirement: being (i) 'a disinterested, dispassionate but otherwise normal person' with (ii) 'vivid awareness of [those facts] which would make a difference to his ethical reaction in [a particular] case' (Brandt 1955: 410). It might be thought quite plausible that *someone* in our world is normal, disinterested, dispassionate, and has vivid awareness of facts that make a difference to whether she approves of a trade agreement between Brazil and Singapore.

This suggestion faces at least three major problems, however. First, it is far from obvious that for *every* ethical issue the actual world happens to contain someone with the right profile. For example, whether lobsters undergo a phenomenally conscious experience is plausibly relevant to whether it is fitting to eat them; but setting aside the fact that nobody *currently* knows whether lobsters are conscious, it might be held that only someone who *has been* a lobster can know whether lobsters are conscious.

Secondly, if ideal observers can vary widely among them in their inferential capacities, disagreements among them are likely to be rife: some would conclude that it is fitting to approve of abortion and some would conclude it is unfitting. This produces a can of worms for the ideal-observer theorist.[27] Thirdly, and most embarrassingly, consider a case where (i) a disinterested actual subject with vivid awareness of the facts regarding crack cocaine approves of legalizing it, while (ii) a perfectly informed perfect reasoner would disapprove of legalizing it. It would be folly to follow the suboptimal reasoner's verdict over the optimal one's. But if so, the suboptimal (actual) reasoner's attitudes should fix attitude-fittingness only when they coincide with the optimal (nonactual) reasoner's.

I have considered four possible assays of ideal observers: as nonactual fully informed perfect reasoners; as ordinary subjects with idealized dispositions; as God; as disinterested actual subjects with vivid awareness of relevant facts. On all four, I have argued, ideal observers are ill suited to serve as ungrounded grounders of actual-world normative facts, including fittingness facts. This casts a long shadow over the 'ideality first' approach to fittingness.

To be sure, the 'ideality first' theorist may choose to offer *no* account of observers' ideality, construing it as primitive and inexplicable. (She is entitled to her own primitives, after all!) But this leaves us with the challenge of how to grasp the nature of observers' ideality without a theoretical explanation of what such ideality consists in. Brentano, we have seen, *has* a story to tell about how we are to grasp the nature of self-imposition in the absence of any theoretical explanation. That story appeals to direct encounter in inner perception, which is self-evident and therefore infallible. For Brentano, there is no way we can have self-evident encounter with the ideality of an observer, since the latter is not an inner-perceptible phenomenon. This is why primitivism about ideality is not as promising, he would claim, as primitivism about self-imposition.

The other alternative to Brentano's self-imposition-based account of fittingness is the 'reasons first' approach, but the latter still has to contend with the WKR problem, which incidentally has no force against Brentano's account. The upshot is that while Brentano himself does not pursue his argument from elimination far enough, leaving 'standing' two alternative versions of FA, these alternatives can be ruled out by additional considerations.

3.3. *A posteriori naturalism*

Gilbert Harman objected to Moore's open-question argument as follows:

...as it stands the open-question argument could be used on someone who was ignorant of the chemical composition of water to 'prove' to him that water is not H_2O...[But, s]ince this argument would not show that water is not H_2O, the open-question argument cannot be used as it stands to show that for an act to be an act that ought to be done is not for it to have some natural characteristic C. (Harman 1977: 19)

The fact that for any natural characteristic C, one can still *meaningfully* ask whether C is good only shows, for Harman, that the thesis that goodness = C cannot be a priori. But it can perfectly well be a posteriori and true, indeed a posteriori and *necessarily* true.[28] This is precisely the tack adopted by Cornell realists (Boyd 1988), who model the reduction of goodness to some natural property on the reduction of water to H_2O.

It will not help here to simply reject the Kripkean approach to necessary a posteriori truths and adopt the more deflationary, 'Australian' approach. According to the latter, every necessary a posteriori truth can be factorized into two claims, neither of which are, both necessary and a posteriori (Jackson 1998: chap. 3). For example, 'Necessarily, water = H_2O' results from the superposition of two ideas: (1) Necessarily, water = the actual occupant of the water role; (2) The actual occupant of the water role = H_2O. Here, 'the water role' means (roughly) the total causal role of water in nature. And the notion that 'water' refers to whatever plays or occupies that role is claimed to be an a priori conceptual truth.[29] Meanwhile, the claims that H_2O is what plays or occupies that role is claimed to be a posteriori but contingent. It is only the fortuitous superposition of one a priori necessary truth and one a posteriori contingent truth, according to this more deflationary account, that produces a composite truth both necessary and a posteriori. The point I want to make here is just that even against the background of this more deflationary account, the open-question argument seems fallacious (Jackson 1998: 150–1). For a naturalist could still argue as follows: (1) Necessarily, goodness = the actual occupant of the goodness role; (2) Natural characteristic C = the actual occupant of the goodness role; so, (3) Necessarily, goodness = C.

Obviously, Brentano did not consider the possibility of this kind of moral naturalism. Accordingly, we are consigned to considering whether arguments completely external to the Brentano corpus could be wheeled in to rescue Brentano's open-question argument for FA. Unfortunately, the topic is too vast and too complex to settle here. I will restrict myself to citing two extant objections to the aqueous bit of reasoning just laid out. I should stress that my contribution to this discussion is nil; I am merely reporting other philosophers' work, work that a Brentanian *could* appeal to in supplementing Brentano's argument against moral naturalism.

Horgan and Timmons (1992) have objected to Premise 1 that there is a deep asymmetry between 'Water = the actual occupant of the water role' and 'Goodness = the actual occupant of the goodness role.' On Twin-Earth, where everything is the same as on Earth except that what plays the water role is not H_2O but XYZ, the word 'water' means something different than it does here. If earthlings and twin-earthlings met one day, they might have an apparent disagreement on what water is, until they realized that they were just using the word differently. They could then all agree that, as long as they speak English, there is no water on Twin-Earth (and if they switched to speaking Twin-English, it would be correct to say 'There is no water on Earth'). Contrast now a third planet, Moral Twin-Earth (MTE), where everything is like on Earth except that the goodness role is occupied by C* and not C. If earthlings and MTEists met one day, they would quickly disagree on whether it is C or C* that constitutes goodness. But here it does not seem that the disagreement is merely verbal, so that everybody might at some point realize that the word 'good' means something different in English and in Twin-English. On the contrary, the disagreement will persist and, if C and C* are sufficiently different, earthlings and MTEists may reasonably war over who is right. The question seems substantive (Horgan and Timmons 1992: 165). This shows that it cannot be in the very *meaning* of 'good' to pick out the *actual* occupant of the goodness role, as Premise 1 claims.[30]

Premise 2 is questionable as well. In the case of water and H_2O, we can point at empirical research designed to expose the molecular composition of water, leading to the empirical discovery that it is H_2O which plays the water role. In the case of goodness, by contrast, it is hard to imagine what empirical research is supposed to identify the occupant of the goodness role (see Huemer 2005: chap. 4).

I conclude that although Brentano's argument by elimination contains two important lacunas, it might admit of suitable supplementation to provide real support for FA_4.

3.4. The basic motivation

We do not fully appreciate the basic motivation for Brentano's FA if we only rely on his open-question argument. The analogy Brentano belabors with his theory of existence is potentially of greater importance.

Recall that according to Brentano, saying that *x* exists amounts to saying that it is fitting to believe in *x* (where the relevant fittingness is ultimately assayed in terms of self-evidence). The basic motivation for this is that there is no property of existence – so that attributions of such a property to objects would result in falsehoods – and yet there is this important difference between 'Ducks exist' and 'Ghosts exist': the former is true while the latter is false. To make sense of the possibility of existential truth, Brentano makes a double move. The first is intended to illuminate the truth of existential *judgments*, the second that of existential *sentences*. The first move is to adopt an attitudinal account of judgments' existence-commitment, so that a judgment could commit to the existence of an object without quite attributing to that object a property of existence. The second move flows directly from this first one. Since the content of an existential judgment is exhausted by the object, and not by the proposition that the object exists, the corresponding existential sentence cannot be understood to simply express the proposition that the object exists. Instead, it must be understood as expressing the idea that the correct judgment to make toward that object is the kind of judgment that commits to the existence, rather than to the nonexistence, of the object.

Consider now the analogy with goodness. As we have seen in that letter to Kraus, Brentano rejects the existence of a property of goodness. It follows that any attribution of goodness to something would result in a falsehood. And yet there is this important difference between 'Genocide is good' and 'Compassion is good': the former is false while the latter is true. How can we make sense of moral truth? The answer proceeds in an analogous two-step fashion. First, we must adopt an attitudinal conception of *mental* goodness-commitment, so that a pro attitude toward an object could commit to the object's goodness without attributing goodness to it. Second, and in consequence, we must understand *linguistic* goodness-commitment as a matter of expressing not the proposition that the object is good, but the more subtle idea that the right attitude to take toward that object is a pro rather than con attitude. This is how we get to a fitting-attitude account of moral (and more generally evaluative) talk.

One weakness here is that it is clear, from a certain perspective, why there could not be a property of existence: things do not divide into those that exist and those that do not! But it is unclear why there should not be a property of *goodness*; things *do* divide, after all, into those that are good and those that are not. Insofar as the basic motivation for FA takes the nonexistence of a property of goodness as its starting point, it seems to beg the question against any form of moral realism, whether naturalist or nonnaturalist. What is missing from Brentano's overall case for his theory of value, then, is an argument against such realism. Here too, we could attempt to supplement Brentano's argumentation with independent considerations, notably the notorious argument from queerness (Mackie 1977). But it is a curious fact that Brentano himself appears to feel no need to provide *reasons* for setting aside moral realism.

4. Problems for Brentano's Metaethics

In this section, I consider three central objections to Brentano's theory of value. I start with the Euthyphro-style objection that the subject-end order of explanation gets things backwards (§4.1). I then consider two objections presented by Moore in a review he wrote of Brentano's *Origin* (Moore 1903b): one objects to Brentano's account of *betterness* (§4.2), the other to the notion of direct grasp of fittingness through inner perception (§4.3).

4.1. A Euthyphro problem

Perhaps the most fundamental liability of Brentano's theory of value is the counterintuitiveness of the subject-end order of explanation. The notion that genocide is bad because it is fitting to have a con attitude toward it strikes us as getting things backwards: surely the reason we should have a con attitude toward genocide is that genocide is so very bad.

One approach to this problem, taken by Ehrenfels for instance, is to *celebrate* the view's counterintuitiveness. For Ehrenfels, the fitting attitude account of value is something of a precious *philosophical discovery*:

It is not that we desire things because we recognize in them this mystical, unfathomable essence 'value,' but rather that we ascribe 'value' to things because we desire them.   (Ehrenfels 1897: 219)

In the background here is the intellectual influence of Austrian economics (see Ehrenfels 1893: 76, Smith 1986, Reicher 2017), one of whose major ideas was the market-based account of *economic* value: the economic value of a thing is a function of how much people actually want it (demand), as well as how scarce it is (supply). People do not want gold because it is valuable; gold is valuable because people want it (and there is not a lot of it). When we move from economic value, which is a *descriptive* notion, to *moral* value, which is a *normative* notion, we may need to also move from the desires people *actually* have to the desires they *ought* to have, that is, the desires it would be fitting for them to have. The result is a fitting attitude account of moral value.[31]

The basic idea behind this unapologetic reaction to the Euthyphro objection is that Brentano cannot shy away from this feature of his theory, since, in a way, it is *the whole point* of the theory. That goodness is actually grounded in fittingness, rather than the other way round, as we might naturally (read: pre-philosophically) assume, is not so much an unwelcome consequence of the view as the view itself!

A second and more substantive line of response distinguishes two nearby intuitions that one might wish to accommodate. Although Brentano cannot accommodate the intuition that it is fitting to oppose genocide precisely because genocide is bad, he *can* accommodate the following nearby intuition: it is fitting to oppose genocide because of *what genocide is like* – where 'what genocide is like' is unpacked in terms of genocide's *nonnormative* properties. Thus Brentano can say that it is fitting to disapprove of genocide because genocide involves the death of so many people, their intentional targeting for their ethnic or racial affiliation, and so on. Seen in this light, the following order of explanation does not seem all that unintuitive: genocide is bad because it is fitting to disapprove of it, and it is fitting to disapprove of it because of what it is like, descriptively speaking. From this perspective, FA boils down to the claim that normativity proper comes into the picture only through the fittingness of pro and con attitudes.[32]

4.2. *The good, the better, and fitting attitudes*

In the same year Moore published his *Principia*, he also published a lesser-known review of Brentano's *Origin*. The review opens thus: 'This is a far better discussion of the most fundamental principles of Ethics than any others with which I am acquainted' (Moore 1903b: 115). Despite its generous opening, the review proceeds to develop a powerful critique of Brentano. A centerpiece of this critique is an attack on Brentano's account of betterness in the image of his account of goodness.

According to Brentano, x is better than y iff it is fitting to prefer (*vorziehen*) x over y (Brentano 1889: 24–6 [25–6]). Now, one might have held that to prefer one thing over another is just to like or love it more; and some have attributed this view to Brentano (Olson 2017). But it seems to me that Brentano explicitly rejects such a reductive account of preference in terms of like/love:

…'the better' seems to be that which is worthy of being loved with a greater love. But is this really so? …Someone will say, perhaps, that the intensity of enjoyment/liking (*Gefallen*) is what we call here the magnitude of love. If so, the better would be that which ought to be enjoyed/

liked with more intense enjoyment/liking. But that would be, upon closer inspection, an absurd definition. It would imply that in every specific case where someone is happy over something, only a certain amount of happiness (*Freude*) is permissible; whereas I should think it could never be objectionable to be maximally (wholeheartedly, as they say) happy over what is really good.   (Brentano 1889: 24–5 [25])

The argument is this. If preference were a matter of greater liking, then fitting preference would be a matter of fitting greater liking. However, there are cases where it is fitting to prefer x over y even though there is no upper limit on how much it is fitting to like y. Even if it is fitting to prefer art to football, it does not follow that it is unfitting for me to like football with the maximum amount of liking I am capable of. Therefore, preference cannot be a matter of greater liking. Instead, it must be a sui generis species (*besondere Spezies*) of interest state (Brentano 1889: 25 [26]).

Moore's main complaint against this is psychological – he thinks preference as conceived by Brentano is just not part of our psychological repertoire:

If, as usual, we mean by 'preference' a *feeling*, it is obviously a feeling *only* towards the thing preferred, *not* towards the thing which is not preferred. When we say that we prefer one thing to another we usually mean either (1) that we *like* the one *more* than we like the other, or (2) that we choose the one and do *not* choose the other: there is no such thing as a single feeling, called 'preference,' directed to *both* the things.   (Moore 1903b: 119; italics original)

If Moore is right that there is no evaluative mental state directed at object-pairs, then Brentano's nonreductive take on preference is doomed.

It is hard to see, however, what motivates Moore's proclamations here. Preferring football to basketball seems very much a mental state directed at both football and basketball. Certainly basketball shows up in the content of the preference; it is hard to see in what sense Moore thinks it is not *directed toward* basketball.

A more perspicacious objection Moore raises connects the nonreductive account of preference with a nonreductive account of betterness:

[Brentano] does not clearly recognize that to know one thing to be better than another must be to know that it has in a higher degree the very property which we mean by 'good in itself.'
(Moore 1903b: 120; see also Ehrenfels 1988)

If betterness is a matter of fitting preference, and (fitting) preference is irreducible to (fitting) relative liking, then betterness is irreducible to greater goodness. But betterness *just is* greater goodness!

This is a much better objection. Suppose art is more valuable than football. Then it would seem to follow that football must have a smaller quantity of goodness than art. But Brentano's theory has no resources to explain or even accommodate this fact.

Brentano's response here would be to bite the bullet. Perhaps he could claim that betterness is not *in general* reducible to greater goodness, though such reduction does work for goods *of the same kind*. If knowledge is intrinsically good (Brentano 1952: 183 [116]), then other things being equal, more knowledge is better than less (knowing both Euclidean and non-Euclidean geometry is better than knowing only Euclidean). In some cases, however, goods belong to categorically different kinds, so that it makes no sense to say that one contains more goodness than the other. One might hold that in such cases no value comparison is possible, but Brentano's view is rather that these are instances of betterness that do not amount to greater goodness:

There are also cases of preferences with the character of correctness where the better is not the greater sum [of good]; rather, the superiority (*Vorzug*) is grounded in a *qualitative difference*. It is evident, for example, that positive knowledge is more valuable than negative, other things being equal.   (Brentano 1952: 213 [134]; my italics)

As we will see in greater detail in the next chapter, Brentano holds that knowing what *is* the case is more valuable than knowing what is *not* the case. Obviously, this is not a case of having more of the same: other things being equal, knowing that the Higgs boson exists is not *more knowledge* than knowing that the ether does not. Moore would say that even though the former bit of knowledge is not *more knowledge* than the latter bit, it does contain *more goodness*. But this might strike one as an arbitrary assertion. Instead, Brentano suggests that the betterness of positive knowledge is irreducible to greater goodness. In a way, for Brentano each kind of knowledge has its own distinct sort of goodness, and one sort is plain better than the other (without being in any sense more plentiful than the other).

Accepting Brentano's nonreductive account of preference (and betterness), one might wonder why Brentano does not consider the opposite reduction: perhaps to have a pro attitude toward x is just to prefer x's existence to x's nonexistence. Thus, to admire Shakespeare is to prefer a world with him to one without him. This would provide for a more unified account of value, reducing goodness to betterness. However, this requires construing preference as a *propositional* attitude, directed not at (pairs of) concrete particulars, but at (existential) states of affairs. As we saw in Chaps. 4 and 6, this is anathema to Brentano. Brentano is stuck, then, with a disunified account of value in terms of mutually irreducible goodness and betterness. Furthermore, in being thus disunified, the account breaks the symmetry between value and truth that Brentano otherwise stresses so much. This is one instance, among many, where Brentano's penchant for unities and symmetries does not blind him to the peculiarities of the phenomena.

4.3. Can we really (inner-)perceive normative properties?

A major disadvantage of Moore's object-end nonnaturalism is its reliance on *intuition* to account for *knowledge* of goodness. The epistemology of intuition is a notorious can of worms, and philosophers aplenty have suspected that direct intellectual acquaintance with abstracta, such as intrinsic goodness and badness, is simply not part of our psychological repertoire.[33]

Brentano's subject-end theory of value appears to enjoy a definite advantage here, as it avoids appeal to intuitional encounter with goodness and badness. For Brentano, our knowledge of good and bad is not direct in this way, but is rather based on prior knowledge of fitting and unfitting. We know something to be good by knowing that pro attitudes toward it are fitting. Knowledge of fittingness is in turn based on knowledge of self-imposingness. It is knowledge of self-imposition that is direct and foundational in our moral knowledge. And our direct encounter with it is through inner perception, not intuition:

> ...when we call certain objects good, and others bad, we are saying thereby nothing more than that whoever loves the former and hates the latter has taken the right stand. The source of these concepts is inner perception, for only in inner perception do we grasp (*erfassen*) ourselves as something which loves or hates.   (Brentano 1952: 144 [90])

It is the central thesis of *Origin* that moral knowledge *originates in* inner-perceptual acquaintance with self-imposingness.

The immediate problem here is that inner-perceiving the items that exhibit self-imposition does not seem to guarantee inner-perceiving self-imposition itself. From the fact that an item is perceptible it does not follow that all its *properties* are perceptible. Thus, one may see a rubber ball at the distance without seeing that it is rubber. Likewise, one may inner-perceive an experience of indignation at Trayvon Martin's murder without inner-perceiving that one's indignation occurs on a Monday – occurring on a Monday is simply not the kind of feature one can pick up on using *inner perception*. And by the same token, one may very well inner-perceive that same indignation without inner-perceiving its self-imposingness.

But there may be a deeper problem lurking here. Self-imposition is not any old property of our inner-perceived pro attitudes – it is a *normative* property. And it is specially mysterious how we could possibly (inner-)perceive normative properties. Recall that Brentano himself branded outer perception of normative properties 'an ad hoc invention' (1952: 119–20 [74]). Why should we be more sympathetic to *inner* perception of such properties? Moore belabors this very point in his review:

> Obviously the conception of 'good,' as Brentano defines it, cannot be derived merely from the experience of *loving*, but only from that of '*right*' loving' – from the perception of the *rightness* [or fittingness] of a love: its *origin* cannot be merely the perception of a love which *is* right, but in which this quality is not perceived, it can only be a perception in which it is itself *contained*. But...The quality of 'rightness' [fittingness] is *not* a psychical content and the perception of it is *not* an impression in the ordinary sense of these words.
>
> (Moore 1903b: 117; italics original)[34]

The claim that fittingness and self-imposition, qua normative properties, should not be directly perceptible is antecedently very plausible. Unless this difficulty can be overcome, any advantage over Moore's appeal to intuition is illusory.

One option for Brentano is to seek inspiration from proponents of moral *outer* perception. Cuneo (2003, 2006), for example, suggests that we perceive normative properties *by* perceiving the nonnormative, natural properties upon which they supervene. Just as I hear my wife's approach *by* hearing her distinctive footfalls, I may also see the goodness of a situation *by* seeing the visible natural grounds of the situation's goodness. For example, I may see a child's delight at receiving a gift and thereby see the prima facie goodness of the gifting. If this works for external perception, a Brentanian might suggest, it should also work for inner perception: perhaps we can inner-perceive the self-imposingness of a pro attitude *by* inner-perceiving (some of) the attitude's subvenient psychological properties.

An immediate question is what purely psychological property might subvene self-imposition – especially given that the latter is ontologically bedrock. One view is that an attitude's normative property of *being* self-imposing supervenes upon that attitude's psychological property of *feeling* self-imposing, i.e., having the felt character of self-imposition. This latter property is surely inner-perceptible. It might be suggested, then, that we can inner-perceive an attitude's being self-imposing *by* inner-perceiving its feeling self-imposing – just as we can outer-perceive a flower's *being* purple by outer-perceiving its *looking* purple.[35]

The main problem with this move is that it undermines the notion of direct grasp (assisted by certain contrasts) of self-imposition. If we inner-perceive an attitude's being self-imposing by inner-perceiving its feeling self-imposing, then the inner perception of being self-imposing is *mediated*: the inner perception of the nonnormative, psychological property of *feeling* self-imposing is *direct*, whereas the inner perception of the normative property of *being* self-imposing is *indirect*. Direct grasp of a normative property seems no longer in the cards. This seems to undermine in turn the 'assisted revelation' theory for the normative property of *being* self-imposing; only the nonnormative property of feeling self-imposing may be revealed.

This result undermines Brentano's entire moral epistemology. Brentano homes in on self-imposition primarily as the 'practical analogue' of self-evidence. Self-evidence, recall from Chap. 5, is more basic than, and guarantees, infallibility – an immunity to mistakes. Likewise, self-imposition should have the advantage of guaranteeing a sort of practical infallibility – immunity to mis*steps*, if you will. And it is this immunity to missteps that bestows on self-imposing attitudes the capacity to serve as foundations of practical knowledge. Once we admit that we enjoy no direct grasp of our attitudes' *being* self-imposing, but only their *feeling* self-imposing, daylight opens between that which is directly grasped and that which guarantees immunity to missteps. An attitude's *feeling* self-imposing does not guarantee immunity to missteps, since it may turn out that the attitude is not *actually* self-imposing. We might put the point this way: by Brentano's own lights, attitudes that merely *feel* self-imposing are not suitable to serve as foundational in our moral knowledge, since they do not exhibit the practical analogue of infallibility; but attitudes which *are* self-imposing cannot serve as foundational either if their being self-imposing is not directly graspable.

The point goes back to the Janus-faced character of self-imposition. It is clear how the property of *being* self-imposing can be irreducibly normative, and also how the property of *feeling* self-imposing can be inner-perceptible; it is much less clear how either property could be *both* normative and perceptible. Certainly Brentano does little to clarify how this could be. The fact that he himself dismisses the possibility of *outer* perception of goodness, hence of the normative status of worldly objects, raises the question of why he sees nothing problematic about inner perception of self-imposition, hence of the normative status of mental states.

❦

My own view is that this is the biggest problem in Brentano's theory of value, perhaps the weakest link in his entire philosophical system. We can get at the daylight between what *appears* right and what *is* right from another angle. The prominent Moore scholar Thomas Baldwin has argued that there is an element of 'wishful thinking' in Brentano's reliance on inner perception to reveal fittingness (Baldwin 2006: 244). There are two complementary concerns here: first, inner perception may fail to detect the fittingness (or unfittingness) of a particular pro attitude; secondly, it may misattribute fittingness to an unfitting attitude or unfittingness to a fitting one. George Washington, a man of rare dignity and courage, who insisted on retiring from the US presidency after only two terms to inspire strong democratic practice in American governance, owned slaves his entire life. Presumably, he harbored a pro attitude toward slave-ownership. This pro attitude was unfitting, but Washington's inner perception failed to detect its unfittingness. Many of us today, including this author, engage in certain meat-eating practices which may well seem in three centuries' time as morally abhorrent as slave-ownership. Presumably, most of us fail to detect the unfittingness of our attitudes toward such meat-eating; many positively attribute fittingness to it. And let us not forget Brentano himself, whose attitudes toward women might raise eyebrows in retrospect:

On the relative positions of the two spouses I would essentially agree with Bentham's judgment. He demands: a) the subordination of the woman. The man should be in charge (*Vormund sein*). It is no good when the legislature and the executive work against each other. In general it may be said that the man's cognitive power (*geistige Kraft*) is greater, not because women are less smart, but rather because most of them have lower endurance for cognitive labor (*geistiger Arbeit*).   (Brentano 1952: 392 [239])

Judging by this passage, Brentano harbored a con attitude toward women 'being in charge,' and a pro attitude toward the subordination (*Unterordnung*) of the wife to the husband. I am going to go ahead and assume that at least one of these attitudes is unfitting. Its unfittingness evidently eluded Brentano's inner perception. In general, much of our lives we are altogether unaware of our attitudes' fittingness or unfittingness. Sometimes we do experience our pro attitudes as fitting or unfitting, but as Baldwin observes, 'we do not have a sufficient understanding of the origins of our feelings to be confident about such an experience of their correctness [or fittingness]' (Baldwin 1999: 237; my translation). If so, for most pro and con attitudes we can contemplate, we are in no position to establish whether they are fitting.

In this respect, Brentano's theory may bear an unfortunate resemblance to the conscience-based ethical systems of certain early British moralists. According to Butler (1726), for instance, conscience is a faculty that monitors one's mental states and actions and approves or disapproves of them.[36] If one held that what makes conscience (dis)approve of an attitude is the latter's (un)fittingness, the view would be extremely close to Brentano's.[37] This resemblance of ethical theory did not escape Brentano, who is happy to regard conscience theory as in some sense a predecessor (Brentano 1952: 157–8 [98–9]). The problem with such ethical systems is brought out compellingly in Jonathan Bennett's 'The Conscience of Huckleberry Fin' (Bennett 1974). Bennett argues that the dictates of conscience lie downstream of moral theory, so that when one's moral theory is misguided one's conscience will be as well. An example is Huck Finn's pangs of conscience upon failing to turn in his runaway-slave friend Jim; another is SS chief Heinrich Himmler's pride at following his conscience in trying to see through the Final Solution despite persistent gut feelings of moral discomfort. The parallel problem for Brentano's position is clear: Huck Finn and Himmler seem to inner-misperceive unfitting attitudes as fitting and fitting attitudes as unfitting.

Three possible responses to this problem should be considered. Hill (1998) suggests that Huck Finn may be misidentifying the voice he hears within him – he thinks it is the voice of conscience, but in reality it is just social conditioning. In a similar vein, Brentano might suggest that although Washington judged his pro attitude toward slavery fitting, that judgment's source was not inner perception but something else – again social conditioning, perhaps (see Gubser 2009). If successful, this move would protect the authority of inner perception.

The price, however, would be to sacrifice any first-person insight into when inner perception (or conscience) is operative. We would be justified in relying on our inner perception, but would have no way to tell when what we are relying on is inner percep-tion. This is precisely the problem Baldwin describes in complaining that we have insufficient understanding of the processes that lead us to judge that our attitudes are fitting or unfitting. In many cases, we have no direct, first-person insight into whether we are undergoing a conscience-driven process or a self-serving one.

A second response is that while inner perception of an attitude's *fittingness* may go awry, inner perception of an attitude's *self-imposingness* cannot. Let us continue to indulge Brentano's supposition that knowledge is an intrinsic good (we will adopt a more critical posture in the next chapter). For Brentano, this must be based on certain deliverances of inner perception: say, that preference for knowing whether 2+2=4 over ignorance as to whether 2+2=4 is a self-imposing preference, a manifestly fitting preference. Brentano may suggest that when we reach such starkly fundamental pro attitudes, to do with intrinsic goodness, we simply cannot inner-*mis*perceive self-imposingness. It is only with respect to much more nuanced pro attitudes, to do with instrumental goodness, that matters start getting obscurer and we lose our ironclad grip on fittingness. A Hutu's pro attitude toward the Tutsi genocide may seem to her fitting, when in fact unfitting, but by Brentano's lights, genocide is probably not *intrinsically bad* (because, as we will see in the next chapter, life is probably not intrinsically, but only instrumentally, good). Accordingly, one must perform various inferences to realize the badness of genocide; the badness of genocide does not impose itself on us the way the badness of (say) simple pain does. That is why the fittingness of such complex attitudes, to do with instrumental goods, must be derived from the more fundamental *manifest* fittingness of much more straightforward pro attitudes to do with intrinsic goods.

The essence of this response is that Huck Finn and Himmler are not counterexamples to a sufficiently restrictive conception of the domain in which we can unquestionably trust our conscience, or our first-person impression of fittingness. However, the original objection had more to it than counterexamples. Even if we restrict ourselves to ostensibly self-imposing attitudes about intrinsic goods, there is still the principled gulf between (a) a psychological impression of self-imposition and (b) real self-imposition in all its normative glory. As we have seen in the first half of this subsection, there are good reasons to think that in truth we can only inner-perceive our attitudes' *feeling* self-imposing. Brentano must argue that when we reflect on what is intrinsically good, the alleged daylight between feeling and being self-imposing starts to evaporate. But this would need to be shown, and I know of nothing in the Brentano corpus that even tries to show it.

A third response to the 'wishful thinking' objection, decidedly non-Brentanian, is to separate the issues of *acquiring* the concept of fittingness (or self-imposition) and *applying* that concept. Consider unlucky Luke, whose life thus far has been subjected to the following double predicament: whenever Luke has encountered a red object, it was through a thin (and very localized) mist that made the object appear pink rather than red; and whenever Luke has encountered a pink object, a strong (and very focal) red light in the vicinity made the object look red rather than pink. For Luke, vision has been an extraordinarily unreliable guide to the distribution of reds and pinks in his environment. Nonetheless, Luke has no other grasp of the *natures* of red and pink but that afforded to him by visual encounter.[38] Moreover, arguably Luke has an *accurate* grasp of the natures of red and pink, despite having a perverse view of their *extensions*. In consequence, Luke is a full possessor of the concepts RED and PINK, misapplying them systematically though he does.[39] Something tragically close to Luke's predicament may well be the human condition when it comes to moral fittingness. We misapply the concepts of fittingness and unfittingness routinely, because of blinding selfishness, social conditioning, wishful thinking, or just what Arendt (1963) called the banality of evil. Nonetheless, we have an accurate grasp of the *natures* of fittingness and unfittingness. Indeed, Himmler and Washington seem to have the very same concept of fittingness that you and I do, despite wildly misapplying it to some of their attitudes. So it is not implausible to hold that we all fully possess the concepts of fittingness and unfittingness, and possess them thanks to inner-perceptual encounter with our (manifestly) fitting and unfitting attitudes – despite inner perception's unreliable *application* of these concepts.

This response protects Brentano's theory from Baldwin's wishful thinking problem more effectively than the previous two, and I endorse it herewith. I note, however, that it sacrifices the role of inner perception of fittingness and self-imposition in providing us knowledge of their *extension*, and therefore its role in guiding our moral conduct. This is a concession Brentano would most emphatically refuse to make: it is clear from the text of *Origin* that his theory is supposed to account not only for knowledge of the *nature* of goodness and badness, but also for knowledge of their *extension* (see, e.g., §25 and §31). All the same, the track record of moral certitude among our conspecifics suggests that dropping the hope for moral guidance would be a wise move for Brentano to make. The upshot would be an account of what value talk comes down to that does not also deliver a moral epistemology: to say that something is good is to say that self-imposing (or manifestly fitting) attitudes toward it would be pro rather than con attitudes; but how we *know* whether a self-imposing attitude toward something would be a pro or con attitude, when we ourselves do not *have* self-imposing attitudes toward the thing, is a separate matter, requiring a separate account.

5. Moral Value, Aesthetic Value, and Brentano's Theory of Beauty

Moore's *main* objection to Brentano is that his fitting attitude account of value is too broad:

> It is certain that many things, e.g., inanimate beautiful objects, possess the quality of being worthy to be loved, in a higher degree than they possess that of 'rightness'; it may even be doubted whether they possess the latter at all. And it is our duty to effect that which is the most 'right' possible, not that which is most worthy to be loved. Though therefore we can agree with Brentano that everything which is good in itself is worthy to be loved, we cannot agree that everything which is worthy to be loved is good.   (Moore 1903b: 116)

It is fitting to approve of El Greco's *Saint Martin and the Beggar*, but the painting is not morally good. According to Moore, this is because although it is fitting to approve of the painting, this does not impose on us a duty to bring it into existence or keep it in existence (in short: a duty to effect existence). So fitting approval cannot ground moral goodness.

As it stands, the objection is not probing. Brentano's is an account of value as such, not of *moral* value. It addresses the metaphysics of goodness, not of moral goodness. Clearly, El Greco's *Saint Martin and the Beggar is* good, though aesthetically rather than morally so. This does raise the question, however, of how Brentano intends to deliver two distinct accounts of moral and aesthetic goodness (i.e., beauty).

There seem to be two general options within the fitting-attitude framework: either we distinguish two kinds of fittingness or we distinguish two kinds of pro attitude. The first option is to distinguish fittingness$_1$ and fittingness$_2$, such that (i) x is morally good iff it is fitting$_1$ to have a pro attitude toward x and (ii) x is beautiful iff it is fitting$_2$ to have a pro attitude toward x. The difference between moral and aesthetic goodness is then a matter of the difference between moral and aesthetic fittingness.

Might Brentano take this approach to account for the difference between moral and aesthetic value? In some respects, the approach is congenial: Brentano could suggest that the difference between these two kinds of fittingness, too, is a difference manifest to inner perception. Indeed, one can take the evident contrast between the fittingness of helping an old lady cross the street and the fittingness of admiring *Saint Martin and the Beggar* as further material for inner-perceptual zeroing in on the kind of fittingness relevant to the constitution of *moral* goodness.

There are two problems with this, however, as an interpretation of Brentano. First, to my knowledge Brentano nowhere distinguishes between moral and aesthetic fittingness. This is significant, since he *does* explicitly distinguish between the fittingness characteristic of interest states ('axiological fittingness,' we may call it) and the fittingness characteristic of judgments ('doxastic fittingness'):

[There is] a fitting loving or hating and an unfitting loving or hating. This may seem like the analogue of fitting acceptance and fitting rejection, but it is essentially different (*wesentlich anderes*).   (Brentano 1907a: 148–9 [144])

The fact that no similar statement is offered for moral and aesthetic fittingness suggests that Brentano does not intend to distinguish moral and aesthetic goodness in terms of two kinds of fittingness.[40]

Secondly, the *reason* the difference between axiological and doxastic fittingness is required is that there is a different standard of fittingness for such essentially different states as interest and judgment. The standard of fittingness for interest states is grounded in the fact that they essentially present-as-good/bad; that for judgment states in the fact that they essentially present-as-true/false. So even if we distinguished between moral and aesthetic fittingness, presumably as two types of axiological fittingness, that distinction would not be basic. It would be grounded in a more basic distinction in the kind of pro attitude we can take toward objects: those that present-as-morally-good and those that present-as-aesthetically-good.

Ultimately, then, the distinction between moral goodness and aesthetic goodness, or beauty, must come down to two different kinds of attitude. More precisely, there must be two different classes of mental state, M_1 and M_2, such that (i) x is morally good iff it is fitting to harbor M_1-type states toward x and (ii) x is beautiful iff it is fitting to harbor M_2-style states toward x.[41] This is indeed the path Brentano chooses. To appreciate how this works, I now turn to present what I take to be Brentano's theory of beauty.

Existence and goodness are constitutively tied to fitting belief-in and fitting pro attitude in Brentano's system. But Brentano's psychology recognizes a third fundamental type of mental state, presentation or contemplation (*Vorstellung*). So might beauty be constitutively tied to fitting presentation or contemplation? After all, plausibly, a beautiful thing is *worthy of contemplation* in somewhat the same sense as a good thing is worthy of being approved of and an existent merits being believed in. The idea, then, might be that something is beautiful just if it is fitting to contemplate it – to train our awareness on it.

This does have the appearance of a vaguely Brentanian account of beauty, but it is *not* in fact Brentano's account. The basic reason is that the constitutive link between existence and fitting belief-in depends on the special attitudinal character of belief-in, which I have winkingly characterized as presenting-as-existent (and similarly for the link between goodness and fitting pro attitude). If the beautiful were simply that which it is fitting to contemplate, contemplation would have to exhibit the right attitudinal character as well – what we might call presenting-as-beautiful. But as we saw in Chap. 3, *Vorstellung* is special in exhibiting a completely neutral attitude of mere-presenting. It is thus *not* beauty-committal in the way belief-in is existence-committal and pro attitude is goodness-committal.

This problem with a fitting-contemplation account of beauty points the way to a better Brentanian account, which is indeed Brentano's. The right strategy is to identify a mental state attitudinally beauty-committal and assay beauty in terms of the fittingness of adopting that state. Brentano calls the relevant state 'delight' (*Wohlgefallen*). Brentano's is a 'fitting delight' account of beauty, then:

> The concept of the beautiful has to do with…[that which] elicits in us a delight with the character of fittingness/correctness (*als richtig charakteriesiertes*).   (Brentano 1959: 17)

So, to say that something is beautiful is to say that it is fitting to be delighted by it.

The question, however, is *what is delight?* In all of Brentano's taxonomic discussion, we have not encountered yet this mental state. If understanding the notion of beauty depends on understanding the notion of delight and its corresponding standard of fittingness, the first order of business is to elucidate the nature of delight. Brentano's account of delight starts from a simple observation about the experience of encounter with the beautiful: it always entrains a measure of enjoyment (Brentano 1959: 123). If one manages to contemplate El Greco's *Saint Martin and the Beggar* joylessly, one cannot be said to experience it as beautiful. This motivates Brentano to construe delight as a compound mental state involving both contemplation and joy – a kind of joyful contemplation. More specifically, delight at x involves (i) a contemplation of x plus (ii) an enjoyment *of the contemplation* of x. It is this compound state that, according to Brentano, embodies attitudinally encoded commitment to the beauty of its object: in the same sense in which a belief-in presents-as-existent and a pro attitude presents-as-good, delight is the state whose very essence is to present-as-beautiful. We may suppose that its contrary is a kind of dejected or wretched contemplation; we might call this 'dismay.' Dismay is the state whose essence is to present-as-ugly its object.[42]

Note that the joy component of delight is a pro attitude – joy belongs in the category of interest states. So delight is a compound state with a presentation component and a pro attitude component. As noted, the joy component is a *second-order* state: it is an enjoyment *of the presenting*. Thus to be delighted with x is to be in a state which is directed contemplation-wise at x and directed enjoyment-wise at the contemplation-of-x. In the same vein, we might say that to be dismayed with x is to be in a compound state wherein one (i) contemplates x and (ii) feels dejection or 'disenjoyment' about this token contemplation.

The fitting-delight account of beauty provides Brentano with resources to respond to Moore's objection. The objection, recall, was that a fitting pro attitude account of moral value is too broad, since it is also fitting to have a pro attitude toward *Saint Martin and the Beggar*, which has no (intrinsic) moral value. The response is that in reaction to *Saint Martin and the Beggar*, what it is fitting to have a pro attitude toward is not the painting itself, but only the contemplation of the painting. The principled distinction between moral and aesthetic value can be drawn, then, in terms of two different kinds of pro attitude it is fitting to adopt in the presence of an object: a first-order pro attitude toward the object itself in the case of the morally good, and a second-order pro attitude toward awareness of the object in the case of the aesthetically good.

This account explains an interesting asymmetry between moral and aesthetic value pointed out by Brentano (1959: 136). Consider that peace is good, as is having a pro attitude toward peace, but mere contemplation of peace is in itself neither good nor bad. For contemplation of peace is compatible with both a pro attitude and a con attitude toward peace. By contrast, the mere contemplation of *Saint Martin and the Beggar* is in itself good. More generally, when an object is beautiful, contemplating it is valuable, whereas when the object is morally good, merely contemplating it is 'neutral' or 'indifferent' – only the adoption of a pro attitude toward it is valuable. (This recovers the sense in which the beautiful is worthy of contemplation.) This asymmetry between the morally good and the beautiful is *predicted* by Brentano's account of the difference between them. Given that a beautiful object merits delight, and a pro attitude toward one's contemplation of the object is a constituent of delight, it goes to the nature of beauty that a pro attitude toward contemplating the beautiful is appropriate. And since for something to be good is for a pro attitude toward it to be appropriate, it follows that the contemplation of a beautiful object is itself good. This flows out of the nature of delight, then – and the fact that delight in the beautiful is always fitting.

The account also explains why there is no sui generis kind of fittingness standard for delight. According to the account, delight is a compound state involving a first-order contemplation and a second-order pro attitude. As noted in Chap. 3, there is no standard of fittingness for contemplation, as mere-presenting is never fitting or unfitting. So the first-order component of delight introduces no standard of fittingness. The second-order component does introduce a standard of fittingness, but it is simply the standard of pro attitudes, not some new and sui generis standard. The standard is met when the first-order contemplative state is indeed good:

Only when a presentation/contemplation is in itself good and joyful (*erfreulich*) do we call its primary object beautiful. (Brentano 1959: 123)

Accordingly, delight fittingness can be accounted for in terms of self-imposition, as follows: it is fitting to be delighted with *x* iff anyone who contemplated *x* and harbored a self-imposing attitude toward that contemplation would harbor a *pro* (rather than con) attitude toward that contemplation.

The account still requires some refinement, however. For while every instance of aesthetic delight may involve contemplation of an object and enjoyment of that contemplation, the converse does not seem to hold. Consider the following joke: two muffins are baking in the oven; one says to the other, 'Man, it's getting hot in here'; the other says, 'What, you can talk too?!' Consider now your state of faint amusement at this joke. The amusement involves a contemplation of the scenario described in the joke, as well as mild enjoyment of this contemplation. So a combination of first-order contemplation and second-order pro attitude characterizes amusement (and its attitudinal character of presenting-as-funny) just as much as delight (and its attitudinal character of presenting-as-beautiful). Also, did you know that the southernmost point in Canada lies south of the northernmost point in California? If you found this tidbit interesting, you probably just experienced a state of curiosity or interest (in the narrow, non-Brentanian sense). Plausibly, your state of interest involved both contemplation of the fact relayed and a measure of pleasure in that contemplation (it *felt good*). So something must distinguish aesthetic delight from such structurally similar states as amusement and interest. A fully developed Brentanian account of delight would tell us what.

Conclusion

Brentano's theory of goodness proceeds in two main steps: a reductive analysis of goodness in terms of self-imposing pro attitudes, and an assisted revelation account of self-imposition. I have attempted to present this position in a sympathetic light, as an elegant, well thought out, and reasonably defensible account of value. At the same time, I have argued that Brentano's theory of goodness is ultimately destabilized by the ambiguous status of self-imposition as a normative and the same time brutally psychological characteristic of mental states.

The discussion has led us to Brentano's account of the beautiful, which complements rather nicely his accounts of the true and of the good. We can appreciate an unmistakable systematicity in Brentano's three accounts. Consider these three statements:

We call something true when the acceptance [belief] concerned with it is correct/fitting (*richtig*).
(Brentano 1889: 19 [18])

We call something *good* when the love [pro attitude] concerned with it is correct/fitting.

(Brentano 1889: 19 [18])

The concept of the beautiful has to do with...[that which] elicits in us a delight with the character of fittingness/correctness (*als richtig charakteriesiertes*).   (Brentano 1959: 17)

Thus truth, goodness, and beauty are all accounted for in terms of the fittingness of certain distinctive mental states.[43]

In one sense, Brentano is a perfect realist about the true, the good, and the beautiful – whether something exists, is good, or is beautiful is not up to us. Nonetheless, when we say that something exists, is good, or is beautiful, all we are saying is that belief in, pro attitude, or delight is the right attitude to take toward that thing. It is just that whether it is fitting or not to take the relevant attitude is an 'objective,' observer-independent matter. This is so even though it is impossible to truly *grasp* the very notions of the true, the good, and the beautiful without prior grasp of belief-in, pro attitude, and delight (and their fittingness). This is why Brentano wrote the following already in his mid-thirties:

We see that...the triad of ideals – the beautiful, the true, and the good – can well be explicated in terms of the system of mental faculties. Indeed, this is the only way in which it becomes fully intelligible (*erklären*)...   (Brentano 1874: II, 122 [263]; my italics)

In this way, in Brentano's thought the philosophy of mind assumes the role of *first philosophy*. And since for Brentano all mental life is conscious, it is the philosophy of consciousness that serves as first philosophy in his system. This is so in the following sense: the understanding of the true, the good, and the beautiful that the system offers is ultimately grounded in the understanding it offers of our conscious life. This is why we opened this book with discussion of Brentano's theory of consciousness.

Despite this *methodological* primacy of the philosophy of consciousness, let us repeat, Brentano's picture of the world is thoroughly realist. In fact Brentano's world contains just so many individual objects – nothing more. When we say, of any of the concrete particulars inhabiting Brentano's world, that it exists, or is good, or is beautiful, we are just saying that it would be fitting to believe in it, have a pro attitude toward it, or delight in it (respectively). It is in this way that the notions of the true/real, the good, and the beautiful enter our worldview. This entry does not entrain, however, a transcendental mind that does the believing, approving, or delighting. Rather, among the individual objects inhabiting this austere world are individual minds, including believing-minds, approving-minds, and delighted-minds, and indeed correctly-believing-minds, rightly-approving-minds, and fittingly-delighted-minds. It is because (and only because) each of us has on occasion *been* a correctly-believing-mind, rightly-approving-mind, or fittingly-delighted-mind, and has *inner-perceived* himself or herself to be such a mind, that each of us is able to experience the world in terms of truth, goodness, and beauty.[44]

Notes to Chapter 8

1. I go for these rather unlovely labels, as opposed to the more straightforward 'objectivism' and 'subjectivism', because the latter come with too much baggage. Certainly 'objectivism' can mean two very different things – that what is (intrinsically) good or bad is absolute and subject-independent, or that there are worldly facts concerning what is (intrinsically) good or bad – one of which Brentano was a fervent proponent of and the other something he was a clear opponent of. More on this later.

2. A related problem is that NN_1 appeals to the notion of a 'natural science', but what makes a science natural is presumably that its subject matter is part of nature – whereas the question we are trying to answer is precisely what makes a phenomenon part of nature.

3. It may well be that only spatiotemporal entities are reductively explicable in terms of spatiotemporal entities, in which case the reductive explanation clause in NN_2 is redundant. But it is worth keeping the clause in, in case there is a relevantly useful notion of reductive explanation by the lights of which some a-spatiotemporal entities can be reductively explained in terms of spatiotemporal ones.

4. In addition, they all appeal to the notion of reductive explanation, which has courted considerable controversy. Nonetheless, we can all agree on paradigmatic instances of reductive explanation – either in the form of a priori reductive analysis or in the form of a posteriori empirical reduction, such as of water in terms of H_2O, heat in terms of mean kinetic energy, and so on. We can then use these paradigms for an intuitive grasp of what reductive explanation is.

5. Note that a subject-end answer can be 'objectivist' in the sense of demanding that approval of generosity be good universally and context-independently, and be not 'up to the subject'.

6. This is not to deny that fitting-attitude accounts have had a presence in twentieth-century metaethics (see Ewing 1939, Chisholm 1981b and 1986, Carson 1984, Lemos 1989 and 1994, Anderson 1993, Mulligan 1998). But it was clearly a recessive strand in metaethical thinking during the twentieth century.

7. Here 'because' is intended not in a causal sense, but in an 'in-virtue-of' sense. FA thus grounds the goodness of things (e.g., generous acts) in the fittingness of pro attitudes (e.g., approval) toward them.

8. The book's title received this English translation in both translations: the first translation in 1902 by Cecil Hague and the 1969 translation by Chisholm and Elisabeth Schneewind. There would be some case for the tidier *On the Origin of Moral Knowledge* as translation of *Vom Ursprung sittlicher Erkenntnis*.

9. Some have argued that fittingness turns out to be whatever makes FA come out true, thus trivializing FA (see Reisner 2009).

10. In §26, Brentano ends his discussion of the contrast between blind and self-evident judgments thus: 'everyone experiences the difference between these two manners of judging (*Urteilsweise*)... [and] the ultimate elucidation [of self-evidence] consists only in a reference to this experience' (Brentano 1889: 21 [20]) – that is, the personal experience of *grasping* the contrast in question. But here the point is raised merely to introduce the pro attitude analog in §27. The section titles have sadly disappeared from the English edition, but in the German §26 is entitled 'Blind and Insightful Judgments' and §27 'Analogous Distinction in the Realm of Pleasure and Displeasure'.

11. Brentano offers no name for this feature that serves as the Archimedean point of his moral philosophy!

12. Note an important and potentially confusing difference between self-evidence and self-imposition. Self-evidence is revealed in (suitably aided) inner perception, but it is also *exhibited by* inner perception. Thus inner perception self-evidently reveals self-evidence. In contrast, inner perception reveals self-imposition but does not exhibit it – only interest states exhibit it. Accordingly, (suitably aided) inner perception self-evidently reveals self-imposition, but it would be a category mistake to say that it self-imposingly reveals self-imposition.

13. I incorporate different examples into Brentano's thought experiment than his, because his presuppose his own first-order ethical commitments, some of which are controversial (we will discuss them in Chap. 9).

14. I translate the key locution *als richtig charakterisierte* as 'with the character of correctness.' This is in contrast with the translation Chisholm has imposed throughout the Brentanian corpus, 'experienced as being correct,' which seems to me excessively interpretive. Hague's 1902 translation remains much closer to the text in offering 'having the character of rightness.'

15. This second possibility is the analogue of non-self-evident but fitting belief: belief in duck is fitting, recall, when it is such that had the subject judged on the existence of ducks with self-evidence, she would self-evidently *believe* in (rather than *disbelieve* in) ducks.

16. In this version of the view, the cashier case helps us home in on the nature of fittingness in its own way, although Brentano's case helps *more*. Both provide inner-perceptible contrasts between fitting and unfitting attitudes, though one does so using a finer contrast. The point is that the direct-grasp approach, when applied to fittingness itself rather than self-evidence or self-imposition, need not be based on a privileged type of contrast. Various different contrasts can be used to shed light from various angles on the single primitive, unanalyzable, fundamental feature that is fittingness.

17. This formulation in terms of *facts* is of course for convenience. As we saw in Chap. 6, Brentano rejects the existence of facts. Ultimately, for Brentano, the sentence 'If anyone had a self-imposing attitude toward generosity, it would be a pro attitude' must be paraphrased into 'There is no person who takes a self-imposing attitude toward generosity and does not take a pro attitude toward generosity' (or, if we are happy to bask in inelegance, 'There is no non-generosity-pro-attitudinizing self-imposingly-generosity-attitudinizing person'). Since this a negative truth, it does not have a truthmaker, that is, an entity in the world that makes it true. All we can say here is that it is fitting to disbelieve in the kind of person (a person who takes a self-imposing attitude toward generosity and does not take a pro attitude toward generosity).

18. This passage appears at the beginning of §4 of chapter1 of Book II of the *Psychology* – the chapter concerned with the demarcation of the mental. By the end of the section, Brentano recommends seeking a different criterion than that of spatiality. However, the reasons for this seem to be heuristic rather than substantive. His reservations about the spatiality criterion are two: that it is a purely negative characterization, and that it is controversial (whereas a demarcation of the mental should command consensus). Still, Brentano does seem to think that this criterion is just as extensionally adequate as the one he ultimately favors, intentionality. It is just that he thinks it is problematic for the community of inquiry to adopt a criterion whose extensional adequacy not everybody appreciates.

19. It is perhaps noteworthy that, despite his devout Catholicism, Brentano explicitly wields his open-question argument against divine command theory (more on this in §3.2).

20. Brentano makes a similar point regarding the parallel question of why we should believe what is self-evident: he claims that such a question would be 'completely laughable,' that is, does not really remain open (Brentano 1889: 21 [20]).

21. What is the 'pertinent' sense? The sense the FA theorist needs, that is, the sense needed for grounding goodness in fitting attitudes. There may be a sense in which it is fitting to adopt a pro attitude toward someone who will kill everybody unless we adopt a pro attitude toward her – but that is not the sense of fittingness that could be then used in an FA account of goodness.

22. Perhaps the most promising approach has been to claim that in the demon scenario, we actually do not have a reason to admire the demon; we only have a related but different reason – a reason to *bring it about* that we admire him, say, or a reason to *want* to admire him (Skorupski 2007, Way 2012). It is questionable whether this response can be fully general, however. Part of its attraction is due to the fact that admiration is not entirely in our control: I cannot simply up and decide to be an admirer of so-and-so. All I can decide is to *try* to become an admirer. But for all that, there may be some other pro attitudes which are directly controllable. If it is true that some pro attitudes we can *adopt*, then we could also *decide to adopt* them and they would be under our control. The other big approach to WKR seeks a further specification of the *kind* of reasons we should appeal to in an account of value, a kind the demon does not provide us with. Here the problem is how to do without circularity. One prominent idea is to distinguish between content-based (or 'object-given') and attitude-based (or 'state-given') reasons for holding an attitude (Parfit 2001, Danielsson and Olson 2007). This faces a number of problems, however, including returning the wrong results in certain cases (Rabinowicz and Rønnow-Rasmussen 2004, Schroeder 2012).

23. According to Scanlon (1998), a reason for j-ing is a consideration that counts in favor of j-ing. The buck-passer could, of course, appeal to this elucidation of reason talk, but then the same worry will arise for the notion of favoring. We can postpone the point at which we confess to our primitives, but eventually we will reach it!

24. Actually, Kauppinen's view is that it is fitting for a subject to hold attitude A toward x just if an ideal observer would endorse holding A toward x. On the assumption that an ideal observer who *endorses* A would actually *adopt* A, however, this leads to the idea that an attitude is fitting when an ideal subject would adopt it.

25. For Kauppinen, this sort of idealization serves two purposes. First, it undermines Enoch's (2005) accusation that idealization moves are ad hoc and unmotivated. Secondly, it provides for a principled speciation of value: different kinds of idealization avoid different kinds of practical problems, corresponding to moral, aesthetic, and prudential species of value.

26. The idealized triggering conditions mean that the disposition may not be *manifested* in the actual world; all the same, it may be routinely *instantiated* in the actual world. Dispositions are often instantiated without being manifested, as when fragility is instantiated by a vase which never breaks.

27. One option is to hold that an attitude is fitting if at least one ideal observer would adopt it; this is likely to result in more attitudes counting as fitting than we are intuitively inclined to accept. Another option is to hold that attitudes are fitting only if *all* ideal observers would adopt them; this will likely result in fewer attitudes counting as fitting than we would intuitively accept. A third option is to hold that when ideal observers disagree it is *indeterminate* whether the attitude in question is fitting; this is likely to result in extraordinarily many cases of fittingness indeterminacy – many more than we would intuitively accept.

28. Pre-Kripke, one might object that if 'Goodness = C' is true, then it is necessarily true, since morality is necessary (there is no possible world where torturing babies for fun is good).

Post-Kripke, however, the ethical naturalist can concede this and still maintain that 'Goodness = C' is true – it is a Kripkean a posteriori necessity akin to 'Water = H_2O.'

29. It is, of course, an empirical truth, discovered by chemists, that the causal role of water is played in the actual world by H_2O; but this empirical truth merely sustains the necessity 'produced' by (1). For the only reason (2) is necessary is that it is explicitly restricted to the actual world (in every possible world it is true *of our world* that H_2O plays the water role in it) – whereas 'Necessarily, Water = H_2O' is not thus restricted.

30. Retreating to (1*), 'Necessarily, goodness = the occupant of the goodness role,' is problematic. For it would lock up with (2*), 'C = is the occupant of the goodness role,' but (2*) is not necessary, since it is not explicitly restricted to the actual world (it is not 'rigidified'). Accordingly, all that would follow is that goodness is C in the actual world – that is, that C is the realizer of goodness in the actual world. No identity claim could be established.

31. It is worth noting that the father of Austrian market economics, Carl Menger, was a colleague of Brentano's at Vienna – and the two seem to have read each other (see Smith 1986).

32. It might be insisted that the intuition that it is fitting to disapprove of genocide because genocide is bad goes beyond the intuition that it is fitting to disapprove of genocide because of what genocide is like. But this is far from obvious, and in any case this extra intuitive content is something that Brentano could flatly deny with much less embarrassment.

33. Naturally, this is not a universal position. A conception of intuition as experiential or quasi-perceptual encounter with abstracta is defended by Bealer (1998) and Chudnoff (2013) among others. For a nuanced variant developed specifically for the moral context, see Huemer 2005.

34. Moore's review is really of the 1902 English translation of *Origin*, wherein *richtig* was translated as 'right' rather than as 'correct' (as it was in the 1969 translation).

35. Note that adopting this move would deprive Brentano of his main reason for rejecting response-dependent accounts of value that appeal to perceptual responses, which was that there is no such thing as perception of value. But the subsidiary, open-question reason probably persists: just as a grand illusion view of color perception is very much on the table, so is a grand illusion view of value perception – which leaves open the question of whether we should endorse what moral perception presents us with.

36. Butler writes: 'The mind can take a view of what passes within itself, its propensions, aversions, passions, affections, as respecting such objects and in such degrees, and of the several actions consequent thereupon. In this survey it approves of one, disapproves of another, and toward a third is affected in neither of these ways, but is quite indifferent. This principle in man by which he approves or disapproves his heart, temper, and actions, is conscience.' (Butler 1726: 13–14) Interestingly, like Brentano, Butler's elucidation of what he has in mind by 'conscience' adverts centrally to a contrast case: 'Suppose a man to relieve an innocent person in great distress; suppose the same man afterwards, in the fury of anger, to do the greatest mischief to a person who had given no just cause of offence. To aggravate the injury, add the circumstances of former friendship and obligation from the injured person; let the man who is supposed to have done these two different actions coolly reflect upon them afterwards, without regard to their consequences to himself: to assert that any common man would be affected in the same way towards these different actions, that he would make no distinction between them, but approve or disapprove them equally, is too glaring a falsity to need being confuted. There is therefore this principle of reflection or conscience in mankind.' (Butler 1726: 15)

37. If one held instead that what makes an attitude (un)fitting is that conscience (dis)approves of it, the resemblance would be weaker but still significant.

38. This is certainly the case if the revelation theory is true, but probably is so regardless. Even if the revelation theory is false, we could set the thought experiment up so that Luke's handle on red and pink is restricted to visual encounter. Thus, we can stipulate that Luke is not a color scientist, is somehow deprived of testimonial evidence, and so on. His *only* access – direct or otherwise – to the realm of colors is via visual experience.

39. Admittedly, there are externalist accounts of concept possession that would rule this out. According to these accounts, the concept Luke employs when he is directly aware of an object that looks like perfect red to you and me is a concept of pink, and the concept he employs when he is aware of what looks to you and me like paradigmatic pink is a concept of red. I take this scenario to be a *reductio* of the relevant externalist accounts!

40. As we will see toward the end of this section, there is good reason for Brentano not to posit a special kind of aesthetic fittingness; the kind of axiological fittingness suitable for pro attitudes in general does all the work his account of aesthetic value needs done, given his account of the special kind of pro attitude implicated in aesthetic appreciation.

41. Note well: it does not follow that the two mental states must be entirely independent, in the sense that neither can be (partially) analyzed in terms of the other. All the strategy requires is that the two be *different* states; what special constitutive relations there might be between them, as two different states, is irrelevant. (I point this out because Brentano's ultimate account will indeed distinguish two kinds of attitude one of which is partially analyzed in terms of the other.)

42. In some places, Brentano seems to construe delight slightly differently: as comprising contemplation of *x* and not just joy in this token contemplation but preference for it over average, unexceptional states of awareness. The result is the following account of beauty: '...in everyday life we call beautiful that of which the presentation could be preferred (for its own sake) over ordinary (*gewöhnlichen*) [i.e., unexceptional] presentations by a preference with the character of correctness...' (Brentano 1952: 193 [122]). The ugly, then, is presumably that with respect to which it is fitting to be in a compound state involving (i) contemplation of *x* and (ii) preference for ordinary contemplations over it. Here I will ignore this slightly more complicated variant, well motivated though it may be.

43. One important disanalogy is that for something to be beautiful, it must *actually elicit* fitting delight. Things that do not in fact elicit fitting delight, but delight at which would be fitting if it occurred, do not qualify as beautiful according to Brentano. This is clearly reflected in the quotation from Brentano 1959: 17. (Thanks to Kevin Mulligan for pointing this out to me.)

44. For comments on a previous draft, I am grateful to Thomas Baldwin, Terence Cuneo, Conor McHugh, Kevin Mulligan, Lylian Paquet, Jack Spencer, Mark Timmons, Benjamin Wald, and Jonathan Way. I have presented material from this chapter at École Normale Supérieure, the Jean Nicod Institute, Tel Aviv University, the University of Liège, and a summer school at Central European University; I am grateful to the audiences there, in particular Géraldine Carranante, Lionel Djadaojee, Mikaël Quesseveur, Denis Seron, Mark Textor, and Justin Winzenrieth.

9

Ethics
The Goods

What is good? Brentano's *formal* answer is: that toward which it is fitting to take a pro attitude. But one may ask the question hoping also for a *material* answer. In other words: toward which things is it fitting to take a pro attitude? Brentano's normative ethics offers an answer to this question. At the heart of his answer is a list of *four* things which are good in and of themselves. Abruptly put, they are: (i) conscious activity, (ii) pleasure, (iii) knowledge, and (iv) fitting attitudes. Everything else is good only insofar as it is instrumental in bringing about one of these four intrinsic goods. The purpose of this chapter is to offer a fuller critical exposition of this ethical system.

1. Consequentialism and the Structure of Ethical Theory

I have mentioned in Chap. 5 the organizing questions of ethics and metaethics. The ethicist asks: What is good? The metaethicist asks: What does it mean to say that something is good? I have noted, however, that these organizing questions do not quite *exhaust* ethics and metaethics. The latter is concerned also, for example, with questions about the basis and justification of moral knowledge. As for the former, a further question normative ethics must tackle can be summarized succinctly: *What to do?* That is, what are we supposed to do in, and with, our lives? This is a question not about what things are *good*, but about what actions are *right*, or what ends it is right for us to pursue. Brentano writes:

> How did we define ethics? We said it was that practical discipline which teaches us about the highest end (*Zweck*) and the choice of means for it.   (Brentano 1952: 88 [55])

Here 'practical discipline' should be thought of on the model of engineering: a discipline whose proper knowledge is knowledge-*how*, and whose body of knowledge-that is subservient to that knowledge-how.

Although the question Brentano attempts to address concerns the right rather than the good, his *answer* to the question is given in terms of the good: to a first approximation, what is right is to maximize the good. In a slogan, 'the right end consists in the best of what is attainable' (Brentano 1952: 134 [84]). Or in a more verbose statement:

> When is a decision directed upon the right end? The answer reads: when the best among what is attainable is chosen.   (1952: 220–1 [138]; see also 1889: 30 [32])

Different courses of action lead to different results – different *states of affairs*, we might say for the sake of convenience (while not forgetting that Brentano denies the existence of states of affairs). These states of affairs are to be evaluated in terms of their relative goodness – some will be better than others, and one (at least) will be best among them. But in every situation, some states of affairs are *attainable* and some are *unattainable*. That is to say: for some, there is an available course of action that will result in them; for others, there is not. Focusing now on those states of affairs for which a course of action is available that will result in them, they too can be evaluated for their relative goodness – some attainable states of affairs are better than others, and one (at least) is best. It is this state of affairs, the best among the attainable ones in a given circumstance, that is the right end for action in that circumstance. That is:

> (RIGHT)   For any agent A, course of action C, and time t, C is the right course of action for A at t iff there is no course of action C*, such that (i) C* is available to A at t and (ii) C* would bring about a state of affairs better than the state of affairs C would bring about.

Thus the right, although in the first instance more central to ethics as a 'practical discipline,' is ultimately understood in terms of the good (or rather in terms of the *better*).

A few clarifications of RIGHT might be useful. First, in some circumstances, there may be a small group of attainable states of affairs which are equally good and better than all others; Brentano appears to hold that ethical theory is neutral on which among them one ought to pursue. We might say that they are all *permissible* within his ethical theory. If so, RIGHT is really an account of *a* right action rather than *the* right action. Secondly, for the purposes of understanding RIGHT, we should take complete inaction to be a course of action always available to the agent; if all action would result in a state of affairs worse than the status quo, inaction would be the right 'course of action.' Thirdly, it is far from obvious what it means to say that a course of action is *available* to an agent, and accordingly that a state of affairs is *attainable* by her. Thus a Brentanian ethic must be supplemented with an analysis of these notions.[1] Fourthly, there is a clear sense in which RIGHT presents a consequentialist account of right action: the value of an action is fixed by the value of its consequences. As Brentano puts it, 'if anyone wants to call [RIGHT] a utilitarian principle, he is free to do so' (1952: 223 [139]; see also 1889: 31 [33]). Finally, although RIGHT is formulated in terms of *states of affairs*, we must keep in mind that in Brentano's reism there are no states of affairs; instead, there are special kinds of individual. So, there is no such thing as the state of affairs of the trolley hitting a fat man, but only the individual fat-man-hitting trolley; it is this special individual that bears whatever amount of intrinsic value we are inclined to assign to the corresponding state of affairs. I will continue to conduct the discussion in terms of states of affairs, to avoid an unnecessary cognitive tax on the reader. (I find it unnatural to think of these matters in terms of the bringing into or taking out of existence of special individuals, and assume it is the same with the reader.)

❧

The rightness of actions is fixed by the goodness of their consequences, then. But in many cases, the goodness of the consequences is itself fixed by the goodness of *their* consequences. It is right to brush one's teeth because the consequence of doing so is having healthy teeth, and having healthy teeth is good; but having healthy teeth is good because the consequence of having healthy teeth is that one can eat more easily in old age, which is itself good; and this latter is good because it has for likely consequence better nourishment. Ultimately, however, some things must be good *in and of themselves*, so that all other good things may derive their goodness from them, in virtue of having them as consequences.

On this picture, there are two very different ways for something to be good. Some things are good *derivatively*, i.e. in virtue of their consequences, while other things are good *intrinsically*, irrespective of their consequences. Crucially, the former's goodness is asymmetrically dependent on the latter's. For what constitutes the derivative goodness of a thing is not just the *existence* of its consequences, but their *goodness*. We might summarize the point as follows:

(GOOD)   For any x, x is good iff either (a) x is intrinsically good or (b) there is a y, such that (i) y is intrinsically good and (ii) y is a consequence of x.

GOOD accounts for goodness in terms of intrinsic goodness plus the consequence relation. Since consequence is a nonnormative notion, intrinsic goodness is the only basic normative notion here. The key normative question becomes, then, What is intrinsically good?

Note, however, that this 'account' of goodness is not substantive so much as analytic: it is an attempt to put order in the conceptual interrelations among various normative notions, not (yet) a contentful injunction to do this or that. We may thus call an ethics based on the combination of RIGHT and GOOD *analytic consequentialism*. According to analytic consequentialism, it is in some sense *trivial* that most actions and states of affairs are evaluated in terms of their consequences. But ultimately, some of these consequences must be evaluated intrinsically, on their own merit so to speak. One obtains a substantive, contentful ethics by taking on substantive commitments about what has intrinsic value or merit; that is, by adopting a specific 'table of goods' (*Gütertafel*) (Brentano 1952: 171 [104]).

First-generation utilitarians such as Bentham had a very simple table of goods, featuring only one item: pleasure. When you plug this table into the conjunction of RIGHT and GOOD, you get hedonic consequentialism: the injunction to act in such a way as to maximize the occurrence of pleasure in the world. For Brentano, however, there is no reason to expect there to be just one ultimate good. Pleasure *is* an intrinsic good, he concedes, but only one among several. To that extent, his is a *pluralistic* analytic consequentialism.[2]

What might tempt one to claim that pleasure is the *only* intrinsic good? Bentham (1789) thought that this followed from *psychological* hedonism, the claim that all action is ultimately motivated by desire for pleasure and aversion to pain. In Brentano's hands, the reasoning becomes this: 1) only pleasure can be loved; therefore, a fortiori, 2) only pleasure can be *fittingly* loved; 3) the good is that which can be fittingly loved; therefore, 4) only pleasure is good. Brentano rejects the first premise in this argument. His main argument against it is the following:

> Were nothing but pleasure loveable, it would mean that every love would have love for an object; however, the loved love would then have to be again directed at a love – and so on ad infinitum! No, for there to be pleasure at all, something other than pleasure must be loveable.
>
> (Brentano 1952: 179 [113])

Pleasure, like all other conscious states, is for Brentano an intentional state. Accordingly, it must be directed at some object. At the same time, pleasure is a species of love (that is, of a pro attitude). So whenever a pleasure occurs, a love state occurs that is directed at some object. At what object? Well, if only pleasure could be loved, it would mean that every pleasure has pleasure as its object. This leads to infinite regress, notes Brentano. In addition, we can note, it seems patently false: sometimes we take pleasure in an ice cream, or are pleased by a football game. Indeed, *most* pleasures are pleasures in things other than pleasure. The point is that psychological hedonism (Premise 1 in the above argument for hedonic consequentialism) appears to presuppose a non-intentionalist account of pleasure. Once one adopts the view that pleasure is an intentional state, psychological hedonism becomes exceedingly implausible.

Not only is there no good reason to expect pleasure to be the only good, then, there is good reason to expect there to be other goods. This aligns nicely with what our moral intuition instructs. Imagine two possible worlds very much like our own, and like each other, but for a very private stretch of thirty seconds in human history. At the beginning of this stretch, Hitler sits alone in his bunker and drinks poison that he knows will take thirty seconds to kill him; he spends the last thirty seconds of his life lying back and reflecting. In one of the two worlds, he spends those thirty seconds in utter glee and pride over all that he had accomplished. In the other, he is suddenly visited by the horrific realization of what he had done, and is tortured by an intense sense of shame, regret, and self-hatred. Hedonic consequentialism returns the verdict that the first world is the morally better of the two, the one we should hope is more similar to the actual world. But moral intuition is firm in its opposite verdict: that the second world is the morally superior, involving as it does the slightest measure of redemption.

2. Brentano's Table of Goods

In this section, I present Brentano's specific list of intrinsic goods (§2.1) and discuss various objections to them – that is, various suggestions for lengthening and/or shortening the list (§2.2).

2.1. The table

As noted, Brentano is happy to concede that pleasure is an intrinsic good. Given Brentano's metaethics, to say that pleasure is an intrinsic good is to say that it is fitting to adopt a pro attitude toward pleasure. More specifically, it is to say that anyone who adopted (what I called in Chap. 8) a self-imposing attitude toward pleasure, would adopt a *pro* attitude. And indeed, when we contrast our actual pro attitude toward pleasure and joy and con attitude toward pain and suffering with an imagined emotional set-up that involves a pro attitude toward pain and sorrow and a con attitude toward pleasure and joy, the former strikes us as preferable in a self-imposing sort of way. Thus pleasure is, qua pleasure, always and everywhere a good (Brentano 1889: 85 [90]).[3]

Importantly, for Brentano not all pleasures are *equally* intrinsically good. A pleasure taken in helping a blind person cross the street is more intrinsically valuable (has greater intrinsic goodness to it) than a(n equal) pleasure taken in torturing kittens for profit. The reason is that the former is a *fitting* pleasure whereas the latter is an *unfitting* pleasure; the right attitude to take toward kitten-torture is that of *dis*pleasure, not that of pleasure.

The overall intrinsic value of a fitting pleasure is in this picture a sum of the value of pleasure and the value of pleasure-fittingness, which means that pleasure-fittingness is another intrinsic good, in addition to pleasure. The fittingness of pleasure is, however, just a special case of the fittingness of any state of 'interest' or emotion:

... all emotions with the character of correctness/fittingness are good in and of themselves. This holds of love and hatred in all forms. So for example a noble pain, say about the victory of injustice, ... is valuable in itself.   (Brentano 1952: 186 [118])

Fitting pain taken in extrajudicial execution of African-Americans by US police is an intrinsic bad insofar as it is a pain, but also an intrinsic good insofar as it is a fitting interest state. Its *overall* intrinsic value is a function of the intrinsic good arising from the state's fittingness and the intrinsic bad arising from the state's painfulness. This raises the thorny question of how we may calculate the *overall* intrinsic value of such a state. The answer depends on the comparative value of (i) pleasure/pain and (ii) interest-fittingness – an issue we take up in §3.

Interestingly, the intrinsic value of pleasure is itself, for Brentano, the sum of two distinct intrinsic goods. Recall that for Brentano, pleasure is a specific kind of conscious experience, one that employs a distinctive mode of presenting the intentional object (I have proposed in Chap. 7 the mode which presents-as-prima-facie-good-here-and-now). According to Brentano, though, presentation as such is already intrinsically good! Brentano writes:

Presentations belong doubtless to what is valuable in and of itself, and indeed, I daresay that every presentation is valuable, taken in and of itself.   (Brentano 1952: 188 [119])

What Brentano seems to have in mind here is that the very occurrence of a conscious state is something good in and of itself. The very existence of conscious activity adds value to the world.[4] For it is always fitting to prefer consciousness over zombiehood:

...every presenting, considered in and of itself, is a good and recognizable as such, because an emotion with the character of correctness/fittingness can be directed at it. Everyone who had to choose between the state of unconsciousness and the having of any presentations whatsoever would, without question, welcome even the poorest [presentation]... (Brentano 1959: 144; see also 1952: 188–9 [119])

This means, in turn, that the intrinsic goodness of pleasure is the sum of the intrinsic goodness of (i) the presentation it is grounded in and (ii) the particular modification of the presenting it employs. We may put this by saying that the intrinsic goodness of a pleasure is the sum of the intrinsic goodness of the presentation and of its pleasantness.[5] Accordingly, the intrinsic value of a *fitting* pleasure is the sum of *three* types of intrinsic goodness: (i) the very occurrence of the presentation as such, (ii) that presentation's being a pleasure, and (iii) that pleasure being fitting.

So far, we have encountered three kinds of intrinsic goodness: conscious activity, pleasure, and interest-fittingness. This list is in fact *almost* exhaustive. Brentano asserts only one other kind of intrinsic good, which he calls alternately knowledge (*Erkenntnis*), insight, or fitting/correct judgment. He writes:

Already Aristotle included knowledge (*Erkenntnis*) in the table of goods...And indeed, if anyone should pose the question why we like knowledge better than error, this would seem to us no less laughable than if we had asked why we would rather enjoy ourselves than suffer pain.
(Brentano 1952: 183 [116]; see also 1889: 22, 28 [22, 29])

Two points bear stressing here. First, Brentano's claim of intrinsic value concerns *Erkenntnis* rather than *Wissen*, so something like knowledge-*of* rather than knowledge-*that*. What kind of restriction this really amounts to is not straightforward, given that for Brentano all belief is belief-in rather than belief-that (as we saw in Chap. 4). Secondly, what separates knowledge-of from mere belief-in is *fittingness*: any fitting belief-in qualifies as *Erkenntnis* for Brentano. Given that the mere occurrence of belief-in is *not* intrinsically valuable for Brentano, in claiming that knowledge is intrinsically valuable, all he is claiming is that the fittingness of beliefs (and disbeliefs!) is an intrinsic good.

In summary, for Brentano there are exactly four things of positive intrinsic value in our world: presentation, pleasantness, interest-fittingness, and judgment-fittingness.[6] Observe that Brentano's 'table of goods' reflects quite closely his fundamental classification of conscious states into presentation, judgment, and interest. Recall from Chap. 3 that while judgment and interest have a standard of fittingness that applies to them, presentations do not. And here we find ourselves with a table of goods three quarters of which consists in the fittingness of judgments, the fittingness of interest states, and the mere *occurrence* of presentations. The only extra element is the *occurrence*

Table 9.1. Brentano's table of goods

	value in occurrence	value in fittingess
Interest-related	pleasure	interest-fittingness
Interest-external	presentations	belief-fittingness

of pleasure, a particular type of interest state. This gives us a table where half the intrinsic goods are a matter of the occurrence of a conscious state and half a matter of the *fittingness* of a conscious state; and where half concern the realm of interest and half the other conscious realms (Table 9.1).

The result is quite a striking ethical theory, one where all value derives from four intrinsic goods, all of which are confined to our conscious life. It turns out, then, that Brentano's moral philosophy, *too*, is grounded in his philosophy of consciousness.

Indeed, if we keep in mind Brentano's reism, it would seem that his four intrinsic goods are just four special kinds of conscious subject. As we saw in Chap. 6, Brentano's world contains nothing but concrete particulars, though some which are quite unusual (namely, the accidents). Of this lot of concrete particulars, a proper subset are intrinsically valuable. The emerging view is this:

(INTRINSIC)   Only four kinds of entity are intrinsically good: presenting-subjects, pleased-subjects, fittingly-interested-subjects, and fittingly-judging-subjects.

Note that presenting-subjects, pleased-subjects, fittingly-interested-subjects, and fittingly-judging-subjects are all accidents in Brentano's ontology. This creates a certain difficulty, since accidents depend for their existence on substances (in this case, persons like you and me, who are doing the presenting, experiencing the pleasure, and so on). There are two ways for Brentano to go here. He may embrace the surprising consequence that no substance is intrinsically valuable. (Substances could still be *instrumentally* good, insofar as their existence is a precondition for the existence of intrinsic goods.) Alternatively, he could claim that the substances on which depend presenting-subjects, pleased-subjects, fittingly-interested-subjects, and fittingly-judging-subjects have intrinsic value as well. On this view, all things considered there are *five* kinds of intrinsically good thing: the four mentioned in INTRINSIC, plus the substances whereupon these depend. Which is the better way to go here? There is certainly a natural inclination to choose the second, valuing the persons themselves at least as much as their valuable accidents. The inclination is nicely captured by Kraus:

It is not for the sake of increasing goods and reducing evils, but rather for the sake of elevating as much as possible the incalculable intrinsic value of the relevant beings, that we seek to make the goods accessible to as many as possible... (Kraus 1937: 275, quoted in Janoušek and Rollinger 2017)

But Brentano may have been harder-nosed than his student here. I am not familiar with any *ethical* text in which Brentano addresses the issue, but in a 1915 dictation on space and impenetrability, of all topics, he says in passing the following:

...the actual thinking [or presenting] added as accident to some soul is incomparably more significant than the soul's substance itself. It is here [in the thinking] that we find the oppositions of knowledge and error, higher love and preference for the bad; so that Aristotle could say that a mind without actual thinking, lost in eternal sleep, would be devoid of all dignity (*Würde*).   (Brentano 1976: 184 [155])

Here Brentano seems to dismiss substances as not themselves endowed with any value. It is not people who have moral weight, but conscious-people, joyful-people, fittingly-interested-people, and correctly-believing-people who do!

A final point: corresponding to Brentano's table of goods will be also a 'table of evils.' Interestingly, however, it would seem Brentano's table of evils would include only *three* items: unfitting belief, unfitting attitude, and pain (or rather unfitting-believers, unfitting-attitudinizers, and pained-persons). Presentation does not have an opposing kind of entity – the only thing we can oppose to the occurrence of a presentation is the nonoccurrence of one. If Brentano's ultimate value-bearers were states of affairs, then he could claim that the state of affairs of a presentation not occurring is something real, which therefore can bear value, including negative value. But since Brentano's ultimate value-bearers are individuals, and he does not countenance nonexistent individuals in his ontology, there can be no fourth item in his table of evils corresponding to presenting-individuals in his table of goods. Thus Brentano's 'table of valuables' will include only seven things – four intrinsic goods and three intrinsic evils.

2.2. Objections to Brentano's table

Objections to Brentano's table of goods divide into two groups: some might claim it is too short, proposing further intrinsic goods; some might claim it is too long, rejecting some of Brentano's alleged intrinsic goods. We can discuss neither in great detail here, but will consider briefly the sort of issues that arise in each case.

Brentano is actually quite tentative about the *exhaustiveness* of his table of goods, but is nonetheless inclined toward it. He writes:

1. Is a virtuous disposition preferable to its opposite? We actually love and admire people more on account of their character than because of isolated moral actions...Are dispositions also therefore valuable in themselves – or are they only due to the activities that result from them? 2. Are plants love-worthy in and of themselves, for their own sake, something to be taken as good in itself?...3. Is each and every thing a good, quite aside from its unfailing instrumentality (*allfälligen Nützlichkeit*)?...One is inclined to answer: No!   (Brentano 1952: 206 [130])

In this passage Brentano considers and tentatively rejects three potential new intrinsic goods.

In the first group are 'virtuous disposition.' Consider a person who does not just harbor a fitting desire right now, but has a stable disposition to harbor fitting rather than unfitting desires. Given that fitting desire is an intrinsic good, the disposition to have such desires is a *virtuous* disposition. Brentano's question is whether (a) having such a virtuous disposition is good in and of itself, or (b) it is only the *manifestations* of this disposition which are intrinsically good, and the disposition as such is merely *instrumentally* good. At bottom, the question is whether two worlds indistinguishable in terms of what actually occurs in them, but where in one Jimmy's fitting desires are grounded in a stable disposition while in the other Jimmy's fitting desires are something of a happy accident, are of equal or differing intrinsic values. If we think the one world is intrinsically better than the other, this must be due to the intrinsic value contributed by the disposition; if instead we think that they are of equal intrinsic value, then we do not assign the mere disposition any intrinsic value. Now, since Brentano's table of goods includes four occurrent intrinsic goods, the same kind of question will arise for four distinct types of virtuous disposition: the disposition to judge correctly, the disposition to emote or will fittingly, a joyful disposition, and the disposition to engage in much conscious activity. On all of these, Brentano is tempted by the view that mere dispositions are only *instrumentally* valuable – valuable insofar as their manifestations are intrinsically valuable. Thus a temperamentally considerate person is in and of itself no better than an inconsiderate person if it just so happens that the two have shown *actual* consideration with equal frequency. If character is destiny, it is only instrumentally so; the *destination* is occurrent conscious life full of intrinsic good.[7]

In addition, Brentano considers whether *life* might be an intrinsic good. This is what the question about plants seems to get at. Unlike animals, who often have a mental life, which Brentano has already accepted as intrinsically valuable, plants have only a nonmental life, hence a life deprived of what he has already accepted as intrinsically valuable. Yet there might be a strong intuition that a pro attitude would be fitting toward the living as such, quite independently of the potential pleasures and insights of the living. (Left-wing environmentalists and right-wing abortion opponents might agree on this point!) Again, Brentano is tempted by the notion that while the environment might be instrumentally valuable (to conscious beings), it is not intrinsically valuable. More specifically, life as such has no intrinsic value: a zombie world with rocks and flowers is no better than a zombie world with rocks only. At the same time, life must be granted enormous instrumental value in Brentano's ethics, insofar as it appears to be a precondition for all conscious activity, hence for pleasure, fitting interest, and fitting judgments.

Finally, Brentano considers and tentatively rejects the notion that as such might be intrinsically valuable. Here too, it might seem that as a precondition of everything, including everything valuable, being as such must be in and of itself valuable. But ultimately Brentano is tempted by the opposite view: a zombie world with more stuff in it is no better than a zombie world with less.

Interestingly, since he is not entirely sure that existence, life, and virtuous disposition are merely instrumentally valuable, Brentano articulates also a fallback position: that these are *intrinsically* valuable, but their intrinsic value is greatly outweighed by the intrinsic value of the four official items on his list (Brentano 1952: 209 [131]). This means that in situations where we have to choose between two intrinsic goods, these potential addenda to the table will typically be overlooked in favor of the four more established items on the table.

Moore (1903a: §50, §55) held that among the intrinsic goods is *beauty*. To that extent, Moore would consider the existence of the right kind of flowers as intrinsically good, not in virtue of the flowers being alive though, but in virtue of being beautiful. Now, Brentano does not cite beauty as such in his list of intrinsic goods. Recall from Chap. 8, however, that Brentano analyzes beauty in terms of fitting delight, that is, a fitting mental state composed of first-order presentation (e.g., of flowers) and a second-order joy taken in that first-order presentation. By its very nature, then, fitting delight is quadruply intrinsically good in Brentano's ethics: (i) insofar as it involves a first-order presentation, (ii) insofar as it involves a second-order presentation of that presentation, (iii) insofar as the second-order presentation is pleasant, and (iv) insofar as that second-order pleasure – a state of interest – is fitting. Insofar as it provokes the instantiation of these four intrinsic goods, the beautiful flower is *instrumentally* good.[8]

Modern consequentialists sometimes focus on more global properties of a good life, such as well-being or welfare (see Sen 1979). The idea is that while pleasure contributes to a person's well-being, so may friendship, satisfaction, meaning, and the like more complex elements. According to welfare consequentialists, it is this more complex phenomenon of welfare that is intrinsically good, and anything which enhances welfare is instrumentally good.[9] Evidently Brentano did not include anything like welfare or well-being in his table of goods. One suspects his motivation for this omission is the conviction that well-being is simply the resultant of his four acknowledged goods, not a distinct fifth good. On this view, a person's well-being is but a function of an active conscious life with pleasure and fitting emotions and beliefs aplenty. In particular, the various other ingredients of a good life that welfarists tend to cite have such intrinsic value as they do in virtue of involving as constituents (some of) Brentano's four intrinsic goods. For instance, friendship might constitutively involve fitting care for one's friends, pleasure in their company, and so on; if the intrinsic value of friendship is *exhausted* by the sum of such intrinsic values already taken into account in Brentano's table of goods, then friendship as such does not inject into the world any proprietary intrinsic value.

It is an open question, of course, whether everything that appears intrinsically good in our world can be seen as just a mixture of Brentano's four fundamental intrinsic goods. The question is obviously too vast to settle here, but I trust that the above discussion clarifies the structure and burden of the kind of pluralist consequentialism defended by Brentano. Evidently, Brentano's bet is on a positive answer, but we have seen he is open in principle to certain supplementations of his *Gütertafel*.

⊷⊱

A completely different challenge Brentano faces is to ensure that none of the four goods in his table is *de trop*. While it is relatively uncontroversial that pleasure as such is in and of itself good, this is less obvious for conscious activity, knowledge, and fitting emotion.

There is no question, of course, that conscious activity is a good. A zombie world is quite plausibly devoid of all meaning and value (Siewert 2013). If so, you cannot have any value in the absence of conscious activity. However, this guarantees at most that conscious activity is an *instrumental* good, on a par with life and existence. After all, for Brentano a lifeless world is devoid of all meaning and value too, as is an empty world. But life and existence derive their value only from the fact that they are preconditions for what is intrinsically valuable. So theirs is a derivative, not intrinsic, value. By the same token, one might suggest that conscious activity is valuable only insofar as it is a precondition for pleasure, say, or knowledge; it is derivatively rather than intrinsically valuable.

As noted, Brentano's main argument for the *intrinsic* goodness of consciousness is simply that anyone in her right mind would prefer consciousness over zombiehood, and it would be very fitting for her to do so (Brentano 1959: 144). But while we can readily agree that it is fitting to have a pro attitude toward an *important* or *interesting* thought, is it so obviously fitting to have a pro attitude toward a *trivial* thought, say a fleeting image of gravel? Imagine two possible worlds that differ only in this detail, that in one of them Jimmy fell asleep at ten o'clock sharp and in the other he fell asleep fifty milliseconds later and had a fleeting image of gravel during that interval. It is hard to tell whether (a) the two worlds are equally fitting to desire or (b) there is an ever so minuscule extra desirability associated with the second world. Likewise, imagine two worlds in which Jimmy suffers from an obsessive-compulsive disorder, which induces him to repeatedly think of octopi (he finds neither special interest nor special displeasure in these repeated thoughts, let us stipulate); it is not obvious that a world in which Jimmy has one more random octopus thought is more fittingly desirable.[10] Now, the very fact that it is *difficult* to tell which is the right position to take on such questions suggests the following conditional: if it turns out that conscious activity *as such* does have intrinsic value, then it may be very limited – greatly outweighed by the other items on the table of goods. (Recall Brentano's fallback position on the value of existence, life, and the virtues.)

The notion that fitting belief, knowledge, or insight is intrinsically good is also contestable. There is no question that the *experience* of insight or understanding, for instance, involves a distinctive highly positive affect that makes it fitting to want. Moreover, the relevant affect is sui generis, in the sense that it is irreproducible by the summation of any number of other kinds of positive affect. No amount of orgasm and cheesecake can replicate quite the same *kind* of good feeling we experience when we suddenly understand something or have a deep insight ('when the scales fall from our eyes'). But this in itself motivates only a much more limited notion: that in assigning intrinsic value to pleasure, we must keep in mind that not only 'bodily' pleasure is at stake – there are certain irreducibly 'spiritual' pleasures that must be recognized as well, including the pleasures of understanding and insight. This was famously Mill's (1863: 11–12) great contribution to the consequentialist tradition. Presumably, however, Brentano has something stronger in mind. In adding to his table of goods knowledge or insight *on top* of pleasure, he seems to suggest that the pleasurable aspect of insight does not exhaust insight's intrinsic value. There is an additional measure of intrinsic value contained in the fact that insight offers a kind of epistemic penetration of reality: the clear and distinct presenting to the mind of how things really are is intrinsically good, quite apart from any pleasure it might involve.[11]

Interestingly, Brentano does not offer much by way of *argument* for the intrinsic value of knowledge or insight. I have already quoted his main support for the claim: 'if anyone should pose the question why we like knowledge better than error, this would seem to us no less laughable than if we had asked why we would rather enjoy ourselves than suffer pain' (Brentano 1952: 183 [116]). For any given belief of yours, your preference for that belief being true over its being false is, *other things being equal*, self-imposing in the sense explained in Chap. 8. (The qualification 'other things being equal' is required to rule out cases where one prefers one's belief to be false because of the pain its truth would occasion – as when one suspects one has been betrayed by a friend. Such preference has to do only with the instrumental value of the belief's truth.)

Brentano's basic thought here might be framed in terms of Nozick's (1974: 42–5) 'experience machine.' Consider the following variant: imagine you are offered to be hooked into a science-fiction machine that (i) predicts your entire future life and (ii) directly stimulates your brain just so as to reproduce the experiences you would have had, but adding a few more positive experiences and dropping a few negative ones. (It might, for instance, take one instance in which your favorite team loses a game and induce in you the illusory experience of your team winning that game.) Most of us seem to prefer living our 'real' life over entering the experience machine – and intuitively, we seem to be rational in so preferring. Likewise, we find it perfectly rational for Neo to choose the red pill over the blue pill in the Matrix film, even though taking the red pill promises to proffer many more units of displeasure. This is essentially the intuition Brentano taps into in holding that awareness of how things really are is intrinsically valuable independently of such pleasure as may be thereby procured.

The intuition is of course very robust.[12] One might nonetheless respond that the untutored intuition of people who have not sufficiently reflected on the question of what is intrinsically valuable should not count for all that much (Feldman 2011). This kind of response is enhanced when combined with a debunking explanation of where the intuition comes from. Here is one potential explanation. When we contemplate *someone else* who thinks her team won a game that in fact it has lost, we feel a measure of derision (however mild) toward her – she is a fool, after all. But now, when we contemplate the experience-machine scenario, we imagine it 'from the outside,' from the third-person perspective. For we do not just imagine experiencing certain things, but in addition imagine that these things are not really happening – something we can only do 'from outside' the machine. As a result, we effectively adopt the same viewpoint we take on others being in that scenario, and consequently experience something of the same derision – but this time toward our own imagined self.

From Brentano's Aristotelian viewpoint, this kind of debunking explanation should not be available to a real philosopher. A philosopher who loves wisdom not for its own sake, but because of some positive titillation she expects it to occasion, is a bad instance of a philosopher. A real philosopher does not seek wisdom in order that she might use it to obtain something else. No activity requires further justification that can be shown to enhance wisdom. For it is through the individual conduct of contemplative lives that the universe progresses toward its fundamental *telos* of reaching self-understanding. All the good feelings in the history of the universe are just so many agreeable occurrences by the roadside of this advance toward the universe's self-understanding. This is why Aristotle took the contemplative life to be the best kind of life.

I am not sure how moved we should be by this line of thought, but am quite sure it animated Brentano's own conduct of his life and undergirds his commitment to knowledge or understanding (as opposed to the pleasures attendant thereupon) as an intrinsic good. This is not the place to settle the issue of whether knowledge (or correct belief, or insight) really is intrinsically valuable. What matters for our purposes is that Brentano evidently takes it to be so, on the grounds that anyone who made a self-imposing decision on whether to enter the experience machine would decide not to.

Brentano's other highest intrinsic good is fitting pro or con attitude. Here a serious problem arises rather immediately: the citing of fitting attitude can help guide us in our moral action only if we are told *which attitudes are fitting*. Qua first-order normative ethicist, Brentano should let us know which attitudes are fitting, or else we have no idea how to pursue the good. So what attitudes *are* fitting?

The natural answer is of course: those pro attitudes are fitting which are directed at what is truly good (and those con attitudes are fitting which are directed at what is truly bad). But what *is* truly good (bad)? Brentano's answer is encapsulated in his table of goods, one of which is precisely fitting attitude. This seems to send us on an explanatory circle. But perhaps the point of the inclusion of fitting attitude is to point at a *recursive specification* of a much longer *full* table of goods (Hurka 2000: 25). This includes: (i) pleasure, (ii) consciousness, (iii) knowledge, (iv) a pro attitude toward pleasure, (v) a pro attitude toward consciousness, (vi) a pro attitude toward knowledge, (vii) a pro attitude toward a pro attitude toward pleasure, ... and so on. Thus, not only pleasure is good, but also the desiring of pleasure and the desiring of desiring of pleasure; not only knowledge is good, but also the approving of knowledge and the approving of approving of knowledge; and so on and so forth. On the present suggestion, this is all there is to the inclusion of fitting attitudes in the table of goods.

It might be objected that if that is all there is to the inclusion of fitting attitudes, then fitting attitudes will not make any distinctive contribution to actual evaluation of competing states of affairs. But this is not true. Thus, we must do justice to the fact that pleasure intentionally brought about is intrinsically better than pleasure accidentally taking place. The inclusion of fitting attitudes is a way of doing justice to that fact: a pleasure intentionally brought about involves not just two intrinsically good things (the conscious state and its pleasantness), but *three* – the fitting intention to bring the pleasure about makes the difference.

A better objection, however, is that the recursive approach to the intrinsic value of fitting attitudes does not return the *right* evaluations in certain cases. Consider again the aforementioned intuition that the sad-Hitler world is better than the happy-Hitler world. The citing of fitting attitude seemed to us to vindicate the intuition: although the world where the final thirty seconds of Hitler's life are spent in shame and self-hatred contains less pleasure than the world where they are spent in pride and elation, the latter world contains more fitting emotions than the former. If it turns out, however, that fitting emotions are just positive emotions toward pleasure, knowledge, or conscious activity, or negative emotions toward displeasure or ignorance, then we can envisage scenarios in which sad-Hitler undergoes an episode of shame which (i) is intuitively fitting but (ii) unfitting by the theory's lights. Suppose sad-Hitler feels momentary shame about ordering the execution of a thirteen-year-old girl. All her family and acquaintances had already been murdered, and her execution was swift, let us stipulate, so her execution occasioned no additional pain, but much glee on the part of the executioners. Had the girl survived the Holocaust, let us further stipulate, the great majority of her beliefs would be false. By the lights of Brentano's theory, sad-Hitler's shame in ordering the execution is unfitting, so the happy-Hitler world is better than the sad-Hitler one. Wrong result.

The other option for Brentano is to identify some monadic characteristic of any pro (or con) attitude, unrelated to *what* it is about, that makes it fitting. If such a characteristic could be found, then the appeal to other items on Brentano's table of goods is not necessary to know which attitudes are fitting. This strategy recommends itself to Brentano, since as we saw in the previous chapter, he understands an attitude's fittingness in terms of the monadic characteristic I called self-imposition – the practical analogue of self-evidence. More specifically, according to Brentano a pro attitude toward x is fitting just if anyone who took a self-imposing attitude toward x would take a pro (rather than con) attitude toward it, where self-imposition is an intrinsic feature of self-imposing attitudes. In recommending that we attempt to maximize fitting attitudes in the world, Brentano's ethics can be interpreted as recommending that we attempt to maximize the occurrence of pro and con attitudes which either (a) are self-imposing or (b) would be the attitudes adopted by someone whose attitudes were self-imposing.

However, this strategy brings up again worries about whether Brentano's ethics can informatively guide us in our moral conduct. If one of our own attitudes is self-imposing, then we can know, according to Brentano, that its occurrence would be self-imposing in anyone who experienced it; so we would be well justified to try to maximize the occurrence of this attitude in the world. It is less clear, however, how we can know, of any non-self-imposing attitude we experience, whether it would be the attitude adopted by someone who enjoyed a self-imposing stance on the matter at hand. Suppose x merits a pro attitude, but you have no attitude toward x. Obviously, you cannot detect self-imposition in an attitude you do not even have (compare Ehrenfels 1988: 216).

You must instead speculate about the attitude taken by someone who did have a self-imposing attitude, pro or con, toward x. Consider again Sartre's student. He evidently does not inner-perceive self-imposition either with respect to the option of joining the war effort or with respect to the option of tending to his mother. What is he to do? Replying 'Pick the option that someone with a self-imposing attitude would pick' would be just cruel.[13]

Might there be some other monadic characterization of pro and con attitudes, not in terms of what they are about, that can 'tag' them as fitting? A Kantian might propose that a fitting attitude is one that treats a person as an end and not merely as a means. On this suggestion, among the intrinsically good things are *respectful* attitudes, where 'respectful' is meant in the sense of Kantian respect for persons, that is, in the sense of treating as an end. The suggestion is on its face rather plausible. On the one hand, having a respectful attitude toward a person – treating her as an end in herself – is clearly a good thing. On the other hand, such goodness as the attitude has does not seem to derive (only) from its consequences; it has to do (partially at least) with the internal character of respectful attitude as such. Furthermore, we may construe the relevant internal character in terms of attitude rather than content. The idea would be that Kantian respect is the kind of mental state which essentially presents-as-end-rather-than-mere-means its object. The occurrence of every such attitude toward a person, it might be suggested, is good in and of itself. Thus one option for a Brentanian is to take a leaf from Kant and identify respectful attitude toward persons as the fourth intrinsic good, complementing pleasure, knowledge, and consciousness.

Needless to say, there is no trace of anything like this in Brentano himself (and given Brentano's general attitude toward Kant, there is not much risk that a manuscript might resurface that developed Brentano's ethics in that direction). More deeply, there is a tension between the fact that Kantian respect is supposed to be directed at persons, on the one hand, and the Brentanian thought, on the other hand, that what is intrinsically valuable is not *persons*, but pleased-persons, knowing-persons, and so on.[14] On the resulting view, persons as such are not intrinsically valuable, but treating them as ends is. One is entitled to wonder: Why should I treat as an end something devoid of intrinsic value? Citing the fact that that thing has immense instrumental value will not do, since valuing something for its instrumental value is precisely valuing it as a means. Thus this Kanto-Brentanian combination seems, at least initially, unstable.[15] Nonetheless, it has the virtue of *illustrating* the kind of move the Brentanian should make to address the problem of guidance: offering a substantive characterization of those attitudes which are fitting so that we know what to do when told that one of the things we need to maximize in the world is fitting attitudes.

I conclude that the inclusion of fitting attitudes in the table of goods is highly problematic, as long as no account is provided of which attitudes, or kinds of attitude, are fitting. More generally, while the injunctions to maximize pleasure, conscious activity, and fitting beliefs are fairly straightforwardly followable, the injunction to maximize fitting attitudes is not (except perhaps insofar as it involves taking pro attitudes toward pleasure, conscious activity, and fitting belief). At the same time, we cannot simply strike fitting attitudes off our table – we need them in order to get the right result in the happy-Hitler/sad-Hitler case. So Brentano's normative ethics clearly needs supplementation here.

This strikes me as the most significant challenge facing Brentano's ethical theory. It is not unrelated, of course, to what is probably the weakest part of his metaethics – the question of how inner perception could pick up not just on an attitude's *feeling* self-imposing (a completely psychological property), but its actually *being* self-imposing (a partly normative property). His entire moral philosophy is thus threatened by a certain elusiveness attending its *Punctum Archimedes* – self-imposition.

3. What To Do

Even if Brentano's table of goods were accepted *as is*, it would not yet deliver an answer to the question 'What to do?' For that, we would need an account of the relative weight or significance of different intrinsic goods. We have seen that what we should do, at any one time, is take whatever available course of action will likely lead to the *intrinsically best* state of affairs. And we have seen what makes a state of affairs intrinsically good to begin with. But to know which state of affairs is intrinsically *best*, we also need an account of what is intrinsically *better* than what. Without that, we *still* receive no guidance from the One True Table of Goods.

In many cases, intrinsic betterness is a matter of *quantitative* superiority: more pleasure is intrinsically better than less, more intense pleasure is intrinsically better than milder pleasure, and so on. Likewise, situations involving several intrinsic goods are better than situations involving a proper subset of those goods: pleasure is better than mere presentation, for instance, given that pleasure involves presentation as a component, so already includes the value of the presentation in it. In those cases, claims of intrinsic betterness seem unproblematic.

The trickier cases are those where quantitative comparison is unavailable. More pleasure is better than less, but is more pleasure better than more *knowledge*? Or is knowledge on the contrary more intrinsically valuable than pleasure? And what methodology are we to use in answering such questions? The difficulties surrounding non-quantitative comparison may inspire an incommensurability approach, whereby there is no way to weigh different intrinsic goods against each other.[16] But incommensurability is not compulsory here. A different approach is to claim that in addition to quantitative superiority, there are facts of the matter regarding *qualitative superiority*, and it is those facts that decide whether pleasure is more intrinsically valuable than knowledge or the other way round. For example, Brentano follows Mill in holding that *mental* pleasure (*geistigen Freude*) is mutatis mutandis more valuable than *bodily* or *sensory* pleasure (*Sinneslust*): pleasure derived from a good poem is (other things being equal) more intrinsically valuable than pleasure derived from a good ice cream (Brentano 1952: 186 [117]). And he makes similar claims for the domains of judgment and interest writ large. Thus, he maintains that *positive* knowledge is mutatis mutandis intrinsically better than *negative* (Brentano 1952: 184, 213 [116, 134]). In telling us how the world *is*, rather than how it is *not*, a fitting belief is of greater intrinsic value than a fitting disbelief. Likewise, not all fitting interest states are equally intrinsically good: fitting love of *x* is intrinsically more valuable than fitting hatred of *y* (Brentano 1952: 213 [134]).[17]

These are cases of qualitative superiority *within* individual types of intrinsic goods. For Mill, there can be no other kind of qualitative superiority, since ultimately there is only one kind of intrinsic good, pleasure. But Brentano is a pluralist here, so he recognizes cases of intrinsic betterness *across* goods. For example, other things being equal, interest-fittingness is more intrinsically valuable than pleasure: it is intrinsically better to experience fitting sorrow about extrajudicial killings of African-Americans than to take unfitting pleasure in it (Brentano 1889: 85 [91]; 1952: 213 [134]).

How might we *justify* such claims of qualitative intrinsic superiority? Mill's (1863: 12-3) argument was that people who know both kinds of pleasure prefer mental over physical pleasures; people who prefer physical pleasure have no real acquaintance with mental pleasure. Setting aside the veracity of this empirical claim, it seems to leave completely untouched the question of whether people who know both types of pleasure *ought* to prefer the mental variety. Some people prefer murder to ice cream. If they succeed in murdering everybody else, they would manage to make it a universal truth that all people prefer murder to ice cream. Yet the claim that murder is better than ice cream would not thereby become true.

Brentano's approach relies not on the preferences certain subjects actually have, but on the preferences they *ought* to have – the preferences it would be *fitting* for them to have. Recall from Chap. 8 that in addition to love and hate, which essentially present-as-good and present-as-bad, Brentano posits a third fundamental interest state, *preference*, whose essence is to present-as-better. Preference in this account is irreducible to love and hate: preferring *x* over *y* is *not* a matter of loving *x* more than one loves *y*. (We have seen the reasons for this in the previous chapter.) Accordingly, for Brentano '*x* is intrinsically better than *y*' does *not* mean 'It is fitting to love *x* more than *y*'; rather, it means 'It is fitting to prefer *x* over *y*.' That, in turn, means something like 'Anyone who adopted a self-imposing comparative attitude toward *x* and *y* would prefer *x* over *y*.' The advantage of preference here, as opposed to greater love, is that while fitting greater love would at best be able to capture *quantitative* betterness, fitting preference has at least the chance of capturing also *qualitative* betterness.

Consider the case of mental versus bodily pleasure. In claiming that the former is more intrinsically valuable than the latter, what Brentano is saying is that, other things being equal, it is fitting to prefer mental pleasure over bodily pleasure. That is, anyone who adopted a self-imposing preference with respect to mental and bodily pleasure would adopt a preference for the former over the latter. Brentano *could* be wrong in claiming that such a person would in fact adopt the preference Brentano says she would. But we can at least see what grounds Brentano can cite in favor of his claim that mental pleasure is, as such, intrinsically better than bodily pleasure. And these grounds speak to what *ought* to be preferred, not only to what *is* preferred.

This approach to qualitative superiority will involve in some cases a kind of second-order fittingness. For to say that positive knowledge is, in itself, qualitatively better than negative knowledge is to say the following: it is fitting to prefer fitting belief over fitting disbelief. Likewise:

Pleasure in the bad is qua pleasure a good, and yet qua incorrect/unfitting emotion something bad…Therefore, in being disgusted with it as something bad [overall], we are actually performing an act of preference whereby the absence of something bad is given preference over something else which is good. And if that disgust is therewith recognized as correct/fitting, it must be because this preference has the character of correctness/fittingness. (Brentano 1889: 85 [90–1]; see also 1952: 213 [134])

That is, to say that fitting pain is intrinsically better than unfitting pleasure – read: that interest-fittingness is more intrinsically valuable than pleasantness – is to say this: it is fitting to prefer fitting pain over unfitting pleasure. Observe that it is this fact that explains why the sad-Hitler world is intrinsically better than the happy-Hitler world: although the latter involves pleasure whereas the former involves pain, the former involves interest-fittingness while the latter involves interest-unfittingness – and it is fitting to prefer interest-fittingness over pleasure.

A further advantage of the fitting-preference approach is that it can be extended to the comparison of *combinations* of intrinsic values. For example, although positive knowledge is more intrinsically valuable than negative, it may well be that the combination of negative knowledge *and pleasure* is more intrinsically valuable than just positive knowledge. For Brentano, this would be the case if it is fitting to prefer that combination over positive knowledge, that is, if anyone who faced the relevant choice and had a self-imposing preference regarding it preferred negative knowledge plus pleasure. Of course, it may also turn out that positive knowledge is in fact fittingly preferable to the combination of negative knowledge and pleasure. The point is that such questions become meaningful within Brentano's framework.

Given that Brentano recognizes four types of intrinsic good, his *complete* ethical theory must take a stand on the qualitative superiority relations between every pair of possible combinations of these. Since there are fifteen such combinations, his complete theory must include thirty claims of the form 'With respect to combinations C_1 and C_2 of intrinsic values, C_1 is intrinsically better than/worse than/equal to C_2.' It will, however, include considerably *more* than those thirty claims, since it will also have to address qualitative superiority relations *within* individual types of intrinsic goods, as well as quantitative superiority relations.

In fact, the complete theory would also have to address value comparisons *between* qualitative and quantitative superiority. Consider the claim that mental pleasure is mutatis mutandis more intrinsically valuable than bodily pleasure. In itself, this claim is totally consistent with the epistemic possibility that, as a matter of contingent fact, human beings' average bodily pleasures are in fact more intrinsically valuable than average mental pleasures. For it may turn out that we tend to experience sufficiently *greater* bodily than mental pleasure, so that the *quantitative* superiority of the bodily pleasure compensates and indeed overrides the *qualitative* superiority of the mental pleasure. Perhaps it is fitting to prefer a hundred perfect cheesecakes to an adequate Emily Dickinson poem, say because the former afford so much bodily pleasure as to overwhelm the moderate mental pleasure afforded by the latter. This kind of claim may seem initially hard to assess, but within Brentano's framework all it would mean is that someone who had a self-imposing preference here would prefer the cheesecakes.

In this way, Brentano's notion of fitting preference allows him to avoid the incommensurability of distinct intrinsic goods, indeed provides him with considerable flexibility in terms of evaluative comparison. At the same time, in some cases incommensurability may be the right way to go, namely, where no fitting preference is achievable. Interestingly, when we have to choose between a fitting pro attitude and a fitting belief, Brentano finds that we are unable to experience *any* self-imposing preference (Brentano 1952: 214–15 [135]).[18] This is so *not* in the sense that we experience a self-imposing neutrality; that would only suggest that fitting attitude and fitting judgment are *equally good*. The idea, rather, is that there is simply no fitting preference to be had (including 'null preference'). This suggests not that fitting attitude and fitting belief are equally valuable, but that their values are incommensurable.

What are the implications of such cases for action? What guidance are we to take from Brentano's theory in cases of incommensurability? Brentano's answer is:

…where it is impossible to establish intrinsic preferability, the latter must be taken out of consideration; it is as good as absent.   (Brentano 1952: 215 [135]; see also 1889: 28 [29])

This seems to suggest that cases of incommensurability will simply not affect the question of which among all attainable states of affairs is intrinsically best. Where two states of affairs differ in value in this way, that difference in value need not figure in our deliberation on which we ought to pursue. And if the two states of affairs differ *only* in this way, and are otherwise equally valuable, pursuing either is *permissible*, indeed right.

What, then, is the intrinsically *best* attainable state of affairs? That which, among all states of affairs one can bring about, it is fitting to prefer over all others. Sometimes two states of affairs may be equally good, or be incommensurable, but better than all others. In such cases, both are best. So, Brentano's account of *an* intrinsically best attainable state of affairs is this:

(BEST)   For any agent A, time *t*, and state of affairs S, S is an intrinsically best state of affairs attainable by A at *t* iff (i) there is a course of action C, such that C is available to A at *t* and C would bring about S, and (ii) for any state of affairs S*, if there is a course of action C* available to A at *t* that would bring about S*, then S* is not fittingly preferable over S.[19]

The fact that S* is not fittingly preferable over S leaves open three possibilities: that S is fittingly preferable over S* (hence S is better), that the null preference is fitting (hence S and S* are equally good), or that no fitting preference state is available (incommensurability). In all three cases, pursuing S is permissible.

Note well: since what BEST addresses is *intrinsic* betterness, the kind of fitting preference at issue is of a special kind: it is fitting preference-for-own-sake. To prefer *x* over *y* for their own sake is to prefer *x* as such over *y* as such. This is different from the kind of *instrumental* preference involved in, say, preferring fork and knife over chopsticks. It is also different from preference simpliciter, which combines both intrinsic and instrumental evaluation. For example, it might be fitting to prefer-for-own-sake *x* over *y*, but there is a *z* such that *y* is instrumental in bringing about *z* and it is fitting to prefer-for-own-sake *z* over *x*. In that case, it may be fitting to prefer simpliciter *y* over *x*. But this would not mean that *y* is intrinsically better than *x*.

Brentano's complete answer to the question 'What to do?' consists of the combination of RIGHT and BEST, with INTRINSIC providing specific content for concrete choices. For my part, I find myself in intuitive agreement with Brentano's various claims about relative intrinsic value ('intrinsic superiority'). Nonetheless, at the risk of repeating myself, let me state that as long as BEST is framed in terms of fitting preference, and fitting preference is unpacked in terms of the preferences of someone whose preferences are self-imposing, I find the resulting bit of moral guidance very unsatisfactory. It is simply hard to know how to follow an advice of the form 'Do what someone with an infallible moral compass would do!'

Conclusion

In summary, Brentano's ethical theory provides an answer to both central questions of normative ethics. To the question 'Which things are good?,' the conjunction of GOOD and INTRINSIC provides the answer: anything is good which is instrumental in bringing about, or else *is*, a pleased-subject, consciously-active-subject, fittingly-judging-subject, and/or fittingly-interested-subject. To the question 'What to do?,' the conjunction of RIGHT, BEST, and INTRINSIC provides a compact answer, but one which holds the key for guiding us through life both locally and globally: locally, in the sense that it hopes to provide in principle a verdict on every possible moral decision; globally, in the sense that it plants clearly before the mind what it is that is intrinsically valuable in life, and to that extent what our moral life is *all about*. I have just voiced my skepticism about the local guidance offered by Brentano's ethics. But the global kind of guidance, which just tells us, and reminds us, what is really good in and of itself, is still of first importance. Arguably, this capacity to keep clear before the mind the difference between our ultimate ends, on the one hand, and the various more instrumental goods we spend our lives chasing, on the other, is the hallmark of *practical wisdom*. It marks the difference between those who rove through life more or less blindly, stumbling from task to task, and those who *lead* their life in an aware way.[20]

Notes to Chapter 9

1. I am unfamiliar with a serious discussion of this issue in the Brentano corpus. For a recent serious discussion, and a proposal for an analysis of the relevant notions, see Dorsey 2013.
2. It should be noted that although Brentano's consequentialism is both pluralistic and analytic, its pluralism is essential to it whereas the analyticity could in principle be given up. (Moore's consequentialism is a precedent, having started out analytic but later acquired a substantive status.)
3. Brentano writes: 'Pleasure in the bad is, as pleasure, a good, and only insofar as it is an unfitting/incorrect emotion something bad.' Even pleasure in, say, a cruel act is, qua pleasure, a good – though qua directed at a cruel act it is also bad. (As we will see later on, unfitting emotion is an intrinsic bad in Brentano's ethics.) This raises the question of how we are to calculate the event's overall value, something we will have occasion to discuss in due course.
4. Since every conscious state is 'grounded in' a presentation – it either simply presents something, or presents-as-F (that is, present in a specific manner) something – we can say that the very occurrence of presentation is intrinsically good.
5. Here I use 'pleasantness' not to denote a potential pleasure taken *in* the presentation, but the modification of the presentation itself that renders it a pleasure-presentation.
6. Recall from Chap. 8 that interest-fittingness and judgment-fittingness are two different things for Brentano (Brentano 1907a: 148–9 [144]). Otherwise we could reduce the table to three items: presentation, pleasure, and fittingness.
7. To that extent, Brentano would not take the *virtues* (such as generosity, consideration, courage, and so on) to be intrinsic goods. At the same time, he qualifies as a virtue consequentialist in the sense of Driver (2001) and Bradley (2005); namely, the sense that a character trait qualifies as a virtue iff *its exercise* increases the amount of (intrinsic) good in the world (see Bradley 2005: 295 for a more precise formulation).
8. In saying this I am opposing Chisholm, who lists beauty among Brentano's intrinsically good things (Chisholm 1986: 60). This is surely a mistake, as is made clear by the way Brentano insists that there is probably no intrinsic good outside the realm of conscious life (Brentano 1952: 206–7 [130]).
9. Note that to represent a genuine alternative to Brentano's consequentialism, it must be friendship or meaning itself, and not the pleasures of friendship or meaning, that are taken to be intrinsically valuable.
10. Brentano has another argument for the intrinsic goodness of consciousness: that when we construct in our mind the idea of a perfect being, we do not attribute to it every belief and every desire, since it will not have false beliefs and unfitting desires, but we do attribute to it every possible idea – as someone who entertains, or apprehends, or is aware of every notion or possibility (Brentano 1952: 189 [119]). Here too, however, it is hard to tell whether the being's perfection requires, or on the contrary is compromised, by the fact that it had not a million but a million and one images of gravel 'floating' in its mind.

11. That this is what Brentano has in mind is further suggested by the fact that Brentano recognizes the intrinsic goodness of 'higher pleasures' of Mill's variety in his discussion of the value of pleasure: pleasure derived from a good poem is more intrinsically valuable than (an equal amount of) pleasure derived from a good ice cream (Brentano 1952: 186 [117]). So he certainly has something more in mind when claiming that knowledge or fitting belief or insight is a further kind of intrinsic good.

12. This can be seen by the extraordinary number of philosophers who take it to be a knock-down refutation of hedonism about well-being, that is, the thesis that what makes a life good is just the pleasure it involves. For a staggering list, see Weijers 2013 n. 4.

13. For the background on Sartre's student, see Chap. 7.

14. Thanks to Kevin Mulligan for pointing this tension out to me.

15. One option is to distinguish two notions of intrinsic value: intrinsic goodness and intrinsic worth. We can then claim that persons as such, although not intrinsic goods, have intrinsic worth, and that in virtue of their intrinsic worth they merit respectful attitudes (that is, attitudes modulated by the awareness of them as ends and not mere means). In this picture, respectful attitudes toward persons are intrinsically good *even though* the things they are attitudes toward – i.e., persons – are not. Note that this involves positing not just a plurality of items with intrinsic value *in the same sense of 'intrinsic value'*, but also positing different senses in which something has intrinsic value. '

16. Indeed, this could be integrated into a fitting-attitude account of intrinsic value, so that comparison of fittingness between certain distinct attitudes is claimed to be impossible (Anderson 1993).

17. One *can* hold that fitting love is better than fitting hate because although both are fitting, love also tends to involve positive affect, whereas hate tends to involve negative affect. If this is why fitting love is taken to be better than fitting hatred, then this would be an instance of quantitative betterness. But there is a clear intuition that even in case a fitting hatred is followed by a certain (fitting) glee, equal to the glee accompanying a fitting love, the latter is still intrinsically better. In that case, we would have to say that this is an instance of qualitative betterness.

18. Likewise, in some cases the amount of pleasure and the significance of knowledge might be such that it becomes impossible to tell which it would be fitting to prefer (Brentano 1952: 215 [135]). A fitting belief about the local tailor's phone number has a certain amount of intrinsic value in virtue of being fitting (independently of its instrumental value, which it has in virtue of the pleasure it may afford when tailoring is needed), and it may be impossible to tell how this amount compares to the pleasure taken in a cheesecake ice cream.

19. This formulation, again, adverts to states of affairs for convenience. In truth we should think of S and S* as ranging over those special Brentanian individuals. A best course of action is the one that brings into existence that among those individuals which bears no less intrinsic good than any other that can be brought into existence on the occasion.

20. For comments on a previous draft of this chapter, I am grateful to Kevin Mulligan, Mark Timmons, and Benjamin Wald.

PART IV

Conclusion

10

Brentano's System
The True, the Good, and the Beautiful

In what is quite possibly the most scholarly English-language overview of Brentano's philosophy, Liliana Albertazzi writes that it 'is the general opinion that Brentano's theories do not constitute a system' (Albertazzi 2006: 295). By content this is a mere sociological remark, but by tone it appears to be also an interpretive comment. In this concluding chapter, I want to suggest that the interpretive claim is false.

Several facts lend support to the interpretive claim. First and foremost is Brentano's vehement rejection of post-Kantian German philosophy, from Kant to Hegel, which is undoubtedly the most system-oriented period in the history of Western philosophy, but which Brentano saw as a period of philosophical decadence (see Brentano 1895). In addition, the fact that Brentano's thought was always in flux, 'never stood still' as Husserl pointed out in his reminiscences (Husserl 1919: 50), does not paint a picture of a systematic thinker drawing out consequences from top-down immutable principles. Finally, the chaotic state of Brentano's literary remains – with its bewildering variety of lecture notes, dictations, fragments, and letters – may also inspire a sense of a philosopher given to bottom-up bursts of ideas.

At the same time, it is worth noting that while Albertazzi's sociological remark is accurate across large swaths of Brentano scholarship, some have seemed to see a systematic streak in Brentano's work. When they were 22, Hugo Bergman and Emil Utitz, two high-school friends converted to philosophy by Anton Marty's courses in Prague, started visiting the ageing Brentano (then 67) at his Schönbühel summer home.[1] In one of three reminiscences of Brentano he composed in his lifetime, Utitz writes:

He, who saw through the nonsense (*Unfug*) of standard systematic philosophy more sharply than anyone else, at the end of the day nonetheless wanted a system, one which would know the answer to all questions.   (Utitz 1954: 84)[2]

More recently, Susan Gabriel writes:

Though he rejected the architectonic, speculative systems of Kant and Hegel, [Brentano] was himself a systematic philosopher with the big picture always in mind. Many useful studies of his thought have focused narrowly on this or that aspect of his system – his theory of intrinsic value, his intentionality thesis, his mereology, and so forth – but...few have paid attention to the overarching themes and their interrelations.   (Gabriel 2013: 247)

In the bulk of this chapter, I want to address Gabriel's 'complaint' by providing a condensed presentation of Brentano's uniform account of the true, the good, and the beautiful.

Utitz and Bergman also help explain away some of the factors inspiring the nonsystematic reading of Brentano. In particular, his distaste for German idealism appears to have been grounded not so much in the latter's systematic character, but in its tendency to reinterpret the phenomena in light of the system in order to protect the latter's stability. From Brentano's perspective, this was a theoretical vice that entrained a sort of dangerous insulation from reality. But as long as one guarded against this danger, systematicity as such was nothing to fear – quite the contrary. Utitz writes:

[Brentano] shattered the systematic character of philosophy, in order to substitute for it concrete local studies (*Einzelforschung*), yet he did not give up as such on the yearning/aspiration for a system (*Systemsehnsucht*).   (Utitz 1954: 86)

It would seem Brentano deemed a bottom-up approach to be more intellectually honest, and at the same time retained the *goal* of producing an all-encompassing system from so many bottom-up investigations. In this respect he embodies the idea of combining careful analysis as a means and grand synthesis as the end. This would explain Brentano's rejection of post-Kantian German philosophy, as well as the fact that his thought was always in flux.

As for the disparate character of his writings, Bergman tells us that 'Brentano did not like to publish books; as he once said, he hated the "secondary work" that was connected with proof-reading, referencing of quotations, etc.' (Bergman 1965: 94).

It is impossible, however, to discuss the question of whether Brentano had a system without getting clear on what it *means* for a philosopher to 'have a system.' A rather minimalist demand is that the philosopher in question have substantive theories in all the traditional areas of philosophy (metaphysics, epistemology, moral philosophy, and so on), or positions on all the classical problems of philosophy (knowledge of the external world, freedom and determinism, why be moral, etc.). A more demanding view of what it takes to have a system would require a measure of *unity* among the philosopher's various theories or positions. Such unity may manifest in recurrent appeal to similar patterns, notions, or 'moves,' or it may manifest in structural symmetries across different theories. In its ideal form, a philosophical system would provide structurally symmetric accounts of the true, the good, and the beautiful.

Looking back at the materials covered in previous chapters, it seems to me that by *all* these measures – including the strictest – Brentano did have 'a system.' For starters, he does have a theory in virtually every area of philosophy. Perhaps the one significant exception is political philosophy, where we have no significant contributions from Brentano to point to. One suspects, however, that this is primarily because Brentano took religion, more than anything else, to underpin the social order (see Brentano 1929: 10 [17]). As for recurring notions and moves, we have seen throughout this book Brentano's patterns of appeal to mereological notions, presentational modes (attitudinal properties), fittingness/correctness, the direct grasp of primitives in inner perception, and the grounding of different areas of philosophy in the philosophy of consciousness. Most interestingly, one can clearly discern in Brentano's writings a systematic, unified approach to the true, the good, and the beautiful. The basic idea is that we understand the true, the good, and the beautiful when we gain a clear grasp of (i) the distinctive mental states targeting them and (ii) what success for such mental states amounts to. As we have seen, the true is that which it is fitting to believe, the good is that which it is fitting to have a pro attitude toward, and the beautiful is that with which it is fitting to be delighted.

✌︎☙

For the third and last time in this book, I am going to quote this passage penned by the 36-year-old Brentano:

> We see that… the triad of ideals – the beautiful, the true, and the good – can well be explicated in terms of the system of mental faculties. Indeed, this is the only way in which it becomes fully intelligible (*erklären*)… (Brentano 1874: II, 122 [263]; my italics)

The 'system of mental faculties' Brentano alludes to is the threefold system of presentation, judgment, and interest. The program is to use presentation, judgment, and interest to render intelligible, respectively, the beautiful, the true, and the good.[3] We have seen how this works at the end of Chap. 8. Here I merely want to recapitulate Brentano's main ideas in a way that highlights their systematicity.

In an important sense, the true does not in fact belong on the same list as the good and the beautiful. Keeping in mind the distinction between intentional act and intentional object, being good and being beautiful are ostensibly attributes of the object, whereas truth is ostensibly an attribute of the act. *If* one held that the intentional objects of judgment and belief are propositions, and propositions are true or false, *then* the true would belong with the good and the beautiful as an attribute of the object rather than the act. But Brentano does not think that the intentional objects of judgment and belief are propositions, and he takes truth to be originally an attribute of the judgments themselves (Brentano 1930: 6 [6]).

This incongruence is resolved by Brentano's theory that all judgments are existential. Since existence is ostensibly an attribute of intentional objects rather than acts, existence belongs on the same plane as goodness and beauty. Ultimately, then, the philosophical theory of the true boils down to the task of rendering intelligible the notion of existence or realness.

Brentano's attempt to render existence intelligible has two facets. The first is destructive: Brentano simply denies that there is any such property as existence. The second is constructive: it aims to show how it can make sense, indeed be *true*, to say that ducks exist (say). The main idea here could be summarized as follows. If a positive existential judgment attributed to a duck the property of existing, then given that there is no such property, the positive existential judgment would be false. Accordingly, a positive existential judgment concerning a duck must commit to the duck's existence without attributing to it the property of existing. In practice, this means that the judgment's existence-commitment must not be part of the judgment's content, but be rather built into its very mode or attitude. Accordingly, when we say that ducks exist, we are not saying that ducks have the property of existing; rather, we are saying that toward ducks it is appropriate to take an existence-committing attitude – in short, that it is fitting to believe in ducks.

This account attempts to render the notion of existence intelligible by analyzing it in terms of two other notions, namely, fittingness and belief-in. It would *succeed* in rendering it intelligible only if it can make us understand (i) what it is to believe in something and (ii) what it is for a belief in something to be fitting. Now, we can try to elucidate these notions in terms of yet others, but ultimately our attempt at rendering existence intelligible must bottom out in certain notions that we understand, but not via analysis. The only way to understand a notion without analyzing it is by grasping directly the nature of the phenomenon it picks out. And indeed, according to Brentano we can understand what it is to believe in something by grasping directly, in inner perception, the felt difference between believing in something and either disbelieving in it or merely contemplating it. (This direct graspability of the nature of belief-in is crucial, because if we instead analyzed belief-in as the existence-committal state, we would be using the notion of existence to elucidate the very same notion.) As for fittingness, we can grasp directly, again in inner perception, the felt difference between *manifestly fitting* (read: self-evident) beliefs and beliefs not so; we can then analyze fittingness in terms of manifest fittingness or self-evidence. At the foundation of our philosophical appreciation of the nature of the true, then is a direct grasp of (i) the character of belief-in and (ii) the nature of self-evidence. Philosophical analysis produces the conceptual bridge between these directly graspable phenomena and the notion of the true.

We find the same plan of attack in Brentano's attempt to render goodness intelligible. Recall the 1909 letter to Kraus:

> It is incomprehensible to me what you seek to gain here with your belief in the existence of goodness with which the emotions are found to correspond.   (Brentano 1966: 207)

That is, there is no such thing as mind-independent goodness. This is the destructive part of Brentano's tack. The constructive part is to show that our evaluative discourse is nonetheless sensible; indeed, we often speak *truly* when we say that such-and-such is, or would be, good.

How could that be? A state of positive interest – of will, positive emotion, or pleasure – involves commitment to the goodness of its object in the same way a positive judgment involves commitment to the reality or existence of its object. Since there is no such thing as mind-independent goodness, any state that attributed goodness to its object would be nonveridical. Thus positives interest states must cast their objects as good, but not by attributing to them the property of goodness. Instead, it must be built into the very mode or attitude of a positive interest state (intention, gladness, pleasure) that it is goodness-committal. Accordingly, when we say that freedom is good, we are not saying that freedom has the mind-independent property of being good; rather, we are saying that toward freedom it is appropriate to take a goodness-committing attitude – in short, that it is fitting to take a pro attitude toward freedom.

To understand the nature of the good, then, we must ultimately understand the nature of pro attitudes and their fittingness. Here again, Brentano offers an analysis of attitude-fittingness in terms of a practical analogue of self-evidence, what I have called self-imposition – a particularly *manifest* kind of attitude-fittingness. However, the nature of self-imposition, as well as the nature of a pro attitude, are to be grasped *directly* in inner perception. More specifically, what is required is inner perception of contrasts between (i) self-imposing attitudes and non-self-imposing attitudes and (ii) pro attitudes and con attitudes (as well as mere contemplations). Ultimately, then, our understanding of the nature of goodness rests on inner-perceptual acquaintance with the natures of pro attitudes and their self-imposition; philosophical analysis creates the conceptual bridge between the notion of goodness and these directly-graspable natures.

It is easy to appreciate the evident symmetry between Brentano's attempts to render intelligible the true and the good. In both cases, direct acquaintance with a distinctive kind of mental state, and the manifest fittingness of entering that state in response to certain things, grounds our grasp of the relevant notion. At the same time, though, Brentano also recognizes an important asymmetry between the true and the good. The domain of value is inherently different from the domain of reality in that while an intentional object is either real or unreal, it need not be either good or bad – objects differ also in their *degree* of goodness or badness (in a way they do not differ in their degree of existence). Correspondingly, however, our interest states divide not only into goodness-committal and badness-committal ones, but include in addition states which are *better*-committal. These are the states Brentano calls 'preference,' and for which there is no analogue in the sphere of judgment. Ultimately, then, understanding the realm of value requires also direct acquaintance with the nature of preference – obtained, naturally, through inner perception of contrasts with mental states other than preference.

The same blend of symmetry and asymmetry attends the domain of beauty, which has its own peculiarities, but nonetheless submits to the same two fundamental Brentanian ideas. First: there is no such thing as a mind-independent property of beauty. But second: there are aesthetic truths, made true by facts about what it is fitting to be delighted with. So far, the account parallels the case of truth and goodness. The big asymmetry here, however, is that the notions of (i) delight and (ii) (manifest) delight-fittingness are mostly analyzable in terms of already familiar notions. Delight itself is analyzed in terms of the combination of first-order presentation and second-order joy in this presentation. Since there is no standard of fittingness for presentations, delight's fittingness reduces to the fittingness of the second-order joy, that is, to the familiar kind of pro-attitude-fittingness. The only new primitive here, not already invoked in the account of the true and the good, is the (first-order) *mere* presentation of the object. Presumably, the nature of mere presentation is to be grasped directly through inner perception of the contrast between merely presenting something and believing in it, disbelieving in it, taking a pro attitude toward it, or taking a con attitude toward it.

In sum, Brentano's program for rendering intelligible the true, the good, and the beautiful depends on the combination of (i) direct inner-perceptual grasp of six phenomena and (ii) philosophical analysis of truth, goodness, and beauty claims in terms of those six phenomena. The six phenomena are: mere-presentation, belief-in, pro attitude, preference, manifest judgment-fittingness (self-evidence), manifest interest-fittingness (self-imposition). The philosophical analysis follows the 'fitting mental response' format in each case.

As I hope this summary makes clear, Brentano's philosophical thought is in reality extraordinarily systematic. If the goal of a philosophical 'grand system' in the style of seventeenth- and eighteenth-century philosophy is to provide a unified, structurally symmetric account of the true, the good, and the beautiful, then Brentano clearly *had* a system. Indeed, in this rather demanding sense of the term, Brentano's may well be the last grand system of Western philosophy. (It is hard to think of a later Western thinker who not only produced theories of the true, the good, and the beautiful, but did so in a way that ensured unity and symmetry among them.) At the same time, Brentano marries this Germanic yearning for a total system with a more British empiricist sensibility: it is crucial to his system that the six primitive, directly graspable notions are *acquired rather than innate*.[4] Interestingly, though, they are acquired not by outer but *inner* perception. Brentano's is to that extent a kind of *introverted* empiricism, baking a certain *Cartesian* orientation into the system as well.

Brentano's system features a number of pressure points, the most notable of which should be collected and highlighted one last time.

First, the notion of a merely distinguishable part is problematic. On the one hand, such parts have no independent existence in the thing itself – they are distinguishable merely in thought. On the other hand, when it is true that *x* is a distinguishable part of *y*, it is true *cum fundamentum in re* – there is something about *y* that makes that statement true. The result, then, is that claims about merely distinguishable parts can be true *cum fundamentum in re*, but the relevant *fundamentum* is not any *part* that exists *in re*. The notion feels unstable. I have suggested on Brentano's behalf that the notion be understood as trying to articulate *structure* which outstrips *partition*. But this is just to open a window on a whole new project of (i) showing that the notion of structure that goes beyond having qualitatively different parts makes sense and (ii) explaining what exactly such structure consists in.

Secondly, Brentano's theory of judgment seems to entail that the psychological reality of a belief that either some baby or some puppy is cute involves the subject disbelieving in a mereological sum of a correct disbelief in a cute baby and a correct disbelief in a cute puppy. Crazy! We are entitled to speculate that someone in the history of humanity has believed that either some baby or some puppy is cute without so much as *possessing* the concept of correct belief.

Thirdly, Brentano's objectual theory of all three basic types of mental state faces the major challenge of explaining the *data* of systematicity. It seems to be a *datum* that no person is capable of grasping the idea that John loves Mary without being able to grasp the idea that Mary loves John. The capacity to grasp the two notions arises simultaneously, and this does not seem to be an accident. By the lights of Brentano's objectual theory, however, one is the capacity to contemplate one individual, a Mary-loving John, while the other is the capacity to contemplate a separate individual, a John-loving Mary. On the face of it, it is unclear why the capacity to contemplate Joe and the capacity to contemplate Schmoe should arise simultaneously as a matter of psychological necessity.

Fourthly, Brentano's theory of existence talk produces a difficulty regarding the assessment of some seemingly straightforward existence truths. According to the theory, to assert that the Eiffel Tower exists is, ultimately, to say that whoever adopted a self-evident doxastic attitude toward the Eiffel Tower would adopt the belief-in attitude. It is unclear, however, how we are supposed to assess the claim that whoever adopted a self-evident doxastic attitude toward the Eiffel Tower would adopt the belief-in attitude, without presupposing that we have an independent grasp on what it means for the Eiffel Tower to exist, given that nobody like us *can* have a self-evident doxastic attitude toward the Eiffel Tower.

Fifthly, there are problems with Brentano's reist ontology, one of the crown jewels of his system (and a retrospective partial justification of his theories of judgment and existence). Outstanding among these problems is the fact that it does not seem to have the resources to recover the compelling idea that *The Spatially Extended Eiffel Tower*, if it is a real concrete particular at all, is one whose existence depends on that of *The Eiffel Tower* – rather than the other way round.

Sixthly, Brentano's theory of will and emotion entails a reclassification of desire as an emotion – a somewhat uncomfortable classification given the felt difference between desire and such paradigmatic emotions as sadness and anger.

Finally, there is the problem of the dual status, or Janus face, of the keystone ethical notion of *self-imposition*. If we insist on objectivism about what is good and what is not, and interpret self-imposition as conceptually linked to goodness objectivistically construed, there is not much chance that self-imposition could be manifest to inner perception. But if instead we insist on the inner-perceptual manifestness of self-imposition, we lose any reasonable hope for objectivism about value. We cannot have it both ways.

There are of course many other difficulties, of various levels of significance, with Brentano's system. But these seven seem to me the deepest and most troubling. There is, in particular, a deep tension in Brentano's attempt to defend a kind of objectivism and observer-independence about existents and goods, while ultimately analyzing existence and goodness in terms of inner-perceptible self-evidence and self-imposition. One *could*, of course, believe in a preestablished harmony between observer-independent existents and goods, on the one hand, and inner-perceptually manifest self-evidence and self-imposition, on the other. But a philosophical system undergirded by this manner of supposition, magnificent though that system might otherwise be, would be little more than an intricate intellectual edifice held together by an act of faith.

The weight of these considerations makes it impossible for me to *accept* Brentano's system. All the same, I think of the system as a monumental intellectual achievement, among the finest of the West. With insight and invention, it brings a vast number of punctilious analyses into stable equilibrium within a unified framework for under-standing the true, the good, and the beautiful. In doing so, it combines exuberant ambi-tiousness regarding the *aims* of philosophical inquiry with painstaking meticulousness with regard to the *pursuit* of those aims. In all these respects, Brentano's philosophical system, even if ultimately hard to embrace, may serve us well as a *model* – a model of a philosophical endeavor both rigorous in its means and exhilarating in its ends.

Notes to Chapter 10

1. Brentano kept up a correspondence with both for the rest of his life (as well as with many other young philosophers hailing from the centers of Brentanian orthodoxy in Prague and Innsbruck). For the historical background, see Baumgartner 2017, Dewalque 2017, Fréchette 2017, and Janoušek and Rollinger 2017.
2. Thanks to Arnaud Dewalque, who pointed this passage out to me. Bergman, meanwhile, included an expansive chapter on Brentano in his last book, tellingly titled *Systems in Post-Kantian Philosophy* (Bergman 1979).
3. Note the unusual order in which the true, the good, and the beautiful are listed in the passage; the reason is that they are listed so as to reflect the order of the types of mental state used to render them intelligible. (Recall that in Brentano's taxonomy, presentation is treated as the most basic mental state, judgment the second most basic, and interest the least basic. The reason is that judgment and interest presuppose presentation but presentation does not presuppose them, while interest presupposes judgment but judgment does not presuppose interest.)
4. Brentano's ardent commitment to empiricism goes back to the very beginning of his career. In his thirteenth habilitation thesis, he already states: 'Nothing is in the understanding that was not earlier in one of the senses' (Brentano 1866: 139).

References

Albertazzi, L. 2006. *Immanent Realism: An Introduction to Brentano*. Dordrecht: Springer.

Albertazzi, L. and R. Poli 1993. *Brentano in Italia*. Milan: Guerini.

Alfonso, M. 2009. 'A Danger of Definition: Polar Predicates in Metaethics.' *Journal of Ethics and Social Philosophy* 3(3).

Anderson, E. 1993. *Value in Ethics and Economics*. Cambridge, Mass.: Harvard University Press.

Anscombe, G.E.M. 1963. *Intention*. Oxford: Blackwell.

Antonelli, M. 2011. 'Die Deskriptive Psychologie von Anton Marty. Wege und Abwege eines Brentano-Schülers.' In A. Marty, *Deskriptive Psychologie*. Würzburg: Konigshausen & Neumann.

Arendt, H. 1963. *Eichmann in Jerusalem: A Report on the Banality of Evil*. New York: Penguin, 2006.

Aristotle. *Physics*. Trans. R. Waterfield. Oxford: Oxford University Press, 1996.

Armstrong, D.M. 1978. *Nominalism and Realism: Universals and Scientific Realism*, Vol. 1. Cambridge: Cambridge University Press.

Armstrong, D.M. 1997. *A World of States of Affairs*. Cambridge: Cambridge University Press.

Armstrong, D.M. 2004. *Truth and Truthmakers*. Cambridge: Cambridge University Press.

Audi, R. 1994. 'Dispositional Beliefs and Dispositions to Believe.' *Noûs* 28: 419–34.

Aydede, M. 2005. 'The Main Difficulty with Pain.' In M. Aydede (ed.), *Pain: New Essays on Its Nature and the Methodology of Its Study*. Cambridge, Mass.: MIT Press.

Ayer, A.J. 1936. *Language, Truth, and Logic*. London: Victor Gollancz Ltd.

Bacigalupo, G. 2015. 'A Study of Existence.' Ph.D Dissertation, University of Lille-3.

Bain, D. 2013. 'What Makes Pains Unpleasant?' *Philosophical Studies* 166: 69–89.

Baker, L.R. 1997. 'Why Constitution is not Identity.' *Journal of Philosophy* 94: 599–621.

Baldwin, T. 1999. 'La valeur intrinsèque chez Brentano et Moore.' *Philosophiques* 26: 231–43.

Baldwin, T. 2006. 'Keynes and Ethics.' In R.E. Backhouse and B.W. Bateman (eds.), *The Cambridge Companion to Keynes*. Cambridge: Cambridge University Press.

Ball, S.W. 1988. 'Reductionism in Ethics and Science: A Contemporary Look at G. E. Moore's Open-Question Argument.' *American Philosophical Quarterly* 25: 197–213.

Baumgartner, W. 2013. 'Franz Brentano's Mereology.' In Fisette and Fréchette 2013.

Baumgartner, W. and P. Simons 1994. 'Brentano's Mereology.' *Axiomathes* 1: 55–76.

Baumgartner, W. 2017. 'The Innsbruck School.' In Kriegel 2017.

Bealer, G. 1998. 'Intuition and the Autonomy of Philosophy.' In M.R. Depaul and W. Ramsey (eds.), *Rethinking Intuition: The Psychology of Intuition and Its Role in Philosophical Inquiry*. Lanham, Md.: Rowman & Littlefield.

Bennett, J. 1974. 'The Conscience of Huckleberry Finn.' *Philosophy* 49: 123–34.

Bentham, J. 1789. *An Introduction to the Principles of Morals and Legislation*. Oxford: Clarendon Press, 1907.

Bergman, H. 1965. 'Brentano on the History of Greek Philosophy.' *Philosophy and Phenomenological Research* 26: 94–9.

Bergman, H. 1966. 'Franz Brentano.' *Revue Internationale de Philosophie* 20: 349–72.

Bergman, S.H. 1979. *Shitoth ba-filosofyah shele' akhar Kant* [*Systems of Post-Kantian Philosophy*]. Jerusalem: Bialik.

Bergman, S.H. forthcoming. 'Franz Brentano.' In G. Fréchette (ed.), *The School of Brentano in Prague*. Berlin: Springer.

Bergmann, H. 1908. *Untersuchungen zum Problem der Evidenz der Inneren Wahrnehmung*. Halle: Max Niemeyer.

Bergmann, H. 1946. 'Briefe Franz Brentanos an Hugo Bergmann.' *Philosophy and Phenomenological Research* 7: 83–158.

Betti, A. 2017. 'The Lvov-Warsaw School.' In Kriegel 2017.

Binder, T. 2017. 'Brentano's Life and Work.' In Kriegel 2017.

Black, M. 1952. 'The Identity of Indiscernibles.' *Mind* 61: 153–64.

Block, N.J. 1978. 'Troubles with Functionalism.' In C. Savage (ed.), *Perception and Cognition: Issues in the Foundations of Psychology*. Minneapolis: University of Minnesota Press.

Block, N.J. 1995. 'On a Confusion About the Function of Consciousness.' *Behavioral and Brain Sciences* 18: 227–47.

BonJour, L. 2000. 'Toward a Defense of Empirical Foundationalism.' In M.R. DePaul (ed.), *Resurrecting Old-Fashioned Foundationalism*. Lanham, Md.: Rowman & Littlefield.

Boyd, R. 1988. 'How to be a Moral Realist.' In G. Sayre-McCord Geoffrey (ed.), *Essays on Moral Realism*. Ithaca, NY: Cornell University Press.

Bradley, B. 2005. 'Virtue Consequentialism.' *Utilitas* 17: 282–98.

Bradley, F.H. 1893. *Appearance and Reality*. London: Swan Sonnenschein.

Brandl, J. 2005. 'The Immanence Theory of Intentionality.' In. D.W. Smith and A.L. Thomasson (eds.), *Phenomenology and Philosophy of Mind*. Oxford: Clarendon.

Brandl, J. 2017. 'Was Brentano an Early Deflationist about Truth?' *The Monist* 100: 1–14.

Brandt, R.B. 1955. 'The Definition of an "Ideal Observer" Theory in Ethics.' *Philosophy and Phenomenological Research* 15: 407–13.

Brentano, F.C. 1862. *Von der mannigfachen Bedeutung des Seienden nach Aristoteles*. Freiburg: Herder. Trans. R. George, *On the Several Senses of Being in Aristotle*. Berkeley: University of California Press, 1976.

Brentano, F.C. 1866. 'Ad Disputationem Qua Theses Gratiosi Philosophorum Ordinis Consensu Et Auctoritate Pro Impetranda Venia Docendi in Alma Universitate Julio-Maximiliana Defendet.' Aschaffenburg: Schipner. Reprinted as 'Die 25 Habilitationsthesen' ['The 25 Habilitation Theses'], in his *Über die Zukunft der Philosophie*. Hamburg: Meiner, 1929.

Brentano, F.C. 1874. *Psychologie vom empirischen Standpunkte* (2 vols.). Leipzig: Meiner, 1924. Trans. A.C. Rancurello, D.B. Terrell, and L.L. McAlister, *Psychology from Empirical Standpoint*. London: Routledge, 1973.

Brentano, F.C. 1889. *Vom Ursprung sittlicher Erkenntnis*. Hamburg: Meiner, 1969. Trans. R.M. Chisholm and E.H. Schneewind, *The Origin of Our Knowledge of Right and Wrong*. London: Routledge & Kegan Paul, 1969.

Brentano, F. 1895. *Die vier Phasen der Philosophie und ihr augenblicklicher Stand*. Stuttgart: Cotta. Trans. B.M. Mezei and B. Smith, 'The Four Phases of Philosophy and Its Current State.' In their *The Four Phases of Philosophy*. Amsterdam: Rodopi, 1998.

Brentano, F.C. 1907a. 'Vom Lieben und Hassen' ['Love and Hate']. In Brentano 1889.

Brentano, F.C. 1907b. *Untersuchungen zur Sinnespsychologie* [*Investigations on Sense Psychology*]. Hamburg: Meiner, 1979.

Brentano, F.C. 1911. *Von der Klassifikation der psychischen Phänomena* [*The Classification of Mental Phenomena*]. In Brentano 1874.

Brentano, F.C. 1917a. 'Vom ens rationis' ['On *Ens Rationis*']. In Brentano 1874.

Brentano, F.C. 1917b. 'Über das Sein im uneigentlichen Sinne, abstrakte Namen und Verstandesdinge' ['On the Term "Being" in its Loose Sense, Abstract Terms, and *Entia Rationis*']. In Brentano 1874.

Brentano, F.C. 1925. *Versuch über die Erkenntnis* [*Essay on Knowledge*]. Hamburg: Meiner, 1970.

Brentano, F.C. 1928. *Vom sinnlichen und noetischen Bewußtsein*. Leipzig: Meiner. Trans. M. Schättle and L.L. McAlister, *Sensory and Noetic Consciousness*. London: Routledge & Kegan Paul, 1981.

Brentano, F.C. 1929. *Vom Dasein Gottes*. Leipzig: Meiner. Trans. S. Krantz, *On the Existence of God*. The Hague: Martinus Nijhoff, 1987.

Brentano, F.C. 1930. *Wahrheit und Evidenz*. Leipzig: Meiner. Trans. R.M. Chisholm, I. Politzer, and K. Fischer, *The True and the Evident*. London: Routledge, 1966.

Brentano, F.C. 1933. *Kategorienlehre*. Leipzig: Meiner. Trans. R.M. Chisholm and N. Guterman, *The Theory of Categories*. The Hague: Martinus Nijhoff, 1981.

Brentano, F.C. 1952. *Grundlegung und Aufbau der Ethik*. Bern: Francke. Trans. E.H. Schneewind, *The Foundation and Construction of Ethics*. London: Routledge & Kegan Paul, 1973.

Brentano, F.C. 1956. *Die Lehre vom richtigen Urteil*. Bern: Francke.

Brentano, F.C. 1959. *Grundzuge der Ästhetik*. Bern: Francke.

Brentano, F.C. 1966. *Die Abkehr vom Nichtrealen*. Bern: Francke.

Brentano, F.C. 1976. *Philosophische Untersuchungen zu Raum, Zeit und Kontinuum*. Leipzig: Meiner. Trans. B. Smith, *Philosophical Investigations on Space, Time and the Continuum*. London: Croom Helm, 1988.

Brentano, F.C. 1982. *Deskriptive Psychologie*. Hamburg: Meiner. Trans. B. Müller, *Descriptive Psychology*. London: Routledge, 1995.

Brentano, F.C. MS N7. 'Zur Lorenz-Einsteinfrage.'

Brentano, F.C. MS XPs5. 'Gegen die "Annahme" als besondere Grundklasse psychischer Beziehung.'

Brentano, F.C. MS XPs12. 'Apodiktigsheit.'

Brentano, F.C. MS XPs53. *Drittes Buch: Von den Vostellungen*.

Brentano, F.C. MS XPs62. 'Für D. Psychologiekolleg.'

Brink, D. 1989. *Moral Realism and the Foundations of Ethics*. Cambridge: Cambridge University Press.

Brück, M. 1933. *Über das Verhältnis Edmund Husserls zu Franz Brentano, vornehmlich mit Rücksicht auf Brentanos Psychologie*. Würzburg: Triltsch.

Butler, J. 1726. *Fifteen Sermons Preached at Rolls Chapel*. London: J. & J. Knapton.

Byrne, A. 1997. 'Some Like It HOT: Consciousness and Higher Order Thoughts.' *Philosophical Studies* 86: 103–29.

Byrne, A. 2001. 'Intentionalism Defended.' *Philosophical Review* 110: 199–240.

Bykvist, K. 2009. 'No Good Fit: Why the Fitting Attitude Analysis of Value Fails.' *Mind* 118: 1–30.

Calosi, C. 2014. 'Quantum Mechanics and Priority Monism.' *Synthese* 191: 915–28.

Campbell, K. 1990. *Abstract Particulars*. Oxford: Blackwell.

Carson, T.L. 1984. *The Status of Morality*. Dordrecht: Reidel.

Caston, V. 2002. 'Aristotle on Consciousness.' *Mind* 111: 751–815.

Cesalli, L. and H. Taieb 2012. 'The Road to *ideelle Verähnlichung*. Anton Marty's Conception of Intentionality in the Light of its Brentanian Background.' *Quaestio* 12: 171–232.

Chappell, R.Y. 2012. 'Fittingness: The Sole Normative Primitive.' *Philosophical Quarterly* 62: 684–704.

Chisholm, R.M. 1952. 'Intentionality and the Theory of Signs.' *Philosophical Studies* 3: 56–63.

Chisholm, R.M. 1957. *Perceiving*. Ithaca, NY: Cornell University Press.

Chisholm, R.M. 1976. 'Brentano's Nonpropositional Theory of Judgment.' *Midwest Studies in Philosophy of Mind* 1: 91–5.

Chisholm, R.M. 1978. 'Brentano's Conception of Substance and Accident.' *Grazer Philosophische Studien* 5: 197–210.

Chisholm, R.M. 1981a. 'Introduction to the Theory of Categories.' In Brentano 1933.

Chisholm, R.M. 1981b. 'Defining Intrinsic Value.' *Analysis* 41: 99–100.

Chisholm, R.M. 1982. *Brentano and Meinong Studies*. Atlantic Highlands, NJ: Humanities Press.

Chisholm, R.M. 1986. *Brentano and Intrinsic Value*. Cambridge: Cambridge University Press.

Chisholm, R.M. 1997. 'My Philosophical Development.' In L.E. Hahn (ed.), The Philosophy of Roderick M. Chisholm. Peru, Ill.: Open Court Publishing.

Chrudzimski, A. 2001. *Intentionalitätstheorie beim frühen Brentano*. Dordrecht: Springer.

Chrudzimski, A. and B. Smith 2004. 'Brentano's Ontology: From Conceptualism to Reism.' In D. Jacquette (ed.), *The Cambridge Companion to Brentano*. Cambridge: Cambridge University Press.

Chudnoff, E. 2013. 'Awareness of Abstract Objects.' *Noûs* 47: 706–26.

Clark, P. 2010. 'Aspects, Guises, Species, and Knowing Something to be Good.' In S. Tenenbaum (ed.), *Desire, Practical Reason, and the Good*. Oxford: Oxford University Press.

Cohen, L.J. 1992. *An Essay on Belief and Acceptance*. Oxford: Clarendon Press.

Copp, D. 2003. 'Why Naturalism?' *Ethical Theory and Moral Practice* 6: 179–200.

Coventry, A. and U. Kriegel 2008. 'Locke on Consciousness.' *History of Philosophy Quarterly* 25: 221–42.

Crane, T. 1998. 'Intentionality as the Mark of the Mental.' In A. O'Hear (ed.), *Contemporary Issues in Philosophy of Mind*. Cambridge: Cambridge University Press.

Crane, T. 2001. *Elements of Mind*. Oxford: Oxford University Press.

Crane, T. 2006. 'Brentano's Concept of Intentional Inexistence.' In M. Textor (ed.), *The Austrian Contribution to Analytic Philosophy*. London: Routledge.

Crane, T. 2009. 'Intentionalism.' In A. Beckermann and B. McLaughlin (eds.), *The Oxford Handbook of Philosophy of Mind*. Oxford: Oxford University Press.

Crane, T. 2013. 'Conscious Thought.' In U. Kriegel (ed.), *Phenomenal Intentionality*. Oxford and New York: Oxford University Press.

Crisp, R. 2000. 'Review of Jon Kupperman, *Value... and What Follows*.' *Philosophy* 75: 458–62.

Cuneo, T. 2003. 'Reidian Moral Perception.' *Canadian Journal of Philosophy* 33: 229–58.

Cuneo, T. 2006. 'Signs of Value: Reid on the Evidential Role of Feelings in Moral Judgment.' *British Journal for the History of Philosophy* 14: 69–91.

Darwin, C. 1859. *The Origin of Species*. Cambridge, Mass.: Harvard University Press, 1964.

Davidson, D. 1963. 'Actions, Reasons, and Causes.' *Journal of Philosophy* 60: 685–700.

D'Arms, J. and D. Jacobson 2000. 'Sentiment and Value.' *Ethics* 110: 722–48.

Danielsson, S. and J. Olson 2007. 'Brentano and the Buck-Passers.' *Mind* 116: 511–22.

Deonna, J. and F. Teroni 2012. *The Emotions*. Abingdon and New York: Routledge.

Deonna, J. and F. Teroni 2015. 'Emotions as Attitudes.' *Dialectica* 69: 293–311.

Devitt, M. 1980. ' "Ostrich Nominalism" or "Mirage Realism"?' *Pacific Philosophical Quarterly* 61: 433–9.

Dewalque, A. 2013. 'Brentano and the Parts of the Mental: A Mereological Approach to Phenomenal Intentionality.' *Phenomenology and the Cognitive Sciences* 12: 447–64.

Dewalque, A. 2014. 'Intentionnalité *in obliquo*.' *Bulletin d'analyse phénoménologique* 10: 40–84.

Dewalque, A. 2017. 'The Rise of the Brentano School.' In Kriegel 2017.

Dokic, J. and S. Lemaire 2013. 'Are Emotions Perceptions of Value?' *Canadian Journal of Philosophy* 43: 227–47.

Dorsey, D. 2013. 'Consequentialism, Cognitive Limitations, and Moral Theory.' *Oxford Studies in Normative Ethics* 3: 179–202.

Dretske, F.I. 1981. *Knowledge and the Flow of Information*. Oxford: Blackwell.

Dretske, F.I. 1988. *Explaining Behavior*. Cambridge, Mass.: MIT Press.

Dretske, F.I. 1993. 'Conscious Experience.' *Mind* 102: 263–83.

Dretske, F.I. 1996. 'Phenomenal Externalism.' *Philosophical Issues* 7: 143–59.

Driver, J. 2001. *Uneasy Virtue*. Cambridge: Cambridge University Press.

Drummond, J.J. 2006. 'The Case(s) of (Self-)Awareness.' In U. Kriegel and K.W. Williford 2006 (eds.), *Self-Representational Approaches to Consciousness*. Cambridge, Mass.: MIT Press.

Dunlap, K. 1900. 'The Effect of Imperceptible Shadows on the Judgment of Distance.' *Psychological Review* 7: 435–53.

von Ehrenfels, C. 1890. 'Über "Gestaltqualitäten".' *Vierteljahrsschrift für wissenschaftliche Philosophie* 14: 249–92. Reprinted as 'On Gestalt Qualities.' Trans. B. Smith. In B. Smith (ed.), *Foundations of Gestalt Theory*. Munich and Vienna: Philosophia Verlag.

von Ehrenfels, C. 1893. 'Werttheorie und Ethik.' *Vierteljahresschrift für wissenschaftliche Philosophie* 17: 76–110. Reprinted in his *Philosophische Schriften*, Band 1. Ed. R. Fabian. Munich: Philosophia, 1982.

von Ehrenfels, C. 1897. *System der Werttheorie*. Reprinted in his *Philosophische Schriften*, Band 1. Ed. R. Fabian. Munich: Philosophia, 1982.

von Ehrenfels, C. 1988. 'Fragen und Einwände an die Adresse der Anhänger von Franz Brentanos Ethik.' In his *Philosophische Schriften*, Band 3. Ed. R. Fabian. Munich: Philosophia.

Einstein, A. 1920. *Relativity*. Trans. R.W. Lawson. New York: Henry Holt & Co.

Enoch, D. 2005. 'Why Idealize?' *Ethics* 115: 759–87.

Enoch, D. 2011. *Taking Morality Seriously: A Defense of Robust Realism*. Oxford: Oxford University Press.

Ewing, A.C. 1939. 'A Suggested Non-Naturalistic Analysis of Good.' *Mind* 48: 1–22.

Farber, M. 1943. *The Foundation of Phenomenology*. Cambridge, Mass.: Harvard University Press.

Falk, W.D. 1945. 'Obligation and Rightness.' *Philosophy* 20: 129–47.

Feldman, F. 2011. 'What Do We Learn from the Experience Machine?' In R.M. Bader and J. Meadowcroft (eds.), *The Cambridge Companion to 'Anarchy, State, and Utopia'*. Cambridge: Cambridge University Press.

Fine, K. 1982. 'Acts, Events and Things.' In W. Leinfellner, E. Kraemer, and J. Schank (eds.), *Sprache Und Ontologie*. Vienna: Holder-Pichler-Tempsky.

Fine, K. 2001. 'The Question of Realism.' *Philosophers' Imprint* 1.

Firth, R. 1952. 'Ethical Absolutism and the Ideal Observer.' *Philosophy and Phenomenological Research* 12: 317–45.

Fisette, D. and G. Fréchette 2013 (eds.). *Themes from Brentano*. Amsterdam: Rodopi.

Fodor, J.A. 1975. *The Language of Thought*. Cambridge, Mass.: Harvard University Press.

Forbes, G. 2000. 'Objectual Attitudes.' *Linguistics and Philosophy* 23: 141–83.

Frankfurt, H. 1971. 'Freedom of the Will and the Concept of a Person.' *Journal of Philosophy* 68: 5–20.

Fréchette, G. 2017. 'Bergman and Brentano.' In Kriegel 2017.

Frege, G. 1884. *The Foundations of Arithmetic*. Trans. J.L. Austin. Oxford: Blackwell, 1974.

Gabriel, S. 2013. 'Brentano at the Intersection of Psychology, Ontology, and the Good.' In Fisette and Fréchette 2013.

Gert, J. 2009. 'Response-Dependence and Normative Bedrock.' *Philosophy and Phenomenological Research* 79: 718–42.

Gibbard, A. 1990. *Wise Choices, Apt Feelings*. Oxford: Clarendon Press.

Gilbert, D.T. 1991. 'How Mental Systems Believe.' *American Psychologist* 46: 107–19.

Giustina, A. 2017. 'Conscious Unity from the Top Down: A Brentanian Approach.' *The Monist* 100: 16–37.

Goldman, A.H. 2017. 'What Desires Are, and Are not.' *Philosophical Studies* 174: 333–52.

Grahek, N. 2007. *Feeling Pain and Being in Pain* (2nd edn.). Cambridge, Mass.: MIT Press.

Gubser, M.D. 2009. 'Franz Brentano's Ethics of Social Renewal.' *Philosophical Forum* 40: 339–66.

Guzeldere, G. 1995. 'Is Consciousness the Perception of What Passes in One's Own Mind?' In T. Metzinger (ed.), *Conscious Experience*. Padborn: Schoeningh-Verlag.

Harman, G. 1977. *The Nature of Morality*. Oxford: Oxford University Press.

Hazlett, A. 2010. 'Brutal Individuation.' In A. Hazlett (ed.), *New Waves in Metaphysics*. Basingstoke: Palgrave-Macmillan.

Heathwood, C. 2008. 'Fitting Attitudes and Welfare.' *Oxford Studies in Metaethics* 3: 47–73.

Helm, B.W. 2002. 'Felt Evaluations: A Theory of Pleasure and Pain.' *American Philosophical Quarterly* 39: 13–30.

Hershenov, D. 2003. 'Can There Be Spatially Coincident Entities of the Same Kind?' *Canadian Journal of Philosophy* 31: 1–22.

Hill, C. 1988. 'Introspective Awareness of Sensations.' *Topoi* 7: 11–24.

Hill, T.E. 1998. 'Four Conceptions of Conscience.' In I. Shapiro and R. Adams (eds.), *Integrity and Conscience*. New York: New York University Press.

von Hillebrand, F. 1891. *Die neuen Theorien der kategorischen Schlüsse*. Vienna: Hölder.

Horgan, T. and M. Potrč 2000. 'Blobjectivism and Indirect Correspondence.' *Facta Philosophica* 2: 249–70.

Horgan, T. and M. Potrč 2006. 'Abundant Truth in an Austere World.' In P. Greenough and M. Lynch (eds.), *Truth and Realism: New Essays*. Oxford: Oxford University Press.

Horgan, T. and M. Potrč 2008. *Austere Realism: Contextual Semantics Meets Minimal Ontology*. Cambridge, Mass.: MIT Press.

Horgan, T. and J. Tienson 2002. 'The Intentionality of Phenomenology and the Phenomenology of Intentionality.' In D.J. Chalmers (ed.), *Philosophy of Mind*. Oxford and New York: Oxford University Press.

Horgan, T., J. Tienson, and G. Graham 2004. 'Phenomenal Intentionality and the Brain in a Vat.' In R. Schantz (ed.), *The Externalist Challenge: New Studies on Cognition and Intentionality*. Amsterdam: de Gruyter.

Horgan, T. and M. Timmons 1992. 'Troubles for New Wave Moral Semantics: The "Open Question Argument" Revived.' *Philosophical Papers* 21: 153–75.

Hossack, K. 2002. 'Self-Knowledge and Consciousness.' *Proceedings of the Aristotelian Society* 102: 163–81.

Hossack, K. 2006. 'Reid and Brentano on Consciousness.' In M. Textor (ed.). *The Austrian Contribution to Analytic Philosophy*. London: Routledge.

Huemer, M. 2005. *Ethical Intuitionism*. New York: Palgrave Macmillan.

Hume, D. 1740. *Treatise of Human Nature*. Nu Vision, 2007.

Hurka, T. 2000. *Virtue, Vice, and Value*. Oxford and New York: Oxford University Press.

Husserl, E. 1901. *Logical Investigations II*. Trans. J.N. Findlay. London: Routledge, 2001.

Husserl, E. 1919. 'Reminiscences of Franz Brentano.' Trans. L.L. McAlister and M. Schättle. In L.L. McAlister (ed.), *The Philosophy of Brentano*. London: Duckworth, 1976.

Husserl, E. 1994. *Briefwechsel*. Dordrecht: Kluwer.

Ierna, C. 2015. 'A Letter from Edmund Husserl to Franz Brentano from 29 XII 1889.' *Husserl Studies* 31: 65–72.

Iglesias, L. 2015. 'La métaphysique psychologique de Brentano.' Ph.D Thesis, Aix-Marseille Université.

van Inwagen, P. 2003. 'Existence, Ontological Commitment, and Fictional Entities.' In M.J. Loux and D.W. Zimmerman (eds.), *The Oxford Handbook of Metaphysics*. Oxford and New York: Oxford University Press.

Jackson, F.C. 1977a. *Perception: A Representative Theory*. Cambridge: Cambridge University Press.

Jackson, F.C. 1977b. 'Statements about Universals.' *Mind* 86: 427–9.

Jackson, F.C. 1998. *From Metaphysics to Ethics: A Defence of Conceptual Analysis*. Oxford: Clarendon Press.

Jacobson, D. 2011. 'Fitting Attitude Theories of Value.' *The Stanford Encyclopedia of Philosophy*, E.N. Zalta (ed.), <http://plato.stanford.edu/archives/spr2011/entries/fitting-attitude-theories/>.

Janoušek, H. and R. Rollinger 2017. 'The Prague School.' In Kriegel 2017.

Johnston, M. 1992. 'How to Speak of the Colors.' *Philosophical Studies* 68: 221–63.

Johnston, W.M. 1972. *The Austrian Mind: An Intellectual and Social History* 1848–1938. Berkeley, Los Angeles, and London: University of California Press.

Jordan, M.C. 2013. 'Divine Commands or Divine Attitudes?' *Faith and Philosophy* 30: 159–70.

Katkov, G. 1930. 'Bewußtsein, Gegenstand, Sachverhalt. Eine Brentanostudie.' *Archiv für die gesamte Psychologie* 75: 459–544.

Kauppinen, A. 2014. 'Fittingness and Idealization.' *Ethics* 124: 572–88.

Kim, C.T. 1978. 'Brentano on the Unity of Mental Phenomena.' *Philosophy and Phenomenological Research* 39: 199–207.

Kim, J. 1992. 'The Nonreductivist Troubles with Mental Causation.' In J. Heil and A. Mele (eds.), *Mental Causation*. Oxford: Oxford University Press.

Kim, J. 2003. 'The American Origins of Philosophical Naturalism.' *Journal of Philosophical Research* 28: 83–98.

Kind, A. 2013. 'The Case against Representationalism about Moods.' In U. Kriegel (ed.), *Current Controversies in Philosophy of Mind*. London: Routledge.

King, J. 2007. *The Nature and Structure of Content*. Oxford and New York: Oxford University Press.

Klein, C. 2007. 'An Imperative Theory of Pain.' *Journal of Philosophy* 104: 517–32.

Kobes, B.W. 1995. 'Telic Higher-Order Thoughts and Moore's Paradox.' *Philosophical Perspectives* 9: 291–312.

Kotarbiński, T. 1929. *Gnosiology: The Scientific Approach to the Theory of Knowledge*. Trans. O. Wojtasiewicz. Oxford: Pergamon Press, 1966.

Kotarbiński, T. 1966. 'Franz Brentano as Reist.' *Revue Internationale de Philosophie* 20: 459–76. Trans. L.L. McAlister and M. Schättle. In L.L. McAlister (ed.), *The Philosophy of Brentano*. London: Duckworth, 1976.

Kraus, O. 1937. *Die Werttheorien*. Brünn: Rohrer.

Kriegel, U. 2003a. 'Consciousness as Intransitive Self-Consciousness: Two Views and an Argument.' *Canadian Journal of Philosophy* 33: 103–32.

Kriegel, U. 2003b. 'Consciousness, Higher-Order Content, and the Individuation of Vehicles.' *Synthese* 134: 477–504.

Kriegel, U. 2008. 'The Dispensability of (Merely) Intentional Objects.' *Philosophical Studies* 141: 79–95.

Kriegel, U. 2009. *Subjective Consciousness: A Self-Representational Theory*. Oxford and New York: Oxford University Press.

Kriegel, U. 2011. *The Sources of Intentionality*. Oxford and New York: Oxford University Press.

Kriegel, U. 2013a (ed). *Phenomenal Intentionality*. Oxford and New York: Oxford University Press.

Kriegel, U. 2013b. 'The Phenomenal Intentionality Research Program.' In Kriegel 2013a.

Kriegel, U. 2013c. 'Two Notions of Mental Representation.' In U. Kriegel (ed.), *Current Controversies in Philosophy of Mind*. London and New York: Routledge.

Kriegel, U. 2015. *The Varieties of Consciousness*. Oxford and New York: Oxford University Press.

Kriegel, U. 2017. *The Routledge Handbook of Brentano and the Brentano School*. London and New York: Routledge.

Kriegel, U. and K.W. Williford 2006 (eds.). *Self-Representational Approaches to Consciousness*. Cambridge, Mass.: MIT Press.

Kripke, S. 1972. 'Naming and Necessity.' In D. Davidson and G. Harman (eds.), *Semantics of Natural Language*. Dordrecht: Reidel.

Kroon, F. 1987. 'Causal Descriptivism.' *Australasian Journal of Philosophy* 65: 1–17.

Kroon, F. 2013. 'Phenomenal Intentionality and the Role of Intentional Objects.' In U. Kriegel (ed.), *Phenomenal Intentionality*. Oxford and New York: Oxford University Press.

Leibniz, G.W. 1686. *Discourse on Metaphysics*. Trans. D. Garber and R. Ariew. Indianapolis: Hackett, 1991.

Lemos, N.M. 1989. 'Warrant, Emotion, and Value.' *Philosophical Studies* 57: 175–92.

Lemos, N.M. 1994. *Intrinsic Value: Concept and Warrant*. Cambridge: Cambridge University Press.

Leśniewski, S. 1916. 'Foundations of the General Theory of Sets,' trans. D.I. Barnett. In his *Collected Works*, ed. S.J. Surma, J. Srzednicki, D.I. Barnett, and F.V. Rickey. Dordrecht: Kluwer, 1992.

Levine, J. 2001. *Purple Haze: The Puzzle of Consciousness*. Oxford and New York: Oxford University Press.

Lewis, D.K. 1972. 'Psychophysical and Theoretical Identifications.' *Australasian Journal of Philosophy* 50: 249–58.

Lewis, D.K. 1973. *Counterfactuals*. Cambridge, Mass.: Harvard University Press.

Lewis, D.K. 1983. 'New Work for a Theory of Universals.' *Australasian Journal of Philosophy* 61: 343–77.

Lewis, D.K. 1986. *On the Plurality of Worlds*. Oxford: Blackwell.

Lewis, D.K. 1989. 'Dispositional Theories of Value.' *Proceedings of the Aristotelian Society* (supplement) 63: 113–37.

Lewis, D.K. 1991. *Parts of Classes*. Oxford: Blackwell.

Lewis, D.K. 2001. 'Truthmaking and Difference-Making.' *Noûs* 35: 601–15.

Loar, B. 1987. 'Subjective Intentionality.' *Philosophical Topics* 15: 89–124.

Loar, B. 2003. 'Phenomenal Intentionality as the Basis for Mental Content.' In M. Hahn and B. Ramberg (eds.), *Reflections and Replies: Essays on the Philosophy of Tyler Burge*. Cambridge, Mass.: MIT Press.

Locke, J. *An Essay Concerning Human Understanding*, ed. P.H. Nidditch. Oxford: Oxford University Press, 1975.

Lowe, E.J. 2008. 'Two Notions of Being: Entity and Essence.' *Philosophy* 83: 23–48.

Lycan, W.G. 1990. 'Consciousness as Internal Monitoring.' *Philosophical Perspectives* 9: 1–14.

McBrayer, J. 2010. 'Moral Perception and the Causal Objection.' *Ratio* 23: 291–307.

McDowell, J. 1985. 'Values and Secondary Qualities.' In T. Honderich (ed.), *Morality and Objectivity*. Boston: Routledge & Kegan Paul.

McHugh, C. 2014. 'Fitting belief.' *Proceedings of the Aristotelian Society* 114: 167–87.

McHugh, C. and J. Way. 2016. 'Fittingness First.' *Ethics* 126: 575–606.

Mackie, J.L. 1977. *Ethics: Inventing Right and Wrong*. New York: Penguin.

Maddy, P. 1981. 'Sets and Numbers.' *Noûs* 15: 495–511.

Mandelbaum, E. 2013. 'Thinking is Believing.' *Inquiry* 57: 55–96.

Marek, J. 2017. 'Meinong and Brentano.' In Kriegel 2017.

Markosian, N. 1998. 'Brutal Composition.' *Philosophical Studies* 92: 211–49.

Markosian, N. 2004. 'A Defence of Presentism.' In *Oxford Studies in Metaphysics* 1: 47–82.

Martínez, M. 2011. 'Imperative Content and the Painfulness of Pain.' *Phenomenology and the Cognitive Sciences* 10: 67–90.

Marty, A. 1908. *Untersuchungen zur Grundlegung der allgemeinen Grammatik und Sprachphilosophie*. Erster Band. Halle: Niemeyer.

Massin, O. 2011. 'Joies amères et douces peines.' In A. Konzelmann Ziv, C. Tappolet, and F. Teroni (eds.), *Les ombres de l'âme. Penser les émotions négatives*. Geneva: Haller.

Massin, O. 2013. 'The Intentionality of Pleasures and Other Feelings: A Brentanian Approach.' In Fisette and Fréchette 2013.

Massin, O. 2017. 'Brentano on Sensations and Sensory Qualities.' In Kriegel 2017.

Meinong, A. 1894. *Psychologisch-ethische Untersuchungen zur Werth-Theorie*. Graz: Leuschner & Lubensky.

Meinong, A. 1902. *On Assumptions*, trans. J. Heanue. Berkeley: University of California Press, 1983.

Meinong, A. 1904. 'On the Theory of Objects.' In R. Chisholm (ed.), *Realism and the Background of Phenomenology*. Glencoe, NY: Free Press, 1960.

Meinong, A. 1906. 'Über die Erfahrungsgrundlagen unseres Wissens.' *Abhandlungen zur Didaktik und Philosophie der Naturwissenschaften* 1: 1–113. Berlin: J. Springer.

Mendelovici, A. 2013. 'Pure Intentionalism about Moods and Emotions.' In U. Kriegel (ed.), *Current Controversies in Philosophy of Mind*. New York: Routledge.

Merlan, P. 1945. 'Brentano and Freud.' *Journal of the History of Ideas* 6: 375–7.

Merricks, T. 2007. *Truth and Ontology*. Oxford: Clarendon Press.

Mill, J.S. 1863. *Utilitarianism* (7th edn.). London: Longmans, Green & Co., 1879.

Millikan, R.G. 1984. *Language, Thought, and Other Biological Categories*. Cambridge, Mass.: MIT Press.

Moore, G.E. 1899. 'The Nature of Judgment.' *Mind* 8: 176–93.

Moore, G.E. 1903a. *Principia Ethica*. Cambridge: Cambridge University Press.

Moore, G.E. 1903b. 'Review: The Origins of the Knowledge of Right and Wrong.' *International Journal of Ethics* 14: 115–23.

Moran, D. 1996. 'Brentano's Thesis.' *Proceedings of the Aristotelian Society* 70: 1–27.

Montague, M. 2007. 'Against Propositionalism.' *Noûs* 41: 503–18.

Montague, M. 2009. 'The Logic, Intentionality, and Phenomenology of Emotion.' *Philosophical Studies* 145: 171–92.

Mulligan, K. 1998. 'From Appropriate Emotions to Values.' *The Monist* 81: 161–88.

Mulligan, K., P. Simons, and B. Smith 1984. 'Truth-Makers.' *Philosophy and Phenomenological Research* 44: 287–321.

Nasim, O.W. 2008. *Bertrand Russell and the Edwardian Philosophers*. Basingstoke: Palgrave-Macmillan.

Neander, K. 1998. 'The Division of Phenomenal Labor: A Problem for Representational Theories of Consciousness.' *Philosophical Perspectives* 12: 411–34.

Newman, M.H.A. 1928. 'Mr. Russell's Causal Theory of Perception.' *Mind* 37:137–48.

Nida-Rümelin, M. 2017. 'Self-Awareness.' *Review of Philosophy and Psychology* 8: 55–82.

Nolan, D. 1997. 'Quantitative Parsimony.' *British Journal for the Philosophy of Science* 48: 329–43.

Nozick, R. 1974. *Anarchy, State, and Utopia*. New York: Basic Books.

Oddie, G. 2005. *Value, Reality, and Desire*. Oxford: Oxford University Press.

Olson, J. 2017. 'Brentano's Metaethics.' In Kriegel 2017.

Papineau, D. 1993. *Philosophical Naturalism*. Oxford: Blackwell.

Parfit, D. 2001. 'Rationality and Reasons.' In D. Egonsson, J. Josefsson, B. Petersson, and T. Rønnow-Rasmussen (Eds.), *Exploring Practical Philosophy*. Aldershot: Ashgate.

Parsons, C. 2004. 'Brentano on Judgment and Truth.' In D. Jacquette (ed.), *The Cambridge Companion to Brentano*. Cambridge: Cambridge University Press.

Parsons, J. 2004. 'Distributional Properties.' In F. Jackson and G. Priest (eds.), *Lewisian Themes: The Philosophy of David K. Lewis*. Oxford: Oxford University Press.

Parsons, T. 1980. *Nonexistent Objects*. New Haven: Yale University Press.

Picciuto, V. 2011. 'Addressing Higher-Order Misrepresentation with Quotational Thought.' *Journal of Consciousness Studies* 18: 109–36.

Pitt, D. 2004. 'The Phenomenology of Cognition; or What is it Like to Think that P?' *Philosophy and Phenomenological Research* 69: 1–36.

Potrč, M. 2002. 'Intentionality of Phenomenology in Brentano.' *Southern Journal of Philosophy* 40 (supplement): 231–67.

Potrč, M. 2013. 'Phenomenology of Intentionality.' In Fisette and Fréchette 2013.

Price, H. 1989. 'Defending Desire-as-Belief.' *Mind* 98: 119–27.

Quine, W.V.O. 1948. 'On What There Is.' *Review of Metaphysics* 2: 21–38.

Quine, W.V.O. 1950. 'Identity, Ostension and Hypostasis.' *Journal of Philosophy* 47: 621–33.

Quine, W.V.O. 1951. 'Two Dogmas of Empiricism.' *Philosophical Review* 60: 20–43.

Rabinowicz, W. and T. Rønnow-Rasmussen 2004. 'The Strike of the Demon: On Fitting Pro-Attitudes and Value.' *Ethics* 114: 391–423.

Recanati, F. 2007. *Perspectival Thought*. Oxford and New York: Oxford University Press.

Reicher, M.E. 2017. 'Ehrenfels and Brentano.' In Kriegel 2017.

Reisner, W.E. 2009. 'Abandoning the Buck Passing Analysis of Final Value.' *Ethical Theory and Moral Practice* 12: 379–95.

Ricœur, P. 1950. *Le volontaire et l'involontaire*. Paris: Aubier.

Rodriguez-Pereyra, G. 2002. *Resemblance Nominalism*. Oxford: Clarendon Press.

Rodriguez-Pereyra, G. 2011. 'Nominalism in Metaphysics.' *Stanford Encyclopedia of Philosophy* (ed. E.N. Zalta), <http://plato.stanford.edu/archives/fall2011/entries/nominalism-metaphysics/>.

Rollinger, R.D. 2012. 'Brentano's *Psychology from an Empirical Standpoint*: Its Background and Conception.' In I. Tănăsescu (ed.), *Franz Brentano's Metaphysics and Psychology*. Bucharest: Zeta Books.

Rosen, G. and C. Dorr 2002. 'Composition as a Fiction.' In R. Gale (ed.), *The Blackwell Guide to Metaphysics*. Oxford: Blackwell.

Rosenthal, D.M. 1990. 'A Theory of Consciousness.' ZiF Technical Report 40, Bielfield, Germany. Reprinted in N.J. Block, O. Flanagan, and G. Guzeldere (eds.), *The Nature of Consciousness*. Cambridge, Mass.: MIT Press, 1997.

Rosenthal, D.M. 2005. *Consciousness and the Mind*. Oxford: Oxford University Press.

Ross, W.D. 1930. *The Right and the Good*. Oxford: Oxford University Press.

Russell, B. 1904. 'Meinong's Theory of Complexes and Assumptions.' *Mind* 13: 509–24.

Russell, B. 1905a. 'On Denoting.' *Mind* 14: 479–93.

Russell, B. 1905b. 'Review of A. Meinong, *Untersuchungen zur Gegenstandstheorie und Psychologie*.' *Mind* 14: 530–8.

Russell, B. 1912. *The Problems of Philosophy*. Oxford: Oxford University Press, 1997.

Russell, B. 1921. *The Analysis of Mind*. London: Routledge, 1995.

Rutte, H. 1987. 'The Problem of Inner Perception.' *Topoi* 6: 19–23.

Sartre, J.-P. 1946. *Existentialism is a Humanism*. London: Methuen, 1948.

Sauer, W. 2006. 'Die Einheit der Intentionalitätkonzeption bei Brentano.' *Grazer Philosophische Studien* 73: 1–26.

Sauer, W. 2017. 'Brentano's Reism.' In Kriegel 2017.

Sayre-McCord, G. 1994. 'On Why Hume's "General Point of View" Isn't Ideal – and Shouldn't Be.' In E.F. Paul, F. Miller, and J. Paul (eds.), *Cultural Pluralism and Moral Knowledge*. Cambridge: Cambridge University Press.

Scanlon, T. 1998. *What We Owe to Each Other*. Cambridge, Mass.: MIT Press.

van der Schaar, M. 2013. *G.F. Stout and the Psychological Origins of Analytic Philosophy*. Basingstoke: Palgrave-Macmillan.

van der Schaar, M. 2017. 'Brentano, Stout, and Moore.' In Kriegel 2017.

Schafer, K. 2013. 'Perception and the Rational Force of Desire.' *Journal of Philosophy* 110: 258–81.

Schaffer, J. 2001. 'The Individuation of Tropes.' *Australasian Journal of Philosophy* 79: 247–57.

Schaffer, J. 2009. 'On What Grounds What.' In D.J. Chalmers, D. Manley, and R. Wasserman (eds.), *Metametaphysics*. Oxford and New York: Oxford University Press.

Schaffer, J. 2010a. 'Monism: The Priority of the Whole.' *Philosophical Review* 119: 31–76.

Schaffer, J. 2010b. 'The Internal Relatedness of All Things.' *Mind* 119: 341–76.Schroeder, M. 2010. 'Value and the Right Kind of Reasons.' *Oxford Studies in Metaethics* 5: 25–55.

Schroeder, M. 2012. 'The Ubiquity of State-Given Reasons.' *Ethics* 122: 457–88.

Schueler, G.F. 1995. *Desire*. Cambridge, Mass.: MIT Press.

Seager, W. 1999. *Theories of Consciousness*. London: Routledge.

Searle, J.R. 1983. *Intentionality*. Cambridge: Cambridge University Press.

Sellars, W. 1963. *Science, Perception, and Reality*. London: Routledge & Kegan Paul.

Sen, A. 1979. 1979. 'Utilitarianism and Welfarism.' *Journal of Philosophy* 76: 463–89.

Seron, D. 2008. 'Sur l'analogie entre théorie et pratique chez Brentano.' *Bulletin d'analyse phénoménologique* 4: 23–51.

Seron, D. 2017. 'Brentano's Descriptive Psychology.' In Kriegel 2017.

Shafer-Landau, R. 2003. *Moral Realism*. Oxford: Oxford University Press.

Sider, T. 2013. 'Against Parthood.' *Oxford Studies in Metaphysics* 8: 237–93.

Sidgwick, H. 1884. *The Methods of Ethics*, 3rd edn. London: Macmillan.

Sidis, B. 1898. *The Psychology of Suggestion*. New York: D. Appleton & Co.

Siegel, S. 2007. 'How Can We Discover the Contents of Experience?' *Southern Journal of Philosophy* (supplement) 45: 127–42.

Siewert, C. 2013. 'Speaking Up for Consciousness.' In U. Kriegel (ed.), *Current Controversies in Philosophy of Mind*. London: Routledge.

Simons, P.M. 1987a. *Parts*. Oxford: Oxford University Press.

Simons, P.M. 1987b. 'Brentano's Reform of Logic.' *Topoi* 6: 25–38.

Simons, P.M. 1990. 'Marty on the Consciousness of Time.' In K. Mulligan (ed.), *Mind, Meaning and Metaphysics*. Dordrecht: Springer.

Simons, P. 2000. 'Truth-Maker Optimalism.' *Logique et Analyse* 43: 17–41.

Simons, P. 2006. 'Things and Truths: Brentano and Leśniewski, Logic and Ontology.' In A. Chrudzimski and D. Łukasiewicz (eds.), *Actions, Products, and Things: Brentano and Polish Philosophy*. Frankfurt: Ontos.

Simons, P. 2008. 'Why the Negations of False Atomic Sentences are True.' *Acta Philosophica Fennica* 84: 15–36.

Simons, P. 2013. 'Brentano, Franz.' In H. Lafollette (ed.), *International Encyclopedia of Ethics*. London: Wiley-Blackwell.

Skorupski, J. 2007. 'Buck-Passing about Goodness.' In T. Rønnow-Rasmussen, B. Petersson, J. Josefsson, and D. Egonsson (eds.), *Hommage à Wlodek* <http://www.fil.lu.se/hommageawlodek/site/papper/SkorupskiJohn.pdf>.

Skyrms, B. 1981. 'Tractarian Nominalism.' *Philosophical Studies* 40: 199–206.

Smith, B. 1986. 'Austrian Economics and Austrian Philosophy.' In W. Grassl and B. Smith (eds.), *Austrian Economics and Austrian Philosophy*. London: Croom Helm.

Smith, B. 1988. 'Gestalt Theory: An Essay in Philosophy.' In B. Smith (ed.), *Foundations of Gestalt Theory*. Munich and Vienna: Philosophia Verlag.

Smith, B. 1994. *Austrian Philosophy: The Legacy of Franz Brentano*. LaSalle, Ill.: Open Court.

Smith, B. 2006. 'The Stages of Reism.' In A. Chrudzimski and D. Łukasiewicz (eds.), *Actions, Products, and Things: Brentano and Polish Philosophy*. Frankfurt: Ontos.

Smith, D.W. 2004. 'Return to Consciousness.' In his *Mind World: Essays in Phenomenology and Ontology*. Cambridge: Cambridge University Press.

Smith, M. 1994. *The Moral Problem*. Oxford: Blackwell.

Smith, N.J.J. 2005. 'A Plea for Things That Aren't Quite All There: Is There a Problem about Vague Composition and Vague Existence?' *Journal of Philosophy* 102: 381–421.

Solomon, R. 1976. *The Passions*. New York: Doubleday.

Sosa, E. 2009. 'Knowing Full Well: The Normativity of Beliefs as Performances.' *Philosophical Studies* 142: 5–15.

de Sousa, R. 1987. *The Rationality of Emotion*. Cambridge, Mass.: MIT Press.

Stalnaker, R. 1984. *Inquiry*. Cambridge, Mass.: MIT Press.

Stampe, D. 1987. 'The Authority of Desire.' *Philosophical Review* 96: 335–81.

Steiner, R. 1917. *Riddles of the Soul*. Trans. W. Lindeman. Liverpool: Mercury Press.

Stocker, M. 1979. 'Desiring the Bad.' *Journal of Philosophy* 76: 738–53.

Stout, G.F. 1896. *Analytic Psychology*. London and New York: Swan Sonnenschein-Macmillan.

Strawson, G. 1989. *The Secret Connexion*. Oxford: Clarendon.

Strawson, P.F. 1950. 'On Referring.' *Mind* 59: 320–44.

Stumpf, C. 1890. *Tonpsychologie II*. Leipzig: Hirzel.

Sutton, J. 2007. *Without Justification*. Cambridge, Mass.: MIT Press.

Szabó Z.G. 2003. 'Believing in Things.' *Philosophy and Phenomenological Research* 66: 584–611.

Tenenbaum, S. 2007. *Appearances of the Good*. Cambridge: Cambridge University Press.

Tenenbaum, S. 2009. 'Knowing the Good and Knowing What One is Doing.' *Canadian Journal of Philosophy* 39 (supplement): 91–117.

Textor, M. 2006. 'Brentano (and some Neo-Brentanians) on Inner Consciousness.' *Dialectica* 60: 411–32.

Textor, M. 2007. 'Seeing Something and Believing IN It.' In M.M. McCabe and M. Textor (eds.), *Perspectives on Perception*. Frankfurt: Ontos.

Textor, M. 2013. 'Brentano on the Dual Relation of the Mental.' *Phenomenology and the Cognitive Sciences* 12: 465–83.

Textor, M. 2015. '"Inner Perception can never become Inner Observation": Brentano on Awareness and Observation.' *Philosophers' Imprint* 15 (10): 1–19.

Textor, M. 2017. 'From Mental Monism to the Soul and Back.' *The Monist* 100: 133–54.

Thomas, A.P. 2003. 'An Adverbial Theory of Consciousness.' *Phenomenology and the Cognitive Sciences* 2: 161–85.

Thomasson, A.L. 2000. 'After Brentano: A One-Level Theory of Consciousness.' *European Journal of Philosophy* 8: 190–209.

Thomasson, A.L. 2015. *Ontology Made Easy*. Oxford and New York: Oxford University Press.

Titchener, E.B. 1912. 'The Schema of Introspection.' *American Journal of Psychology* 23: 485–508.

Twardowski, K. 1894. *On the Content and Object of Presentations*. Trans. R. Grossmann. The Hague: M. Nijhoff, 1977.

Tye, M. 1990. 'A Representational Theory of Pains and Their Phenomenal Character.' *Philosophical Perspectives* 9: 223–39.

Utitz, E. 1954. 'Erinnerungen an Franz Brentano.' *Wissenschafliche Zeitschrift der Martin-Luther-Universität Halle-Wittenberg* 4: 73–90.

Valentine, E.R. 2003. 'The Relation of Brentano to British Philosophy.' *Brentano Studien* 10: 263–8.

Van Cleve, J. 2007. 'The Moon and Sixpence: A Defense of Mereological Universalism.' In T. Sider, J. Hawthorne, and D.W. Zimmerman (eds.), *Contemporary Debates in Metaphysics*. Oxford: Blackwell.

Van Gulick, R. 2006. 'Mirror Mirror – is that All?' In Kriegel and Williford 2006.

Velleman, D. 1992. 'The Guise of the Good.' *Noûs* 26: 3–26.

Wallace, R.J. 1999. 'Addiction as a Defect of the Will.' *Law and Philosophy* 18: 621–54.

Way, J. 2012. 'Transmission and the Wrong Kind of Reason.' *Ethics* 122: 489–515.

Weijers, D. 2013. 'An Assessment of Recent Responses to the Experience Machine Objection to Hedonism.' *Journal of Value Inquiry* 47: 461–82.

Weisberg, J. 2008. 'Same Old, Same Old: The Same-Order Representational Theory of Consciousness and the Division of Phenomenal Labor.' *Synthese* 160: 161–81.

Weisberg, J. 2011. 'Misrepresenting Consciousness.' *Philosophical Studies* 154: 409–33.

Whitehead A.N. and B. Russell 1913. *Principia Mathematica*. Cambridge: Cambridge University Press.

Williams, D. 1953. 'The Elements of Being: I.' *Review of Metaphysics* 7: 3–18.

Williams, J.R.G. 2010. 'Fundamental and Derivative Truths.' *Mind* 119: 103–41.

Williamson, T. 2002. 'Necessary Existents.' In A. O'Hear (ed.), *Logic, Thought, and Language*. Cambridge: Cambridge University Press.

Wodehouse, H. 1909. 'Knowledge as *Presentation*.' *Mind* 18: 321–9.

Woleński, J. 1994. 'Brentano, the Univocality of "Thinking", "Something", and Reism.' *Brentano Studien* 5: 149–66.

Woleński, J. 2012. 'Reism.' *Stanford Encyclopedia of Philosophy* (Ed. E.N. Zalta) <http://plato.stanford.edu/archives/sum2012/entries/reism/>.

Zahavi, D. 2004. 'Back to Brentano?' *Journal of Consciousness Studies* 11: 66–87.

Zangwill, N. 1998. 'Direction of Fit and Normative Functionalism.' *Philosophical Studies* 91: 173–203.

Zimmerman, D. 1992. 'Could Extended Objects Be Made Out of Simple Parts?' Ph.D Dissertation, Brown University.

Zimmerman, D. 1996a. 'Could Extended Objects Be Made Out of Simple Parts? An Argument for "Atomless Gunk".' *Philosophy and Phenomenological Research* 56: 1–29.

Zimmerman, D. 1996b. 'Indivisible Parts and Extended Objects.' *The Monist* 79: 148–80.

Zimmerman, M.J. 2001. *The Nature of Intrinsic Value*. Oxford: Rowman & Littlefield.

Index